The
SCOTS WORD BOOK

WILLIAM GRAHAM

THE RAMSAY HEAD PRESS EDINBURGH

© 1977 William Graham

First published in 1977 by
The Ramsay Head Press
36 North Castle Street
Edinburgh EH2 3BN

Second Edition, 1978
Third revised Edition, 1980

Printed in Scotland by
W. M. Bett Ltd, Tillicoultry

ISBN 0 902 859 714

THE SCOTS WORD BOOK

Preface

"WHAT is the meaning of the Scots word **ettle**?" Any of the existing Scots-English dictionaries will immediately supply the answer. But how would one go about finding the Scots word for **intend**? One would have to scan one hundred and fifty-nine pages of Chambers's Scots Dictionary, or three whole volumes of the Scottish National Dictionary before one finally arrived at the word **ettle**.

It is hoped that this Word Book will present a way out of the difficulty and at the same time provide a key to some little part of the treasury of the Scots language as contained in Jamieson's and Chambers's dictionaries, and in the magnificent ten volumes of the recently completed S.N.D.

The book had its beginnings many years ago in a list of English words with their Scots equivalents pencilled in alongside. Then as it grew bigger and ever more useful—to acquaintances as well as myself—it was suggested that I might have it published.

The problem was that meantime the list had grown into a fifteen-hundred-page monster which not even the gargantuan efforts of my good friends Dr George Philp and Professor W. Watson Buchanan could find a publisher to tackle. The only feasible project, I was told, was to produce a greatly abridged version, together with a Scots-English section for easy reference, and an introductory chapter or chapters on the subjects of Scots Grammar, Idiom, Spelling, and Pronunciation. And this I have finally done.

The book is not a dictionary.* The all-important question of space has made it impossible to include, for example, the names of less common animals, birds and flowers, and in the English-Scots section I have had to omit a number of quite common English words where synonyms appear elsewhere in the word book. Again, in the Scots-English section the general guideline has been to admit only those words that have been in regular conversational or literary use over the past two centuries, and to conserve space even further, alternative spellings of which there are all too many in Scots writing have been quite often ignored. A simple example is the Scots spelling of the word **stand**. A glance at the vowel-change list on page 9 will immediately

* See Preface to Third Edition.

direct the reader's attention to **staun**, and the less suitable alternative **stawn** is excluded.

On the other hand, I have not hesitated to include a number of obsolete Scots words that I have thought worth preserving, or where I have known of no more satisfactory equivalent.

Of course there is scope for criticism. There will be errors, and some will consider that there are far more omissions than there ought to have been, even within the confines that the book has set itself. And of course a much better-known authority should have been entrusted with the task of compiling such a work.

My simple answer is—no such authority has come forward. Meantime, with the Scots tongue "dying before our eyes," someone had to tackle the job. Surely.

In conclusion I wish to acknowledge my great indebtedness to the Scottish National Dictionary, to Chambers's Scots Dictionary (Alexander Warrack), and to Jamieson's Dictionary of the Scottish Language, all of whose pages I have consulted freely.

WILLIAM GRAHAM

Preface to the Third Edition

In the introduction to the first edition I observed that *The Scots Word Book* could scarcely claim the title of dictionary, since so much material was omitted through lack of space. The present edition contains a-33 page Supplement which goes some considerable way towards supplying the missing vocabulary in the English-Scots section and, in its Scots-English counterpart, furnishes at least enough "new" vocabulary to provide the average reader with as comprehensive a glossary of Scots words as he will normally require.

The list of verbs with their Past tenses and Past participles has also been extended, and the Scots Idiom section has been enlarged by some ninety more examples.

Considering how well sales have been maintained since the book appeared three years ago, I feel bound to thank the public at home *and* abroad, for their support. I would thank the critics, too, for their generous reviews, also the many friends who have taken the trouble to pass on to me a host of useful words and suggestions.

W. G.

Contents

CONSONANTS

The **b** in English **mb** words is replaced in Scots with a second **m**—**fummle** (fumble), **grummle** (grumble), **mummle** (mumble), **timmer** (timber), **trummle** (tremble).

English **ch** at the beginning or end of a word sometimes becomes **k** or **c**—**birk** (birch), **kirk** (church), **poke** (pouch), **sic** (such).

On the other hand, English **ch** is retained in form and sound in words like **chaff** (chafe), **chaumer** (chamber), **chaunt** (chant), **chaw** (chew), **cheeny** (china).

English **d** is often omitted in such words as **ahin** (behind), **blin** (blind), **caunle** (candle), **frien** (friend), **haun** (hand), **kennle** (kindle). Here as elsewhere the insertion of an apologetic apostrophe is to be deplored.

Scots retains the **f** where certain English nouns ending in **f** and **fe** form their Plurals by changing the ending to **ves**—**knifes** (knives), **leafs** (leaves), **loafs** (loaves), **wifes** (wives).

English **dge** is replaced by **g** in **brig** (bridge), **rig** (ridge), **seg** (sedge), **draig** (dredge).

English **gh** is replaced by the guttural digraph **ch** in words like **fricht** (fright), **licht** (light), **micht** (might), **ocht** (ought), **sicht** (sight), **slauchter** (slaughter), **wecht** (weight).

The letter **h** is inserted in such words as **shinner** (cinder), **creish** (grease), **gushet** (gusset), **shew** (sew).

English **l** is often omitted from the middle of a word when preceded by a back vowel—**cowt** (colt), **faut** (fault), **gowd** (gold), **haud** (hold), **poupit** (pulpit), **saut** (salt), **sodger** (soldier).

The **ll** ending is dropped in such words as **ball**, **call**, **fall**, **wall**, and either an apologetic apostrophe is substituted as was the custom before the appearance of the Style Sheet in 1947, or the **a** vowel is doubled—**baa**, **caa**, **faa**, **waa**—with the original **aw** sound retained. In fact a few writers favour a simple change from **a** to **aw**—**baw**, **caw**, **faw**, **waw**—in order to make the pronunciation quite clear to the reader.

The letter **r** sometimes changes place with the preceding or following vowel as in **brunt** (burnt), **crib** (kerb), **cruds** (curds), **kirsen** (christen), **scart** (scratch), **shaird** (shred), **warsle** (wrestle).

English **sl** words sometimes appear in their Scots version with an inserted **c** or **k**—**sclander** (slander), **sclate** (slate), **sclice** (slice), **sklent** (slant).

English **w** disappears before the vowel in words like **athout** (without), **oo** (wool), **soum** (swim), **soup** (sweep).

Spelling and Pronunciation

THE fact that there are so many different spellings and pronunciations in different parts of Scotland poses the problem of how to present, in a book such as this, a system of spelling and pronunciation that will not by its incompleteness do very grave injustice to the Scots tongue in all the richness of its various dialects.

On the other hand, such is the chaotic state of Scots orthography that not only does each writer have his own favourite manner of spelling, but quite often one finds the same person serving up the same word in two or three different forms. There is therefore at least some scope for a regularising of Scots spelling without having to interfere overmuch with dialect words in all their colourful variety.

The system employed here is based partly on the Makars' Club proposals made in Edinburgh in 1947, partly upon observation of the spelling practice of leading contemporary Scots writers, and partly upon word spelling as given in the pages of the Scottish National Dictionary.

A key to spelling and pronunciation is given below, while the pronunciation of individual words that may cause difficulty appears in brackets immediately after the head-word in the Scots-English section of the Word Book. Unless where otherwise stated, vowel and consonant sounds are generally the same as in standard English.

A in the Scots pronunciation of such words as **want, warm, wash, water** retains the more usual **a** sound as in **arm**.

Aa=English **aw** as in **lawn**, but more open—**aa, baa, caa, faa**.

Ai=English **a** as in **fate**—**brainch, cairt, mair, sair**.

Ei, ie=English **e** in **me**—**dreip, seik, steir, scrieve**.

Eu, as in **sheuch**, is pronounced **yoo** in the Lothians and other districts, and **yu** (shyuch) elsewhere. Other examples are **deuk, neuk, heuk, eneuch**.

Ey, y=English **i** as in **mine**—**gey, Mey, stey, syne**.

I in the Scots version of a number of English words of two or more syllables is pronounced **ee** as in **sweet**, and some writers indicate this in their spelling—**adverteesement, feenish, parteeclar, exhibeetion, peety, rideeclous, speerit**.

Scots and Standard English

IT is remarkable how many people regard Scots as merely a degraded form of standard English, when the fact is that each is derived from a distinct dialect of the Germanic tongue brought to England by the Teutonic invaders who settled along the east coast in the fifth and sixth centuries.

By the middle of the seventh century, the dialect of the Angles of Northumbria had extended with the conquests of King Edwin as far north as the Firth of Forth, and under the name of Inglis gradually took over from Gaelic as the main language of the Scottish Lowlands. The resultant Celtic and Scandinavian contacts greatly increased the difference between Inglis as spoken in Scotland and the Anglian speech of Northumbria, and after the year 1494 the principal tongue gradually came to be known as **Scottis** instead of **Inglis.**

Lowland Scots vocabulary consists partly of words drawn from the same, mainly Anglo-Saxon, source as their standard English equivalents, and partly of words quite foreign to the vocabulary of the English language.

The main points of distinction between Scots and English words of obviously common origin are set out below.

VOWELS

English **a** becomes:

(1) **ai** (pronounced as in English **gate**) in such words as **airt** (art), **aix** (axe), **cairry** (carry), **cairt** (cart), **faither** (father), **raither** (rather), **tairt** (tart), **yaird** (yard);

(2) **au** (pronounced as in **raw**) in words like **baur** (bar), **caur** (car), **faur** (far), **haunle** (handle), **saumon** (salmon), **scaur** (scar), **staun** (stand);

(3) **e** in words such as **gled** (glad), **gless** (glass), **gress** (grass), **lether** (ladder), **seck** (sack), **sterve** (starve).

The vowel **a**, with its normal **a** sound as in **arm** is retained in Scots in words like **want, warm, wash, water.**

The vowel **a** is retained in certain English **a**-consonant-e words, but the terminal **e** is discarded and the pronunciation is altered accordingly—**cam** (came), **mak** (make), **shak** (shake), **tak** (take).

English **e** becomes:

(1) **a** in **dwall** (dwell), **wal** (well), **wast** (west), **wat** (wet), **wather** (weather), **whan** (when);

(2) **ai** (pronounced as in **gate**) in **mairchant** (merchant), **saicont** (second), **thaim** (them);

(3) **ei** (pronounced as in **feet**) in **deivil** (devil), **seiven** (seven), **streitch** (stretch), **weit** (wet).

Note that the English **ee** sound is generally spelt **ei** in Scots, less frequently **ie**, or **ee** "according to old usage" (Makars' Club Style Sheet, 1947).

English **i** becomes:

(1) **ei** in **dreip** (drip), **seik** (sick), **steir** (stir);

(2) **u** in **hull** (hill), **mull** (mill), **whun** (whin), **whup** (whip), **whurl** (whirl), **whustle** (whistle), **wrunkle** (wrinkle).

Note that the **i** sound in **mine** is often represented in Scots by the letter **y**.

English **o**, when preceded or followed by a lip consonant, becomes **a** in Scots—**aff** (off), **gab** (gob), **pat** (pot), **sab** (sob), **tap** (top).

Note that the **o** sound as in **lot** becomes an **oa** sound as in **board** in such Scots words as **cost** (pronounced **coast**), **lost**, **order**, **scholar**.

English **oi** becomes **i**, pronounced as in **mine** and often spelt **y** as in **byle** (boil), **hyst** (hoist), **pynt** (point).

English **oo** becomes **ui** or **u**-consonant-e in a number of Scots words, these being pronounced in the Ayr-Clyde-Forth area like **i** in **bit**, and in certain other areas more like the **u** in the French word **plume**. Examples are—**fuil** (fool), **guid** (good), **mune** (moon), **ruit** (root), **spune** (spoon), **stuid** (stood).

English **ou** and **ow** pronounced as in **now** generally have the **ou** spelling in Scots, but are pronounced like **oo** in **soon**—**broun** (brown), **flouer** (flower), **hou** (how), **hous** (house), **mous** (mouse), **shouer** (shower), **toun** (town).

On the other hand, English **ow** as in **row** (of houses) becomes **aw** in words like **blaw** (blow), **awe** (owe), **shaw** (show), **slaw** (slow), **saw** (sow).

English **u** or **o** with a **u** sound becomes **i** in **brither** (brother), **dizzen** (dozen), **mither** (mother), **simmer** (summer).

Five (five)	fift (fifth)
Sax (six)	saxt (sixth)
Seiven (seven)	seivent, seiventh (seventh)
Aicht, aucht, echt (eight)	aicht (eighth)
Nine (nine)	nint
Ten (ten)	tent (tenth)
Eleiven (eleven)	eleivent (eleventh)
Twal (twelve)	twalt

Groups of people engaged in some activity are denoted by the addition of **some** to the Cardinal Number:

> Hou about makkin a fowersome at cairds?

Still under Numeral Adjectives, **a small number more** becomes **a pickle mair**, or **a wheen mair**, and **a considerable number more** becomes **a guid wheen mair**, or **a hantle mair**, or **a sicht mair**.

On the other hand, **a small amount more** becomes **a thocht mair**, or **a wee tait mair**, and **a considerable amount more** becomes **a guid pickle mair**, or **a sicht mair**.

These Demonstrative Adjectives are also to be noted:

Definite		Indefinite	
Singular	**Plural**	**Singular**	**Plural**
This	thir, thur	Onie (any)	onie
That	thae	Ae, yae (a certain)	—
Thon (yon)	thon	Anither (another)	ither
Sic (such)	sic		
The tither (the other)	the tither		

PRONOUNS

Although the Personal Pronouns are much the same in Scots as in English, some writers use the following forms as being nearer to popular pronunciation:

First Person, Masculine or Feminine
Nominative Singular   a, aa (I)
Possessive Singular   ma, mine's

While the Objective Singular is **me**, the Plural **us** or **'s** is used in its place in colloquial speech—Gie's (give me) a piece.

Second Person, Masculine or Feminine
Nominative Singular   ye, you (emphatic)
Possessive Singular   yur, your (emphatic)
Objective Singular   ye, you (emphatic)

Third Person, All Genders
Nominative Plural   thae
Objective Plural   thaim

15

The English Indefinite Demonstrative Pronoun, **one**, becomes **a body** in Scots.

The Scots equivalent of both Nominative and Objective cases of the Interrogative Pronoun **who** is **wha**, and of **what sort of** is **whatna**.

That is the word used for all relative pronouns, Nominative and Objective cases, **wha** and **wham** having largely fallen into disuse.

VERBS

To quote the Style Sheet on the Spelling of Scots, 1947, "Past tenses and Past participles of weak verbs end in **it, t** and **ed** according to euphony—**flypit, skailt, garred, snawed, loued.**"

Verbs ending in vowel sounds form their Past tenses and Past participles by adding **d** to the Present tense form—**gaed, gied, peyd**. Past tense **loued** in the Style Sheet quotation is, however, preferable in order to avoid confusion with the adjective **loud**.

As to strong verbs (i.e. verbs which form their Past tenses and Past participles by changing the inside vowel instead of adding a final **it, t** or **ed**), the following list may be of some assistance in view of the fact that problems of space have made it impossible to include Past tenses and Past participles in the Word Book. The list is taken from the compiler's Teach Yourself Scots articles in the magazine, *Lallans*.

Present	Past	Past Participle
bear	bure	borne
	buir	
beat	bate	beaten
		baten
begin	begoud	begoud
bid	bad	bidden
bind	band	bun
byde	bid	bidden
(dwell)	bade	
brek	brak	brak
(break)	bruik	braken
bring	brocht	brocht
	brung	brung
burst	brast	bursen
can	cud	cuid
catch	cotch	cotch
	catched(w)	catched(w)

Ou, oo=English **oo** in **moon**—**broun, flouer, hou, hous, nou, smoor**.

Ow, owe=English **ow** in **down.** Unlike English, Scots never uses **ou** for this sound—**bowel, growe, lowe, sowl, thow**.

Ui and **u**-consonant-**e**=English **i** in **bin** in areas south of the Forth and Clyde. In other areas it is more like the **u** in the French word **plume**. However, in such words as **muir, puir** where **ui** precedes the consonant **r**, it is pronounced like English **a** in **fate**—**fuil, guid, ruit, stuid, mune, spune**.

Ch and **gh** have a guttural **kh** sound quite lost to English—**fricht** (fright), **licht, nicht, micht, richt, sicht, ergh, brugh**. On the other hand, the English **ch** sound as in **chin** is retained at the beginning or the end of words such as **chaumer** (chamber), **chaunt, chairge, fleich** (flatter), **streitch**.

Ng is pronounced as in English **singer**, with the **g** sound completely suppressed. This is an important distinction, especially in the pronunciation of words common to both English and Scots—**anger, finger, hunger, single**.

R has a much more prominent sound in Scots than in English, the Scots "rolled **r**" being well enough known not to require further mention.

Scots Grammar

SINCE Scots and English are derived from sister dialects, their grammars have many points of similarity. The main differences are as follows:

NOUNS

While the Plural number is formed in most cases by adding **s** to the Singular, nouns of time, space, measurement and number often retain the Singular form, as in "Twa bag o tatties," "Twa acre o grun."

On the other hand, such nouns as **parritch, brose, broth** are followed by a plural verb as if, like the English noun of Multitude, it were intended to denote the constituent parts:

> The parritch are rale guid this mornin.

Again, where in English those nouns that end in **f** or **fe** generally form their Plurals by changing the **f** or **fe** to **ves**, Scots simply follows the general rule of adding **s** to the Singular—**wifes, knifes, lifes, loafs, sheafs**.

ADJECTIVES

As in English, the degrees of comparison are formed by adding **er** and **est** in the case of single syllable words, and **mair** (more) and **maist** (most) to most words of two or more syllables. The following irregular comparisons are however to be noted:

Guid (good)	better	best
Ill (bad)	waur	warst
Hin (rearward)	hinner	hinmaist
Monie (many)	mair	maist
Muckle (much)	mair	maist

Key Cardinal and Ordinal Adjectives are:

Ae, yae (one)	furst (first)
Twa, twae (two)	saicont (second)
Thrie (three)	thurd (third)
Fower (four)	fort (fourth)

clim (climb)	clam	clum
come	cam	cam
creep	crap	cruppen
	creepit(w)	creepit(w)
ding	dang	dung
(beat)		
drink	drank	drunken
		drucken
drive	drave	driven
dae	did	dune
eat	ett	etten
faa	fell	faan
fecht	faucht	fauchten
	focht	fochten
	feuch	feuchen
fin(d)	fan(d)	fun(d)
get	got/gat	gotten
gie	gae	gien
	gied(w)	gied(w)
greit (weep)	grat/gret	grutten
grup	grap	gruppen
(seize)	gruppit(w)	gruppit(w)
hae	had/hid	haen
hide	hade	hodden
	hidit(w)	hidit(w)
hit	hat	hutten
		hitten
lat	loot	latten
(let)	luit	lutten
lauch	leuch	lauchen
(laugh)		leuchen
	laucht(w)	laucht(w)
leap	lap	luppen
lowp		lowpen
(leap)	lowpit(w)	lowpit(w)
mistak	misteuk	mistaen
pit	pat	pitten
		putten
	pit(w)	pit(w)
pruive		proven
	pruived(w)	pruived(w)
quit	quat	quat

rise	rase	risen
rive	rave	riven
(rend)	rived(w)	rived(w)
seek	socht	sochten
sell	sauld	sauld
	sellt(w)	sellt(w)
set	suitt	setten
	set(w)	set(w)
shak	sheuk	sheuken
(shake)	shuik	shuiken
	shakit(w)	shakit(w)
shape	shoop	shapen
	shapit(w)	shapit(w)
shaw (show)	shew	shawn
	shawed(w)	shawed(w)
shear	shuir	shorn
sink	sunk	sunk
sit	sat	sitten
	sut	sutten
slide	slade	slidden
slyte (slit)	slate	slitten
speak	spak	spoken
		spak
staun	stude	stude
(stand)	stuid	stuid
steal	staa	stown
stride	strade	stridden
strike	strak	strucken
strive	strave	striven
sweit	swat	swutten
(sweat)	sweitit(w)	sweitit(w)
tak	tuik	taen
teach	taucht	taucht
tell	tauld	tauld
	tellt(w)	tellt(w)
think	thocht	thocht
thraw (twist)	threw	thrawn
	thrawed(w)	thrawed(w)
thrive	thrave	thriven
tyne	tint	tint
(lose)	tyned(w)	tyned(w)

18

wash	wuish	washen
	wush	wushen
	washt(w)	washt(w)
weir (wear)	wuir	worn
weive (weave)	wuive	wuven
win	wan	wan
		wun
work	wrocht	wrocht
wynd (coil)	wand	wund
write	wrate	written
	wrat	
yield	yald	yowden

The Scots Present participle is another case where the apologetic apostrophe is used quite needlessly. Instead of the common **ing** ending of the English Present participle and Verbal noun, Scots makes a distinction and replaces **ing** with **an** and **in** respectively. So, even if more and more writers are using the **in** ending for both Participle and Verbal noun—probably to avoid being pedantic— there is absolutely no reason for taking this as just another example of speech slovenliness.

The use of the Present tense of the verb **to be** along with a Present participle to express a state of doubt or wonder is to be noted— **I'm wondering/I'm doubting whither** for **I wonder/I doubt whether.** . . .

The Present tense of the verb **to be** is the same in Scots as in English, but the Past tense is—I wis, you/ye wur, he/she/it wis, we wur, ye wur, they wur.

The Scots forms of the Auxiliaries **shall, should** and **have** are **sal, soud** and **hae**.

ADVERBS

In many cases where English adds **ly** to an adjective to form the adverb, Scots uses the same form for both parts of speech. Thus **to caa canny** means **to proceed cautiously**—and **I'm awfu tired** means **I'm extremely tired**.

OTHER PARTS OF SPEECH are as detailed in the Scots-English Vocabulary.

Scots Idiom

IDIOMS are those special forms of expression that capture in their own peculiar phraseology the vivid colloquial speech of a people going about its everyday business. They give life and character to a language. Scots is particularly rich in idiomatic expressions, and a selection is given below, arranged in the alphabetical order of key words. A supplementary list of idioms will be found on page 30.

Aa (all)	Aa ae oo	All the same
Aabody (everybody)	Aabody's body	A sycophant; a sail-trimmer
Able	No able for	Having no appetite for; incapable of
Aff (off)	Aff the gleg	Off the mark
Efter (past, of time)	Five efter ten	Five minutes past ten
Agley (askew)	To gang agley	To go astray
Ahint (behind)	Ahint the haun	Overdue
Ail	What ails ye at . . . ?	What do you dislike about . . . ?
An aa (also)	I hae yin an aa	I have one also
An (if)	He'll gie me a haun, an he's a man at aa	He'll help me, if he's a man at all
As (than)	I wad raither dae oniething as ask ye	I would rather do anything than ask you
At (of)	Ask at him what he's ettlin to dae	Ask him what he intends doing
At (with)	He's angry at me	He's angry with me
At (=scold)	She's aye at me	She's always scolding me
Atween (between)	Atween the wind and the waa	In dire poverty
Auld (old)	Auld i the horn	Astute
	Auld claes and parritch	Routine
	Auld langsyne	Bygone times
Back	Back and fore	One way or another

Back (shortly after)	I'll see ye the back o thrie	I'll see you shortly after three o'clock
Baurley (respite)	Cry baurley-fummil	Ask for a truce
Beck (bend)	Beck and bou	Curry favour
Bent (coarse grass)	Gae to the bent	Abscond
Better	Mak a better o	Improve upon
Better (completely healed)	The wound's aa better	The wound is quite healed
Biddin (invitation)	A fiddler's biddin	A last-minute invitation
Bit (decisive point)	Whan it comes to the bit, naebody cares	Nobody cares, when it comes to the crucial moment
Bit (small)	He was only a bit laddie	He was only a little lad
Bit (somewhat)	I'm feelin a bit wabbit	I'm feeling somewhat tired
Blaw (blow)	Blaw i the lug	Wheedle
Black (extremely)	I feel black affrontit	I feel deeply ashamed
Blink (instant)	In a blink	In an instant
Bonny (large, of sum of money)	It'll cost ye a bonny penny	It'll cost you a great deal of money
Born	I've never seen the like in aa my born days	I've never seen anything like it in my whole life-time
Bou (bow)	Bou ane's hoch	Sit down
Brae (downward slope)	To gae doun the brae	To deteriorate in health or circumstances
Bree (brunt)	He got the bree o't	He bore the brunt of it
Brither (the like; find the like of)	Ye'll no fin the brither o't/brither it in monie a lang day	You won't find its like for a very long while
Brou (liking)	I hae nae brou o this	I have no liking for this
Bug, let bug (show sign)	He never let bug	He gave no indication
But (outside, outer room)	But and ben	Outside and inside; front and back
By (over and done with)	It's aa by nou	It's all over and done with now

By (past)	He's by his best	He's past his best days
Bygaun (bygoing)	I'll drap in on ye i the bygaun	I'll call in to see you in the passing
Byde (wait; tarry)	Will ye no byde a wee?	Will you not tarry for a short time?
Caa (proceed)	Caa canny	Proceed carefully
Cadger (tinker)	A cadger's curse	A worthless thing
Cauf (calf)	Cauf kintra	Native district
Cauld (cold)	Cauld comfort	Niggardly hospitality
Cheek	Cheek up	Be insolent
	Cheek for jowl	Side by side
Chow (chew)	Chow the chafts	Gnash the teeth
Claes (clothes)	Guid claes	Best clothes
	Auld claes and parritch	Routine
Claw (scratch)	Claw somebody's back	Flatter someone
Cleik (catch hold)	Cleik in wi	Associate with
Coals	Tak owre the coals	Call to account
Cock (raise)	Cock the wee finger	Drink; tipple
Come	Come speed	Make progress
	Come tae	Recover from a faint
	Come throu	Recover from an illness
	Come the peter owre	Dictate to
Common	He was only a common five-aichts	He was only an ordinary person
Concait (opinion)	To hae a guid concait o anesel	To have a good opinion of oneself
Cowp (upset)	Cowp somebody's hurly	Upset someone's plans
	Cowp the cran	Be ruined
Cowp (deal)	Nae great cowp	Not much worth
Crack (instant)	In a crack	In an instant
Crack (gossip)	Caa the crack	Chat
	Get on the crack wi	Start a conversation with
	Gie's your crack	Give me your news
	Turn the crack	Change the subject
Crap (top)	Crap and ruit	Entirely
Craw (crow)	Craw crouse	Talk confidently
	Crouse i the craw	Confident in speech

Creep	Creep in/out	Shorten/lengthen, of daylight
Creish (grease)	Creish the luif	Bribe; give gratuity
Cruppen (crept)	Cruppen doun	Bent with age
Cry	Be cried	Have marriage banns read in church
	Cry at the cross	Make public
Daft	Daft Days	Period of festivity at Christmas and New Year
Day	Day and day about	On alternate days
Dear	Dear keep us!	God keep us!
Dee (die)	Dee a fair strae daith	Die a natural death
Deid (death)	Deid o the year	Winter
Deil (devil)	Deil a haet did I get	Not a whit did I get
	Deil kens!	Goodness knows!
Doun (down)	Doun i the mou	Downcast
dram (glass of spirits)	Caa a dram	Order a drink
Draw	Draw tae	Take a seat at table
Dree (endure)	Dree ane's weird	Suffer one's fate
	Dree out ane's life	Drag out one's existence
Dreipin (dripping)	A dreipin roast	A good source of income
Dreip (let oneself down)	Dreip a dyke	Let oneself down from a wall with arms stretched
Drink	Nae smaa drink	Of no small consequence, of a person
Drive	Drive a prey	Make a cattle raid
	Drive on	Pass by, of time
Droun (drown)	Droun the miller	Put too much water in whisky
Easy	Be easy til	Be amenable to
Ee (eye)	Hae an ee til	Covet: have a liking for
	Pit somebody's ee out	Supplant someone
Eeran (errand)	Anes/yince eeran	On one special errand; for one special purpose
Egg	A peeled egg	A piece of good luck
	Aff ane's eggs	Uncomfortable; nervous

End	At the hinner end	In the long run
Faa (fall)	Faa aff ane's feet	Lose one's balance
	Faa out on	Lose one's temper with
	Faa throu ane's claes	Grow very thin
Fair	Fair to middlin	Quite well
Faurer (farther)	Nae faurer gane than	As recently as
Faut (fault)	In faut	At fault
Faut (lack)	For faut o	For want of
Feck (majority)	The feck o	The most of
Ferlie (wonder)	Nae ferlie	No wonder
Fettle (state; humour)	In grand fettle	In excellent condition/ spirits
Few	A guid few	A good many
Fiddler	A fiddler's biddin	A last-minute invitation
	Fiddler's news	Stale news
Fidgin (fidgeting)	Fidgin fain	Fidgeting with anticipation
Flee (fly)	Flee laich	Be unambitious
Fuit (foot)	Abune ane's fuit	Beyond one's means
	Aff the fuit	Morally astray
	Fuit for fuit	Side by side
	Gie up ane's fuit	Rebuke one
	Tyne a fuit	Lose one's foothold
Gae/gang (go)	Gae doun the brae	Deteriorate in health or circumstances
	Gang agley	Miscarry
	Gang to the gate	Be ruined
Gate (way)	Come the gate o	Present oneself at
	Gang ane's ain gate	Go one's own way
	Tak the gate	Depart
Gee, pronounced "jee" (stir)	Gee ane's ginger	Bestir oneself; bother oneself
Gee (pique)	Tak the gee	Take the huff
Gentry	Put on the gentry	Give oneself airs
Get	Get into a job	Familiarise oneself with a job
	Get mends o/upside wi	Get even with
	Get on to	Rebuke
	Get yokit tae	Get started on

Gie (give)	Gie somebody his coffee	Rebuke someone
	Gie somebody the gunk	Disappoint someone
	Gie somebody up his fuit	Scold someone
Go	Go on the bash	Go on a drinking bout
Greek	Short o the Greek	Stuck for words
Guid (good)	The unco guid	Extremely self-righteous people
Guilt	Tak guilt to anesel	Be conscience-stricken
Haet (particle)	No a haet	Not a whit
Hale (whole)	The hale jingbang/ hypothec/ rickmatick	The whole concern
	Gang hale-heidit for	Be absolutely en-grossed in
Haud (hold)	Haud in wi	Curry favour with
	Haud the stick owre	Dominate
	Haud up	Keep fair, of weather
	Haud wi	Acceed to
	Haud hame	Make for home
	Haud wide o	Keep clear of
Haun (hand)	Ahint the haun	In arrears
	Haun for nieve	Abreast
	Tak ane's haun aff	Strike with one's hand
	A haun's turn	A stroke of work
Heave	Gie somebody the heave	Dismiss someone from his job
Heels	Heels owre gowdie	Heels over head
Heid (head)	On the heid o	Occupied with
Hert (heart)	Steik ane's hert	Harden one's heart
	Tak the hert	Affect deeply
High	High i the bend	Haughty; ambitious
Hing (hang)	Hing in wi	Curry favour with
Hover (pause)	Hover a blink	Wait a moment
Humph (back)	Come up ane's humph	Come into one's mind
Hungry	A hungry welcome	A poor reception
Ilk (family)	Of that ilk	Of the same name
Ill (badly)	Tak something ill out	Be upset about some-thing
Juist (just)	Juist that	Quite so

Kaim (comb)	Kaim ane's hair backwards	Annoy one
Keen	Be keen o	Be fond of
Keep	Keep in wi	Keep on good terms with
Kee-vee	On the kee-vee	On the alert
Ken (know)	Fine I ken	Well I know
	A kent face	An acquaintance
Kist (chest)	Kist o whissles	Pipe organ
Lad	Lad o pairts	Talented youth
Laldie (beating)	Get laldie	Get a beating
Lang (long)	At lang and last	At length
Leese (be pleased)	Leese me on	I take delight in
Len (loan)	Tak the len o	Make a fool of
Licks (beating)	Get ane's licks	Get a beating
Loaf	Speak pan loaf	Speak with an affected English accent
Loss (lose)	Loss the heid	Lose one's temper
Lugs (ears)	Hing the lugs	Mope
	Warm the lugs	Box the ears
	Owre the lugs	Completely absorbed
Luif (palm)	Creish the luif	Bribe; tip
Made	Made up wi	Pleased with
Mail (rent)	Pey the mail	Pay the penalty
Meat	Like ane's meat	Well-fed looking
Mill	Mak a kirk or a mill o't	Make or mar it
Monie (many)	Monie's the . . .	Many a . . .
Munelicht (moon-light)	Munelicht flittin	A decamping by night to escape creditors
Nae (no)	Nae ferly	No wonder
	Nae faurer gane than	As recently as
Naither (neither)	Naither eechie nor ochie	Neither one thing nor another; not a cheep
	Naither wonder	No wonder
No (not)	No in	Abstracted in mind
Notion (liking)	Tak a notion o	Develop an affection
Or	Or that	Or the like [for
Out	Out o thocht	Beyond belief
Pease-brose (porridge made from pease-meal)	Pease-brose and pianaes	State of genteel poverty

Penny	A braw penny	A large sum of money
Peter	Put the peter on	Put a stop to
Pith (energy)	Aa ane's pith	With all one's might
Plug	Play the plug	Play truant
Plunk (be absent)	Plunk the schuil	Be absent from school without leave
Raither (rather)	I wad raither dae this as that	I would rather do this than that
Rax (stretch)	Rax somebody's neck	Hang someone
Rin (run)	Rin the gless	Use up allotted time
Road	Get the road	Be dismissed
	In the road	In the way
		Pregnant
Room	In room o	In place of
	The guid/best room	The sitting-room
Sake	For onie sake	For goodness' sake
Saut (salt)	Saut somebody's brose	Get one's revenge on someone
	Mak saut to ane's kail	Earn a living
Shavin (shaving)	To a shavin	To a nicety
Sheepshank (sheep's leg)	Think anesel nae sheepshank	Consider oneself of no small importance
Shouther (shoulder)	Thring the shouther	Shrug the shoulder
Sin	Sin ane's mercies	Show ingratitude for heaven's favours
Smaa (small)	Nae smaa drink	Of no small importance
	Smaa folk	People of humble rank
Sorrow	The sorrow a scrap	Not a whit
Souch (sigh; murmur)	Keep a calm souch	Keep quiet
	Hae aye the auld souch yet	Keep to the old ways
Souk (suck)	Souk in wi	Ingratiate oneself with
Stab (stob)	Stab and stow	Completely
Staun (stand)	Staun guid for	Be surety for
	Staun somebody's pairt	Take somebody's part
Steik (shut)	Steik ane's gab	Be silent
	Steik ane's hert	Harden one's heart
Stick	Haud the stick owre	Hold in subjection
	Stick and stow	Completely

27

Stickit (stuck)	Stickit minister	One who has failed in his profession
Stoup (stake)	Stoup and roup	Completely
Taen (taken)	Taen on wi	Attracted by
	Taen to the fair	Taken aback
	Taen up wi	Absorbed in
	Taen wi	Affected by
Tak (take)	Tak a guid bucket	Be a heavy drinker
	Tak a rise out o	Make fun of
	Tak inowre	Take advantage of
	Tak somebody doun a hack	Humble someone
	Tak somebody on	Pull someone's leg
	Tak something ill out	Be offended at some-thing
	Tak tent	Take heed
	Tak the dorts/drunts/gee	Sulk
	Tak the gate	Depart
	Tak the gow	Decamp in debt
	Tak the len o	Take advantage of
	Tak til anesel	Feel remorse
	Tak the rue	Feel remorse
Tap (top)	Be on ane's tap	Be constantly criticising one
	The tap-rung	The highest point
Think	Think lang for	Be long expecting; pine for
	Think shame	Feel ashamed
Thocht (thought)	To a thocht	To a nicety
Throu (finished)	Are ye throu?	Have you finished?
Thrapple (throat)	Redd the thrapple	Clear the throat
Thraw (twist)	Thraw a gruntle	Make a wry face
Time	This side o time	In this world
	It'll be yon time afore . . .	It'll be a long time before . . .
Trail	Trail the poke	Beg
	Trail a wing	Have an illicit love affair
Tryst (appointment)	Haud tryst	Keep one's word
Turn	On the turn	Beginning to curdle
Twa (two)	Be at twa	Be at variance
	Twa in a raw	Two abreast

Tyne (lose)	Tyne ane's fuit	Lose one's foothold
	Tyne the gate o	Lose the knack of
	Tyne the road	Lose one's way
	Tyne time on	Waste time on
Up	Up to	Equal to; able for
Wait	Wait on	Wait for
Want (defect)	Hae a want	Be mentally defective
Waur (worse)	The waur o	The worse for
Wear	Weir in	Pass by slowly
Wee (little)	A wee	A short time/distance/degree
	Haud a wee	Stop a moment
Weill (well)	Weill at anesel	Plump and healthy
	Weill-dune-tae	Well-treated
	Weill on	Drunk
	Weill tae	Well on time
	No weill	Unwell
Weird (fate)	Dree ane's weird	Endure one's fate
Wey (way)	Aa weys	In every respect
	Nae weys	In no respect
	In the wey	Pregnant
	In the wey o	About to
	Be in the wey o	Be in the habit of
	By his wey o't	According to him
	Mak wey o anesel	Commit suicide
	The richt wey o't	The true version of it
What-for	You'll get what-for	You'll be punished
Wheesht (hush)	Wheesht!	Be silent!
	Haud ane's wheesht	Be silent
While	This while back	For some time past
	A while syne	A while ago
Win (succeed)	Win owre	Fall asleep
	Win awa	Die
Wind	Brek the wind	Relieve flatulence
Winter	We never dee'd o winter yet	We'll survive
Wits	Wauk ane's wits	Sharpen one's wits
Wud (mad)	Rin wud	Go mad
Wulkies	Birl the wulkies	Turn somersault
Yince/ance (once)	For yince and aye	For ever

SUPPLEMENT

Aa (all)	Aa his/her/their lane	All alone
Atween (between)	Atween the een	Face to face
Auld (old)	The auld hech-howe	The old routine
Back	A while back	Some time ago
	Back o beyont	Out of the way
Bane (bone)	Near the bane	Miserly
Bash/batter	On the bash/batter	On a drinking bout
Bargain	A blin bargain	A pig in a poke
Ben (inside)	Be faur ben	Be in great favour
Bind	Naither to haud nor to bind	Uncontrollable
Blink (instant)	Hover a blink	Wait a moment
Byle (boil)	On the byle	At boiling point
Cheese	Never say cheese	Say nothing
Collie	Never as much as said, "Collie, will ye lick?"	Failed to give invitation to take food
Come	Come back on	Repeat, of food
	Come guid for	Be surety for
	Come o	Become of
	Come owre	Happen to
Dram (drink of (spirits	Be somebody's dram	Pay one's share of the drinks
Drap (drop)	A drap o the auld kirk	A small amount of whisky
Draw	Draw to rain	Tend to rain
Drink	A big drink o water	A tall, lanky person
Ee (eye)	A drappie in the ee	Enough drink to make slightly inebriated
Faa (fall; befall)	Faa tae	Start eating
	Fair faa . . .	A blessing upon . . .
Faiple (lower lip)	Doun i the faiple	Downcast
	Hing the faiple	Look downcast
Fore (front)	Be to the fore	Be alive and active
Fou (full)	As fou's a wulk	Very drunk
Hum	Hum and hae	Prevaricate
Hunger	A hunger or a burst	A feast or a famine
Like	Be like one's meat	Be well-fed looking
Mill	Gae throu the mill	Undergo an ordeal
Miss	A great miss	A great loss
	Miss oneself	Miss something good

Mistake	In a mistake	By mistake
Morn	The morn's mornin	Tomorrow morning
Mou (mouth)	Doun i the mou	Dejected
	Pit on a puir mou	Complain of poverty
Nane (none)	Nane o the twa	Neither of the two
Oor (hour)	A strucken oor	A whole tedious hour
Out	Is your cup out?	Is your cup empty?
Pan (skull)	Knock your pan out	Work to exhaustion
Peter	Come the Peter owre	Act the bully with
Pig (potsherd)	To pigs and whussles	To wreck and ruin
Pit (put)	Pit ane's gas at a peep	Deflate one
	Pit tae your haun	Set to; begin
	Pitten about	Upset
	Sair pitten til	Hard-pressed
Preens	Sittin on preens	On tenterhooks
	No worth a preen	Of very little **value**
Price	It's the price o him	It serves him right
Rag	Loss the rag	Lose the temper
Rise	Risin fower	Approaching four o'clock
	An early rise	A getting **out of bed** early
Roar	Roar and greit	Weep loudly
Saft (soft)	Hae a saft side tae	Have a liking for
Sairin (a helping)	Get ane's sairin	Get one's deserts
Sax (six)	Sixes and saxes	Six and half-a-**dozen**
Say	I wadna say but what . . .	I daresay . . .
See	I've seen me . . .	There have been times when . . .
	See me that brush	Hand me that brush
Shift (change)	Get shiftit	Change from working togs
	Shiftin claes	Clothes one changes into after work
Speed	Come speed	Make good progress
Speir	Speir a body's price	Ask what one will charge
Steik (stitch)	No a steik	Not one article of wear
Stick	Stick up to	Stand up to; defy
Stour (dust)	Rin like stour	Run at full speed

Swatch (sample)	Tak a swatch fae	Follow the example of
Tak (take)	Tak up hous	Start off in one's own house
	Tak the haun aff	Smack
	Tak up to, of water	Reach up as far as
Teeth	Hae aa ane's back teeth	Have all one's wits
Tell	D'ye tell me that!	Indeed!
Turn	Tak a turn	Take a walk
	No a haun's turn	Not a stroke of work
Vex	Be vext for	Be sorry for
Wale (choice)	The wale o	The pick of
Watch	Watch yoursel	Be on your guard
Will (wish)	Hae ane's will o	Have one's way with
Word	Say/pit up a word	Say a prayer
Wrang (wrong)	Get the wrang sou by the lug	Take the wrong meaning
	Rise aff the wrang side	Get out of bed in a bad mood

Vocabularies

English-Scots
Scots-English

Abbreviations

adj.	.	.	adjective/participial adjective/adjectival phrase
adv.	.	.	adverb/adverbial phrase
conj.		.	conjunction
interj.	.	.	interjection
intrans.	.	.	intransitive
n.	.	.	noun/noun phrase
nom.		.	nominative
part.	.	.	participle
pa. t.	.	.	past tense
prep.		.	preposition
pron.	.	.	pronoun
sing.		.	singular
trans.		.	transitive
v.	.	.	verb

* Word also appears in list of Scots idioms

English - Scots Vocabulary

Supplementary list begins on page 123.

Aback, adv., arselins; backies; backlins: **take aback,** v., tak aff.

abandon, v., dishaunt; forleit; forhoo, of a bird its nest.

abase, v., bemean: **abase oneself,** v., hunker doun.

abash, v., bumbaze; confoun: **abashed,** adj., hingin-heidit/luggit.

abate, v., ease; dachen, of wind: **abatement,** n., let; still.

abattoir, n., butch-hous; shamells.

abbreviate, v., dock; touk.

abdomen, n., wame; kyte; painch.

abduct, v., wyse: **abduction,** n., rapt.

abet, v., airt: **abettor,** n., airter.

abhor, v., laithe: **abhorrent,** adj., scunnersome: **abhorrence,** n., grue.

abide, wait for, v., byde: **endure,** v., byde; thole; dree: **remain,** v., byde: **dwell,** v., byde; dwall; stop; win: **abode,** n., dwallin.

abject, adj., fuit-lickin; inhaudin.

ablaze, adj., ableize; alowe.

able, adj., feckfu; feirdy: **be able/ unable,** v., dow/downa: **able-bodied.** adj., feirdy; yauld: **ability,** n, fushion ; ingyne (injyne).

abnormal, adj., byornar; orra.

abolish, v., owre-thraw: **erase,** v., dash: **end,** v., mak throu wi.

abort, v., misgae; pick; slink.

abound, v., hatter; hotch: **abundance,** n., feck; lashins; rowth; galore: **abundant,** adj., rowth; ruch/rouch.

about, prep., anent; o; on.

above, prep., abune; owre.

abreast, adv., abreist: **keep abreast of,** v., keep til.

abroad, adv., abreid; furth; outby.

abrupt, adj., aff-haun; cuttit: **abruptly,** adv,, swippert.

abscess, n, ingrowth ("as in now"); rinnin.

abscond, v., gae to the bent/gate; tak the gow.

absentee, n., fugie (foodjie); plunker: **absent oneself,** v., play the plug; plunk: **absent-minded,** adj., no in: **absentmindedness,** n., forget.

absolute, adj., clean; fair: **absolutely,** adv., clean; fair; black.

absolve, v., purge; quat.

abstain, v., gae frae; haud by: **bout of abstinence,** n., starve/sterve.

abstemious, adj., scrimpit; canny; furthy.

abstract, summarise, v., resume: **summary,** n., abbreviate; pirlicue.

abstruse, adj., kittle.

absurd, adj., daftlike; ridiclous.

abuse, v., abuise; hash; n., snash: **abusive,** adj., ill-moud.

abysmal, adj., boddomless.

accede to, v., gae in wi; haud wi.

accent, n., souch; tuin: **speak with affected accent,** v., speak pan loaf.

access, n., ingate; withgate: **accessory,** adj., pertinent.

accident, n., mishanter: **accidental,** adj., by-hand: **meet with accident,** v., mishanter.

accommodate, v., up-pit: **accommodation,** n., up-pittin: **space,** n., waygate.

accompany, v., convoy; follow: **accompanist to singer,** n., sang-tilter.

accomplish, v., win throu: **accomplished, skilled,** adj., airtie; faur seen: **accomplished person,** n., dab haun.

accord, v., haud wi: **in accordance with,** adj., conform til.

accost, v., tackle.

account, reckon, v., reck: **value,** v., priz; ereckoning, n., lawin: **report,** n., sae-say; tell: **account book, n.,** count/tammy book.

accumulate, v., see amass.

accurate, adj., leal; perqueer.
accursed, adj., fey; weirdit.
accuse, v., wyte: accusation, n., wyte.
accustom, v., yaise; cuddom.
ache, v., gowp; stound; birl; n.,
stound; stang.
achieve, v., get roun; throch: achievement, n., fait; tap-pickle (crowning).
acid, adj., tairt; sour; sharrow.
acknowledge, v., awn.
acme, n., tap-rung.
acorn, n., aicorn; aiknut.
acquaint, v., acquant: acquaintance, n.,
kent face: acquainted, adj., acquant.
acquire, v., come by; win.
acquit, v., free; quat: acquittance, n.,
dischairge.
acrid, adj., snell; reikit.
acrimony, n., ill-feeling.
across, prep., athort; throu; adv.,
athort.
act, v., n., ack: act recklessly, v.,
gilravage: act energetically, v., lay/
link at: active, adj., steirin; swack:
activity, n., thrang; fyke.
actual, adj., rale.
acumen, n., glegness; gumption; ingyne
(injyne).
acute, adj., sherp; gleg.
adapt, v., adap; sort: adaptable, adj.,
handy.
add, v., eik: addition, n., eik: in addition, adv., forby.
adder, n., edder.
addle, v., n., aidle: addle-brained, adj.,
aidle.
address a letter, v., back: address of a
letter, n., backin.
adequate, adj., eneuch; enow, of number.
adjourn, v., continue.
adjudge, v., jeedge; redd.
adjunct, n., pertinent; pendicle.
administer, v., guide; helm: administra-
tion, n., guidal: administrator, n.,
guider.
admire, v., respeck.
admit, own, v., awn.
ado, n., adae; buff; steir; stramash.
adolescent, adj., halflin.
adroit, adj., canny; gleg; knacky.
adult, n., man/woman body; adj.,
man/woman-grown.
adultery, n., houghmagandie.

advance, v., win forrit: promote, v.,
forder: advancement, n., forderance;
lift: well advanced, adj., forrit: in
advance, adv., afore.
advantage, n., fordel; fore: be of
advantage, v., mak for.
advent, n., hithercome; oncome:
adventitious, adj., by-hands; fremmit
(foreign).
adventure, v., anter/aunter; n., ploy:
adventurous, adj., fordersome.
adverse, adj., thrawn; thrawart: adversity, n., mishanter. ·
advertise, v., adverteese: advertise-
ment, n., adverteesement.
advise, v., guide; wyse; speak a word
to: adviser, n., guider.
advocate, v., rede; avise: n., fore-
speaker; lang goun (legal).
adze, n., eitch; hack.
aerated waters, n., ginger; scoosh.
affable, adj., couthie; furthie: affabil-
ity, n., couthiness.
affair, n., maitter: the whole affair, n.,
the hale rickmatick/hypothec.
affect, v., daur upon; tak the hert:
affected in manner, adj., mim-moud;
primsy: affected by, adj., taen wi:
talk affectedly, v., speak pan loaf.
affection, n., kindness; fainness:
affectionate, adj., lousome; fain; sib.
affinity, n., sibness: blood relationship,
n., sibness; kind.
affirm, v., threip; uphaud: affirmation,
n., threip; sae-say.
afflict, v., ding; fash: affliction, n.,
fash; pyne.
affluent, adj., bien; weill-gethert; ruch/
rouch.
afford, v., affuird; stand.
affront, v., ruffle; snash; n., dunt;
snash.
afire, adv., alowe.
afoot, adv., afuit; agate.
afraid, adj., feart; frichtit; eerie/oorie,
of supernatural.
after, prep., adv., efter: afternoon, n.,
efternune (-nin); afterwards, adv.
syne.
again, adv., ance/yince mair.
against, prep., agin.
age, n., eild: equals in age, n., eildins;
yealins.
agent, n., factor; troker: act as agent,

v., factor.

aggravate, v., gaw; rile.

aggression, n., onding; set: **aggressive,** adj., randy; ruch-haundit.

aggrieve, v., fyke; skaith.

aghast, adj., dumfounert.

agile, adj., souple; swack; spree; fittie.

agitate, v., forfluther; jummle: **agitation,** n., curfuffle; fash, mental.

ago, adv., syne; sinsyne: **some time ago,** adv., a while back.

agony, n., rack; mairtyrin.

agree, v., gree; haud wi: **agreeable,** adj., greeable: **agreement,** n., greement.

aground, adv., agrun.

ague, n., trummles.

aid, v., forder; gie a heize; pit tae ane's haun; fore.

ail, trouble, v., fash; sturt: **ailing,** adj., badly: **ailment,** n., trouble.

aim at, v., ettle at; haud for: **intend,** v., ettle: **aimless,** adj., knotless.

air, suffocating, n., smeik; smoor: **warm, damp air,** n., moch: **scornful air,** n., geck: **a tune,** n., fit; spring.

ajar, adv., agee (ajee).

alacrity, n., blytheness; glegness.

alarm, v., flauchter; sturt; raise; n., sturt.

alas, interj., ochone; wae's me.

alcove, n., bole; neuk.

ale, n., yill; nappy; swats; pennywheep: **alehouse,** n., yill-shop; chynge.

alert, adj., gleg; sprack; vieve; birkie; smert.

align, v., raw.

alike, adj., adv., equal-aqual.

alive, adj., quick; to the fore.

all, n., adj., adv., aa.

allay, v., lay; slocken, thirst.

allege, v., threip; depone.

alleviate, v., lichten; dave; sowther.

alley, n., close; entry; wynd.

allocate/allot, v., lot; stent: **allocated task,** n., stent.

allow, v., lat/lat be; thole; leave: **be allowed,** v., get.

ally, v., part-take; n., stoup; part-taker.

almighty, adj., almichty.

almost, adv., maist.

alms, n., aumous.

aloft, adv., abune; alaft.

alone, adj., alane: **quite alone,** adj., burdalane.

along, adv., prep., alang: **alongside,** prep., alangside; anent.

aloof, adj., aff-staunin; fremmit; adv., abeich.

alphabet, n., abbacee.

already, adv., alreadies; else.

also, adv., alse; an aa; tae.

altar, n., offran-stane.

alter, v., chynge.

alternative, adj., tither: **alternately,** adv., time about; tyde betyde.

although, conj., tho; suppose.

altogether, adv., aathegither; outthrou.

always, adv., aye.

amalgamate, v., gae thegither; meng.

amass, v., rake; scart, in niggardly way.

amateur, adj., halflin.

amaze, v., bamboozle; bumbaze; dumfouner: **amazed,** adj., dumfounert.

ambition, n., ettle: **ambitious,** adj., ettlin; high-bendit.

ambush, v., forlay; n., lour.

amenable, adj., handy: **be amenable,** v., be easy said til.

amiable, adj., couthie; gracious; cosh.

amiss, adv., aff the reel; out o theat: **taken amiss,** adj., ill-taen.

am not, v., amna.

among, prep., amang; mang.

amount, large, n., feck; wecht: **small amount,** n., lick; wee tait/pickle.

ample, adj., rife; rowth; ruch/rouch: **large,** adj., sonsie.

amputate, v., demember.

amuse, v., enterteen: **amusement,** n., ploy.

analyse, v., backspeir.

anarchy, n., heeliegetee.

ancestors, n., forefowk.

anchor, n., heuk.

ancient, adj., auld-warld; auncient; langsyne.

anger, v., rile; thraw; n., birse; dander: **very angry,** adj., dancin mad.

angle, n., sklent: **at an angle,** adj., sklentit.

anguish, n., rack; mairtyrin.

animal, n., beast.

animation, n., birr; smeddum: **animated,** adj., birkie; skeich; vieve.

an le, n., cuit; shackle.

annex, v., skech; hanch.

annihilate, v., nil; perish: **annihilation,** n., wrack.

announce, v., annunce; lat ken: **public announcement,** n., placket.

annoy, v., fash; fyke; rile: **annoying,** adj., angersome: **annoyance,** n., fash.

annuity fund, n., tamteen.

anoint, v., smairg; straik.

anomaly, n., gley.

another, adj., anither.

answer, v., repone; reparty; n., repone; wirr, angry.

ant, n., eemock: **ant-hill,** n., eemock-pile.

antics, n., ongauns; heeliegoleeries.

anticipate, v., forestaw: **expect,** v., ettle; lippen.

anti-clockwise, adv., widdershins.

antique, adj., auld-warld: **antiquated,** adj., auld-farrant.

anvil, n., stiddie.

anxious, adj., careous (care-ous); fain; fond: **anxiety,** n., cark; wanrest.

any, pron., adj., onie: **anyhow,** adv., oniehou/wey: **anything,** n., ocht.

apart, adv., apairt; abreid.

apartment, n., en/end: **one-apartment house,** n., single end.

apex, n., tap; toupic.

aphorism, n., owrecome; threne; say.

apiece, adv., the piece.

apoplexy, n., plexie; apoplectick.

appal, v., fley; daunton.

apparatus, n., graith.

apparent, adj., sensible: **apparently,** adv., appearinly.

apparition, n., ghaist; bogle.

appear, v., kythe: **appearance,** n., cast; seem.

append, v., eik: **appendage,** n., perti-nent: **appendix,** n., eik.

appetite, n., gab: **appetiser,** n., kitchen: **without appetite for,** adj., no able for.

apple, n., aipple.

apply, v., lay til: **apply for,** v., put in for.

appoint, v., stent: **appointment to meet,** n., tryst.

apposite, adj., concaity; brief.

appreciate, v., taste.

apprehend, v., nab; grip: **understand,**

v., ken: **apprehension,** n., kennin: apprehension, fear, n., dreid; ergh: **apprehensive,** adj., timorsome.

apprentice, v., prentice; n., prentice-haun; halflin; boy.

approach, v., mak til; n., oncome: **approach a certain time,** v., weir til.

appropriate, v., skech; thig; adj., con-caity; wycelike.

approve, v., approbate: **approve of,** v., sustain.

approximately, adv., back and forrit.

April, n., Aprile: **April fool,** n., hunt-the-gowk.

apron, n., brat; awpron; scoggie.

apt, adj., concaity; brief: **aptitude,** n., ingyne (injyne); turn.

arbiter, n., thirdsman; sidesman: **arbitrate,** v., redd.

arbour of roses, n., roseir.

arch, v., bou; n., bou; pend.

archaic, adj., auld-fangle; auld-warld; auntient.

ardent, adj., aiverie: **ardour,** n., birk; greeshoch; instancy.

arduous, adj., dour; kittle.

arena, n., rink.

argue, v., argie-bargie; threip: **argu-ment,** n., argie-bargie; threip.

aristocrat, n., laird; duke-ma-lordie.

arithmetic, n., counts: **do arithmetic,** v., count.

arm, n., airm: **armpit,** n., oxter: **walk arm in arm,** v., cleik.

army, n., airmy.

aroma, n., waff; oam.

around, prep., adv., roun.

arouse, v., wauken; raise.

arrange, v., sort; kind; ted.

array, v., graith: **equipage,** n., feir: dress, n., cleidin; graithin.

arrears, n., by-rins: **in arrears,** adj., back-lyin: **be in arrears,** v., rin ahin.

arrest, v., grip; nab.

arrive at, v., win at/tae: **arrival,** n., hithercome; income.

arrogance, n., pauchtiness: **arrogant,** adj., pauchty; heich-heidit.

arrow, n., arra; flane: **arrowhead,** n., prick.

arson, n., rid cock.

art, n., airt: **artful,** adj., airtie; drauchtie: **artfulness,** n., sleeness.

article, n., eetim; objeck.

artificial, adj., made-like; simulate: **artificial flowers**, n., gumflouers.

artist, n., airtist.

ascend, v., munt; speil; sclim: **ascent**, n., speil; sclim.

ascertain, v., mak siccar.

ash tree, n., aish; rodden tree (mountain ash).

ashes, n., aise: **ashbox**, n., baikie: **ashpit**, n., aise-midden.

ashamed, adj., affrontit: **be ashamed**, v., think shame.

aside, adv., sidelins.

ask, v., speir; ax: **ask after**, v., speir for: **ask of**, v., speir at.

askance, adv., asklent: **look askance**, v., sklent; gledge.

askew/aslant, adv., skew; asklent.

asleep, fall asleep, v., faa owre.

asparagus, n., sparrygrass.

aspect, appearance, n., cast; seem: **view**, n., vizzy; swype; whuff.

aspen, n., quakin aish.

asperity, n., nebbiness; ruchness.

aspersion, n., sclander: **cast aspersions**, v., miscaa; ill-speak.

ass, n., cuddy: **silly ass**, n., cuddy; gype.

assail/assault, v., yoke/set on; lay til.

assay, v., n., sey.

assemble, v., forgether; gae in, of school: **assembly**, n., forgetherin.

assent, v., gree.

assert, v., threip; yammer: **assertion**, n., threip; sae-say.

assess, v., stent: **assessment**, n., stent.

assign, v., destinate; dispone: **assignation/make assignation**, n., v., tryst.

assist, v., forder; gie a heize; put tae ane's haun.

associate with, v., cleik in wi; forgether wi; collogue: **association of neighbours**, n., manawdge.

assort, v., kind; sammer.

assume, v., ettle; jalouse; tak.

assure, v., assuir; wat: **assured**, adj., crouse: **assuredly**, adv., certes.

asthma, n., asthmatics: **asthmatic**, adj., pechie: **be asthmatic**, v., slocher.

astir, adv., asteir; agate.

astonish/astound, v., bamboozle; bumbaze; dumfouner.

astray, adv., aff the reel: **go astray**, v., gley; gang agley.

astride, adv., aspar; stridelegs: **sit astride**, v., striddle.

astronomer, n., starnwatcher; astrologian.

astute, adj., able; canny; pawkie: **astuteness**, n., gumption; pawkiness.

asylum, n., girth: **lunatic asylum**, n., loonie-hous.

at all, adv., ava.

athwart, prep., athort.

atlas, n., mapamound.

atmosphere, suffocating, n., smoor; smeik: **atmosphere, hot damp**, n., moch.

atom, n., haet: **atoms**, n., smithereens.

atrocious, adj., hangished; enorm.

attach, v., festen; twine; yoke: **adhere**, v., clap.

attack, v., yoke/set on; lay til; n., onding; grip, of pain.

attain, v., win; fetch.

attempt, v., hae a crack/skelp/whup at.

attend, be present, v., tend: **attend to**, v., see efter; tent: **pay attention**, v., tak tent: **attentive**, adj., eydent; tentie: **inattentive**, adj., no in: **attention**, n., tent: **attendant**, n., dirder.

attic, n., laft: **attic ceiling**, n., cumseil.

attitude, n., set; souch: **dogmatic attitude**, n., threip.

attorney, n., writer.

attract, v., tyce; wyse: **attractive**, adj., bonny; winsome; eesome.

attraction, n., tae-draucht.

attribute, v., even; pit on: **assign**, v., destinate; foreset.

auction, n., rowp; unction: **auctioneer**, n., unctioneer: **proclaim an auction**, v., cry a rowp: **livestock auction building**, n., mart.

auger, n., wummle.

aught, pron., aucht; ocht.

augment, v., biggen; eik to: **augmentation**, n., eik.

augur, n., weirdman: **augury**, n., bode; warnin: **of good augury**, adj., canny.

aunt, n., auntie: **great aunt**, n., auld auntie.

austere, adj., dour; fell; stour: **austerity**, n., dourness.

authentic, adj., rale; leal; soothfast: **authenticity**, n., lealty.

authority, n., heid-room: **person in**

authority, n., heid yin; the maister.
autocrat, n., maister and mair.
autograph, n., haun o wryte.
autumn, n., back-end; hairst.
avail, v., dow: available, adj., patent.
avalanche, n., hooloch; shot brae.
average, n., mids; adj., owreheid: on an average, adv., owreheid.
averse, adj., ill-willie; shy: aversion, n., scunner; staw: cause/get a feeling of aversion, v., scunner: avert, v., weir: avert the eyes, v., gley.
avid, adj., aiverie; cadgy.
avoid, v., jouk; eschew.
await, v., byde; wait on.
awake, v., adj., wauken: stay awake, v., wauk.
aware, adj., waur: be aware of, v., ken: make aware of, v., avise.
awash, adj., rinnin: be awash, v., sail.
away, adv., awa; abeich; hyne; aff: away from, prep., furth o.
awe, n., dreidour; awe-inspiring, adj., awesome; fearsome; grugous.
awkward, adj., ackwart; hielan; gawkit.
awl, n., brog; elshin.
awry, adj., gley; thorter; adv., agee; gley; skew: make awry, v., thraw.
axe, n., aix.
axle, n., aixtree.

Babble, v., blether; cleck; haiver; n., blethers; haivers.
baby, n., babby.
back, rear, n., hinside: backbone, n., rigbane: backache, n., ripple: backside, n., bum; dowp; erse: back to front, adv., arselins: backward, adj., back, of crops; backart: timid, adj., blate; bauch: backwards, adv., backiewards: backwards and forwards, adv., back and forrit.
bad, evil, adj., wicket; ill: faulty, adj., fauty: badly, adv., bad; ill; sair: bad-tempered, adj., crabbit; thrawn.
badge, n., taiken.
badger, n., brock.
baffle, v., dumfouner; bumbaze.
bag, n., pock; seck: baggage, n., trammels; stuff.
bail, n., caution.
bailie, n., beylie.
baker, n., baxter.

balance, lose balance, v., faa aff ane's feet: evenly balanced, adj., equalaqual.
bald, adj., beld.
bale, of straw, v., n., turse.
balk, v., thorter.
ball, n., baa: bounce, of ball, v., n., stot.
ballad, n., ballant.
balloon, n., wind-baa.
balm, n., baum.
ban, v., dischairge.
band, tie, n., whang: band of people, n., core; curn: musical band, n., baun.
bandage, v., rowe.
bandit, n., cateran.
bandy words, v., giff-gaff: the bandying of words, n., giff-gaff.
bandy-legged, adj., bou-leggit/hocht; bowlie.
bang, v., dad; dird; n., dad; dird; bung.
banish, v., fleem.
bank, overhanging, n., brae-hag; brou: steep bank, n., scaur.
bank, 'kitty', n., puggie: penny bank, n., lucky-box: banker, n., banquier.
bankrupt, n., dyvour; abbey laird; adj., broken: bankruptcy, n., brak.
banner, n., standart; waff: banneret, n., thane.
banns, n., cries: have banns read in church, v., be cried.
banquet, n., blaw-out; belly-rive.
banter, v., chairge; taigle; n., bantry.
baptise, v., kirsen.
bar, v., baur; snib; n., baur: wooden bar, n., stang; tram: fire bar, n., rib.
barb, n., whutter.
barbarous, adj., landart; raucle.
bard, n., makar; schenachy.
bare, quite bare, adj., bare nakit/scuddie: barefooted, adj., barefuit.
bargain, v., niffer; cowp; troke: bargain-making, n., thoum-lickin.
barge, v., stave on; waumle.
barge, boat, n., scow.
bark, v., n., bowf.
barley, n., bere: ear of barley, n., aicher.
barn, n., corn-laft.
barnacle goose, n., claik.
barometer, n., mercury.
barrel, n., bowie; easin-butt, for roof drips; hogget, a cask.

barren, adj., yeld/yell: **barren, of soil,** adj., histy; dour; deif.

barrier, n., backhaud.

barrow, n., barra: **barrow shaft,** n., tram: **two-wheeled barrow,** n., hurly.

barter, v., n., cowp; niffer; troke.

base, n., found; laroch; steid: **basement,** n., dunny; grun-hous.

base, adj., fouty; snool-like.

basement, n., dunny.

bashful, adj., blate; bauch; ergh: **bashfulness,** n., blateness.

bask, v., beik.

basket, n., creel; skep; ruskie, of straw; spale basket, of wood strips.

bass, singer, n., base.

bastard, n., bastert; get.

bat, n., baukie bird.

bathe, v., douk: **bite of food after bathing,** n., chitterin-bit.

batten, n., clug; spaik.

batter, v., blaud; clour.

battle, v., fecht; n., fecht; tulzie; stour.

bauble, n., falderal; whigmaleerie.

bawd, n., auntie: **bawdy-house,** n., borthel; gaillie.

bawl, v., n., rowt; yelloch.

bay, n., bey; hope; wick, small.

bay, keep at bay, v., weir aff.

beach, n., foreland.

beacon, n., ward-fire.

beak, n., neb.

beaker, n., bicker.

beam of wood, n., tree; caber: **crossbeam on house,** n., bauk.

bear, v., cairry: **endure,** v., thole; dree: **hard to bear,** adj., dreich.

beard, n., baird; phizz.

beat, v., beatle; bleach; leather: **beat quickly, of heart,** v., dunt; gowp: **beating,** n., beatlin; leatherin: **beat, outdo,** v., bang; cow; ding; lick.

beauty, n., bonniness; lousomeness: **beautiful,** adj., bonny; braw; wally.

becalm, v., dill; lowden.

become, v., come; faa: **become of,** v., come o: **become, suit,** v., seem; set.

bed, put/go to bed, v., skep/get skeppit: **bedroom,** n., chaumer: **bedridden,** adj., bedfast: **four-poster bed,** n., fower-stoupit bed.

bedaub, v., clart; claister; slaiger; splairge.

bedraggle, v., bedraigle; glaurie.

bee, bumble, n., bummle; bumbee; fogie-bee: **bee-hive,** n., skep.

beef, shoulder and loin, n., sey: **hind leg,** n., hoch: **salted beef,** n., mairt.

beer, n., swats; nappy: **small beer,** n., tippenny; wheep yill.

beetle, n., clock; bumclock, humming; golach.

befall, v., faa; come owre; happen; tide.

befit, it befits, v., it sets: **befitting,** adj., wycelike.

before, prep., afore; forenent; gin, of time; conj., afore; or; gin.

beg, v., cadge; trail the poke: **beseech,** v., fleich (fleetch); prig: **beggar,** n., gaun/orra body; gaberlunzieman.

beget, v., get.

begin, v., faa/set/yoke tae: **beginning,** n., affset; fore-end.

begrime, v., coum; elt.

beguile, v., begunk; geck.

behave badly, v., cairry on; ill-dae: **bad behaviour,** n., cairry-on.

behind, adv., prep., ahin; ahint: **behindhand,** adj., back.

behold, v., behaud; leuk til: **beholden to,** adj., behauden to.

belch, v., bock; rift; n., rift.

believe, v., hae; trew: **belief, doctrine,** n., lair: **beyond belief,** adj., past aa.

belittle, v., doun-cry; lichtlie.

bell, n., skellat; clinkum bell, church: **ring, of a bell,** v., n., jow.

belle, n., bab; tip.

bellicose, adj., randy; ettersome; clammersome.

bellow, v., n., belloch; gowl; buller.

bellows, n., bellises.

belly, bulge, v., bag: **stomach,** n., wame; kyte; painch.

belong, v., belang: **belongings,** n., guids and gear.

below, adv., prep., ablow.

belt, n., baudric.

bench, n., binch; bink; sunk.

bend, v., bou; kink: **bow,** v., bou; beck; courie: **twist,** v., camshachle.

beneath, adv., prep., aneath.

benediction, n., blessin; sain.

beneficial, adj., canny.

benefit, n., buit; fore.

benign, adj., canny; couthie; honest.

bent, inclination, n., turn; genie

(jeenee).

benumb, v., daiver; denum: **benumbed**, adj., dozent; fundit.

bequeath, v., will; legate: **bequest**, n., testment; gilbow (jilbow).

bereave, v., twine; reive.

beseech, v., fleich (fleetch); prig.

beside, prep., aside; nearhaun: **besides**, adv., prep., forby.

besiege, v., ligger.

beslobber, v., slaiger; slairg; slorach.

besmear, v., clag; clart; claister; slaiger; splairge.

besot, v., bedunder; daumer: **besotted**, adj., dozent; fond.

bespatter, v., draigle; slaister; splairge; spark.

bespeak, v., forespeak: **bespoken**, adj., trysted.

bestir oneself, v., steir anesel; gèe (jee) ane's ginger.

bet, v., n., wad; wissel.

betide, v., befaa; faa; come owre.

betray, v., begeck; mislippen; swick.

betroth, v., tryst: **betrothed**, adj., trysted.

better, get better, v., mend: **get the better of**, v., ding; get owre.

between, prep., atween.

bevy, n., kivin.

bewail, v., murn; mane.

beware, v., bewaur; tak tent.

bewilder, v., bumbaze; dumfouner: **bewildered**, adj., dumfounert; dozent.

bewitch, v., beglaumer; cast ill on: **bewitched**, adj., fey; elf-shot.

beyond, adv., prep., ayont; outwith: **beyond boundaries of**, prep., furth o.

bias, n., sklent; swee/swey: **biassed**, adj., tae-sided.

bib, n., brat; daidle.

Bible, n., the Auld Buik: **family Bible**, n., haa-bible.

bid, invite, v., seek: **bid at sale**, v., n., bode.

big, adj., muckle; sonsie; wallopin: **very big person/thing**, n., beezer.

bigoted, adj., nerra-nebbit; kirk-reikit.

bile, n., gaw.

bill, account, n., lawin: **an IOU**, n., ticket: **display bill**, n., placket.

bin for corn, n., ark; girnel; gruip.

bind, v., tether; thirl; twine; wap.

birch, the tree, n., birk: **made of birch**, adj., birken.

bird, n., burd: **unfledged bird**, n., gorb; gorlin; wallydraigle, youngest in nest.

birth, give birth to, v., cast; drap: **birth certificate**, n., burth-brief: **birthplace**, n., cauf kintra.

biscuit, n., bake.

bit, little bit, n., bittie; bittock; kennin.

bite, v., nip; chack; n., nip; pick, of food: **biting, of wind**, adj., snell.

bitter, adj., sharrow; sour; wairsh: **bitter, of weather**, adj., snell.

bittern, n., bluiter.

bitumen, n., pick.

black, adj., bleck: **black-looking**, adj., wan: **blackbird**, n., blackie: **blackguard**, n., blagyaird: **blackmail**, n., skaith-mail: **blacksmith**, n., ferrier; burnewin: **blacksmith's workshop**, n., smiddy.

bladder, n., blether.

blame, v., n., faut; wyte.

bland, suave, adj., fair-faced/spoken: **mild**, adj., lythe; maumie.

blanket, n., bed-plyde; hap.

blast, n., blaff; gird: **blast of wind**, n., blaw; bluffert.

blaze, v., n., bleize.

bleak, adj., dour; gurly.

bleat, v., n., bah; mae.

blemish, v., smit; tash; n., gaw; smitch.

blench, v., flaunter; flench.

blend, v., meng; n., mixter; complouter.

bless, v., sain: **blessing**, n., sain; bethankit.

blight, v., scowther; scaum; frap; n., scaum.

blind, v., adj., blin.

blink, v., blinter; glint.

bliss, n., seil: **blissful**, adj., seily.

blister, v., blush; n., blushin; blether.

blithe, adj., cadgy; canty; crouse.

blizzard, n., rowster; stour.

bloat, v., swal; flozen: **bloated**, adj., fozie.

blob, n., blab; drib.

block, v., stap: **block of wood**, n., clug.

blond, adj., fair-avised.

bloom, v., n., flourish; blaw.

blot, n., blab; mote: **blotting paper**, n., blot-sheet.

blotch, n., plouk; slaik.
blow, v., blaw; flaff, in gusts; fuff, gently; blouster, roughly.
blow, n., bash; beff; clash; clour; dad; dirl; dunt: **deal a blow**, v., clour.
blubber, v., bubble: **whale blubber**, n., spick.
blue-grey, adj., blae: **bluebell**, n., blawort: **bluebottle**, n., bummer.
bluff, v., gie the glaiks; adj., raucle.
blunder, v., bummle; ramstam, headlong: **blunderer**, n., bummler; staumrel.
blunt in manner, adj., off-haun; raucle.
blur, v., mirk: **blurred**, adj., mirk; dern.
bluster, v., blouster; gouster: **blustery**, adj., gurly; tashy; tousy.
boar, n., chattie; gaut, castrated.
board, n., brod; buird: **board and lodging**, n., keep.
boast, v., n., blaw; bum; craw: **boastful**, adj., vaunty; vogie: **boaster**, n., bum.
boat, canal, n., scow: **dredger**, n., dregboat; glabbery punt: **tender**, n., clory: **salmon-fishing boat**, n., coble: **boat-mast**, n., staing.
bob, v., bab; hap.
bobbin, n., babbin; pirn.
bodice, n., shirt-goun.
body, the living body, n., corpus: **body-snatcher**, n., resurrector.
bog, n., flow; lair; moss: **boggy**, adj., lairy; mossy: **bog myrtle**, n., gall.
boggle with fright, v., gloff: **equivocate**, v., flaunter.
boil, v., hotter; seeth; wallop.
boil, n., beilin; byle.
boisterous, adj., bousterous; raucle; rantin; gurly.
bold, adj., braisant; bardy; forritsome.
bolster, n., bowster.
bolt, v., n., bowt; sneck; snib: **run off**, v., tak the gate.
bond, n., band, of marriage; thirl-ban: **bonds, fetters**, n., thairms.
bone, n., bane: **funny-bone**, n., dirlie/yeukie-bane.
bonfire, n., banefire.
bonnet, n., bannet; bunnet: **peaked bonnet**, n., skippit bannet; doolander.
onus, n., bountith; cudiech.

book, n., buik: **book-board**, n., batter; brod: **do the books**, v., keep counts.
boor, n., carl; tyke: **boorish**, adj., carlish; hill-run.
boost, v., forder.
boot, n., buit: **bootnail**, n., tacket.
booth, n., buith; crame.
booty, n., fang; spulyie; grab; scaff.
border, n., mairch: **edge**, n., selvedge.
bore, v., thirl: **weary**, v., deave: **boring**, adj., tedisome: **become bored**, v., weary.
borecole, n., green kail.
borough, n., brugh: **burgher**, n., brughman.
borrow, v., thig: **act of borrowing**, n., thig.
boss, chief, n., heid bummer/deister.
botch, v., bootch; broggle; moger.
both, pron., adj., conj., baith.
bother, v., fash; fyke.
bottom, n., boddom; grun: **backside**, n., bum; erse; dowp; droddum.
bough, n., brainch; snag.
boulder, n., bowder.
bounce, v., stot; bunce.
bound, limit, n., stent; tether; scowth: **boundary**, n., mairch; landemeer.
bounty, n., bountith.
bouquet, n., flouer.
bow, knot, n., bab; doss: **bow-legged**, adj., bou/bowly-leggit; bou-hocht.
bow, curtsy, v., beck; bou; lout; n., beck; bou.
bowels, n., painches: **evacuate bowels**, v., scour; fyle.
bower, n., bour.
bowl, receptacle, n., bicker; coggie; luggie.
bowl along, v., hurl; trinnle: **bowl, in game**, v., n., bool.
bow-string of fiddle, n., thairm.
box, n., buist; kist: **put in box**, v., kist.
box the ears, v., warm the lugs: boxing, n., nieves.
boy, n., laddie; callan: **boy-friend**, n., laud: **boyhood**, n., laddie-days.
brace, v., ticht: **bracing**, adj., caller; snell: **braces**, n., gallowses.
bracken, n., breckan; fern.
bracket, n., uphaud; bilget.
bradawl, n., brog.
brag, v., n., blaw; bum; craw.
braid, n., traiss: **trim with braid**, v.,

passment.

brains, n., harns.

bramble, n., brammle: **brambleberry**, n., brammle; gaitberry.

branch, n., brainch; snag: **branch of river**, n., grain.

brand, v., n., buist: **branding iron**, n., burn-airn: **brand new**, adj., brent-new.

brandish, v., swee/swey; swap; wadge.

brass, n., bress.

brat, n., gaitlin; get.

brave, adj., bauld; wight: **bravely**, adv., dauntingly: **bravery**, n., spunk; manheid; smeddum: **have the bravery to**, v., dow: **bravado**, n., blaw.

brawl, v., tulzie; wap; n., collieshangie; ruction; stramash.

breach, n., brak; slap, in wall.

bread, n., breid: **piece of bread and jam**, n., jeelie piece.

breadth, n., breid; braidness.

break, v., brek: **break down**, v., n., founder: **breakwater**, n., fleit-dyke.

breakfast, n., brakfast; parritch.

breast, n., breist; crap; brisket: **woman's breasts**, n., bubbies.

breath, n., braith; wind: **breath of wind**, n., sowff: **breathe heavily**, v., pech; smocher; wheezle: **breathing space**, n., baurley.

breed, v., cleck: **good breeding**, n., gentrice.

breeze, n., souch; sowff: **stiff breeze**, n., skirl o wind; stour.

brew, v., mask: **brewer**, n., browster: **a brewing**, n., maskin; browst.

briar, n., breer: **briar pipe**, n., gun.

bribe, v., creish the luif; n., cudiech.

bridesmaid, n., best maid.

bridge, n., brig.

bridle, v., n., brank.

bright, adj., bricht; licht; skyre: **bright in manner**, adj., gleg; sprack; vieve: **brighten**, v., brichten: **brighten up**, v., cantle up.

brilliant, adj., skinklin: **brilliance**, n., glister.

brim, n., brou; lip: **brimful**, adj., lippin/reamin fou.

brimstone, n., brunstane.

brine, n., brime; brack.

bring, v., fesh.

brisk, adj., sprack; spree; vieve; cadgy.

bristle, v., birsle; stairt, of hair; n., birse: **bristly**, adj., birsie.

brittle, adj., bruckle; frush.

broad, adj., braid.

broil, v., birsle; brander.

broker, n., cowper; troker.

bronchitis, n., brounkaties.

brooch, n., hesp; tie.

brood, n., cleckin; flauchter, of birds.

broom, n., brume: **broomstick**, n., besom.

broth, n., kail; bree.

brothel, n., borthel; gaillie: **brothel-keeper**, n., auntie.

brother, n., brither; billy: **brother-in-law**, n., guid-brither.

brow, n., brou.

brown, adj., broun.

bruise, v., n., bash; birse; brizz; stave.

brunt, n., birst; bree: **bear the brunt of**, v., get the bree o.

brush, n., besom; souper: **brushwood**, n., hag.

brusque, adj., aff-haun; cuttit.

brute, n., bruit.

bubble, v., hotter; plapper; wallop; n., blab; sapple.

bucket, n., bowie; sey; stowp.

buckle, v., buttle; n., spang; tash: **buckler**, n., target.

budge, v., moodge; fitch: **cause to budge**, v., fitch.

buffers, n., dunchers.

bugbear, n., fash; wurricow, source of terror.

build, v., big: **build, physique**, n., set: **building**, n., biggin.

bulge, v., bag; shoot, of walls, etc.

bulk, n., bouk: **bulky**, adj., boukie; great.

bull, n., bul; jock: **bullock**, n., stirk; stot.

bullfinch, n., bullie (bu-lly).

bully, v., gouster; n., gouster; bangster.

bulwark, n., deck-buird.

bumble, v., blabber; gulder: **bumble-bee**, n., bumbee; fogie-bee.

bump, v., n., dunch; dunt.

bun, n., cookie, soft; sweetie-scone, sugar-coated.

bunch, n., bob, of flowers; strap; tass: **tie in bunch**, v., strap.

bundle, v., truss; wap; n., truss; wap; fang.

bung of barrel, n., dook; spicket.
bungle, v., n., bootch; broggle; moger: bungler, n., fouter; clatch.
bunion, n., werrock.
buoy, n., blether: buoyant, adj., canty; gaucy; lichtsome.
burden, v., fraucht; n., cairry; birn: burdened, adj., dounhauden.
bureau, n., buroo.
burly, adj., muckle-boukit; strappin.
burn, v., birsle; scaum; scad; n., scaum; scad: burnt, adj., brunt; brent.
burr in speech, n., crout: speak with burr, v., crout; whurr.
burrow, v., howk; n., bourie.
burst, v., brust; rive: burst open, v., lowp.
bury, v., lair; yird: burial, n., bural; yirdin: burial plot, n., lair.
bus station/halt, n., stance.
bush, n., buss: stunted bush, n., scrag: bushy, adj., bussie.
business, n., troke; handling: do business with, v., niffer/troke wi.
bustle, v., n., bizz; fyke; fissle; n., thrang; stour; stramash.
busy, adj., thrang; gaun.
butcher, n., flesher: butcher-meat, n., flesh.
butt, v., dunch; box; n., dunch.
butt, mark, n., bob.
buttermilk, n., sour douk: butter dish, n., butter ark/crock.
buttocks, n., dock; dowp; hurdies; curpin.
buttress, n., hallan; jamb.
buxom, adj., fodgel; sonsie.
buy, v., coff.
buzz, v., n., bizz; bum.
buzzard, n., gled.
by, prep., of time, come; gin: by and by, adv., belyve.

Cabbage stalk, n., kail runt.
cabinet, n., aumrie: cabinetmaker, n., square-wricht.
cable, n., towe.
cache, v., n., plank; pose.
cackle, v., n., keckle; claik.
cadence, n., lilt.
cadge, v., mouch (mootch); skech; scaff; sorn.
calamity, n., mishanter; wanchance.

calculate, v., upcast.
calf, n., cauf: calf of leg, n., cauf.
call, v., n., caa; cry.
callous, adj., dowf.
callow, adj., green; neip-green.
calm, v., caum; dill; n., caum; lown; adj., caum; lown; lythe; quait.
can, v., dow.
candid, adj., evendoun; fair-spoken.
candle, n., caunle: candlestick, n., chandler.
candy, n., claggum; gundy; gob-stopper; glessie; treacle.
cane, v., n., wattle; swabble.
cannot, v., canna; downa.
cant, n., auld souch; dichty water.
cantankerous, adj., cankert; fykesome; thrawn.
canvas, n., cannas.
cap, n., bunnet.
capable, adj., feckfu; fendie; skeelie.
capacious, adj., gutsy; sonsie; scouthie.
cape, headland, n., craig; scaur.
caper, v., fling; flisk; fyke; n., fling; flisk.
caprice, n., norie; gee (jee); whig-maleerie: capricious, adj., flauntie; flea-luggit; hallirackit: capricious person, n., flichter-lichtie.
capsize, v., cowp; whummle.
capstan, n., kempstane.
carcase, n., carkidge; bouk.
card, n., caird: playing cards, n., cairts.
care, v., n., fash; rack; tent: care for, v., tent; see efter: take care, v., tak tent: careful, adj., canny; tentie: careless, adj., tentless.
career, v., scrieve.
caress, v., cuitle; dawt; straik, with hand.
caretaker, n., janitor, school; dirder, animal.
carnival, n., birlin; gilravage; gaudy-aumous.
carol, n., carle.
carouse, v., birl; go on the bash/skite; n., birlin; splore; spree.
carp, v., threip; yatter.
carpenter, n., jyner; wricht.
carrion, n., cabbrach.
carry, v., n., cairry; cadge, loads: carrier, n., cairrier; cadger: carriage, n., cairriage: carry on/keep on, v., haud on.

45

cart, n., cairt: **carter,** n., cairter: **cart-horse,** n., aiver.

cartilage, n., birsk.

carve, engrave, v., scart: **carving knife,** n., whittle.

cascade, v., plash; sten; n., linn; spout.

casement, n., fenester; shot, shuttered.

cask, n., bowie; hogget, large; knag, small.

cast-iron, n., pot/run metal.

castor of chair, n., whurlie.

castrate, v., cut; lib.

casual, adj., by-haun; orra, of a job.

cat, n., baudrons; poussie-baudrons; cheety: **catgut,** n., thairm.

cataract, n., linn; spout.

catch, v., grip; nab; cleik.

category, n., kinkind.

cater, v., meat.

caterpillar, n., grannie; oobit; kail-worm.

catkin, n., poussie-willow.

cattle, n., beasts; nowt: **cattleman,** n., byreman: **cattle shed,** n., byre.

cause, v., gar; n., occasion; wey.

causeway, n., causey.

caution, n., tent; rack: **cautious,** adj., canny; tentie.

cease, v., deval; gie owre; quat, work.

ceiling, n., ruif: **having sloping ceiling,** adj., coomceiled.

celebrated, adj., faur-kent: **celebration,** n., gaudy-aumous.

cellar, n., grun-hous.

cement, n., lime.

cemetery, n., kirkyaird; howf.

censure, v., flyte; check; faut.

centipede, n., jenny-hunder-feet; thousan-taes.

ceremony, pomp, n., adae; fashery; flumgummery.

certain, adj., shair, siccar: **a certain man,** n., yae man: **certainly,** adv., certes.

certificate, n., line; brief.

cesspool, n., aidle dub; jaw-hole.

chafe, v., chaff; freit; gaw.

chaff, n., caff; stour: **banter,** v., chairge; n., bantry; heize.

chaffinch, n., shilfa.

chair, n., sait: **armchair,** n., big/muckle chair: **small chair,** n., creepie chair: **chairman,** n., preses.

chalk, n., cauk.

challenge, v., brag; n., brag; coorgy (coorji): **challenge the truth of,** quarrel: **a blow as a challenge to fight,** n., courdy-lick.

chamber, n., chaumer: **chamber-pot,** n., chanty; po; jordan.

champion, v., staun somebody's pairt; n., kemp.

chance, n., tid; adj., antrin: **chancy,** adj., wanchancy.

change, v., chynge: **changeable,** adj., kittle: **changeling,** n., witch-wean.

channel for water, n., gang; lade; gaw, of drain.

chaos, n., heeligetee; potterskink: **chaotic,** adj., mixter-maxter.

chapel, n., chaipel.

character, spirit, n., fushion; smeddum; spunk.

charge, v., n., chairge.

charm, spell, n., cantraip; brief.

chase, v., win efter.

chasm, n., cleuch.

chastise, v., dicht; sort: **chastisement,** n., licks; forslitting.

chat, v., crack; claiver; n., crack; claivers.

chatter, v., blether; claiver; n., blethers; claivers.

cheap, adj., chaip.

cheat, v., geck; begunk, n., cheatrie; chate: **deceitful,** adj., swicky.

check, restrain, v., crib; snib; n., awe-band; snib: **reverse,** n., backset.

checkmate, v., stell.

cheek, n., chowk; chaft: **impudence,** n., impidence; snash: **cheeky,** adj., impident; braisant.

cheer up, v., birk/chirk up: **cheerful,** adj., cadgy; canty; crouse.

cheese, a cheese, n., kebbuck: **oily cheese,** n., greitin cheese.

chemise, n., sark.

cherish, v., dawt; browden.

cherry, wild cherry tree, n., gean (gee-an).

chest, n., kist; bink; aumry: **thorax,** n., kist.

chew, v., n., chow.

chicken, n., chookie; chucken: **chick-weed,** n., chickenweed.

chief, adj., heidmaist: **head man,** n., guidman.

child, n., bairn; wean (wane): **child-**

hood, n., bairntime: **childbirth,** n., shouting.

chilly, adj., cauldrife; snell; allerish.

chimney, n., lum; chimla: **chimney top,** n., lumheid; craw-heid.

chin, n., gash.

china, n., cheeny; pig: **china dog,** n., wally dug.

chink, n., bore; gaig, in wood; gell, in wood.

chip, v., pick: **chip of wood,** n., spail.

chirp, v., n., cheip; pleep; chirl.

chisel, n., furmer.

choice, n., chyce; wull.

choir, n., core; baun.

choke, v., kink; smoor, for air.

choose, v., chap; choise; wale.

chop, v., chap; hack; hag; sned.

chores, n., scodgies.

chorus, n., owrecome.

christen, v., kirsen.

Christmas, n., Auld Yule: **Christmas present,** n., Christmas.

chronicle, n., back-leuk.

chubby, adj., chuffy; sonsie; baffy.

chuckle, v., keckle.

chunk, n., hack; fang; whang.

church, n., kirk: **church officer,** n., beadle: **churchyard,** n., kirkyaird.

churn, v., kirn; jummle; n., kirn.

cinder, n., coal; aizle; dander.

cipher, n., ceepher.

circumference, n., laggin-gird.

citizen, n., brughman.

civil, adj., discreet; weill-bred.

clamber, v., clammer; sprauchle.

clammy, adj., mochie; wauch.

clamour, n., dirdum; stramash; rammy.

clang, v., stoun.

clank, v., clunk.

clasp, v., hesp: **clasp hands,** v., chap hauns: **clasp-knife,** n., durk.

class, n., cless; kinkind, category: **classify,** v., kind; sammer.

clatter, v., n., dirl; dunner.

claw, v., n., claut; cleuk.

clay, n., cley.

clean, v., dicht: **clean out,** v., redd; scour; muck, a byre.

clear, adj., fair, of weather; skyre, of liquid: **clear away,** v., redd.

cleave, v., rive.

clench, v., nieve, the fist; chirt, the teeth.

clerk, n., clark.

clever, adj., able; auld-farrant; gleg; wyce.

cliff, n., craig; heuch; scaur.

climb, v., n., sclim; speil.

cling, v., grip to.

clinkers, n., danders.

clip, v., cow; rump: **clipped in speech,** adj., dockit.

clique, n., clan; fry; set.

clock, n., nock: **wall clock with pendulum,** n., wag-at-the-waa.

clog, v., clag: **clogs,** n., clugs.

close, v., steik; gae tae: **close, stifling,** adj., firy; smoory: **close-fisted,** adj., near-the-bit: **close-fitting,** adj., jimp: **close beside,** prep., aside; nearhaun.

clot, v., lapper; n., lapper, of blood; clat, of dung; sclatch, of mud.

cloth, n., claith: **piece of cloth,** n., clout: **clothe,** v., busk; cleid: **clothes,** n., claes; clouts; duds; brats: **best clothes,** n., braws.

cloud, n., clud: **driving clouds,** n., wrack: **clouded,** adj., drumly.

clover, n., claver: **clover flowers,** n., soukies.

clown, n., carl; dobbie.

cloy, v., staw: **cloying,** adj., fousome; ugsome.

club, n., timmer; tree: **club foot,** n., bool-fuit.

cluck, v., claik; clock, of broody hen; n., claik.

clue, n., meith.

clumsy, adj., fouterin; hochlin; gawkit: **be clumsy,** v., fummle.

cluster, n., bourock.

clutch, v., n., cleik; claucht.

clutter, v., cluther; clamper; n., cluther.

coagulate, v., earn; cruddle; lapper; barken.

coal, a live coal, n., aizle: **coal bucket,** n., baikie: **coal cellar,** n., coal neuk: **coal dust,** n., gum: **coal pit,** n., cleuch; heuch.

coarse, adj., courss; raucle; brosy: **coarse in texture,** adj., groff.

coax, v., phraise; whillywha.

cobble-stone, n., causey-stane.

cobbler, n., soutar.

cockroach, n., clock.

cocksure, adj., gleg-shair.

codicil, n., eik.
coffin, n., deid-kist; fir goun/fecket.
cognomen, n., eikname.
cohabit, v., bundle: cohabitation, n., clash-tae.
coil, v., fank; wup: coil of rope, n., fank; wuppin.
coin, n., cuinyie: small coin, n., bawbee; boddle; doit.
cold, adj., cauld; cauldrife; snell; ettersome: cold-blooded, adj., cauldwamed.
colewort, n., kail.
colic, n., bats; bellythraw.
collapse, v., brek; founder: cause to collapse, v., founder.
collect, v., gether; tak up: collector, n., uplifter.
collide, v., bairge.
colour, n., ure: colourless, adj., fauchie; heauveless, in personality.
colt, n., cowt; staig: coltsfoot, n., dishilago.
comb, v., n., kaim.
combat, n., fecht; brulzie; bicker; set-to.
combine, v., gae thegither.
come, v., win.
comely, adj., braw; dainty; weill-faured; wycelike.
comfort, n., easedom: comfortable, adj., canty; cosh.
commerce, n., tred; traffick; troke.
commit, v., play: commit oneself to, v., haud wi.
committee, n., comitee; buird.
commodious, adj., gutsy; scouthie: commodities, n., gear; graith; troke.
commonsense, n., gumption; mense.
commotion, n., bizz; steir; stew; caathrou; collieshangie.
communicate, v., traffick; troke: communication, n., traffick; troke.
compact, adj., ticht; snod.
companion, n., crony; fier; maik; billy.
company of people, n., core; getherin; clamjamfry, contemptuous.
compare, v., even: compared with, prep., besides; by; to.
compass, point of compass, n., airt.
compel, v., gar.
compensate, v., upmak: compensation, n., mends; upmak.
compete, v., kemp; pingle: competent,

adj., habile; weill-seen.
complacent, adj., greeable; weill-willie.
complain, v., compleen; girn; channer; yammer: complaint, n., girn.
complete, adj., hale: absolute, adj., clean; fair: completely, adv., fair.
complexion, n., hue: dark-complexioned, adj., black-avised.
complicate, v., wimple: complication, n., wimple.
compliment, v., phraise.
comply, v., gree; haud wi.
compose, v., dite; mak: composer, n., makar: regain composure, v., come tae.
compunction, n., ilta; efterstang.
compute, v., upcast.
concave, adj., howe.
conceit, n., concait; pauchtiness: conceited, adj., concaity; pauchtie.
conceive, form in womb, v., cleck.
concentrate upon, v., stick into.
concern, n., regaird; kindness: concerning, prep., anent.
concise, adj., cuttit.
conclude, v., feenish: infer, v., draw.
concoction, n., rummle.
concubine, n., callet; lie-by: live with concubine, v., bundle.
concur, v., complowter; say thegither.
condensation, n., oam.
condescend, v., lout: condescending, adj., high-i-the-bend.
condition, n., case; wey: in good/bad condition, adj., tifty/fozie.
condole, v., mane: condolence, n., mane.
condone, v., excaise; forgie.
conduct, v., convoy: conduct church singing, v., precent: conduct, n., gate; backgate, immoral; glaikery, foolish: conductor, n., precentor.
conduit, n., cundy.
confectionery, n., sweeties: confectionery shop, n., sweetie shop.
confer, v., collogue: conference, n., collogue.
confess, v., awn.
confide, v., lippen: confidence, n., traist: confident, adj., crouse.
confine, v., stent; tether; n., mairch: confinement, n., ward.
confirm, v., upbear; sustain; sowther.
confiscate, v., inbring.

conflict, v., n., fecht; warsle.
conform, v., gree; haud wi: **conformably to,** prep., conform til.
confound, v., owrethraw; whummle; dumfouner.
confuse, v., dumfouner; bamboozle; bumbaze: **confused,** adj., dozent; in a creel: **confusion,** n., habble; mixter-maxter.
congeal, v., geal (jeel); set; cruddle.
congenial, adj., couthie; kindly.
congruous, adj., confeerin; habile.
conjecture, v., ettle; jalouse.
connect, v., conneck: **in connection with,** prep., anent; o.
connoisseur, n., cunning man.
conscience, n., inwit: **conscientious,** adj., eydent.
conscious, **be conscious of,** v., fin: **recover consciousness,** v., come again.
consecrate, v., sain.
consent, v., gree.
consequence, n., eftercast: **importance,** n., force.
conserve, v., hain.
consider, v., think on: **considerable,** adj., bonny; braw; gey; dainty/denty: **consideration, regard,** n., tenderness: **considering,** conj., sith.
consign, **transfer,** v., have over: **entrust,** v., lippen.
console, v., mane.
consolidate, v., sowther; sadden.
consort, v., haunt; lig wi; n., fier; marrow.
conspicuous, adj., kenspeckle; weillkent.
conspire, v., collogue; traffic.
constant, adj., leal; close.
consternation, n., fley; sturt.
constitute, v., estaiblish: **appoint,** v., destinate.
constrain, v., gar.
constrict, v., strait.
construct, v., big: **construct badly,** v., rickle.
consult, v., see/inquire at.
consummate, v., throu; adj., perfite.
contagion, n., smit: **contagious,** adj., smittal: **infect by contagion,** v., smit.
contain, v., conteen: **restrain,** v., kep.
contaminate, v., fyle; smit.
contemplate, v., think on; panse.
contemporaries, n., yealins.

contempt, n., geck; laith: **express contempt,** v., geck: **contemptible,** adj., measly; shitten: **contemptible person,** n., nyaff; blastie; shargan.
contend, v., kemp; pauchle; wrastle: **contention,** n., widdle.
content, v., ser; pleisure: **contented,** adj., canty; cosh.
contest a fact, v., quarrel: **contest,** n., kemp; pingle; set-to.
continue, v., haud/win on: **continually,** adv., ever and on.
contort, v., thraw; wamble.
contract, v., n., contrack: **shrink,** v., gae in; cling; crunkle.
contradict, v., thraw; conter: **contradictory,** adj., thrawn.
contraption, n., whigmaleerie.
contrary, adj., contrair; thrawn: **contrariwise,** adv., withershins.
contravene, v., thraw; conter.
contribute, v., mak: **contribution,** n., inpit.
contrite, adj., manefu: **contrition,** n., efterstang; rue.
contrive, v., feck; mak up: **contrivance,** n., graith; tirly-wirly.
control, v., guide; n., guidal; pouer.
controversy, n., argie-bargie; stushie.
conundrum, n., guess.
convene, v., forgether: **convention,** n., forgetherin.
convenient, adj., hanty.
converse, v., caa the crack; claiver: **conversation,** n., speak; gab.
convert, v., chynge; transmue.
convict, v., fyle.
convince, v., insense.
convivial, adj., hertie; sosh.
convulse, v., thraw: **convulsion,** n., kink.
coo, v., croodle.
cook, v., cuik.
cool, v., adj., cuil; caller.
coop, v., n., crib; cavie.
co-operate, v., complowter: **co-operative store,** n., sosh.
copestone, n., capestane: **coping,** n., tablin; crib.
coppice, n., shaw.
copulate, v., mow: **copulation,** n., mow.
copy, v., transcrieve; double; swatch; n., double.
cord, n., hank; hemp; theat; widdie.

cordial, adj., canty; kindly; guid-willie.

cormorant, n., black douker; sea-craw.

corn, bunion, n., warrock.

corn bin, n., ark; kist: **ear of corn,** n., icker: **handful of corn,** n., rip: **corn-crake,** n., skirlcrake: **cornflower,** n., blawart.

corner, n., neuk; cunyie.

corporal punishment, n., licks.

corpse, n., corp; lyke.

correct, v., correck; uptak; adj., correck.

correspond, v., scrieve; corrie, inti-mately.

corridor, n., throu-gang.

corroborate, v., upbear; sustain.

corrode, v., roust; freit: **corrosion,** n., roust.

corrupt, v., thraw: **taint,** v., fulyie.

cost, n., chairge; damage.

costume, n., outrig; habuliment.

cosy, adj., bieldy; cosh; bien; couth; lown.

cottage, n., biggin; shieling; but and ben, two-roomed.

cotton-wool, n., caddis.

couch, n., sunk.

couch-grass, n., wrack; creepin-wheat-grass.

cough, v., n., hoast; craighle.

could, v., cud.

council, n., buird.

counsel, v., n., wyse; rede.

count, v., figur: **countless,** adj., un-kennable.

country, n., kintra; adj., landart.

couple, v., kipple; n., twasome.

courage, n., spunk; smeddum; man-heid.

course, n., adj., courss: **direction,** n., airt: **layer,** n., lachter.

court, v., gae wi; tryst: **courteous,** adj., mensefu; gentie: **courtyard,** n., close: **court building,** n., court-hous.

cousin, n., kizzen.

covenant, n., band; tryst.

cover, v., n., hap; bield: **coverlet,** n., quitin.

covet, v., hae an ee til; eyst: **covetous,** adj., gair.

cow, n., cou; quey, young cow: **cow dung,** n., shairn: **cow-house,** n., byre.

cow, intimidate, v., daur; counjer; snool.

coward, n., feartie; couardie; coucher: **cowardly,** adj., feart.

cower, v., cour; courie; hurkle.

cowl of chimney, n., whurlie; grannie.

coy, adj., willin-sweirt.

crab, n., partan: **crabbed,** adj., crabbit; carnaptious.

crack, v., n., gaig; gell: **cracked,** adj., crackit.

crackle, v., crunkle; crump; reishle.

cradle, n., creddle.

craft, skill, n., skeil; can: **trade,** n., tred: **cunning,** n., sleeness.

crag, n., heuch; cleuch; scaur.

cram, v., stap; stech; stow.

cramp, v., strait.

crazed, adj., daft; gyte; wud.

crest, n., tappin: **crested,** adj., tappit: **crestfallen,** adj., hingin-luggit.

crew, mob, n., canailyie.

cricket, insect, n., cheiper; chirper.

crimson/crimson cloth, n., cramasie.

cringe, v., cour: **cringing,** adj., fuit-lickin: **cringing person,** n., snool.

crinkle, v., crunkle.

cripple, v., shachle; n., clincher; bedral.

crisp, adj., crumpie.

critic, n., pick-faut: **critical,** adj., tuithy: **critical point,** n., bit.

croak, v., craik; craighle; n., croup.

crockery, n., piggery.

croft, n., craft.

crone, n., carlin.

crook, v., n., cleik; cruik; n., bowl: **crooked,** adj., bowlie.

croon, v., croodle.

crop, v., n., crap: **crop hair,** v., cow: **nibble,** v., moup; nip.

cross, n., rude; adj., thrawn: **cross-examine,** v., cross-speir: **crossroads,** n., fower-weys.

crouch, v., cour; courie; hurkle.

crow, v., n., craw: **carrion crow,** n., blackneb: **hooded crow,** n., hoodie.

crowd, v., thrang; hotter; n., thrang; clamjamfry; cleckin.

crown, v., n., croun.

crude, adj., hamespun; raploch; ruch-some.

cruel, adj., fell; ill: **treat cruelly,** v., mischieve.

crumbs, n., crums; crottles.

crumble, v., crummle; murl; muilder:

crumbly, adj., bruckle; frush; murly.
crumpet, n., crimpet; drapscone.
crunch, v., crinch; runch; crump:
crunchy, adj., runchie.
crush, v., champ; dunt; broozle.
crust, n., scruif.
crutch, n., stilt; oxter staff.
cry, v., n., mane; skreich; yammer:
shed tears, v., greit: cry for, v., craik.
crystal, adj., kirstal.
cuckoo, n., gowk.
cudgel, n., timmer; tree.
cue, n., meith; mint.
culprit, n., ill-doer.
cult, n., lair.
cultured, adj., sneith; pretty.
culvert, n., cundie.
cunning, adj., slee; airtie; drauchty.
cup, n., bicker; caup: cupboard, n.,
aumrie; cubbart; press.
cur, n., tyke; messan.
curb, v., stent; crub: bridle, n., brank.
curd, n., cruds: curdle, v., turn; lapper;
yirn.
curio, n., ferlie; knick-knacket.
curious, adj., careous (care-ous);
funny; strange.
curl, v., n., kink; wimple: curling
match, n., bonspiel: curling-stone,
n., whun.
curlew, n., whaup; earn-bleater.
currant, n., curran.
current, n., tide-race; rin: current of
air, n., guff.
curry favour, v., beck and bou; mool wi.
curt, adj., aff-haun; cuttit.
curtail, v., jimp; snib.
curtsy, v., beck; kurchie; lout; n.,
kurchie; beck.
curve, v., n., bou; wimple.
cushion, n., cod; cushin.
custody, n., ward: take into custody,
v., lift; tak in.
cut, v., n., sneck; snib; whittle; cow,
of hair: cut in slices, v., shave.
cynical, adj., seirie.
cyst, n., knurl.

Dabble, v., dauble; moger; plowter, in
water.
daff, v., geck; jink.
dagger, n., durk.
dainty, adj., pernickety; pretty; dainshoch: dainties, n., fine things.

dairy, n., milk-hous: dairymaid, n.,
dey: renter of dairy cows, n., bouar.
daisy, n., gowan.
dale, n., den; hallie.
dally, v., fyke; geck: dallying, n.,
daffin; fyke.
dam, n., caul.
damage, v., skaith.
damp, adj., mochie; saft, of weather.
dance, v., birl; bob; jink; shak the
fuit; n., birl; bob; fuit-shakin.
dandelion, n., pee-the-bed: dandelions
in seed, n., clocks.
dandle, v., diddle; jink.
dandruff, n., scruif.
dandy, n., whup-ma-denty: dandified,
adj., dink; prinkie.
danger, n., jeopardie: dangerous, adj.,
crankie, insecure; wanchancy.
dangle, v., wammle; shoogle.
dapper, adj., sprush; trig.
dappled, adj., fleckit.
dare, v., n., daur: daring, adj., gallus:
daredevilry, n., daredeviltry.
dark, n., adj., daurk; mirk: grow dark,
v., daurken; gloam: in the dark, adv.,
daurklins.
darling, n., daurlin; hinnie; wee thing.
darn, v., n., dern.
dart, v., dert; jink; wheich; n., dart.
dash about, v., skelp: dash with force,
v., dad; wap: dashing, adj., branksome.
daughter, n., dochter.
daunt, v., ding.
dawdle, v., daidle; slogger.
dawn, v., daw; n., gray licht; keek-o-
day.
daydream, n., dwam: daylight, n., daylicht: day-labour, n., darg.
daze, v., dumfouner; bumbaze; daiver;
stound: dazed, adj., dumfounert.
dazzle, v., glaik; glamour: dazzling,
adj., glairy.
dead, adj., deid: strike down dead, v.,
fell.
deaf, adj., deif; dull o hearin: deafen,
v., deifen; deave.
deal, a great deal, n., hantle; muckle.
deal, v., dale; cowp; niffer; troke:
dealer, n., daler; cowper.
dear, expensive, adj., saut: dearness,
n., dearth: dear one, n., jo.
dearth, n., scant and want.

51

death, n., daith; deid: death throes, n., deid-thraws.
debase, v., margullie.
debate, v., n., argie-bargie.
debauch, v., fyle; n., birlin; spree.
debonair, adj., gentie; pretty.
debris, n., redding.
debt, n., ill peyment: in debt, adj., sucken: clear debt, v., outredd.
decade, n., daiken.
decamp, v., tak the gow: a decamping by night, n., munelicht flittin.
decant, v., skink: decanter topped with hen's comb, n., tappit hen.
decay, v., dow; foust; dwyne; muilder: decayed, adj., moulie; frush.
decease, n., daith; deid.
deceive, v., begunk; geck.
decent, adj., daicent; honest.
decide, v., conclude.
decipher, v., spell.
declaim, v., bleize out; gie mou.
declare, v., ledge; depone; legal.
decline in health, v., n., fail; dwyne: a downslope, n., dounfaa.
decompose, v., chynge.
decorate, v., busk; set up: decorous, adj., douce; wycelike.
decoy, v., gow.
decrease, v., dwyne.
decree, n., word.
decrepit, adj., decripit; forfairn.
decry, v., faut; fyle.
dedicate, v., sain.
deduce, v., draw.
deed, exploit, n., docht: deedbox, n., kist.
deer, n., hairt.
deface, v., fyle; blaud.
default, v., n., failyie.
defeat, v., lick; bang; ding; waur; n., waur.
defect, n., defeck; faut; gaw: defective, adj., fauty.
defend, v., fend; weir: defence, n., fend; weir.
defer, v., aff-pit.
deferential, be, v., sing smaa.
defiant, adj., bardy; crouse: defiance, n., crouseness; foreheid.
deficient, adj., scrimpit: be deficient in, v., want: deficiency, n., want.
defile, v., fyle; clart.
define, v., descrive: fix limits, v., stent; mairch.
deflect, v., welr.
deformed, adj., camshach; gemm: deformity, n., eelist.
deft, adj., knacky; slee.
defy, v., thraw.
degenerate, v., dwinnle; dwyne.
degrade, v., even; bemean; tash.
degree, rank, n., gree: confer degree upon, v., laureate.
deject, v., dump: dejected, adj., disjaskit; dowie: dejection, n., waeness.
delay, v., taigle; n., taiglement: causing delay, adj., taiglesome.
delectable, adj., lousome.
deliberate, v., rede; reck; adj., canny.
delicate, adj., peelie-wallie; dwyny: delicacies, n., fine things; sunkets.
delicious, adj., mou-frauchty.
delight, v., n., delyt: delightful, adj., lousome.
delinquent, n., ill-doer.
delirious, adj., deleerit; heich: delirium, n., deleeritness.
deliver, save, v., redd.
delude, v., begunk; geck: delusion, n., begunk; mirligo.
deluge, v., blash; n., plump; blash.
delve, v., dell; howk.
demean, v., bemean; even: demean oneself, v., lout; hunker.
demeanour, n., cast.
demented, adj., daft; gyte; wud.
demolish, v., wrack; cowp.
demon, n., worricow.
demoralise, v., thraw; bemean; dumfouner.
demur, hesitate, v., swither: object, v., backspeak.
demure, adj., primsie; douce.
denominate, v., cry.
denounce, v., miscaa.
dense, adj., blin, of fog; ruch, of growth; goamless, of understanding.
dent, v., n., dunt; clour.
denude, v., tirl.
deny, v., forsay; na-say: denial, n., na-say.
depart, v., depairt; tak the gate; skail: departure, n., wa-gaun.
depend, v., lippen: dependable, adj., steive; siccar.
deplete, empty, v., tuim: reduce, v., howe.

deplore, v., mane.
deposit, v., plank; pose, for concealment.
depraved, adj., gallus.
depress, v., dump; daunton; ding.
deprive, v., twine; reive.
derelict, adj., dishauntit.
deride, v., lichtlie; geck at.
descend, v., gang doun: descent, stock, n., etion (eshun): descended from, prep., aff.
describe, v., descrive.
desecrate, v., fyle.
desert, v., dishaunt; forleit; forhoo, of a bird its nest.
deserve, v., work for; want; faa: deserts, n., fairin; sairin.
design, intend, v., n., ettle: designing, adj., deep-drauchtit.
desire, v., grien; hanker efter; weary on; n., crave; ettle: desirous, aiverie; grienin: desire the male, v., eisen.
desist, v., quat; lat be.
desk, n., buird.
desolate, v., spulyie; adj., dreich; gowsty; wull.
despair, n., wanhope.
desperate, adj., foregone.
despicable, adj., footie; donsie: despicable people, n., dirtrie.
despise, v., lichtlie: despite, n., ilta; laith.
despoil, v., spulyie; reive; rype.
destine, v., weird: destined, adj., weirdit: destiny, n., weird.
destitute, adj., forfairn; sackless: destitution, n., puirtith.
destroy, v., wrack; perish.
detach, v., lowse.
details, n., particularities: taken up with details, adj., pernickety.
detain, v., taigle.
detect, v., airt out.
deteriorate, v., dwinnle; dwyne; gae doun the brae, in health.
determine, resolve, v., conclude: determined, adj., bentset; steive.
detriment, n., skaith.
devastate, v., wrack; perish.
develop, v., rax: development, n., oncome.
deviate, v., twyne: deviation, n., side-cuttin: slidin, moral.

device, fanciful, n., whigmaleerie.
devil, n., deil; fient: devilry, n., deviltry.
devise, v., think on.
devoid, adj., boss; tuim.
devote, dedicate, v., sain: devote oneself to, v., stick into.
devour, v., worry.
devout, adj., gospel-hertit; gracie.
dew, n., dagg: drenched with dew, adj., dew-droukit.
dexterous, adj., knacky; gleg; ready-haundit.
dialect, n., leid.
diarrhoea, n., scoot; backdoor-trot: have diarrhoea, v., skitter.
diary, n., diet-book.
dictate to, v., come the peter owre.
dictionary, n., dictionar.
die, v., dee; slip/win awa.
differ in opinion, v., cast out: difference, n., differ; odds.
difficult, adj., kittle; dour; fickle: difficulty, n., adae; habble.
diffident, adj., blate.
dig, v., dell; howk.
dignify, v., heicht; heize: dignity, n., mense.
dilapidated, adj., crazed: dilapidated building, n., rickle.
dilatory, adj., aff-pittin.
dilemma, n., swither; snurl.
diligence, n., eydence; virr.
dilute, v., tak doun.
dim, adj., bleert, of eyes; drumly.
diminish, v., dwyne; faa.
dimple, v., n., benkle.
dine, v., denner: dinner, n., denner.
dip, v., n., douk.
diploma, n., brief; line.
dire, adj., sair.
direct, v., airt; wyse: direction, n., airt; road; wey: direct road, n., craw road: director, n., guider: in opposite direction, adv., withergates.
dirge, n., dredgie; mane.
dirk, n., durk.
dirt, n., clart; fulyie: dirty, v., clart; fyle; adj., clarty; fousome.
disagree, v., cast out: disagreeable, adj., fousome; thrawn, of weather: disagreement, n., cast-out; curfuffle.
disappear, v., vainish; saunt: disappearance, n., waygate.
disappoint, v., begeck; begunk: dis-

appointment, n., begeck; begunk; chaw.

disarrange, v., tousle; camshachle; shevel.

disaster, n., mishanter; wanchance: **disastrous**, adj., gray.

discard, v., shauchle aff.

discern, v., fin; tell; distan: **discerning**, adj., lang-heidit.

discharge, v., dischairge.

discipline, v., sort; dicht; tairge.

disclaim, v., owregie; renunce.

disclose, v., let dab/bug.

discomfort, n., wanease.

disconcert, v., pit about; tak to the fair.

discontented, adj., worm-etten; freiting; wanrestfu.

discord, n., stour; sturt.

discourage, v., daunton; ding.

discover, v., fin; get.

discredit, v., affront; tash.

discreet, adj., mensefu: **discretion**, n., mense.

discriminate, v., fin; tell; distan.

discuss, v., set tongue to.

disdain, v., lichtlie; geck at.

disease, n., pest; trouble: **venereal disease**, n., glengore; glim.

disembowel, v., gralloch.

disentangle, v., unfankle; redd.

disfavour, n., ill-will; scunner; staw.

disfigure, v., gruggle.

disgorge, v., boke.

disgrace, v., n., affront: **disgraceful**, adj., awfu.

disgust, v., n., scunner; staw: **disgusted**, adj., scunnert: **disgusting**, adj., fousome; scunnersome; ugsome.

dish, n., coggie; luggie: **dish-cloth**, n., dish-clout: **dish-rack**, n., bink.

dishearten, v., daunton; ding: **disheartening**, adj., dishertsome.

dishevel, v., tousle; raivel: **dishevelled**, adj., tousy.

dishonest, adj., swicky; fleichin (fleetchin).

dishonour, v., n., affront; tash.

dislike, v., hae an ill-will at; n., ill-will; scunner.

dislocate, v., rack.

dismal, adj., dowie; daurksome; gray.

dismay, v., n., fley; sturt.

dismiss, v., skail, from meeting; seck,

from job: **dismissal**, n., skailin; seck.

disobey, v., misanswer: **disobedient**, adj., thrawn; waywart.

disorder, n., habble; mixter-maxter: **in disorderly manner**, adv., reel-rall.

dispel, v., fleg; fley.

dispense, v., dale: **dispense with**, v., get by.

disperse, v., skail: **dispersed, of meeting**, adj., out.

display, v., set aff; n., splairge; outset.

displease, v., displeisure: **displeasure**, n., displeisure.

dispose, incline one towards, v., set: **dispose of**, v., pit by; wyse awa: **well-disposed**, adj., weill-willie: **disposition**, n., kind; strynd; turn.

dispossess, v., herry out o.

disprove, v., evert; redargue.

dispute, v., argie-bargie; differ; n., argie-bargie; dirdum; stushie.

disrepute, n., ill name: **disreputable**, adj., guidless; ill-daein.

dissemble, v., guise; jouk.

dissent, v., quarrel; cangle.

dissipate, v., perish; ware: **dissipated**, adj., gallus; randy.

distaff, n., rock.

distance, n., faurness; streitch: **short distance**, n., bittock: **to a distance**, adv., hyne: **distant**, adj., outby; hyne-awa.

distend, v., hove; kyte.

distil, v., sype: **distil whisky**, v., run.

distinct, adj., dividual; sindry: **distinction**, n., distance.

distinguish, v., ken; tell: **distinguished**, adj., marked.

distort, v., thraw; skew; camshachle: **distortion**, n., thraw.

distress, v., fash; pit about; n., fash.

distribute, v., dale.

distrust, v., misdout; mislippen; n., misdout.

disturb, v., fash; steir: **disturbance**, n., habble; steir.

ditch, n., gruip; sheuch; stank; syver: **ditchwater**, n., aidle.

dither, v., n., swither.

diverge, v., twyne.

divide, v., dale, share; twin, break up; half, into two or more parts.

divulge, v., let on.

dizzy, adj., licht-heidit; waumish.

54

do, v., dae: **do not**, v., dinna.

dock, harbour, n., ree.

dock, the plant, n., docken.

doctor, n., mediciner.

doctrine, n., lair; licht.

document, n., brief; wryte: **documentary proof**, n., evident.

dodder, v., dotter; fitter.

dodge, v., jouk; blink.

dog, n., dug; messan; tyke: **dogfight**, n., collieshangie.

doggerel, n., crambo-clink; rat-rhyme.

doleful, adj., dowie; oorie; wae.

doll, n., dall; wheerum.

dolphin, n., gairfish; mereswine.

dolt, n., dult; gowk.

domestic, adj., hamely.

dominate, v., haud the stick owre.

dominion, n., ryke.

dominoes, game of, n., penny chap.

done for, adj., awa wi't; by: **done with**, adj., past.

donkey, n., cuddie; neddy.

doom, n., weird: **doomed**, adj., fey; weirdit.

door catch, n., sneck; snib: **doorstep**, n., doorstane: **doorway**, n., door-cheek.

dote, v., dawt: **doting**, adj., daft; fond.

double, adj., twa-fauld: **double handful**, n., gowpen: **double up**, v., fauld.

doubt, v., n., dout; swither: **doubtful**, adj., doutfu; doutsome.

dough, n., daich: **doughy**, adj., daichy.

douse, plunge in water, v., sowse: **extinguish**, v., smuir, a light.

dove, n., doo; cushie-doo, wild: **dovecot**, n., dooket.

down, under-plumage, n., doun.

down, adj., prep., doun: **down the road**, adv., doun-by.

downpour, n., onding; plump; blaud.

downright, adj., black; evendoun.

dowry, n., tocher: **dower**, v., tocher: **dowerless**, adj., tocherless.

doze, v., dover: **doze off**, v., dover owre.

dozen, n., dizzen.

draft, n., draucht, of money; scantlin, rough plan.

drag, v., n., harl; rug.

draggle, v., draigle.

dragonfly, n., adder-bell.

drain, v., sype; n., gruip; sheuch; syver: **dig a drain**, v., cast a drain.

drape, v., hap; cleid.

draught of air, n., souch; waff: **draught of liquor**, n., waucht; whitter.

draughts, the game, n., dams: **draughtboard**, n., dambrod.

draw, v., harl; rug: **drawback**, n., pitback; thraw i the raip.

drawl, v., draunt.

dread, v., dreid; n., dreidour; eeriness: **inspiring dread**, adj., fearsome.

dreary, adj., dowie; gray.

dredge, v., n., dreg: **dredger**, n., dregboat; clabbery punt.

dregs, n., sypins; dribs: **full of dregs**, adj., grummly.

drench, v., drouk; slounge: **drenched**, adj., droukit.

dress, v., busk; dicht; graith; n., claes; cleidin: **dressy**, adj., fussy: **smartly dressed**, adj., braw; tosht up: **dressing-gown**, n., wrapper.

dribble, v., driddle; slabber; slever.

drift, v., pander; poosk: **drift of argument**, n., string: **driftwood**, n., wrackwuid.

drill, v., n., dreel: **furrow**, n., dreel; furr.

drink, v., wauch; skink; sowp; n., dram, of spirits: **heavy drinker**, n., drouth.

drip, v., dreip; driddle; sab; n., dreip.

drive, v., caa; ding; dad, of wind: **energy**, n., gurr; smeddum.

drivel, v., slever/slaiver: **driveller**, n., gyter.

drizzle, v., n., smirr; drow.

drone, v., n., bum; snore.

droop, of flowers, v., sab; stint.

drop, v., drap; n., drap; jaup.

dross, n., gum; coum.

drought, n., drocht; drouth.

drove, n., drave; drift: **drove of sheep**, n., caa.

drown, v., droun.

drowse, v., dover.

drub, v., mell; skelp; dicht: **get a drubbing**, v., get laldie; get ane's licks.

drudge, v., drodge; scodge; n., ashypet; scodgie: **drudgery**, n., trauchle.

drug, v., n., drog: **druggist**, n., droggist.

drunk, adj., fou; tozy; weill on: **make drunk**, v., fill fou: **drunkard**, n., drouth; drunkart: **bout of drinking**, n., burst; spree.

dry, adj., drouthy; histy, of soil: dry-ness, n., drouth.
dual, adj., twa-fauld.
dubious, adj., doutfu; doutsome.
duck, lower head, v., jouk: ducking, n., doukin.
duck, n., deuk: duckpond, n., deuk-dub.
due, adj., auchtin: dues, n., stents.
dull, stupid, adj., diffy; dowf: prosy, adj., dreich: dull, of weather, adj., mirk.
dump, v., plank: rubbish dump, n., cowp.
dunce, n., dult; gowk.
dung, n., shairn, cow; muck; fulyie: dunghill, n., midden.
duplicate, v., adj., double.
durable, adj., lasty; teuch.
dusk, n., gloamin; daurkenin.
dust, n., stour.
duty, tax, n., mail.
dwarf, n., nirl; croot; droich: dwarfish, adj., nirly.
dwell,. v., dwall; byde; stey; win: dwelling, n., dwallin.
dwindle, v., dwyne.
dye, n., gree; corklit, red/purple; crottle, brown: dyer, n., dyester.
dynamic, adj., feckfu; forcie.
dysentery, n., rush.

Each, adj., ilk/ilka: each one/each other, pron., ilk ane/ilk ither.
eager, adj., fain; gleg; aiverie: eager-ness, n., ettlin.
eagle, n., earn.
ear, n., lug: earwig, n., forkie/hornie golach.
earl, n., yerl.
early, adj., adv., air.
earn, v., win; work for: earnings, n., winnins.
earth, n., yird; yirth: earthquake, n., yird-din: earthenware vessel, n., crock; pig.
ease, n., saucht: easy, adj., eith: easily, adv., eithly.
eastern, adj., eastlin: eastwards, adv., eastlins.
eat dirtily, v., slorp; slaiger: eat greedily, v., worry; lay into: eat quickly, v., gansh: eat sparingly, v., smeucher: eaten, adj., etten.

eaves, n., easin: eavesdrop, v., dirken; harken.
ebb, v., brust: ebbtide, n., brust.
eccentric, adj., daft-like; droll; flea-luggit; maggoty-heidit.
echo, v., n., aich.
economy, n., hainin: economical, adj., canny; gair: economise, v., hain.
ecstasy, n., rap.
eddy, v., swurl; n., swurl; weil.
edge, n., lip; selvedge.
edict, n., word.
educate, v., edicate; leir: educated, adj., buik-leired: education, n., buik-leir.
eerie, adj., oorie; weirdly.
effect, n., effeck: effects, n., gear; plenishin: effective, adj., feckfu.
effeminate, adj., lassie-like; sapsy: effeminate man, n., jessie; faizart.
effervesce, v., ream: effervescent, adj., fizzy.
efficient, adj., feckfu; purposefu: efficiency, n., purpose.
effigy, n., stookie man; mawmet.
effusive, adj., phraisy: effusiveness, n., phraise.
egg, addled, n., fun/squaw egg: sit on eggs to hatch, v., clock.
egotistical, adj., inbigget.
eider-duck, n., dunter-guse.
eight, n., adj., aicht; echt; aucht: eighty, n., adj., aichty.
either, pron., adj., conj., aither.
elaborate, adj., fykie; perqueer.
elastic, n., adj., elaskit.
elate, v., upheize: elated, adj., big; cairrit; crouse.
elbow, v., oxter; n., elba; elbuck.
elder tree, n., bourtree.
elderly, adj., eldern.
elegant, adj., gentie; pretty.
eleven, n., adj., eleiven.
elf, n., wurf; fane: elfland, n., elfin.
eligible, adj., habile.
eliminate, v., redd.
elope, v., gang owre the mairch.
eloquent, adj., glib-gabbit; clever.
elsewhere, adv., ithergates.
elude, v., jouk: elusive, adj., joukie.
emaciated, adj., poukit; shilpit.
emasculate, v., lib.
embankment, n., waterdyke.
embarrass, v., pit about; habble.
ember, n., aumer; aizle; gleid.

56

embezzle, v., pauchle.

emblem, n., whitter.

embrace, v., hause; n., chirt; Scotch grauvat.

embroider, v., flouer; flourish: embroidery, n., flouerin.

embroil, v., insnorl.

emergency, n., stress.

eminent, adj., marked.

emotion, n., hert-rug: causing emotion, adj., hert-scaudin.

employ, v., fee: employees, n., warkfowk.

empty, v., tuim; cowp, by overturning; adj., tuim; boss; howe; deif.

enamel, n., amel.

enamour, v., glamour: enamoured, adj., browden.

enchant, v., glamour: enchantment, n., glaumerie: enchanting, adj., glaikie.

encircle, v., gird; faddom, with arms.

enclose, v., garth; hain, with fence: enclosure, n., garth; haining.

encourage, v., gie a heize: encouraging, adj., hertsome.

encroach, v., owrelowp.

end, v., mak throu wi: end of day's work, n., lowsin-time.

endeavour, v., n., endaivour; ettle.

endure, v., thole; dree; byde: endurance, n., thole; bydin.

enemy, n., fae; unfrien.

energy, n., birr; pith; smeddum; fushion: energetic, adj., bauld; furthie; throu-gaun: lacking in energy, adj., feckless; thowless; fendless.

enfeeble, v., tak doun; craze.

enfold, v., enfauld; rowe.

engage a servant, v., fee; speak for: engage to meet/marry, v., tryst.

engender, v., cleck; get.

English, adj., Suddron; Southron: English language, n., Southron: speak in affected English, v., speak pan loaf.

engrave, v., indent; scart.

engross, v., uptak: be engrossed in, v., be taen up wi.

enigma, n., guess.

enjoy, v., bruik.

enlarge, v., biggen; eik to.

enlighten, v., enlichten.

enmity, n., feid; ill-will.

enormous, adj., wappin.

enough, adj., eneuch; enow, of number.

enrol for a class subject, v., tak out.

ensign, n., brattach.

enslave, v., thirl.

ensure, v., mak siccar.

entangle, v., fankle; insnorl.

enterprise, undertaking, n., ploy; ontakkin.

entertain v., see amuse.

enthusiasm, n., heize; thrift; greeshoch: enthusiastic, adj., weill-willed.

entice, v., tyce; wyse.

entrails, n., harigals; gralloch, of deer.

entrance, n., ingate.

entreat, v., prig; fleich (fleetch).

entrust, v., lippen, something to somebody.

entry, n., ingang: obtain entry, v., win in.

entwine, v., plet; wample.

envelop, v., rowe in.

envy, v., eyst; n., bane; ill-will.

epidemic, n., pest.

epitaph, n., memorandum.

equal, v., n., brither; marrow; piel: equals in age, n., yealins: equally, adv., equals-aquals: without equal, adj., maikless.

equip, v., busk; graith: equipment, n., gear; graith.

equivocate, v., flaunter.

erect, v., ereck; cantle; adj., steive; upset.

eroticism, n., rumple-fyke; keist.

err, v., mistak anesel; sklent, in beliefs; step aside: error, n., mistak.

errand, n., eeran.

eruption, n., outbrak.

escape, v., jouk; win free: escapade, n., ploy; splore.

escort, v., n., convoy.

essential, n., necessar.

establish, v., estaiblish: established, adj., sted.

estate, rank, n., gree: of high estate, adj., muckle.

esteem, v., respeck.

estimate, v., size up; upcast: rough estimate, n., scance.

etiquette, n., mense; havings.

evacuate, v., tuim.

evade, v., jouk: evasive, adj., joukie; slidderie.

evaluate, v., size up.

evanescent, adj., waff.

even, regular, adj., evenly: even, adv., een: even now, adv., eenou: get even with, v., get upsides wi; get mends o.

evening, n., eenin; forenicht: in the evening, adv., at een.

eventually, adv., hinnerly.

every, adj., ilk/ilka: everyone, pron., aabody; ilkane: everything, pron., aathing: every way, adv., aaweys: everywhere, adv., aa-roads.

evict from, v., herry out o.

evidence, n., evident, written; taiken: give evidence on oath, v., depone.

evil, n., ill; wicketness; adj., guidless; wicket: evil-doer, n., ill-doer.

evoke, call to mind, v., mynd.

ewe, n., yowe: two-year-old ewe, n., gimmer.

exact, adj., exack: exacting, adj., fykie.

exaggerate, v., blaw; whid: exaggeration, n., blaw; whid; bloust.

exalt, v., heicht; heize: exaltation, n., heize.

examine, v., exem; sicht; vizzy: thorough examination, n., througaun.

exasperate, v., rile; towt.

excavate, v., howk: excavation, n., howk.

exceed, v., owrelowp; owregae: exceedingly, adv., awfu; unco; richt.

excel, v., bear the gree: excellent, adj., grand; rare.

except, prep., excep; forby; binna: exceptional, adj., byous; forby.

excess, the excess, n., the owremuckle: excessive, adj., overly.

exchange, v., chynge; cowp; niffer; troke; n., niffer; troke.

exciseman, n., gager.

excite, v., raise; kittle up: excitable, adj., flochty: excited, adj., cairrit: move about excitedly, v., fidge: excitement, n., adae; stew; curfuffle.

exclude, v., baur out.

excommunicate, v., cut aff.

excrement, n., fulyie; keech; shite: void excrement, v., keech; shite.

excursion, n., outin; jant.

excuse, v., excaise; faik; n., aff-pit.

exercise book, n., jotter.

exert oneself, v., rax anesel; fyke: exertion, n., stress; faucht.

exhaust, v., founder; tew: exhausted, adj., forfairn; forfochen; wabbit.

exhibit, v., set aff: exhibition, n., outset.

exhilarate, v., heicht; heize: exhilaration, n., heize.

exhort, v., be at; eggle.

exist, v., be to the fore: scrape an existence, v., fend.

exit, n., outgate; waygate.

exonerate, v., assoilyie; quat.

expand, v., rax; hove.

expatiate, v., expawtiate.

expect, v., expeck; ettle; dout: expectation, n., ettle.

expedient, n., pit-by; adj., habile; wycelike.

expedite, v., heize: expedition, speed, n., throu-pit: expeditious, adj., fordersome.

expel, v., fleem; turn to the door.

expend, v., ware: expenditure, n., outpit: expense, n., damage.

experience, v., pree; pruive; n., kennin; skeil: experiment, n., preein.

expert, n., dab haun; cunning man; adj., canny; cunning; perfite.

expire, v., souch awa: expiration of breath, n., pech; souch.

explain, v., expound; rede, a riddle.

explicit, adj., fairfurth.

explode, v., flist; fuff: explosion, n., flist; fuff.

exploit, n., docht; ploy; splore.

expose, v., discover: exposure of a place, n., lie.

express, v., put words to: express oneself, v., word anesel.

exquisite, adj., rare; denty; grand.

extempore, adj., adv., aff-haun; affluif.

extend, v., streitch; rax: extension, n., eik: extent, n., boun; streitch.

exterminate, v., perish; wrack.

extinct, adj., wede awa.

extinguish, v., douse; slock; smuir, a light.

extort, v., herrie; herrie out o.

extra, adj., mair; mae.

extraordinary, adj., byornar; unco: extraordinarily, adv., byornar; unco.

extravagant, adj., spendrife; wasterfu:

extravagance, n., wastrie.

extreme, adj., awfu: **extremely**, adv., awfu; unco; dooms.

extricate, v., howk out; outred.

exuberant, adj., cadgy; in grand fettle.

exude moisture, v., sab; greit, of cheese.

exult, v., craw; rejyce.

eye, n., ee: **eye-brow/lashes/sight**, n., ee-brou/winkers/sicht.

Fable, n., rane.

fabric, texture, n., grist: **fabricate**, v., mak up: **fabrication**, n., mak-up.

face, accost, v., tackle: **face**, n., gizz; grunzie: **facing**, prep., forenent.

facetious, adj., couthy.

fact, state of affairs, n., sae.

factory, n., machinery; mill: **factory worker**, n., mill haun.

faculty, n., genie (jeenee); ingyne (injyne).

fad, n., norie; fyke; freit.

fade, v., dow; dwyne; wally.

fail, v., misgae; stick: **fail to accomplish/happen**, v., miss: **failing in body**, adj., gatty: **failed in one's profession**, adj., stickit.

faint, v., n., fent; swound; dwam; adj., wauch; waumish: **faint-hearted**, adj., chicken-hertit: **attack of faintness**, n., turn; soum.

fair, adj., bonnie; braw; eesome: **fair-complexioned**, adj., fair-avised: **keep fair, of weather**, v., haud up: **fair play**, n., fair hornie.

fair, market, n., tryst; feein fair, for engagement of servants.

fairy, n., fane; wurf: **fairies**, n., guid folk: **fairy ring**, n., elf-ring.

faith, n., lippenance: **faithful**, adj., leal; soothfast.

fake, v., n., jouk; n., adj., cheatrie.

falcon, peregrine, n., blue gled.

fall, v., n., faa: **fall heavily**, v., dad doun; ding, of rain: **fall down flat**, v., flap: **fall over**, v., cowp: **fall with a crash**, v., clash: **noisy fall**, n., clash: **heavy fall of rain**, n., onding; plump.

fallow, v., adj., fauch: **fallow land**, n., lea.

false, adj., fause; cheatrie: **falsehood**, n., whid; flaw; clype: **falsify**, v.,

wrang: **play false**, v., jouk.

falter, v., flaunter; staumer; stoiter, in speaking.

fame, n., gree; wind: **famous**, adj., faur-kent.

familiar, adj., weill-kent; hamely: **familiarise oneself with**, v., get into; yaise anesel wi: **familiarity**, n., couthiness; hameliness.

family, n., faimily; cleckin: **members of a family**, n., fowk.

famine, n., hership; scant and want: **time of famine**, n., dear-meal.

famish, v., faimish; hunger: **famished**, adj., tuim; howe.

fan, v., flaff; waff; n., flaffer; winnister, for corn.

fancy, liking, n., notion: **whim**, n., falderal; whigmaleerie; freit.

fantastical, adj., feenichin; pawkie.

far, adj., faur; outland, remote; adv., faur; a guid sicht: **farthest**, adj., faurest: **as far as**, prep., the lenth o.

fare, happen to, v., faa: **fare, food**, n., farin: **fare for carriage**, n., fraucht: **faring well/badly**, adj., weill/ill aff.

farewell, n., fareweill: **farewell feast**, n., foy.

farm, n., ferm; toun; mains, home farm: **farmhouse**, n., haa; steading: **farm buildings**, n., steading: **farm-yard**, n., fermyaird; close: **farm bailiff**, n., grieve: **farm servants' quarters**, n., bothy.

fascinate, v., glamour: **fascination**, n., glamourie.

fashion, manner, n., gate: **design**, n., mak: **fashionable**, adj., new-fanglt.

fast, adj., fest; slippy; clever: **fast, of clock**, adj., forrit.

fasten, v., festen; twine: **fasten with hook**, v., cleik.

fastidious, adj., perjink; pernickety; fashious.

fat, n., creish; saim; adj., chuffy; fodgel: **fatty**, adj., creishy: **fat of face**, adj., brosy-faced: **blob of fat**, n., starn.

fate, n., weird: **fated**, adj., fey; weirdit.

father, n., faither: **father-in-law**, n., guid-faither.

fathom, v., n., faddom.

fatigue, v., tyauve; trauchle: **fatigued**, adj., forfochen; forjeskit.

fault, n., faut: faulty, adj., fauty: find fault, v., faut: fault-finding, grummly; calshie: at fault, adj., in faut.

favour, n., gree, goodwill; cudiech, bribe: favourable, adj., towardsome: favourite, n., dawtie: curry favour of, v., hing/haud in wi.

fawn, v., flether; foonge: fawner, n., fuit-licker: kiss-ma-luif.

fear, v., dout; dree; dreid; n., dreid; dreidour: cause to fear, v., fley.

fearsome, adj., awesome; eerie: fearful, adj., timorsome: fearless, adj., bauld.

feast, n., belly-rive; blaw-out: feast riotously, v., gilravage.

feat, n., fate; kittle, difficult feat; prattick, daring feat.

feather, n., fedder; pen.

feature, lineament, n., draucht; meith: characteristic, n., particularity.

February, n., Februar.

feeble, adj., feckless; peely-wally; fushionless: feeble-minded, adj., dottle; silly: make feeble, v., craze.

feed, v., meat; corn, horse; fother, cattle.

feel, v., fin: feeling, attitude, n., souch.

feign, v., let on; fenyie.

feint, v., n., mak on.

fell, v., founder.

fellow, n., carl; chiel; block; billy.

female, n., she; wumman-body.

fence, v., n., palin: fence post, n., palin stab: gap in fence, n., slap.

fend off, v., aff-fend; weir aff: fend, provide, v., fen; mak a fen.

ferment, v., quicken; wark; n., barm: over-fermentation, n., fire.

ferocious, adj., farouchie; gurly; wud.

ferret, n., foumart.

fertile, adj., fat; growthie (as in "now"): fertility, n., growthiness.

fervent, adj., aiverie: fervour, n., birk; greeshoch; instancy.

fester, v., beil: festering sore, n., beilin.

festive, adj., mirthsome; rantin: festive gathering, n., rant; play.

fetch, v., fesh.

fetlock, n., cuit.

fetter, n., hapshackle: fetters, n., airns; grips.

feud, n., feid.

fever, n., fivver.

fibre, n., taw: fibrous roots, n., taws.

fickle, adj., kittle; flichtery.

fictional, adj., leefu: work of fiction, n., lee-buik.

fiddler, n., thairm/gut-scraper: fiddle string, n., thairm.

fidelity, n., lealty.

fidget, v., fidge; fyke; hotch: fidgety, adj., fidgin; fykin.

field of grass, n., park: fieldfare, n., feltie.

fierce, adj., farouchie; fairce; gurly; wud.

fiery-tempered, adj., ettery; spunkie; bauld.

fifteen, n., adj., fyfteen: fifth, n., adj., fift.

fight, v., fecht; n., fecht; brulzie; rammy: brave fighter, n., bonnie fechter.

figure, v., n., figur.

file, v., n., risp.

fill, v., fou; full (fu-ll): fill to capacity, v., stap; stow: one's fill, n., sairin.

film, n., scaum; scruif: cover with a film, v., scaum.

filter, v., n., felter; sythe: filter through, v., sype.

filth, n., clart; fulyie; muck: filthy, adj., clarty; fousome.

final, adj., hinmaist: finally, adv., at lang and last; at lang lenth.

finance, n., siller; gear.

find, v., fin; get: find out by seeking, v., airt out.

fine, goodly, adj., braw; denty; gey: finery, n., braws.

finger, v., pawt: fingernail, n., nail-horn: little finger, n., pinkie.

finicky, adj., fashious; perjink; pernickety.

finish, v., n., feenish: finished, adj., throu: finish off, v., snod aff.

fiord, n., voe.

fir cone, n., curldoddy.

fire, n., ingle: catch fire, v., lunt; tak lowe: kindle fire, v., kennle; firebar, n., rib: fireside, n., chimla-lug; fire-en; ingle-cheek: firewood, n., eldin: firework, n., squeeb: on fire, adv., alowe.

firm, adj., steive; siccar: firmness, n., siccarness.

first, adj., forehand: firstly, adv.

firstlins: **first-rate**, adj., grand.

fish, v., n., fush: **fish garbage**, n., fish gowries: **fish lie in river**, n., fish currie: **fish spear**, n., leister: **fishing boat**, n., coble; cowan; scaff: **fishing village**, n., fish toun: **small dried fish**, n., speldin: **catch fish by groping with hands**, v., guddle.

fissure, n., cleavin; rive; skeoch, in cliff.

fist, n., nieve.

fit, v., ser, of clothing: **fit out**, v., outrig: **badly-fitting**, adj., shauchlin: **fit**, adj., macklike, suitable; habile, qualified.

fit of anger, n., fleein passion; tirrivee: **fitful**, adj., towtie; waywart.

flabby, adj., daichie; fozie.

flag, ensign, n., brattach; waff: **flagstaff stone**, n., borestane.

flagon, n., stowp.

flagstone, n., plainstane.

flail, n., flingin-tree.

flair, ability, n., ingyne (injyne); farrach.

flake, n., flauchter, of snow; flaw, of fish flesh.

flame, n., lowe; gleesh, bright.

flannel, n., flannen.

flap, v., flaff; waff; n., flype, of garment; lug, of bonnet.

flare up with anger, v., flyre; bleize; flee up: **flare, of candle**, v., sweil.

flash, v., flist; gliff; n., glisk; gliff: **flash of lightning**, n., flaucht: **in a flash**, adv., in a dunt/glint.

flask, n., flecket, for whisky.

flat, n., adj., flet: **flat, of drink**, adj., dowd: **dull and prosy**, adj., fushionless: **lie flat**, v., clap; grouf, on belly: **ground-floor flat**, n., streethous: **flat on the face**, adv., bellyflaucht.

flatten, v., clap doun; buff.

flatter, v., fleich (fleetch); flether; claw the back: **flatterer**, n., fuit-licker; kiss-ma-luif: **flattery**, n., fleichin; flethers.

flatulence, n., wind: **relieve flatulence**, v., brek the wind.

flaunt, v., flird.

flavour, v., kitchen; saur; gust.

flaw, n., gaw; eelist; smitch.

flax, n., lint; tow: **bundle of flax on**

distaff, n., tap; rock: **flax-dresser**, n., heckler: **flax-dressing board**, n., heckle-board: **flax mill**, n., lintmill: threid-work: **flaxen-haired**, adj., towy-heidit.

flay, v., flypeshard.

flea, n., flae; flech.

fledge, v., feather.

flee, v., fugie (fyoodjie); tak the gate.

fleece, n., fleesh.

fleet, adj., slippy; clever; swippert.

flesh, decayed, n., cabbrach: **poultry flesh**, n., white meat.

flexible, adj., souple; dwaible; waffle.

flick, v., feg; spang; n., flisk.

flicker, v., chitter; flauchter; n., flauchter.

flight, n., flicht; flaucht, of birds: **take flight**, v., flicht: **put to flight**, v., fley: **flighty**, adj., skeerie; glaikit.

flimsy, adj., flindrikin; silly.

flinch, v., flaunter; staumer; stoiter.

fling, v., thraw; fung; wap.

flint rock, n., clint: **flinty**, adj., clinty.

flippant, adj., glaikit; daft.

flirt, v., daff; jink; gallant; n., squeef, male; flirdoch.

flit, dart about, v., flochter; jicker about.

float, v., soum; fleit.

flock, n., hird, cattle; hirsel, sheep; drift, birds.

flog, v., leather; belt: **flogging**, n., leatherin; licks.

flood, v., n., flude: **flooded**, adj., flodden: **in flood**, adj., up; great.

floor, n., flair.

flop, v., n., flap; wallop.

flotsam, n., redd: **flotsam and jetsam**, n., wrack and waith.

flounce, v., n., flunce; flird: **flounce of dress**, n., squirl.

flounder, the fish, n., fleuk.

flourish, v., blaw; blume: **thrive**, v., forder; dae guid: **flourishing**, adj., guid-gaun: **flourish in writing**, n., tirly-wirly; squirl.

flout, v., flyre; geck at; lichtlie.

flow, v., fleit; wimple, gently; trot, swiftly.

flower, n., flouer.

fluctuate, v., swither; waff.

fluent, adj., glib-gabbit; clever.

fluff, n., ooss; caddis.

flurry, v., flister; pit about; n., flister; flirr.

flush, become red, v., ridden.

fluster, v., flister; pit about.

flute, n., whussle; fliet: **play flute,** v., whussle; wheefle.

flutter, v., flaff; flichter; n., flaff; flauchter.

fly, v., flee: **fly, insect,** n., flee: **fly-wheel,** n., thorl.

foam, v., n., faem; freith.

fodder, n., fother; feed.

foe, n., fae.

fog, n., haar; dawk; rouk: **foggy,** adj., haary; roukie.

foil, v., thraw; thorter.

foist, v., pawm; thrummle.

fold, shelter, v., n., bucht; crue; fauld.

fold, crease, v., n., fauld; ply; plait.

foliage, n., fullyerie.

folk, n., fowk.

foment with hot water, v., plot.

fond, adj., fain; daft: **be fond of,** v., be keen o: **fondle,** v., dawt.

food, n., meat; bite; chuck: **supply food,** v., meat.

fool, n., fuil; gowk; cuif; eediot: **foolish,** adj., fuil; daft; glaikit; gyte: **foolishness,** n., daftness; gyteness: **fool's errand,** n., gowk's eeran.

foot, n., fuit/fit: **foothold,** n., fuit; fuitin: **footstep,** n., fuit: **footmark,** n., fuitsteid: **footpath,** n., fuit-pad: **footstool,** n., creepie-stuil: **lose one's foothold,** v., tyne a fuit: **travel on foot,** v., pad.

footling, adj., feckless; fouterie.

fop, n., whupmadenty: **foppish,** adj., dink; prinky.

forage, v., sorn; n., fother.

foray, n., creagh; rode; spreath.

forbear, v., haud by.

forbid, v., refuise; dischairge: **forbidding,** adj., dour; fell; stour.

force, n., birr; virr; bensel: **force to do,** v., gar: **forceful,** adj., forcie.

forceps, n., nippers.

ford, v., fuird; wade; n., fuird.

fore-, prefix, **forebode,** v., spae; weird: **forecast,** v., hecht; spae; **forefathers,** n., aulders; forefowk: **forefront,** n., forebreist: **forehead,** n., brou.

fore-, prefix, *contd.,* **foreleg,** n., fores-paul: **foreman,** n., owresman: **foremost,** adj., foremaist: **forenoon,** n., forenuin: **foreshore,** n., ebb; grun-ebb, lower: **forestall,** v., forestaw: **foretaste,** n., arles: **foretell,** v., spae; weird; freit: **forewarning,** n., forecast.

foreign, adj., fremmit.

forfeit, v., n., tyne; wad.

forge, n., smiddie; stiddie: **forged, counterfeit,** adj., ill.

forget, v., forleit: **forgetful,** adj., no in.

forgive, v., forgie.

fork, farming implement, n., graip.

forlorn, adj., forfairn; waff.

former, adj., umquhile: **formerly,** adv., aforesyne.

formidable, adj., awesome: **formidable person,** n., warmer.

fornication, n., houghmagandie.

forsake, v., dishaunt; forleit; forsak.

fort, n., dun; keir; peel.

forth, adv., furth: **forthwith,** adv., eenou.

fortnight, n., fortnicht.

fortune, n., fortoun; weird; faa: **fortunate,** adj., canny; chancy.

forward, impetuous, adj., baurdy: adj., braisant: **forward,** adv., forrit.

foster, v., forder; forrit.

foul, adj., dichty; fousome: **foul-mouthed,** adj., ill-gabbit.

found, lay foundation of, v., steid: **foundation,** n., found; laroch.

fountain, public, n., spriggit: **fountain-head,** n., spring-heid.

four, n., adj., fower: **company of four,** n., fowersome: **fourth,** adj., fort.

fox, n., tod: **foxglove,** n., deid man's bells: witches' thummles.

fraction, n., mention.

fractious, adj., fashious; fykesome; kittle.

fragile, adj., bruckle; frush.

fragment, n., crottle; nirl: **fragments,** n., smithereens.

fragrance, n., oam; waff.

frail, adj., frush; silly.

frame, moulding, n., muller: **support,** n., sock; tress.

frank, adj., evendoun; fair-spoken: **frankness,** n., furthiness.

frantic, adj., dancin mad.

fraud, n., cheatrie; cheatery-packery:

fraudulent, adj., cheatrie.

fray, v., tash: **frayed**, adj., tasht; fozie, of rope.

freak, caprice, n., norie; whigmaleerie: **curiosity**, n., unco.

freckle, v., spreckle: **freckles**, n., fernie-tickles.

free, exonerate, v., quat: **get/set free**, v., win free: **free of**, adj., quat/redd o: **freedom**, n., scouth.

freeze, v., geal (jeel): **freeze to death**, v., stivven.

freight, v., fraucht; n., fraucht; draucht.

frenzy, v., n., raise: **frenzied**, adj., ree; maukin-mad.

frequent, v., crowder; howff: **frequently**, adv., aft/aften.

fresh, adj., caller; green; sweet, of butter: **freshen**, v., brisken up.

fret, v., channer; yammer; fash; fyke: **fretful**, adj., girnie.

friable, adj., bruckle; free; murly.

friend, n., frien; fier; billy; marrow: **friendly**, adj., frienly; great; chief; thrang; faur ben.

fright, n., fleg; fley; fricht: **take fright**, v., fley; startle: **frighten**, v., fricht; fley: **frightened**, adj., feart; frichtit: **frightful**, adj., frichtsome.

frigid in manner, adj., offish; off-staunin; tuithy.

frill, ruffle, n., frull; bord.

fringe, n., selvedge.

frippery, n., feegarie; pelfry.

frisk, v., flisk; whid: **frisky**, adj., skeich; flisky.

frivolous, adj., freevolous; glaikit; daft: **piece of frivolity**, n., flagarie.

frizzle, v., skirl.

frog, n., puddock: **frog spawn**, n., crud; toad-spue.

frolic, v., daff; glaik; jink; n., tare; splore; spree.

from, prep., fae/frae; furth.

front, n., foreside: **in front of**, prep., afore; forenent.

frost, n., cranreuch, hoarfrost: **frosty**, adj., nippy; sherp.

froth, v., n., freith; faem.

frown, v., n., froun; glower; glunch.

frugal, adj., canny; hainin.

fruitful, adj., breedy; growthie (as in "now").

frustrate. v.. thraw; thorter.

fry, v., skirl.

fuel, n., fire; eldin.

fuggy, adj., smuchty.

fugitive, n., fugie (foodjie).

full, adj., fou: **full to the brim**, adj., lippin/reamin fou.

full cloth, v., wauk: **fuller**, n., wauker.

fulsome, adj., fousome; phraisy, fawning.

fumble, v., fummle.

fumes, emit fumes, v., reik; smeik.

fun, n., daffin: **piece of fun**, n., tare; ploy.

fund, n., found.

fundamental, adj., necessar.

funeral, n., buryin; bural: **attend funeral**, v., show respeck.

fungus, n., nild.

funnel, n., filler, for liquids; rone, for air.

funny, amusing, adj., queer: **funny-bone**, n., dirlie-bane; yeuky-bane.

furnish, v., plenish: **furnishings**, n., plenishin; graithin; sticks.

furrow, n., furr; gaw; sheuch.

further, v., forder; adj., adv., faurer; forder.

furtive, adj., datchie; thieftie.

fury, n., feim; tirrivie: **furious**, adj., dancin mad.

furze, n., whin: **furze-covered**, adj., whinny.

fuss, v., fyke; fizz; feist; n., adae; sang; steir: **fussy**, adj., pernickety.

fusty, adj., fousty; mochie: **grow fusty**, v., foust.

futile, adj., knotless.

Gabble, v., gitter; yabble.

gable, n., gavel: **steps on gable-end**, n., corbie/craw steps.

gad, v., traik; stravaig; gallivant.

gadfly, n., cleg.

gaff, v., cleik: **salmon gaff**, n., cleik.

gain, attain, v., win; fetch.

gainsay, v., forsay.

gait, n., gang.

gaiters, n., spats; cuitikins; gramashes.

gale, n., blouster; skirler; whusker.

gall, v., n., gaw.

gallery, n., laft; cock-laft.

gallop, v., wallop; skelp.

gallows, n., widdie; dule-tree: **gallows**

bird, n., hempie.
gamble, v., gammle.
gambol, v., flisk; whid.
game, n., gemm; play; spiel: **game-keeper**, n., gemmie.
gander, n., gainder.
gang, n., core: **gangster**, n , wido
gangway, n., gang.
gannet, n., basser-guse.
gap, n., slack, between clouds; slap, in fence; want, in teeth, etc.
gape, v., n., gant; gawp.
garb, n., claes; cleidin; graithin.
garbage, n., fulyie.
garden, n., gairden; yaird; **market gardener**, n., mail gairdener.
garish, adj., gairy; roarie; skyrin.
garment, n., clout: **garments**, n., claes; clouts; duds.
garret, n., gaillie.
garrulous, adj., gabbie; windy: **garrulous person**, n., blether.
garter, n., gairten.
gash, v., scaur; gulliegaw.
gasp, v., pech; whaisk; fetch; n., pech.
gate, n., yett; slap: **gateway**, n., bow; port.
gather, v., gether: **gathering**, n., getherin; convene; shine, social.
gaudy, adj., gairy; roarie; skyrin: **gaudiness**, n., skyrishness.
gaunt, adj., poukit; shangie.
gawk, v., gant; gawp; n., hochle; gamaleerie: **gawky**, adj., gamaleerie.
gay, adj., cadgy; lichtsome; skeich: **gaiety**, n., daffery.
gaze, v., glower; goave; n., glower; vizzy.
geld, v., dress; lib: **gelding**, n., staig.
gender, n., gener (jener).
genealogy, n., etion (eshun).
generation, n., kith-end.
generous, adj., furthie; ruch-haundit: **generosity**, n., rowthness.
genial, adj., couthie; honest; guidwillie.
genius, n., genie (jeenee); ingyne (injyne).
genteel, adj., gentie; gentle.
gentle, adj., canny; douce; lythe: **gentility**, n., gentrice: **gentry**, n., knabbery: **gentlemanly**, adj., genty.
genuine, adj., rale: **sincere**, adj., evendoun; leal.

geologist, n., stane-chapper.
germinate, v., acherspyre; breird.
gesture, n., gester; offer; sain, of goodwill.
get, v., come by: **get ahead**, v., win forrit: **get the better of**, v., get owre.
gew-gaw, n., gee-gaw; wheeram; wheegee.
ghastly, adj., grugous.
ghost, n., ghaist; bogle: **ghostly**, adj., ghaistly; eerie; eldritch.
giant, n., etin; gyre-carlin.
gibe, v., flyre; geck at; lichtlie.
giblets, n., emmlins.
giddy, flighty, adj., daft; glaikit: **turn giddy**, v., soum; swurl: **state of giddiness**, n., dwamminess; soum.
gift, n., aumous, charitable; fairin, from fair; handsel, for luck.
giggle, v., n., geegle; keckle.
gills of fish, n., chollers (as in "chin").
gimlet, n., brog; gemlet; wummle.
gimmick, n., whigmaleerie.
ginger, n., ginge: **gingerbread**, n., gingebreid (jinj-).
gipsy, n., caird; tinker; gaun-body.
girl, n., lassie; quean/quyne: **giddy girl**, n., glaik; kittock: **undisciplined girl**, n., limmer: **mischievous girl**, n., clip: **girlhood**, n., lassie days.
girth, n., girt; grist.
give, v., gie: **give me**, v., gie's; see me: **give and take**, n., giff-gaff.
glad, adj., blythe; fain; gled: **gladness**, n., gledness; fainness.
glamour, n., glaumour.
glance, v., n., keek; glisk; glint: **glance sideways**, v., gley; sklent: **fly off obliquely**, v., skite: **kindly glance**, n., blink.
glare, v., glower; n., gliff; glower: **glaring**, adj., glairy.
glass, n., gless: **pane of glass**, n., lozen: **glazier**, n., glassier.
gleam, v., n., leme; gliff; skinkle.
glean, v., screenge: **gleaner**, n., stibbler: **gleanings**, n., screengins.
glee, n., blytheness; fainness.
glib, of the tongue, adj., souple; weill-hung: **glib-tongued**, adj., glib-gabbit.
glide, v., skiff; skimmer; snuive.
glimmer, v., blinter; skimmer; n., skimmer.
glimpse, v., glisk; skyme; n., blink;

gliff; glisk.

glint, v., n., gliff; leme.

glisten, v., skinkle; sheen.

glitter, v., blinter; skinkle; sheen; n., skinkle.

globules of fat in soup, n., een.

gloom, n., mirkness: **gloomy,** adj., drumly; mirk; wan.

glory, v., n., glore.

gloss over, v., fard: **glossy,** adj., brent; glaizie.

glove, n., haunshae.

glow, of fire, v., n., leme: **glowing fire,** n., greeshoch: **red glow in sky,** n., scaum: **sudden glow of heat,** n., gliff; scaum.

glum, adj., dowf; dowie; disjaskit.

glut, v., ser; staw: **glutted,** adj., sert; stawed.

glutton, n., bellygut; guts; ged: **gluttonous,** adj., gutsy.

gnarled, adj., scroggie; wirly.

gnash the teeth, v., chow the chafts; gansh.

gnat, n., midge: **swarm of midges,** n., simmer-cout.

gnaw, v., nirl; gnap; yackle.

gnomes, n., gray folk.

go, v., gae; gang; win: **go slowly, aimlessly,** v., dawdle; slogger: **go carefully,** v., caa canny: **go quickly,** v., skelp: **go towards,** v., mak tae: **go, energy,** n., smeddum: **go-ahead,** adj., forritsome; furthie.

goad, v., prog; n., prog; gaud.

goal, the goal, n., dell; dull: **goalkeeper,** n., goalie: **goal line,** n., hail line.

gobble up, v., gollop; hanch; snack up.

goblet, n., tassie.

goblin, n., bogle; trow; worricow.

God, n., Guid; the Almichty: **godliness,** n., guidliheid.

gold, n., gowd: **golden,** adj., gowden: **goldfinch,** n., goldie; gowdspink.

golf, n., gowf: **golf club,** n., gowfin stick.

gonorrhoea, n., glim.

good, adj., guid; honest, worthy: **goods,** n., gear; graith: **good-fornothing,** adj., waff: **good-for-nothing people,** n., dirtrie: **good-looking,** adj., braw; wycelike: **good-tempered,** adj., weill-natured: **goodwill,** n.,

gree; soind: **good evening/night,** interj., guid-een/nicht: **good luck,** interj., fair faa: **goodness knows,** interj., deil kens.

goose, n., guse.

gooseberry, n., grozet.

gore, v., stick.

gorge, v., stow; stap; stech.

gorgeous, adj., braw; grand.

gorse, n., whin.

gosling, n., gaislin.

gossamer, n., mous-wab.

gossip, v., claiver; clash; clatter; crack; n., blethers; claivers; clash; clatter: **a gossip,** n., blether; sweetiewife.

gouge, v., n., gudge: **gouge out,** v., stap out.

govern, v., guide; wald: **restrain,** v., haud.

gown, n., goun; mantie, loose; strodie, tight.

grab, v., claucht; cleik; nick.

grace, n., gentiness: **grace after meal,** n., bethankit: **gracious,** adj., couthy: **grace note,** n., tirly-wha: **say grace for,** v., lowse.

grade, n., rang: **gradual,** adj., canny: **graduate,** v., come out.

grain of anything, n., corn: **grain, cereal,** n., mealcorn; victual: **ear of grain,** n., icker: **topmost ear of grain,** n., tap-pickle: **eared, of grain,** adj., aichert: **full of grains,** adj., curny.

grain, texture, n., awte, of wood or stone; grist, of wood.

granary, n., girnel; corn-laft.

grand, adj., rare: **grand-aunt,** n., auld auntie: **grandchild,** n., bairn's bairn: **grandfather,** n., auld-faither; granfaither; **grandmother,** n., auldmither; grannie: **grandson,** n., oe.

grapple. v., graipple; rive; n., graipple: **grapple with,** v., warsle wi.

grasp, v., n., claucht; cleik: **grasping,** adj., grabby; grippy.

grass, n., gress; girse: **couch-grass,** n., wrack: **land in grass,** n., lea: **tuft of grass,** n., hassock: **long, reedy grass,** n., bent: **withered grass stalk,** n., windlestrae: **grasshopper,** n., gerslowper.

gratuity, n., guidwill; fairin: **gratuitous,** adj., gien; gratis.

grave, n., lair; mools; grun: **grave-digger**, n., grave-howker; bedral: **gravestone**, n., heidstane; lairstane.

grave, adj., douce; drummure; gargrugous.

gravel, n., graivel; grush; chingle.

gravy, n., bree.

graze, touch lightly, v., skiff.

graze, nibble grass, v., moup; stou; gnap: **pasture**, v., girse.

grease, v., n., creish; tauch: **greasy**, adj., creishy; tauchie.

great, very big, adj., gey; muckle; unco; bonny: **greatcoat**, n., big-coat.

grebe, n., douker.

greed, n., covetice; gutsiness: **greedy**, adj., grabby; grippy; gutsy.

green, adj., emerant: **greengrocer**, n., kail-seller: **greenfinch**, n., green lintie.

greet, v., goam; halse, with embrace.

grey, adj., gray: **streaked with grey**, adj., lyart; haizert.

greyhound, n., grew.

griddle, n., girdle.

gridiron, n., brander.

grief, n., dool; tein; wae: **cry of grief**, n., mane: **source of grief**, n., scaud: **utter sounds of grief**, v., grane: **grief-stricken**, adj., sair.

grieve, v., greit; mane; yammer: **grieve, vex**, v., fash; fyke: **grievance**, n., gaw-i-the-back: **recall a grievance**, v., cast up: **grievously**, adv., sair.

grill, v., n., brander.

grim, adj., grugous; gash; stour, in manner.

grimace, v., shevel; mak a mou; n., girn; grue, of disgust.

grime, n., coum; smush: **grimy**, adj., coumy.

grin, v., girn.

grind, v., grun; grush; runch: **grindstone**, n., grunstane.

grip, v., n., grup; fang; glaum.

grisly, adj., ugsome; grugous; gash.

grist, n., girst.

gristle, n., girsle.

grit, n., grush: **gritty**, adj., sherp: **grit teeth**, v., cramsh.

grizzled, adj., lyart; haizert.

groan, v., n., grane.

groin, n., laich o the belly; lisk.

groom, v., whisk; n., staig-chiel.

groove, v., n., nick; den.

grope, v., graip; fummle; guddle.

gross, adj., gutty; groff.

ground, n., grun; mool: **fallow ground**, n., lea.

groundsel, n., grunsel.

group, n., core; curn.

grouse, n., whircock: **male/female of red grouse**, n., muircock/hen.

grout, sediment, n., gruns.

grow, v., growe; rax: **fast-growing**, adj., growthie (as in "now"); grushie.

growl, v., gurl; gowl.

grudge, n., grummle; pick: **bear a grudge**, v., hae a pick at.

gruel, n., skeelie; skink.

gruesome, adj., gastrous; grugous; ugsome.

grumble, v., grummle; girn; channer; molligrant; yammer; n., grummle; girn.

grumpy, adj., grumphy.

grunt, v., n., grumph; gruntle.

guarantee, v., caution; staun guid for; n., caution; warranty.

guard, v., n., gaird; weir.

guess, v., ettle; jalouse.

guffaw, v., n., gaff; gaffaw.

guide, v., airt; wyse: **guidance**, n., guidal.

guile, n., pawkiness; sleekitness; adj., pawkie; sleekit.

guillemot, n., sea-hen; gulliemaw.

guillotine, n., maiden; shear; rase, paper trimmer.

guilt, n., sak: **guiltless**, adj., sackless; free.

gull, v., begunk; geck.

gull, n., maw; goo: **young gull with brown feathers**, n., sugarie Willie.

gullet, n., craig; hause; wizzen.

gully, n., gill; heuch; glack.

gulp, v., gawp; gowp; gollop.

gun barrel, n., ratch: **gun hammer**, n., frizzel: **gunpowder**, n., gunpouther.

gunwale, n., wyle.

gurgle, v., n., glock; glugger; gurl.

gush forth, v., bock; pish; stroan; ush.

gusset, n., eik; gair; gushet.

gust of wind, n., flaff; swap: **blow in gusts**, v., flaff; whidder: **gusty**. adj., gowsty.

gusto, n., gust; virr.
gut, n., thairm: **guts,** n., painches: **courage,** n., spunk; smeddum.
gutter, n., gruip; sheuch; syke; syver.
gym shoes, n., gutties.

Habit, n., cast; gate: **routine,** n., hechhow: **bad habits,** n., etts; ill-gates: **be in the habit of,** v., be in the wey o.
hack, v., n., haggle; hag; chack.
hackle, n., heckle.
haddock, n., haddie: **smoked haddock,** n., Finnan haddie.
hag, old woman, n., luckie; runt; carlin.
haggard, adj., oorlich.
haggle, v., cangle; niffer; prig.
hair band, n., snood; **haircut,** n., cow: **lock of hair,** n., flaucht; tait: **false hair,** n., curlyfuffs: **cut hair,** v., cow: **part hair,** v., shed.
hale and hearty, adj., freck; yauld.
half, n., adj., adv., hauf: **half-drunk,** adj., hauf-fou: **halfpenny,** n., bawbee: **half-wit,** n., natural: **half-witted,** adj., fuil; gyte; saft.
halibut, n., turbot.
hall, n., haa.
hallow, v., sain.
hallucination, n., blawflum.
halo round moon, n., broch; faul; gow.
halt, v., n., deval; stap.
halve, v., half.
halyards, n., tows.
hamlet, n., clachan; toun.
hammer, v., chap; nap; n., haimmer.
hamper, v., hinner; taigle.
hams of legs, n., hunkers: **squat on hams,** v., hunker.
hand, n., haun; luif: **clenched hand,** n., nieve: **handful,** n., haunfu; claucht; gowpen; double: **hand-cart,** n., hurly: **handwriting,** n., haun o wryte: **palm of hand,** n., luif; pawm: **at hand,** adv., forrit.
handicap, n., doun-draucht; scouth, in a game.
handkerchief, n., naipkin; snotterclout.
handle, v., haunle; fitch; thrummle, too much; **manage,** v., guide: **handle,** n., haunle; heft; shank; steil.
handshake, golden, n., nieve-shakin.
handsome, adj., braw; weill-faured;

wycelike.
handy, adj., hanty; naitie.
hang, v., hing: **hang loosely,** v., trollop: **hangman's noose,** n., tow; widdie.
hanker for, v., weary on; ettle efter: **hankering,** n., crave.
haphazard, adj., antrin.
happen, v., faa; tide: **happen to,** v., come owre: **happenings,** n., ongauns.
happy, adj., blythe; fain; seilfu: **happiness,** n., blytheness.
harangue, n., screed.
harass, v., hash; taigle; tew: **harassed,** adj., forfochen; fyauchled.
harbour, n., hyne; ree; inner; shore.
hard, difficult, adj., dour; ill; sair; teuch: **hard-pressed,** adj., sair dung: **hard-up,** adj., ill-aff: **hardly,** adv., haurdly; barelies.
hardy, adj., stuffy.
hare, n., cuttie; mawkin; donie: **harebrained,** adj., cairrit; glaikit.
harebell, n., bluebell; blawart.
harlot, n., hure (hoor).
harm, v., hairm/herm; n., hairm; ill; skaith: **harmless,** adj., sackless.
harmony, n., greement: **live in harmony,** v., gree.
harness, v., n., graith; yoke.
harp, v., threip; yap; n., hairp; clarsach.
harridan, n., tairge; skelpy-limmer.
harrow, v., link; n., grubber; drag.
harry, v., herry; reive; rype; spulyie.
harsh, adj., dour; fell; stour, of voice: **make harsh sound,** v., scraich; scrunt.
harvest, n., hairst: **harvest home,** n., kirn; winter: **harvest home feast,** kirn supper: **last sheaf of harvest,** n., clyack; kirn; maiden.
haste, v., brattle; faird: **hasten,** v., skelp; leather; heize.
hat, n., bash hat, soft; straw basher, straw; skip hat, brimmed.
hatch, v., cleck: **hatching,** n., cleckin.
hatch, trapdoor, n., trap.
hate, n., venim; ill-will.
haughty, adj., big; dorty; heichheidit; high-i-the-bend.
haul, v., harl; hyke: **haul of fish,** n., drave.
haunches, n., hainches; hunkers; hurdies: **haunch-bone,** n., hainch-

67

bane.

haunt, v., n., howff.

have, v., hae: **have not**, v., haena; hinna.

haven, n., hyne.

havoc, n., dirdum; wrack.

hawk, n., gled.

hawk, clear the throat, v., redd the thrapple.

hawk, sell from door to door, v., cadge: **hawker**, n., cadger; gaun-body.

hawthorn, n., haw; thorn.

hay, n., hey: **haycock**, n., cole: **rick of hay**, n., hey-ruck.

haze, n., gum; loom; ure; simmercout; shimmering summer haze: **hazy**, adj., fozy.

head, n., heid; noddle: **headache**, n., sair heid: **headland**, n., ness; strone: **headlong**, adv., ramstam: **headstrong**, adj., ramstam; raucle: **headway**, n., endwey; weygate: **headmaster**, n., heidmaister.

heal, v., hale; sort; sain: **healed**, adj., aa better.

health, n., hale: **healthy**, adj., hale: **in bad health**, adj., badly: **ask about the health**, v., inquire for: **be in good health**, v., keep the gate.

heap, v., bing; n., bing; cairn, of stones: rickle, loose; humplock, small.

heart, n., hert: **good-hearted**, adj., weill-hertit: **heartsore**, adj., hertsair: **hearty**, adj., sonsie; guidwillie: **flutter, of heart**, v., wallop.

hearth, n., chimla.

heat, n., stove, sudden; swither, great; ure, oppressive; muith, damp: **heat haze**, n., halta dance: **be in heat**, v., spree.

heave, v., n., heize.

heavy, adj., wechty; daichy, of food; lourdie, of clouds.

hedge, n., dyke: **hedgehog**, n., hurcheon: **hedge-sparrow**, n., bluedykie.

hedge, v., flaunter; hum and hae.

heed, v., tak tent: **heedful**, adj., tentie: **heedless**, adj., tentless.

heifer, n., quey.

height, n., hicht; heichness: **heighten**, v., hichten; heicht.

helm, n., tillie.

helmet, n., basnet, steel; magirkie, woollen.

help, v., forder; gie a heize; pit tae ane's haun; n., fore: **helping of food**, n., serin/sairin: **helpless**, adj., daeless; mauchtless.

helter-skelter, adv., ramstam.

hem, n., bord; waltin: **hem in**, v., tack in.

hemp, n., tow: **hemp rope**, n., tow raip.

hen, n., chookie; howdie, young: **brood hen**, n., clocker: **hencoop**, n., cavie: **hen droppings**, n., hen-pen.

herd, v., hird; wark, animals; n., hird; drift.

here, interj., heh: **hereabouts**, adv., hereawa.

hernia, n., douncome; rimburst.

hero, n., kemp.

heron, n., hern; cran.

herring, n., herrin; spirlin, young: **herring measure**, n., cran.

herself, pron., hersel: **by herself**, adv., her lane.

hesitate, v., swither; druther; dackle: **hesitancy**, n., swither; dackle.

hew, v., hag; sned.

hiccup, v., n., hick; yesk.

hide oneself, v., dern: **hide a smell**, v., smuir: **hidden, secret**, adj., datchie; dern: **hiding-place**, n., hidie-hole.

hide, skin, n., leather; flaucht.

hideous, adj., gash; eldritch, of sound.

higgledy-piggledy, adv., mixtie-maxtie.

high, adj., heich: **highest**, adj., heichmaist: **high-born**, adj., gentie: **high-spirited**, adj., spunky; gallus: **highway**, n., highgate.

Highlander, n., teuchter, contemptuous.

hilarious, adj., glorious, with drink; heich.

hill, n., brae; tap; munt, tree-covered; barr, large: **hillock**, n., hullock: **hilltop**, n., brae/knowe-heid: **hills and dales**, n., heichs and howes.

himself, pron., his-sel: **by himself**, adv., his lane.

hinder, v., hinner; taigle: **hindering**, adj., taiglesome: **hindrance**, n., taiglement.

hindmost, adj., hinmaist.

hinge, n., huidin; lith: **hinge pins**, n., charnle-pins.

hint, v., let bug/dab; mint; n., cheip; inklin; mint.

hips, n., hurkles; hurdies: **hip-bone**, n., hurkle-bane.

hire, v., n., fraucht: **hire oneself out to**, v., fee wi: **hire in advance**, v., tryst: **hired, of a servant**, adj., in fee.

hit, v., n., wap; skelp, with flat weapon; skite.

hitch, knot, n., hotch: **difficulty**, n., whaup i the raip: **hitch up**, v., hotch up.

hither, adv., hereawa: **hither and thither**, adv., hither-and-yon.

hive of bees, n., byke; skep.

hoard, v., hain; pit by; n., pose; stockin.

hoarfrost, n., cranreuch.

hoarse, adj.. hairse; ruch; crowpy: **hoarseness**, n., crowp; crichle.

hoax, v., cod; tak a rise out o; n., rise; geg; blawflum.

hob on grate, n., hab; bink.

hobble, v., hirple; hauchle; n., hap-shackle; tam-taigle.

hobnail, n., tacket: **hobnailed boots**, n., tackety buits.

hobnob, v., habnab.

hockey, n., shammy.

hod, n., hud.

hodge-podge, n., gallimaufry.

hoe, v., howe; scutch; n., howe.

hoist, v., n., heist; heize.

hold, v., n., haud: **lay hold of**, v., grip; catch grip o.

hole, n., bore; slap, in fence.

holiday, n., haliday; play.

hollow out, v., howk: **hollow**, n., adj., hallie; howe; boss: **hollow in hills**, n., corrie; merse: **hollow between corn rigs**, n., bauk.

holly, n., hollin.

holm, n., howm; haugh.

holy, adj., halie; sanctly.

home, n., hame: **home-made**, adj., hameart: **homesick**, adj., hamedrauchtit: **homespun cloth**, n., hoddin; raploch: **homestead**, n., toun.

hone, whetstone, n., setstane.

honest, adj., aefauld; evendoun; fair-furth: **honesty**, n., evendounness.

honey, n., hinnie: **honey-comb**, n., hinnie-kaim: **honeysuckle**, n., hinnie-sickle.

honour, n., guidliheid; mense: **a prize**, n., gree: **honourable**, adj., honest.

hood, n., huid: **hooded**, adj., huidie.

hoof, n., cloot; cliv.

hook, v., n., cleik; heuk: **hook barb**, n., wicker: **hook for hanging pot over fire**, n., cruik; ess, s-shaped.

hoop, n., gird; girr.

hop, v., n., hap: **hopscotch**, n., peevers.

hope, v., n., howp: **hopeful**, adj., howpfu: **hopeless**, adj., wanless.

hopper of mill, n., happer.

horde, n., fleesh.

horizon, n., easin; laggin: **horizontally**, adv., flatlins.

horn, trumpet, n., stock; touter: **play a horn**, v., tout.

horrible, adj., gastrous; grugous; ugsome.

horse, n., cuddy; yaud, old; garron, sturdy hill; skybal, worn-out: **horse collar**, n., brecham: **horse dealer**, n., cowper: **horse-fly**, n., cleg: **horse-play**, n., gilravage: **horse's belly-band**, n., wame-gird: **horse shoes**, n., airns: **patch of white on horse's forehead**, n., starn.

hospice, n., spital.

hospitable, adj., guid-willie: **hospitable house**, n., fou hous.

host, crowd, n., thrang; clamjamfry; menzie.

hostile, adj., feidfu; ill-willie: **hostility**, n., feid.

hot, adj., het; sweltry, very: **hot-headed**, adj., birsie; ettery.

hound, v., hund; shore; n., hund; messan; tyke.

hour, n., oor: **hours of sleep**, n., blin oors.

house, n., hous; biggin: **household articles**, n., plenishin: **dry-stone and turf house**, n., black hous: **house site**, n., hous-steid: **house removal**, n., flittin: **outer/inner part of house**, n., but/ben: **master/mistress of household**, n., guidman/guidwife: **one-apartment house**, n., single-en.

hovel, n., bourach; cruive.

hover, v., steady; fidder: **hover indecisively**, v., swither.

how, adv., conj.. hou.

howl, v., n., yowl; gowl.

hub of wheel, n., trinnle.

huddle, v., hudder; smacher.

hue, n., ure.

huff, v., tak the dorts/drunts/gee (jee); n., drunts; towt.

hug, v., hause.

huge, adj., wappin.

hull of boat, n., howe.

hum, v., bum: hum a tune, v., diddle; souch: hum, n., bum; souch.

human, n., body: human beings, n., fowk.

humane, adj., canny; kindly: humanity, n., naitral-hertitness.

humble, v., tak doun a hack/peg; adj., hamespun; hummle; semple.

humdrum, adj., hech-how; dreich; dryward.

humid, adj., mochie.

humiliate, v., affront; bemean: humiliation, n., affront; dountak.

humour, v., uimour; tid: mood, n., uimour; tid; wey.

hump, n., humph: hump-backed, adj., bou/humphie-backit.

hundred, n., adj., hunder/hunner.

hunger, n., worm; scant and want: hungry, adj., tuim; aiverie, ravenously.

hunt about, v., splore: hunt for, v., fork for: hunt through, v., rype.

hurdle, n., wattle, as stop-gap; flake, as temporary gate.

hurl, v., let fly; whurl.

hurly - burly, n., whurlie - birlie; strooshie.

hurricane, n., dreel o wind; doister.

hurry, v., leather; skelp: hurry off, v., scoot: hurry, n., brattle; faird.

hurt, v., skaith; brain, seriously; n., skaith.

hurtle, v., hurl.

husband, n., man; guidman.

hush, v., n., wheesht: hush up, v., wheesh up: hush, interj., wheesht.

husk, n., cod; huil.

husky, adj., crowpy; whaisky: huskiness in throat, n., crowp; roup.

hussy, n., hizzy; skelpie-limmer.

hustle, v., dreel; fluister; hirsel.

hut, n., shieling; cruive.

hutch, n., cray: box on wheels, n., hurly.

hydrant, n., toby.

hypnotise, v., dumfouner.

hypocrite, n., scoug; whillie-goleerie: hypocritical, adj., sleekit.

I shall, v., I'se.

ice, n., geal (jeel): iceberg, n., ice-hill: icicle, n., ice dirk; ice-shogle: half-congealed ice, n., goor; grue.

idea, n., concait; freit, whimsical; plisky, wild; whigmaleerie, foolish.

identify, v., ken; own, as owner.

idiosyncrasy, n., makdom; particularity.

idiot, n., naitral.

idle, v., daidle; mouch; slouth; adj., slouthfu: idler, n., moucher; waster.

idol, n., eedol; mawmet.

if, conj., an; gin; gif.

ignoble, adj., nyabble; ill-willie: of low birth, adj., semple.

ignominy, n., affront.

ignorant, adj., unacquant; unkennin; faur back.

ignore, v., blink: ignored, adj., disrespeckit; untentit.

ill, adj., badly; no weill: very ill, adj., faur throu: become ill, v., tak ill: ill-behaved, adj., ill-daein: ill-bred, adj., menseless; misleird: ill-disposed, adj., ill-intentit: ill-fated, adj., ill-weirdit: ill-feeling, n., umrage: ill-humour, n., dorts; drunts: ill-humoured, adj., thrawn; tuithy; crabbit: ill-natured person, n., ettercap: ill-omened, adj., unchancy; unsonsie: ill-to-please, adj., dorty: ill-treat, v., hash: attack of illness, n., turn; brash: slight illness, n., towt.

illegal, adj., unleisome.

illegitimate, adj., ill-gotten: illegitimate child, n., bastert; get.

illicit intercourse, n., houghmagandie.

illuminate, v., lichten.

illusion, n., blawflum.

illustrious, adj., marked.

image, n., spit; maik.

imagine, v., jalouse: imagination, n., fantice.

imbecile, n., daftie.

imbibe, v., seip in.

imitate, v., tak a swatch frae: imitate English speech, v., knap Suddron.

immature, adj., green.

immediately, adv., straucht; in a crack.

70

immense, adj., wappin.

immodest, adj., heich-kiltit; foutie.

immoral, adj., ill-leevin; waff: **immoral conduct**, n., ill-leevin.

imp, n., limb o Satan.

impact, n., dunt.

impaired in health, adj., failed.

impatient, adj., whippert; mainless: **be impatient with**, v., fash at.

impeccable, adj., fautless.

impede, v., hinner; taigle: **impediment in speech**, n., mant.

impend, v., owrehing.

impertinent, adj., impident; braisant.

impetus, n., virr; swecht: **impetuous**, adj., raucle; forcie.

implement, n., gibble; wark-lume.

imponderable, adj., dowless.

import, v., inbring: **signify**, v., bear: **importance**, n., force.

importune, v., fleich (fleetch); prig: **importunate**, adj., untimeous.

impostor, n., impoustor.

impotent, adj., daeless; mauchtless: **be sexually impotent**, v., fummle.

impoverish, v., herry; tak doun.

impress, v., daur upon; n., steid: **impressive**, adj., vaudie.

imprison, v., jyle; nick.

impromptu, adv., aff-luif.

improve, v., impruive; haud forrit: **improve upon**, v., mak a better o.

imprudent, adj., uncanny; unwyçelike.

impulse, n., stunder: **impulsive**, adj., furthie; raucle.

impute to, v., pit on.

in, prep., i.

inactive, adj., daeless; thieveless; thowless.

inadvertently, adv., unwittins.

inane, empty, adj., tuim; boss: **senseless**, adj., wutless.

inattentive, adj., tentless; tapetless.

incapable, adj., weirdless; heauveless: **incapable of**, adj., no able for.

incessant, adj., uncessant; eend-on.

incident, n., outfaa: **incidental payment**, n., casualty.

incite, v., airt; put up to: **inciter**, n., airter.

inclement, adj., gurly; hashy.

incline, v., airt; wyse: **inclination**, n., mynd: **slope**, v., n., sklent.

incoherent, adj., ravelled: **talk incoher-**

ently, v., yabble.

incompetent, adj., feckless; haunless; weirdless.

inconvenient, adj., unhanty; fashious: **inconvenience**, n., fash.

increase, v., eik to; n., eik: **increase charges**, v., heicht.

indebted, adj., behauden.

indecent, adj., heich-kiltit; foutie.

indecision, n., ramscooter; whillywha: **indecisive**, adj., whether-or-no.

indeed, adv., deed; atweel; interj., d'ye tell me that.

indicate, v., shaw; lat see: **indication**, n., inklin; meith.

indict, v., libel: **indictment**, n., dittay; libel.

indifferent, adj., cauld-water; jeck-easy: **of middle quality**, adj., middlin.

indignity, n., affront.

indirect, adj., sidelins: **indirectly**, adv., sidelins.

indiscreet, adj., unwycelike.

indiscriminately, adv., frimple-frample.

indisposed, adj., no weill: **indisposition**, n., towt.

indistinct, adj., drumly; mirk.

indolent, adj., sweirt: **indolent person**, n., snaiker: **indolence**, n., sweirness.

indoors, adv., inby.

induce, v., wyse; tid.

indulge, v., spyle; waste; dawt.

industry, n., eydence; virr: **industrious**, adj., eydent; warlike.

ineffectual, adj., thowless; thieveless.

inefficient, adj., haunless.

inequality, n., odds.

inevitably, adv., sune or late.

inexpert, adj., prentice.

infant, n., wean (wane); getlin.

infatuated, adj., fond; begottit.

infect, v., infeck; smit: **infection**, n., smit: **infectious**, adj., smittle.

infer, v., gether.

infertile, of soil, adj., deif; dour: **infertile, of eggs**, adj., aidle.

infest, v., owregae; strik: **be infested with**, v., hotch wi.

infinite, adj., stentless.

inflame, v., kennle; raise, infuriate: **inflame with rubbing**, v., scaud.

inflexible, adj., steive; stour.

influence, v., wark; n., wecht.

inform, v., acquant.

infuriate, v., raisc.
infuse, v., mask.
ingenious, adj., airty: **ingenuity**, n., ingyne (injyne).
ingratiate oneself with, v., souk in wi: **ingratiating**, adj., inhaudin.
inhabitant, n., indwaller: **inhabitants**, n., fowk.
inhale, v., snuff; snifter; waucht.
inherit, v., heir.
inhospitable, adj., uncouthy: **inhospitality**, n., cauld comfort.
injure, v., skaith; brain: **injury**, n., ill; skaith: **injurious**, adj., skaithfu.
injustice, n., wrength.
inland, adj., landward; upthrou.
inlet of sea, n., wick.
inn, n., chynge-hous: **innkeeper**, n., chynge-keeper.
inner, adj., ben: **innermost**, adj., benmaist.
innocent, adj., ill-less; sackless; silly.
innovation, n., new-fangle ("ng" as in "sing").
inoffensive, adj., sackless.
inquire of, v., speir at: **inquiry**, n., speir: **inquisitive**, adj., nebby.
inscribe, v., scart.
insecure, adj., immis; shooglie; unsiccar.
insensible, adj., dirr; feel-less: **insensitive**, adj., dowf; timmer.
insert, v., inpit.
inside, adv., ben; inby; prep., ben.
insidious, adj., foutie; sneukit.
insight, n., kennin.
insignificant, adj., nochtie; shitten: **insignificant person**, n., nyaff.
insincere, adj., sleekit; twa-faced: **insincerity**, n., sleekitness.
insipid, adj., fushionless; wairsh; sautless.
insist, v., threip; prig.
insolent, adj., pauchtie; bardy: **insolence**, n., pauchtiness; gash.
inspect, v., sicht; vizzy.
inspire, v., spirit: **inspiration**, n., gell; tift.
instant, n., blink; crack; whuff: **instantly**, adv., in a blink/crack/whuff.
instead, adv., insteid.
instigate, v., airt; wyse: **instigator**, n., airter.

institute, v., estaiblish.
instruct, v., learn; leir; wyse.
instrument, n., wark-lume.
insufficient, adj., scrimp; ergh: **insufficiently**, adv., ergh.
insult, v., ruffle; snash; n., dunt.
insure, v., staun guid for.
integrity, n., strauchtforitness; aefauldness.
intellect, n., intelleck; ingyne (injyne): **be of weak intellect**, v., hae a want.
intelligent, adj., gleg; wyce: **intelligence**, n., mense; uptak; wut.
intend, v., ettle: **intent**, n., ettle; adj., eydent; tentie.
intensely, adv., awfu; sair.
intercept, v., kep.
intercourse, n., traffick; troke; houghmagandie, illicit sexual.
interest, regard, n., regaird: **bank interest**, n., onwal; use.
interfere, v., pit in ane's spune: **interfering**, adj., beddy; nebby.
interior of house, n., ben.
intermediary, n., midsman.
intermediate, adj., halflin.
intermittently, adv., aff and on.
interpret, v., expound; spell.
intersect, v., half.
intertwine, v., plet; wample.
interval, n., spell; baurley, for rest; sklent, in storm.
interview, n., collogue.
intestines, n., harigals.
intimate, n., cummer; goss; adj., big; faur ben; thick; thrang; pack.
intimate, v., annunce; lat ken.
intimidate, v., daunton; counger (coonjer).
into, prep., intae; intil.
in-toed, adj., hen-taed.
intolerable, adj., past aa; untholeable.
intonation, n., souch; tuin; luid.
intrepid, adj., bauld; wight.
intricate, adj., fykie; kittle: **intricacy**, n., wimple.
intrinsic, adj., necessar.
introspective, adj., inbigget.
intrude, v., ingyre: **intruder**, n., incomer; sneckdrawer.
intuition, n., can: **flash of intuition**, n., glint.
inundate, v., fleit.
invade, v., set/yoke on.

invalid, ineffective, adj., feckless; knot-less: weakly, adj., peelie-wally.
inveigle, v., insnorl.
invent, v., cleck; feinyie, forge: invention, n., upmak.
investigate, v., speir into: investigation, n., speir.
invite, v., bid; speir: invite in, v., cry in: inviting, adj., temptsome.
invoke, v., weird: invocation, n., incalling.
iota, n., haet; perlicket.
irascible, adj,. attery; carnaptious.
iris, n., seg; shallock: iris leaf, n., swurd.
iron, n., v., adj., airn: sheet-iron, n., white-airn: flat-iron, n., guse.
irregular, adj., raggled; mistimeous, unpunctual: irregularity, n., gley.
irrelevant talk, n., buff; buller.
irrigate, v. weit.
irritate, v., rile; towt; gaw, chafe: irritable, adj., carnaptious; towty.
I shall, v., I'se.
island, n., inch.
is not, v., isna.
isolated, adj., lane; backabout.
issue, v., ush; spark: issue, result, n., affcome.
isthmus, n., tarbet.
itch, v., n., kittle; yeuk: itchy, adj., yeuky.
item, n., eetim.
itinerant, adj., gangrel: itinerant person, n., gangrel body.
itself, pron., itsel: by itself, adv., its lane.
vy, n., eevie; bindwood.

Jab with sharp instrument, v., brog; jog.
jabber, v., gitter; yabble.
jackdaw, n., kae.
jacket, n., jaiket; cartoush, woman's short; carseckie, light summer.
jade, n., jaud; callet; limmer: jaded, adj., forjeskit.
jagged, adj., knaggit; stabby.
jail, v., jyle; nick; n., jyle; nick; tol-booth, old town jail.
jam-pot, n., jeelie-jaur.
jamb, n., door-cheek.
jangle, v., jow.
January, n., Janwar.

jar, v., n., dirl.
jar, vessel, n., jaur; crock; pig.
jaunt, v., jant; n., jant; outin.
jaunty, adj., crouse; vaunty.
jaw, n., chowk; chaft: having projecting lower jaw, adj., shan-gabbit.
jealous, adj., chawed: be jealous, v., eindle: jealousy, n., taid's ee.
jeer, v., geck at; lichtlie.
jelly, n., jeelie: piece of bread and jelly, n., jeelie piece: jelly-fish, n., seal-skitter; follieshat.
jerk, v., n., yirk; hotch: jerk head side-ways, v., fling.
jest, n., pliskie; shavie.
jetty, n., jet; tress, small.
jib, v., hick; reist.
jibe, v., geck at; lichtlie.
jilt, v., jouk; begunk.
jingle, v., n., jink; ting.
job, n., speil; turn; ontak, big: mean household jobs, n., scodgies: badly done job, n., broggle: fiddling job, n., fouter: odd-job man, n., orraman.
jog, v., n., dunch; jundie; shog: jog along, v., dodge on; daiker.
join, v., jyne: joiner, n., jyner; wricht: joint of beef, n., roast.
joist, n., bauk; jeist.
joke, n., baur; farce, funny story: practical joke, n., pliskie; shavie.
jolly, adj., gaucy; crouse: jollification, n., splore; spree.
jolt, v., n., dad; dunch; jundie; shog.
jot, n., haet; dottle.
journey, v., trevel; n., vaige; gate.
jovial, adj., gaucy; wally.
joy, n., fainness: joyful, adj., blythe; gaucy; rantin.
judge, v., jeedge; redd; n., dempster; lang goun.
jug, n., joug; pourie, for cream; stowp.
juggle, v., joogle.
juice, n., bree: juicy, adj., sappy.
jumble, v., n., jummle; hatter.
jump, v., n., lowp; spang; stend.
jurisdiction, n., pouer.
just, adj., richt-like: just, newly, adv., juist; new.
jut, v., ledge; skail, of wall.
juvenile, adj., green; halflin.

Keen, adj., fain; gleg: keen-edged, adj. gleg.

73

keep, v., kep: **keep in with**, v., haud in wi.

keg, n., cag; tree.

kerb, n., crib.

kettle, n., byler: **kettle spout**, n., stroup.

kick, v., n., fung; fling: **kick about**, v., wallop.

kill, v., end; pit doun, of animal.

kiln, n., kill: **kiln fireplace**, n., killogie.

kilt, n., philabeg; bottomless breeks: **kilt-wearer**, n., kiltie.

kin, n., bluid-friens; sib: **kinship**, n., sibness: **kinsman**, n., frien.

kind, sort, n., swatch; thing.

kind, adj., couthie; furthie; guid-willie: **kindness**, n., couthiness.

kindle, v., kennle; beit; lunt, catch fire.

kingdom, n., kinrik.

kink, n., thraw; lirk.

kipper, n., speldin.

kiss, v., pree the lips; slaik, wetly; n., cheiper; slaik; smurach, stolen.

kitchen, n., kitchie: **kitchen drudge**, n., scodgie.

kite, the bird, n., gled: **boy's kite**, n., draigon.

kitten, n., kittlin.

kitty, jackpot, n., puggie.

knack, n., gate; hing.

knead, v., kned; bake; tyauve.

knee-bone, n., knap-bane: **knee-cap**, n., knap-shell.

knick - knacks, n., bonny - wallies; trantles; whigmaleeries.

knife, n., whittle; gullie, large; cuttie, small.

knight, n., knicht.

knit, v., weive; work: **knitter of stockings**, n., shanker; weiver.

knob, n., knag; snag; tappiloorie, ornamental.

knock, v., n., chap; caa; dad; dunt; knap: **knock-knees**, n., baxter legs.

knot in wood, n., knap; knar: **knot in ribbon**, n., bob: **knotty**, adj., knaggie; nirlie; wirlie: **become knotty**, v., knurl.

know, v., ken; wat: **knowing**, adj., skeely; wyce: **knowledge**, n., ken; leir.

knuckle, n., knurl: **knuckles**, n., nicks: **knuckle-bone**, n., shackle-bane.

Labour, v., n., wark; darg; swink:

Labour Exchange, n., Buroo.

lace, n., perlin; stringin: **bootlace**, n., steiker; whang, of leather.

lack, n., want; airgh; scant: **be lacking**, v., want.

lackadaisical, adj., mauchtless.

lackey, n., flunkie.

laconic, adj., cuttit.

lad, n., laud; callan; halflin; chiel: **smart lad**, n., boy.

ladder, n., lether: **ladder in stocking**, n., lowpen-steik.

ladle, n., divider; scoup.

lady, n., leddy: **ladybird**, n., clock-leddy; sodger: **lady's smock**, n., kerses.

lair, n., bourie.

lake, n., loch; water.

lame, adj., gemm-leggit; happity; paulie: **walk lamely**, v., hirple.

lament, v., cry dool; greit; mane; molligrant; yammer; n., dredgie; coronach: **lamentation**, n., molly-grant; yammer.

lamp, n., cruizie; glennie, safety: **lamplighter**, n., leerie.

land, n., lan; grun: **flat land by river**, n., carse; merse: **sandy, bent-covered land by shore**, n., machair: **small landowner**, n., bunnet laird: **landmark**, n., mairch-stane: meith: **landlady of inn**, n., guidwife; lucky.

lane, n., loaning: **lane between houses**, n., vennel; wynd.

language, n., leid: **English language**, n., Southron.

lank, adj., scranky: **lanky**, adj., skemmlie; ganglin.

lantern, n., bouet: **lantern-jawed**, adj., shan-gabbit: chandler-chaftit.

lap, v., lapper; souk: **lap up**, v., slab up.

lapse, n., lowpen steik.

lapwing, n., peesweep; teuchat.

larceny, n., stouthrie.

larch, n., larick.

lard, n., creish; saim.

larder, n., aumrie; pantry.

large, adj., muckle; gey; dainty/denty: **large specimen**, n., cleisher.

lark, n., laverock.

lascivious, adj., horny; keisty.

lash, v., leish; whang; n., cracker; leish; whang.

lass, n., lassie; quean/quyne; bird.

last, v , lest; staun; weir: **endure**, v., thole: **long-lasting**, adj., lasty.

last, adj., hinmaist: **last night**, n., yestreen: **at last**, adv., at lang and last.

latch, n., sneck; pin; hasp.

late, adj., ahin-haun; adv., ahin: **deceased**, adj., umquhile.

lath, n., strap; spail.

lathe, n., turnin-lume.

lather, v., freith; n., freith; graith; saip sapples.

latrine, n., shunkie; dirt-hous; wee hous.

latter, adj., hinner: **latterly**, adv., at the hinner-en.

laugh, v., n., lauch; keckle; snicker, jeer; flyre, jeer: **laugh loudly**, v., gaff: **loud laugh**, n., gaff: **fit of laughter**, n., kink.

lavatory, n., shunkie; wee hous.

lavish, adj., spendrife; wasterfu.

lawful, adj., leifu: **lawsuit**, n., plea: **lawyer**, n., writer.

lawn, n., green.

lax, adj., slaw; thowless: **loose**, adj., lowss.

laxative, n., scour.

lay, v., lig: **lay aside**, v., pit by: **lay hold of**, v., claucht; grip.

layer, n., fauld; ply; scruif; skliff: **cover with thin layer**, v., scruif.

lay-out, n., outsettin: **well laid out**, adj., snod.

lazy, adj., sweirt; mauchtless; dowless: **very lazy**, adj., bone/horn lazy.

lea, n., meedie; loaning.

lead, the metal, n., leed.

lead, v., guide; wyse: **leader**, n., guider; heid yin.

leaf, cabbage, n., blade: **potato/turnip leaf**, n., shaw.

leak, v., rin out; seip; skail; n., seip: **leak through drought**, v., gizzen.

lean-to, n., tae-faa; tirvin.

lean, adj., rigwiddie; scranky; thin-ribbit.

leap, v., n., lowp; spang; stend.

learn, v., leir: **learned**, adj., buik-leared: **learning**, n., buik-leir.

lease, v., tack: **leaseholder**, n., tacks-man.

leave, v., lae; quat; win awa, depart: **leave off**, v., deval; gie owre: **leave undisturbed**, v., lae alane: **leave-taking**, n., wa-gaun.

leavings, n., brock; dichtins; orras; smush.

leaven, v., raise.

lecher, n., dowp-skelper: **lecherous**, adj., keisty; horny.

lecture, n., lesson; bensel, rebuke.

ledge, n., ledgin; cantle; dass.

leech, n., souker; gell.

leer, v., n., flyre; gledge.

leeward side, n., lythe.

left, adj., caur: **left hand**, n., caurry haun: **left-handed**, adj., caurry-haundit: **left-handed person**, n., caurry-fister.

leg, n., shank; pin; spaul: **long thin legs**, n., spinnle-shanks: **bandy-legged**, adj., bowlie-leggit: **weak-legged**, adj., sheep-shankit.

leggings, n., leggins; gramashes.

legacy, n., testment; heirskip: **give a legacy**, v., legate.

legend, n., auld threip; stoil.

legitimate, adj., weill-comed.

leisure time, n., by-oors.

lemonade, n., scoosh.

lend, v., len.

length, n., lenth: **lengthen**, v., lenthen; eik, of clothes; creep out, of nights: **lengthy**, adj., lenthie; langsome: **lengthwise**, adv., endlang: **at length**, adv., at lang and last: **at full length**, adv., endlang.

lens, n., lozen.

leopard, n., libbard.

leper, n., spilt man.

lest, conj., case be; or.

let, allow, v., lat: **let alone**, v., lat be; lae alane.

letter, postal, n., scrieve; screed: **capital letter**, n., double letter.

level, adj., plain; evenly; soun: **put on level with**, v., even to.

lever, n., pinch; gavelock.

levy, v., n., cess.

liar, n., leear; fleggar.

liberal, adj., guid-willie; hertie; furthie: **liberality**, n., rowthness.

liberate, v., win free.

liberty of movement, n., scouth.

licence, leave, n., freedom: **licentious**, adj., ill-daein; horny.

lichen, n., corkir, for red dye; crottle,

75

for brown; staneraw, for purple; hazleraw, as cure for lung diseases.

lick, v., slaik; slammer, dirtily; n., slaik.

licorice, n., sugaraullie; alicreish.

lid, n., brod.

lie, tell lies, v., lee; whid; n., lee; whid.

lie, v., lig: **lie stretched out,** v., spalder.

lifeless, adj., steirless: **lifelike,** adj., vieve: **lifetime,** n., born days.

lift, v., heize; heist; heicht: **lift, borrowed ride,** n., cairry.

light, n., licht; lunt, from match; glaik, streak of light; gloam, faint light; winkie, flickering light: **light up,** v., licht; enlichten.

light, not heavy, adj., licht; frauchtless: **light and flimsy,** adj., flindrikin: **light-headed,** adj., daft; cairrit: **make light of,** v., lichtlie.

lightning, n., lichtnin; fire-flaucht; wulfire; levin.

like, equal, n., maik; spit: **liken to,** v., even to.

liking, n., fainness; kindness; notion: **well-liked,** adj., weill-likit.

limb, n., spaul.

limit, v., n., stent: **beyond the limits of,** prep., furth o.

limp, flaccid, adj., souple; waffle; mauchtless.

limp, v., hirple; habble; hauchle; n., hirple.

limpet, n., lampit.

limpid, adj., skyre.

line up, v., raw: **out of line,** adv., agee (ajee); agley; asklent; skew.

lineage, n., kin; stryne: **of same lineage,** adj., sib.

linen, n., harn; hagabag, coarse; twal/seiventeen-hunner, fine / very fine linen: **household linen,** n., naiprie.

linger, v., hing/wait on.

liniment, n., rubbins.

linnet, n., lintie.

linoleum, n., waxcloth.

linseed, n., linset.

lint, surgeon's, n., caddis.

lintel, n., owretree.

lip, n., gam: **having thick underlip,** adj., spune-gabbit.

liquid, n., bree: **thin, insipid liquid,** n., jilp; slush.

liquor, n., bree; skink; wheich: **pour out liquor,** v., skink.

list of candidates, n., leet.

listen, v., tent: **listen to,** v., tak tent tae; hark at.

listless, adj., thowless; mauchtless; smerghless.

literary, a literary work, n., quair.

lithe, adj., souple; gleg; swack.

litter, n., cleckin; ferry, of pigs.

little, adj., wee; smaa; peerie: **a little,** n., a pickle; a thocht, of amount: a wee, of time/distance/degree: **little bit,** n., bittock.

live, v., leeve: **reside,** v., byde; win; dwall; stop: **a living,** n., leevin: **poor living,** n., fend; throu-pittin: **livestock,** n., cattle-beasts; bestial.

lively, adj., birkie; skeich; vieve; steirin.

livid, adj., blae.

lizard n., ask.

load, v., fou; lade; fraucht; n., lade; draucht; fraucht; back-birn.

loaf, n., brick; ruchie, wholemeal: **yesterday's loaf,** n., cutting loaf.

loaf, v., mouch (mootch); sotter: **loafer,** n., moucher; waster.

loan, v., n., len.

loath, adj., laith; sweirt.

loathe, v., laithe: **loathing,** n., scunner; ug: **loathsome,** adj., scunnersome; laithsome; ugsome: **object of loathing,** n., scunner.

lobby, n., throu-gaun; trance.

lobster, n., labster; firy-tangs: **lobster trap,** n., creel.

locality, n., gate-end.

lock, v., key: **locked,** adj., lockfast.

lodge, v., byde/stop wi; ludge: **lodging,** n., ludgins; up-pittin.

loft, n., laft; bauk.

log, n., clug.

logical, adj., connect.

loiter, v., slogger; daidle.

lonely, adj., lane; lanesome: **remote,** adj., backabout.

long, adj., lang; langsome: **long-winded,** adj., dreich: **long ago,** adv., lang-syne.

look, v., leuk; gley, sideways; glint, sideways: **look after,** v., mynd; tent: **look foolishly,** v., gawp: **look sulkily,** v., glunch; glower.

loom, n., lume.

loop, v., hank; n., hank; latchet; kinch; slung.

loose, adj., lowss: loosen, v., lowse.

loot, v., herry; spulyie; n., fang; spulyie; reif.

lop, v., sned.

lop-eared, adj., lap-luggit: lop-sided, adj., skellie.

lord, n., laird.

lorry, n., larry.

lose, v., loss; tyne: loss, n., skaith: cause the loss of, v., tyne o.

lot, portion, n., faa; weird.

lot, n., muckle; hantle.

lottery, n., lucky-poke.

lounge, v., mouch (mootch); sotter: lounger, n., moucher; waster.

louse, n., lous: louse egg, n., nit: lice, n., cattle.

lout, n., cuif; cowt; gowk; dobbie.

love, v., lou; luve; n., luve; fainness: lovable, adj., lousome: lover, laud; jo: lovers' go-between, n., blackfuit: love glance, n., love blink.

low, adj., laich: lowest, adj., dounmaist: low-born, adj., semple: lower, v., laichen: lowland, adj., lallan: Lowland Scots tongue, n., Lallans.

low, of cattle, v., rowt; belloch.

lower, of weather, v., mirken: lowering, adj., mirk; cankert, of a look.

loyal, adj., leal; siccar.

lubricate, v., creish.

luck, n., thrift; sonse: bad luck, n., ill-chance: lucky, adj., chancy; sonsie: unlucky, adj., donsie; unsonsie: good luck, interj., fair faa ye.

lug, v., humph: luggage, n., trammels; traps.

lukewarm, adj., luewarm; dowd.

lull, v., ease; dachen; n., let; still.

lullaby, n., cradlie-baa; hush-a-baa.

lumbago, n., cleiks.

lump, n., daud; claut: protuberance, n., knag; knurl.

lunatic, n., loonie.

lunch, packed lunch, n., denner-piece; chat.

lungs, n., buffs; pluffies; windwarks.

lurch, v., swey; rowe; hotch; n., swey; rowe.

lure, v., wyle; wyse.

lurid, of sky, adj., glowert.

lurk, v., lour; scouk; snoove.

luscious, adj., maumie.

lush, adj., growthie; grushie: lushness, n., growthiness (as in "now").

lustre, n., skinkle: lustrous, adj., skinklin; glistery.

luxuries, n., fineries: luxuriant, adj., growthie; grushie.

lye of urine for bleaching linen, n., bouk.

Macabre, adj., gastrous; grugous; ugsome.

machinery, n., graith.

mackerel, n., maukrel.

mad, adj., deleerit; gyte; wud: madden, v., craze; frenzy.

maggot, n., mawk: maggoty, adj., mawkit.

magic, n., glamourie; weirdrie; adj., weirdly: magician, n., warlock.

magistrate, town magistrate, n., bailie.

magnanimity, n., gentrice.

magnificent, adj., rare.

magpie, n., pyat.

maid, n., lass; burd; quean: maid-servant, n., girzie; servant-lass.

mail, postal, n., post.

maim, v., demember; mang.

main, adj., heidmaist: mainly, adv., feckly: main street, n., toun gate.

maintain, v., fend: maintenance, n., uphaudin.

majesty, n., glore: majestic, adj., michty; buirdly.

majority, n., feck; ruch.

make, v., mak: compel, v., gar: make do, v., pit by.

malady, n., ill.

malefactor, n., ill-doer.

malevolent, adj., ill-hertit; ill-willie: malevolence, n., ill-will.

malice, n., ilta; venim: malicious, adj., ill-hertit; ill-willie.

mallard, n., gray duck.

mallet, n., mell; knapper.

malt, n., maut.

man, n., man-body; chiel; carl; mannie, little: foolish old man, n., doddard: small bumptious man, n., cockie-bendie: manhood, n., manheid.

manage, cope, v., mak a fen: administer, v., guide: manage to reach, v., win: managing, adj., fendie: manager, n., guide; grieve, of farm.

manger, n., heck.

mangle, v., haggle; hash.

mania, n., deleeritness; wudness.

manifest, make manifest, v., kythe: **manifestation,** n., kythin.

manipulate, v., feugle; pauchle.

manner, n., wey; gate: **manners,** n., mainners: **mannerisms,** n., pirlicues.

manoeuvre, v., n., jouk: **manoeuvre in a certain direction,** v., wyse; airt.

mantelpiece, n., chimla-brace.

manure, n., dung; muck.

many, adj., monie: **many-coloured,** adj., gairy.

map, n., cairt.

mar, v., spyle; hash; connach.

marble, boy's, n., bool; chuckie; stanie; cleyie; jaurie; glessie: **game of marbles where winnings are returned/kept,** n., funny/keepy.

march, v., mairch.

mare, n., meir.

margin, n., selvedge.

mark, butt, n., bob; gog.

mark, stain, v., fyle; tash: **make mark on surface,** v., scart: **distinguishing mark,** n., meith.

market, n., mairket; mart; mercat: **market place,** n., tron: **market garden,** n., mail gairden: **present brought from market,** n., fairin.

marry, v., wad: **ask in marriage,** v., speir: **marriage,** n., mairriage; waddin: **coins thrown to children at marriage,** n., baa-siller: **marriage certificate,** n., mairriage lines: **trial marriage,** n., handfast.

marrow, n., smergh.

marsh, n., flow; lair; moss: **marshy,** adj., lairy: **marsh-marigold,** n., puddock-flouer.

martyr, n., mairtyr.

marvel. v., ferlie; mairvel: **marvel at,** v., strange at.

mash, v., champ; chap; n., mush.

mask, n., fause-face.

mason, n., dorbie: **masonry,** n., aislerwark; stanewark.

masquerade, v., n., guise: **masquerader,** n., guiser.

mass of matter, n., claut; clitter, wet; slaiger, wet; hotter, seething.

mast of boat, n., stang.

master, v., get roun; owregae; n., maister; guidman: **mastery,** n., owrance.

mat, v., tawt; n., thresh, of rushes; flet, straw: **door mat,** n., bass.

match, v., brither; marrow; n., maik; marrow: **a game,** n., spiel; bonspiel, curling: **matchless,** adj., maikless: **not matching,** adj., neibourless.

match, n., spunk; lunt: **strike a match,** v., scart a match.

mate, n., maik; marrow.

material, n., stuff; stuffrie: **materialise,** v., sowther.

matrimony, holy, n., haly band: **join in matrimony,** v., sowther.

matter, pus, n., bealin; atter.

mature, adj., maumie, of fruit; man-grown: **become mature,** v., set.

maul, v., mell; rive.

maximum, adj., outmaist.

may not, v., mauna: **maybe,** adv., aiblins; mebbe; belike.

May, the month, n., Mey.

mead, n., bragwort.

meadow, n., meedie; loaning.

meagre, adj., stintit; scrimpy; jimp: **meagreness,** n., scrimp.

meal, last meal from crop, n., disty-melder: **meal-bin,** n., ark; kist; girnel: **meal of food,** n., mail; pick; stechin, hearty; twal-piece, light meal at noon: **mealtime,** n., crowdie-time; diet-hour.

mean, base, adj., fouty; shitten; measly; wee: **meanness,** n., fouti-ness: **stingy,** adj., gair; grippy; nippit: **stingy person,** n., skin-a-lous.

mean, intend, v., ettle: **meaningless,** adj., rhymeless.

means, n., graith; gear.

meander, v., wimple.

measure, v., mizzure; faddom; spang, by pacing; tak aff, for suit: **measurement,** n., grist.

meat, n., mait; slink, second-rate: **leg of meat,** n., shank: **meat scraps,** n., stottin bits: **meat market,** n., shamells: **meat safe,** n., gardymang.

mechanical contrivance, n., whurlie; wark machine: **mechanism,** n., intimmers.

meddle, v., put in ane's spune: **meddling,** adj., beddy.

mediator, n., midman; gang-atween.

medicine, n., feesick.

meditate, v., lay the brains asteep: meditative, adj., pensy.

medium, adj., middlin.

medley, n., menzie; mixter-maxter: medley of sound, n., mang.

meek, adj., hummle.

meet, v., forgether: encounter, v., meet in wi: agree to meet, v., tryst wi: meeting, n., forgetherin; convene: meeting place, n., howff.

melancholy, n., dowfness; dowieness; adj., dowie; oorie; wae.

mellow, adj., maumie.

melody, n., tuin.

melt, v., mouten; sowther; render, dripping.

membrane, n., striffin; hind, over white of egg.

memento, n., myndin.

memoranda, n., notandums.

memory, n., mynd.

menace, v., boast; shore.

mend, v., men; help; fettle.

menial, n.. scodgie: menial work, n., scodgie wark.

mental deficiency, n., want: mental vigour, n., fushion.

mention, v., let dab.

merchant, general, n., Johnnie-aa-thing: merchandise, n., merchandie; trokerie.

mercy, n., guid gree: a mercy, n., a guid's blessin.

merge, v., gae thegither; meng.

mermaid, n., selkie-wife.

merry, adj., blythe; canty; crouse: make merry, v., daff; splore; spree: merrymaking, n., daffin; splore; spree.

mesmerise, v., dumfouner.

mess, n., guddle; hash; moger: sloppy mess, n., slaister; slitter: messy, adj., clarty; slittery: make a mess of, v., bullox; mak a munsie o; hash.

message, n., send: messenger, n., send; caddie.

metal worker, n., hammerman: fit with metal rims, v., shae.

metaphor, n., scairie.

meteor, n., staur-glint.

method, n., gate; wey; road: methodi-

cal, adj., purposefu.

meticulous, adj., perjink; pernickety.

mew, v., n., myow; yarm.

midden, n., dungstead.

middle, n., mids.

midges, swarm of, n., simmer-cout.

midnight, n., howe o the nicht; lang oor.

midway, adv., halflins.

midwife, n., cummer/kimmer; howdie.

might, v., micht.

might, n., micht; maucht: mighty, adj., michty; mauchty; wight.

mild of temperament, adj., lythe; meith: of weather, adj., saft; maumie.

mildew, n., foust.

milk, n., mulk: curdled milk, n., lappert milk: milk container, n., boyne: milk pail, n., hannie; laiglen: milk strainer, n., mulsy; milk-sey: sour milk, n., sour douk: milking place, n., loaning.

mill, n., mull: mill-pond, n., dam: millrace, n., mill-lade: mill grinding stone, n., quern.

mimic, v., gamf; manner.

mind, n., mynd: bear in mind, v., keep mynd o.

miner, n., coallier.

minnow, n., mennen: red-breasted minnow, n., bluid-hert.

minstrel, n., bard.

minute, n., meenit.

minute, adj., tottie; peerie-weerie.

mire, n., clart; clabber; muck: miry, adj., clarty; clabbery; claggy.

mirror, n., keekin-gless.

mirth, n., daffery; blytheness; crouse-ness.

miscall, v., caa; miscaa.

miscarry, of plan, v., gang agley; mis-gae.

miscellaneous, adj., orra: miscellany, n., geddery; variorum.

mischance, n., mishanter; snapper.

mischief, n., ill; deviltry: mischief, injury, n., skaith: piece of mischief, n., cantraip; prattick: mischievous, adj., gallus; tricky.

misdemeanour, n., step-aside; ill-daein.

miser, n., gear-getherer; scrunt; skin-a-lous: miserly, adj., grippy; near-the-bit; moulie; nippit.

miserable, adj., sairie; weary: misery,

n., dool; wanjoy.
misfortune, n., begunk; mishanter; snapper.
mishap, n., begunk; mishanter; snapper.
misinform, v., misleir.
mispronounce, v., thraw; miscaa.
miss, fail to hit, v., tyne: **pass over,** v., hap; miskip.
missel-thrush, n., feltie; storm-cock.
misshape, v., mismak: **misshapen,** adj., shauchled; wrang.
misspent, adj., ill-spent.
mist, n., drow; driffle; haar; reik: **misty,** adj., daggy; haury.
mistake, v., n., mistak: **mistake one's meaning,** v., forestaw.
mistress of household, n., guidwife; hersel: **"mistress",** n., doxy.
mistrust, v., n., mistrue.
misunderstand, v., misken; misunnerstaun: **misunderstanding,** n., differ.
misuse, v., hash; disabuise.
mitten, n., pawkie; humlie.
mix, v., mell; meng: **mixed confusedly,** adj., mixtie-maxtie: **mixture,** n., complowter; rummle: **mix-up,** n., complowter; mashle.
moan, v., n., mane; souch.
moat, n., dub; stank.
mob, n., canailyie.
mock, v., flyre; geck at; lichtlie: **mocking,** adj., mockrife.
model, n., marrow; maik.
moderate, adj., canny; handy, in price; middlin: **moderation,** n., mense.
modest, adj., blate; bauch; lown.
moist, adj., mochie; wauch: **moisten,** v., slocken: **moisture,** n., wat; weit.
molasses, n., blackstrap.
mole, n., mowdie: **molehill,** n., mowdiehill.
mole on skin, n., hinnie drap.
molest, v., steir; sturt.
mollicoddle, v., dawt; browden; fraik; n., jessie.
moment, n., blink; crack; whuff.
momentum, n., virr; wecht.
money, n., siller; gear; bawbees: **large sum of money,** n., braw penny: **money-grubbing,** n., catch-the-plack: **ready money,** n., dry siller.
mongrel, n., messan; tyke.
monkey, n., puggy.

monopolise, v., thirl to anesel.
monotonous, adj., dreich; weary **monotonous talk,** n., thrum.
monster, n., etin; gyre: **monstrous,** adj., grugous; ugsome.
mood, n., wind; tid; tuin: **moody,** adj., stounie; tifty.
moon, n., mune: **moonlight,** n., munelicht: **moon halo,** n., brocht; faul.
moor, n., muir.
moor a boat, v., tether.
mop up, v., dicht; swaible.
mope, v., hing the lugs; mump.
moral excellence, n., grace: **moral relapse,** n., way-sliding: **moral stain,** n., smitch: **morally astray,** adj., glendergane; aff the fuit.
morbid, adj., unhalesome; ill.
more, adj., mair: **more or less,** adv., back or fore.
morsel, n., crum; nirl; pick.
mortar, n., lime.
mortgage, n., thirl-ban; wadset.
mortify, v., gunk.
mortuary, n., deid/lyke-hous.
moss, n., fog: **mossy,** adj., foggie.
most, adj., maist: **mostly,** adv., maistly; fecklins.
mote in eye, n., flicht.
moth, n., moch; nicht-hawk, large white; shelly-coat, tortoise-shell.
mother, n., mither; mammy; maw: **mother-in-law,** n., guidmither.
motion, n., steir: **rocking motion,** n., coble: **motionless,** adj., stane-still.
motley, adj., mixtie-maxtie: **motley crowd,** n., ragabash.
mottle, v., marl; spreckle: **mottled,** adj., mirlie; marled; spreckled.
motto, n., ensenyie.
mould, v., n., foust: **mouldy,** adj., fousty; moulie: **moulder,** v., mouler.
mould, frame, n., muild; caum.
moult, n., pouk.
mound, n., humplock; hullock.
mount, v., munt; speil: **place in position,** v., stell.
mountain, n., ben: **mountain pass,** n., balloch: **mountain ash,** n., rodden tree.
mourn, v., murn; mane; greit: **mournful,** adj., doolfu; dowie.
mouse, n., mous: **mouse-coloured,** adj., din.

mouth, n., mou; gab/gub/gob: **mouthful,** n., mouthfu: **having crooked mouth,** adj., gley-moud: **shut one's mouth,** v., steik ane's gab.

move/cause to move, v., muive; steir; moodge: **move from one place to another,** v., flit: **move laboriously,** v., warsle: **move quickly,** v., jink; link; skelp: **move stealthily,** v., scouk: **movement,** n., steir.

mow, v., maw.

much, adj., muckle/meikle; adv., muckle; geylies.

mucus, nasal, n., snotters: **mucus, throat,** n., sloch; glit.

mud, n., glaur; clabber; muck; clart: **muddy,** adj., clarty; glaurie; drumly: **bedaub with mud,** v., slaister; slaiger.

muddle, v., guddle; bootch; n., guddle; bootch; fankle.

mug, n., stowp; joug; tinnie.

muggy, adj., mochie.

multi-coloured, adj., pyat; sprittle.

multitude, n., menyie; hirsel.

mumble, v., mummle; mump.

mummer, n., guiser: **go mumming,** v., guise.

mumps, n., branks; buffets.

munch, v., ramsh; cramp; scrump.

murky, adj., mirk; gowrie.

murmur, v., chirm; souch; n., curmurrin; souch.

muscle, n., thow.

mush, n., powsowdie: **reduce to mush,** v., poach.

mushroom, n., mushie; flab.

music, n., maisic: **music school,** n., sang-schuil: **music festival,** n., sangschaw.

mussel, n., mushle; clabbydoo, large; yam, large.

must, v., maun; buist, had to.

muster, pass muster, v., ser.

musty, adj., fousty; mochie.

mute, adj., tongue-tackit.

mutilate, v., demember; mang.

mutter, v., mump; yabble.

mutton, leg of, n., gigot (jigot).

mutual aid, n., giff-gaff: **mutual aid club,** n., manawdge.

mysterious, adj., uncanny; unyirdly.

mystify, v., bumbaze; dumfouner.

Nag, n., naig.

nag, v., natter; yammer; yap; yatter.

naked, adj., nakit: **quite naked,** adj., bare-nakit; bare-scuddie.

name added to surname, n., eikname: **name after,** v., caa efter.

nap, v., n., dover; snooze.

napkin, n., naipkin: **baby's napkin,** n., babby-clouts.

narrate, v., tell owre: **narrative,** n., sae-say: **narration,** n., throu-gang.

narrow, adj., nerra; strait: **make narrow,** v., strait.

nasty, adj., nesty.

native, adj., hameward: **native district,** n., cauf-country/kintra.

natural, adj., naitral: **nature,** n., naitur.

naughty, adj., ill-daein; wangracie.

nausea, n., scunner; staw; ug: **nauseate,** v., scunner.

nearest, adj., nearmaist: **nearly,** adv., near.

neat, adj., nait; trig; dink; feat; snod: **make neat,** v., snod; tosh; trig.

necessary, adj., necessar: **necessity,** n., maundae; need-be.

neck, n., craig; hause; thrapple.

need, necessity, n., caa: **needy,** adj., needfu; sairie.

needle for darning, n., stocken-needle: **point of needle,** n., starn: **needlewoman,** n., shewer: **needlework,** n., shewin.

ne'er-do-well, n., dae-nae-guid; waster; wangrace.

nefarious, adj., guidless; ill; wangracie.

neglect, v., n., negleck; slicht.

negotiate, v., transack; troke; throu: **negotiable, of currency,** adj., gangable: **negotiation,** n., transack; troke.

negro, n., bleck.

neigh, v., n., nicker.

neighbour, n., neibour: **neighbourhood,** n., gate-end.

neither, pron., adj., conj., naither.

nephew, n., brither/sister-son.

nervous, adj., timorsome; skeer; crappy: **nervousness,** n., swither.

nest, plunder nest, v., herry: **nestling,** n., gorlin: **nest-egg,** n., sorting.

nestle, v., courie; squattle: **nestle closely,** v., croodle.

net for hair, n., snood: **salmon net stretched across river,** n., stell-net.

nether, adj., enner: **nethermost,** adj.

ennermaist.
nettle with sting, n., day-nettle: **dead-nettle,** n., soukie sou.
never, adv., ne'er: **nevertheless,** adv., for aa that; still and on.
new, brand new, adj., brent/sprush new: **new-fangled,** adj., new-farrant: **newcomer,** n., outland/unco body: **newly,** adv., new.
news, n., word; wittins; uncos: **get news of,** v., hear tell o: **tell one's news,** v., gie ane's crack: **newspaper,** n., paper; news.
next, adj., adv., prep., neist.
nibble, v., moup; nip; stou.
nice, adj., canty; couthy: **nicety,** n., perjink: **to a nicety,** adv., to a thocht.
niche, n., neuk.
nick, notch, v., n., sneck; nag.
nickname, n., eik-name; tae-name.
niece, n., brither/sister-dochter.
niggard, n., scrunt; skin-a-lous: **niggardly,** adj., grippy; near-the-bit.
nigger, n., neeger; bleck.
night, n., nicht: **last night,** adv., yestreen: **nightgown,** n., goun: **nightcap,** n., hoomet: "**nightcap**", n., bowster-cup: **nightfall,** n., dayset; nicht-faa: **pass the night,** v., nicht.
nimble, adj., souple; gleg; swack: **move nimbly,** v., spank; skelp.
ninepin, n., kyle: **game of ninepins,** n., kyles.
nip, v., nirl: **nip off,** v., stou: "**nippy**", adj., nebby.
nipple, n., tit.
no, adj., nae: **say no,** v., na-say: **no fear,** interj., fient a fear.
noble, adj., gentie; gentle; buirdly; sneith: **nobleman,** n., laird; duke-ma-lordie.
nobody, n., naebody.
noise, n., dirdum; buller; bellum: **make noise,** v., brattle, clattering; chirk, grinding; buller, gurgling.
noisome, adj., fousome; scunnersome; ugsome.
noncommittal, adj., tory; twa-and-twae.
none, pron., nane.
nonentity, n., fley-the-doos; smaa-drink; stookie.
nonsense, n., blethers; claivers; haivers:

talk nonsense, v., haiver.
nook, n., neuk.
noon, n., nune; twal-oors.
noose, n., fank; kinch.
normal, adj., naitral; warldlike.
northern, adj., norland: **northward,** adv., northwart.
nose, n., neb; grunzie, contemptuous: sharp-nosed, adj., coulter-nebbit: **nose mucus,** n., snotter: **nose about,** v., snowk: **speak through nose,** v., snuil.
nosegay, n., bab; flouer.
not, adv., no; nae: **not any,** pron., nane.
notable, adj., kenspeckle; marked.
notary, n., writer.
notch, v., n., sneck; nag.
note, musical, n., spatril: **memorandum,** n., notandum: **note down,** v., mark: **take note,** v., tak tent: **noteworthy,** adj., particlar.
nothing, n., naethin; nocht; nowt.
notice, v., tak tent: **intimation,** n., word; warnin: **notice board,** n., buird.
notion, n., concait; freit, whimsical; whigmaleerie, foolish.
nourish, v., meat: **nourishment,** n., meat; fushion.
novice, n., greenhorn.
now, adv., nou: **just now,** adv., the nou: **now and then,** adv., whyles.
nowhere, adv., naewhaur; naewey.
nudge, v., nidge; shog.
nuisance, n., humbug; scunner.
numb, adj., feel-less: **go numb,** v., stivven.
number, v., n., nummer: **number of,** n., wheen: **considerable number,** n., guid few; hantle: **large number,** n., thrang; pouer: **numerous,** adj., monie.
nurse, v., cuiter; tak about; trowe wi; n., nurice.
nurture, v., fesh up.
nut, n., nit.
nuzzle, v., nuisle; snoozle.

Oaf, n., cuif; cowt; dobbie; gowk.
oak, n., aik.
oats, n., aits; corn: **oatcake,** n., bannock; farl: **oatmeal and water,** n., crowdie; cauld steirie: **oatmeal fried**

with onions, n., skirl-i-the-pan.

oath, n., aith.

obdurate, adj., dour; thrawn; dursy.

obedient, adj., biddable: obey, v., dae ane's biddin.

obeisance, n., beck; bob: make obeisance, v., beck; bob; lout.

object, v., objeck; n., ettle, purpose: objection, n., backjar: objectionable, adj., scunnersome.

oblige, v., obleege: obliged, adj., behauden: obliging, adj., discreet; greeable: obligement, n., obleegement.

oblique, adj., sidelins; skew: obliquely, adv., sidelins; asklent.

obliterate, v., smoor/smuir.

obscene, adj., foutie; randy: obscenity, n., sculdudry.

obscure, v., smoor/smuir; adj., dern; drumly; mirk.

obsequious, adj., inhaudin; souple-neckit: be obsequious, v., foonge.

observe, v., leuk til; tent: observant, adj., tentie.

obstacle, n., backhaud; stick.

obstinate, adj., dour; thrawn; willyart: obstinacy, n., thrawnness.

obstreperous, adj., misbehauden; outstrapalous; tousy.

obstetrician, n., wamesmith.

obstruct, v., hatter; mar: obstruction, n., hinder; mar.

obtain, v., come by: obtain by craft, v., skech; wyse.

obvious, adj., sensible.

occasion, chance, n., tid: need, n., caa: occasional, adj., antrin; daimen.

occur to, v., come up ane's humph: occurrence, n., hap; outfaa.

odd, occasional, adj., antrin; orra; daimen: strange, adj., droll; unco: odd person, n., ticket: odd-job-man, n., orra-man: odds and ends, n., trantles.

odour, n., guff; goo; smeik; waff.

of, prep., o.

off, adv., prep., aff: off the mark, adv., aff the gleg.

offal, n., faa; emmledeug.

offend, v., short; tramp on ane's taes: easily offended, adj., saft-skinned: take offence, v., tak ill out; flee up: offensive, adj., nesty.

offer, v., hecht; shore: offer at sale, v., n., bode.

offhand, careless, adj., jeck-easy: impromptu, adv., aff-luif.

office, give up office, v., demit: officer, n., officiar.

officious, adj., offeecious; powterin.

offspring, n., bairn; get, derogatory.

often, adv., aft; aften.

ogle, v., flyre.

ogre, n., gyre; gyre-carlin.

oh that, interj., gin: oh yes, interj., oay.

oil, v., ile; n., ile; eelie; uily: oily, adj., ilie; glittie: oil-can, n., pourie: oil lamp, n., cruizie: oilskin, n., iliecoat.

ointment, n., eyntment; saw; gree.

old, adj., auld: old age, n., eild: old-fashioned, adj., auld-fanglt; auld-farrant, wise: old-looking, adj., auld-like: grow older, v., weir on.

omen, n., bode; warnin.

omit, v., owreleuk: omission, n., forget; owreleuk.

once, adv., ance; yince: at once, adv., aff-haun; straucht.

one, pron., ane; yin; adj., ae; ane: one another, pron., ilk ither: one-sided, adj., tae-sided.

onion, n., ingan; sybie, young.

only, adj., ae; yae; adv., anerly.

onset, n., oncome; onding.

onward, adv., forrit.

ooze, v., seip; sype; n., glit; glaur: ooziness, n., glittiness.

open, v., adj., apen; adj., agee, partly: opening, n., apenin; slap, in wall.

opinion, n., think; souch; braith; concait.

opponent, n., fae; unfrien: formidable opponent, n., breenger.

opportune, adj., tiddy; timeous: opportunity, n., tid.

oppose, v., conter; thraw: opposite, adj., contrair; prep., forenent.

oppress, v., dounhaud; thraw: oppressive, of weather, adj., firy; glorgy.

optimistic, adj., weill-hertit.

ordain, v., destinate; weird, by fate.

ordeal, n., throu-come.

order, command, n., word: arrangement, n., ray; skik: condition, n., tuin; tiff: in good working order, adj., guid-gaun: set in order, v., redd; snod; sort.

ordinary, adj., ornar; ordinar.

organ, pipe, n., kist o whistles; mill: **barrel organ**, n., whurly organ: **organist**, n., whussle grinder: **internal organs**, n., intimmers.

orgy, n., gilravage.

origin, n., springheid.

ornament, v., set up; fineer: **ornaments**, n., targets; wallies: **ornamental flourish in writing**, n., pirlicue; squirl.

orthodox, adj., soun.

osprey, n., sea-gled; water-earn.

other, adj., ither: **the others**, n., the lave: **otherwise**, adv., else.

otter, n., tyke.

ought, v., ocht; boost.

ounce, n., unce.

ourselves, pron., oursels.

out of, prep., out frae; furth: **out of doors**, adv., outby.

out-, prefix, **outburst**, n., outbrak: **outcast**, n., outland body: **outcry**, n., sang; yammer: **make an outcry**, v., yammer: **outdo**, v., lick; bang; ding: **outlaw**, n., fugie (foodjie): **outlay**, n., oncost; outgang: **outlet**, n., affgate: **outline**, n., scantling: **outlive**, v., see awa: **outlying**, adj., outby: **outpace**, v., cappilow: **output**, n., throu-pit: **outset**, n., affset: **outside**, adj., adv., prep., outby; prep., furth: **outspoken**, adj., raucle; free: **outward**, adj., adv., outwith: **outwit**, v., circumvene; ravel.

outrageous, adj., enorm; heronious.

ovary of fowl, n., lay-bag.

oven, n., oen; een.

over, adv., prep., atour: **over and above**, adv., prep., forby.

over-, prefix, **overall**, n., slug: **overawe**, v., counger (coonjer); daunton: **overbalance**, v., cowp: **overbearing**, adj., heich-heidit; high-i-the-bend: **overboiled**, adj., slubbery: **overburden**, v., trauchle: **overcast**, adj., hingin; mirk: **become overcast**, v., lour; mirken: **overcoat**, n., big/tap coat: **overcome**, v., lick; ding; waur: **overcome with fatigue**, adj., forfochen; forjeskit; wabbit: **overdue**, adj., ahint the haun: **overflow**, v., skail: **overgrow**, v., owregang: **overhaul**, n., throu-gaun: **overlap**, v.,

owrelowp: **overlook**, v., owreleuk: **over-ornamented**, adj., fantoosh: **overpower**, v., owrethraw; whummle: **overreach**, v., owre-rax: **overrule**, v., collie: **overrun**, v., owre-rin: **overseer**, n., gaffer; heid bummer: **oversensibility**, n., parritch-hertitness: **oversight**, n., forget: **oversleep**, v., sleep in: **overstep**, v., owrestap: **overstrain**, v., owrerax: **overtake**, v., mak up on; owretak: **overthrow**, v., owrethraw; whummle: **overturn**, v., cowp: **overwhelm**, v., whalm; whummle: **overwork**, v., hash; stress.

owe, v., awe; be due: **owing**, pres. part., awn.

owl, n., houlet.

own, possess, v., awn; aucht: **confess**, v., awn: **owner**, n., awner: **what is owned**, n., aucht; haddin: **ownership**, n., aucht.

own, adj., ain.

ox, n., owse; stirk; stot: **oxen**, n., owsen; nowt.

oysters, n., oyse: **oyster bed**, n., scalp: **oyster-catcher**, n., pictarnie.

Pace, step, n., pass; spang: **speed**, n., course; raik: **steady pace**, n., dodge; jundie: **pace hither and thither**, v., reinge.

pacify, v., cullie.

pack, v., stow; stech; stap: **packman**, n., chapman.

paddle, v., paidle; plowter.

paddock, n., loan; loaning.

padlock, n., hingin lock.

pail, n., luggie; bowie; hannie; leglen.

pain, v., rack; stoun; n., pyne; rack; stang, shooting: **painful**, adj., sair: **alleviate pain**, v., dirr: **take pains**, v., fash; fyke.

paint, v., n., pent.

pair, v., sort; n., twasome.

palate, n., mouth-ruif: **palatable**, adj., mou-frauchty; tuithrife.

palaver, v., claiver; n., fracaw; ontak.

pale, adj., fauchie, of liquid; gash, ashen: **pale with grief**, adj., waewan.

paling post, n., palin stab.

pall, n., mort-cloth.

palm of hand, n., luif: **palm off**, v., pawm aff.

palm, prize, n., gree.
palpitate, v., dunt; flaff; flichter: palpitation, n., dunt; gowp.
palsy, n., trummles.
paltry, adj., fouterie; auchimuty.
pamper, v., dawt; browden; waste.
pamphlet, n., track.
pan, n., skellat: pancake, n., pan-scone.
pane of glass, n., lozen.
pang of pain, n., stang; stound: of remorse, n., efterstang.
panic, n., fray; swither; wuddrum: panic-stricken, adj., fear-fangit.
panorama, n., swype.
pant, v., pech; fetch; fuff; n., pech.
pantry, n., aumry.
paralyse, v., palsify: paralysed, adj., paulie: paralytic stroke, n., shock.
paramour, n., callet; dunty.
parapet, n., selvedge; lanstell.
parasite, n., atemeat; sorner: live parasitically, v., sorn.
parcel, n., paircel.
parch, v., birsle; wizzen: parched, adj., druchtit; gizzen.
pardon, v., forgie.
pare, v., scaup; skive; flauchter, turf.
parish, n., pairish.
park for vehicles, n., rest: side-road parking place, n., ingaunce.
parliament, n., paurliament: member of parliament, n., inler; parlementer.
parlour, n., spence; haa.
paroxysm, n., shouer; rapture.
parrot, n., papingo; paurrot.
parry, v., fend; kep; waur.
parsley, n., persley.
part, n., pairt: one of two unequal parts, n., half: partly, adv., halflins.
part, v., pairt; sinder; twin: parting drink, n., deoch-an-dorus; stirrup-dram: parting of ways, n., shedding.
particle, n., crum; curn; haet.
particular, special, adj., particlar: fastidious, adj., pernickety; fykie; perjink: particulars, details, n., particularities.
partisan, n., pairt-taker.
partition, n., hallan; brattice; parpane.
partner, n., marrow; pairtner.
partridge, n., paitrick.
party, n., pairty: social meeting, n., shine; splore: party of people, n., core; curn.

pass, of time, v., drive on; weir in: pass away, v., win awa: passable, of road, adj., gangable: passing bell, n., deid-bell: password, n., tryst-word.
passageway, n., throu-gang; trance: between houses, n., close; vennel.
passion, n., tirrivee; rampage; frennishin: passionate, adj., flisty; ettery: in a passion, adj., dancin mad: fly into a passion, v., flist; fuff.
passive, adj., dowf; thowless.
paste, n., batter; pap, flour and water: pastries, n., sweet-breid.
pastime, n., play; ploy.
pasture, v., gress; n., gress park; loaning: pasturage, n., grassing.
pat, v., clap; n., clap; tig; straik.
patch, v., n., clout; eik: patched, adj., cloutie.
path, n., pad; gang.
pathetic, adj., sairie: pathetic expression, n., puir face.
patience, n., tent; thole: patient, adj., patientfu.
patron, n., stoup.
pattern, n., patren; muild; set.
paunch, n., bag; haggis.
pause, v., hover: respite, n., blaw; baurley.
pave, v., causey: pavement, n., plain-stanes.
paw, v., pawt; claw; n., mag; luif.
pawn, v., n., wad/wadset: pawnshop, n., pawn.
pay, v., n., pey; siller: payment, n., peyment; siller.
pea-pod, n., huil; shaup: flour of ground peas, n., pease-meal.
peace, n., saucht; lown; lythe: peaceful, adj., lown; lythe.
peal, v., n., jow; rowt, of thunder.
peanut, n., puggy nit.
pear, n., peir.
peasant, n., loun.
peat, n., moss: a peat, n., truff; turr: heap of peats, n., peat bing/stack: peat bog, n., moss: peat hole, n., hag.
pebble, n., peeble; chuckie-stane: pebbles, n., chingle.
peck, v., n., pouk; dab; dorb.
peculiar, adj., geylike; unco; orra: peculiarities, n., perjinketies.

pedantic, adj., lang-nebbit.
pedestrians, n., fuit-folk.
pedlar, n., chapman; packie; tinker.
peel off, v., flype; scruif.
peep, v., n., keek; glint: peep-hole, n., keek/vizzy hole.
peer, equal, n., maik: nobleman, n., laird.
peer, v., keek: peer at sideways, v., slee at
peevish, adj., fashious; girny; thrawn.
peewit, n., peesweep; peesie; teuchat.
pell-mell, adv., ramstam; throuither.
pelt, v., blatter; peeble, with stones.
pen worn small, n., stumpie: stroke of pen, n., straik.
pen, enclosure, n., bucht; cruive; fank; cray: pen up, v., bucht; fank.
penalty, n., skaith; wyte: pay the penalty, v., pey the mail.
penance, n., mends.
pencil, n., keelivine: slate pencil, n., slate-caum.
pendant, n., target.
pendulum, n., leed; pendle: pendulum rod, n., pendle shank.
penetrate, v., throuch: mental penetration, n., ingyne (injyne); fushion.
penis, n., cod; pizzel; whang.
pennant, n., pinnet; thane.
penniless, adj., sillerless.
pension, n., louance.
people, n., fowk: company of people, n., core; getherin; clamjamfry.
perceive, v., tell; fin; distan.
perch, v., perk; n., spaur; perk.
percolate, v., seip; sype.
peregrine falcon, n., blue gled.
perfect, adj., perfeck; perfite.
perfidious, adj., brek-faith; slidderie.
perforate, v., hole; thirl.
performance, n., play.
perfume, n., fume.
perhaps, adv., aiblins; mebbe; belike.
peril, n., joepardie.
period of time, n., track; sketch, short; tift, tedious.
perish, be lost, v., torfle; tyne.
perjure, v., missweir.
perk up, v., keckle up; spunk up: perky, adj., clippie; forritsome.
permit, v., lat; thole: permission, n., freedom: permissible, adj., leifu.
perpendicular, adj., parpin: out of perpendicular, adj., toltery.

perpetual, adj., eend-on; uncessant.
perplex, v., bumbaze; fyke; stunder: perplexity, n., stew; swither.
perquisites, n., chances; fores; sprecherie.
persecute, v., hash; taigle; tew.
persevere, v., stick in: persevering, adj., throu-gaun.
persist in, v., haud at/tae: persistent, of a cold, adj., sittin doun.
person, n., body; wicht; bauchle, short-legged; blawflum, pretentious; blellum, silly talkative; blether, garrulous; clart, slovenly; cock-abendy, small perky; cuif, stupid; dreip, spiritless; drochle, puny; eastie-wastie, vacillating; ettercap, bad-tempered; feartie, cowardly; fidge, restless; flaiper, foolishly dressed; flairdie, wheedling; fichter-lichtie, light-headed; fodgel, fat; foggie, old out-of-date; fouter, aimless; gamaleerie, foolish clumsy; gawkie, stupid; ged, greedy; gilpin, big stout; girn, peevish; gomeril, stupid; gowk, stupid; jumpin-jake, unstable; lathron, lazy; neip-heid, stupid; nipper, sharp unscrupulous; nirl, puny; nizzart, sharp-faced; nyaff, insignificant; perjink, fastidi-ous; prickmadenty, affected; rummle, clumsy; runt, dwarfish; safty, stupid; scrunt, emaciated; shargan, scraggy; skybal, contempt-ible; slaister, slovenly; sneck-drawer, sly; snirt, insignificant; spunkie, quick-tempered; stumpie, squat; sumph, clumsy; teuchter, uncouth; ticket, odd-looking; tinker, disreputable; trailach, slovenly; tumfie, boring insensible; wally-draigle, ill-developed; wullcat, ill-tempered.
perspire, v., sweit: state of perspiration, n., stew.
persuade, v., perswad; wyse: moral persuasion, n., thraw.
pert, adj., clippie; forritsome.
perturbation, n., fash; stour.
perverse, adj., dour; thrawn; conter-macious: pervert, v., thraw.
pester, v., fash; haud at; scaud.
pet, v., browden; dawt; n., dawtie: petted, adj., dawtit; browdent.

pet, huff, n., drunts; gee (jee); towt: **go off in a pet**, v., fling.
petition, n., crave; asking.
petticoat, n., weé coat.
petty, adj., freevolous; measly; shitten.
petulant, adj., dorty; tifty.
pew, n., dask.
phlegm, n., fleem; glit; sloch.
phosphorescence, n., wildfire; sea-fire.
photograph, n., draucht.
physique, n., set.
pick, in all senses, v., pyke: **select**, v., chaps; wale.
pickaback, n., shouderie.
picket, n., outwatch.
pickpocket, n., poucher.
Pict, n., Pecht.
picture, n., pictur.
piddle, v., pee; stroan.
pie, meat pie, n., bridie.
piebald, adj., pyat; skybal.
piece, large, n., dawd; fang: **small piece**, n., nip; nirl: **to pieces**, adv., to smithereens.
pied, adj., fleckit.
pier, n., jet; shipping.
pierce, v., thirl; prog, with sharp point.
pig, n., gruntie; grumphie; sou, sow; gryce, young: **pig's mouth**, n., gruntle; grunzie: **pigsty**, n., cray; sou-cruive.
pigeon, n., doo; cushie-doo, wild pigeon.
pike, the fish, n., ged.
pile, v., bing; n., bing; humplock, small; cairn, of stones; rickle, loose.
pilfer, v., pauchle; skech; snick.
pill, n., peel.
pillage, v., herry; reive; spulyie; n., herryment.
pillar, n., stoup; syle: **support with pillars**, v., stander.
pillory, n., cock-stuil.
pillow, n., cod.
pilot, v., airt; n., lodesman; guider.
pimple, n., plouk; girran: **pimply**, adj., plouky.
pin, n., preen/peen: **pin-point**, n., neb: **pin-cushion**, n., preen-cod.
pinafore, n., peenie; daidlie; tinty-sarket.
pincers, n., clams; pinchers.
pinch, v., tweeze: **steal**, v., skech: **stint**, v., scrimp: **pinched-looking**, adj.,

poukit; shilpit: **pinch, small amount**, n., fingerfu; nip.
pine, v., dwyne.
pinnacle, n., tappietourie; toupic.
pious, adj., guid-leevin; gracie.
pipe for tobacco, n., cutty, clay: **stem of pipe**, n., stapple.
pipe-clay, n., stookie; caumstane; rubbin-stane.
pique, n., thraw.
pit, n., cleuch; coal heuch: **pit shaft**, n., heuch; sink.
pitch, bitumen, n., pick: **pitch dark**, adj., deid-mirk; mirk-daurk.
pitch, v., thraw; fung; lab; n., thraw: **pitch, of boat**, v., howd.
pitch, station, n., stance.
pitcher, n., pig.
pith, n., smergh: **vigour**, n., fushion; smeddum: **pithless**, adj., fushion-less.
pity, v., rue on; mane: **pitiable**, adj., pitifu; sairie.
pivot, n., pinion; gudge, of bell.
place, v., staun; stell; n., bit; pairt; steid.
placid, adj., lown; sonsy, of person.
plagiarise, v., thig.
plaice, n., splash; spottie.
plaid, n., plyde; faik; brat, shepherd's.
plain, adj., hamely: **downright**, adj., braid: **plain-spoken**, adj., aff-haun.
plain by river, n., carse; howe.
plaintive, adj., manerife.
plan, v., ettle; n., draucht; plottin.
plane, carpenter's, n., halflin.
plank, n., buird.
plant, v., pit doun; set: **bed of plants**, n., toft: **plantation**, n., plantin.
plash, v., n., jaup.
plaster, v., plaister; claister; slairg; n., plaister.
plate, n., ashet, large oval; truncher, large: **plate rack**, n., bink.
platter, n., troch; truncher.
plausible, adj., fair-farand; mealy-moud.
play, v., daff; jink; spiel: **playmate**, n., play-fier: **plaything**, n., die (dye).
plead, v., prig.
please, v., pleisure; fit: **pleasing to the eye**, adj., ee-sweet: **pleasure**, n., pleisure: **pleasant**, adj., canty; dainty/denty; fine.

87

pleat, v., plet; warp; n., plet; touk.
pledge, v., n., tryst; wad/wadset.
plenty, n., fouth; galore; rowth: plentiful, adj., rowth; ruch/rouch.
pliable, adj., souple; dwaible; waffle.
pliers, n., pinchers.
plight, n., snorl; pickelty; tiff.
plod, v., widdle; stodge.
plop, v., n., plowp: make plopping noise, v., plump.
plot of land, n., gleib.
plot, v., collogue; n., draucht; plottin.
plough, v., n., plou; pleuch: plough handles, n., stilts; stiels: plough-share, n., sock: iron cutter on front of ploughshare, n., coulter.
plover, n., peesie; peesweep; teuchat.
pluck, v., pouk; touk; yank.
plug, n., stapple; dook, in wall to take nail; tap, for tub.
plum, n., ploum.
plume, n., fedder; pen.
plump, adj., sonsie; gaucy; weill at anesel.
plunder, v., reive; herry; rype; spulyie; n., fang; herryment; sprecherie.
plunge, v., n., slounge; douk: plunger, the instrument, n., plumper.
ply, n., faik; fauld.
pneumoconiosis, n., stourie lungs.
poach, v., nick; skech; spoach: poacher, n., poachie.
pocket, n., pouch.
poet, n., makar: poetry, n., musardrie; rhyming-ware.
point, v., n., pynt: critical point, n., bit: point of compass, n., airt.
poison, v., n., pousion/pizzen.
poke, v., guddle, with hands; prog; rype; n., brod; prog; rype.
pole, n, stang; wand; stab; tree; caber, fir tree trunk.
polecat, n., foumart.
policeman, n., polis: police force, n., the polis.
policy, n., draucht.
polished, adj., burnist; polished in manner, adj., sneith.
polite, adj., mensefu; discreet: polite-ness, n., mense; discretion.
pollute, v., fulyie.
pomp, n., paraffle; effeir: pompous, adj., fou-breekit: pomposity, n., pauchti-ness.

pond, n., pownd; dub; waterhole.
ponder, v., refleck; think on.
pony, n., pownie; naigie; sheltie, Shetland.
pool, n., puil; hole, in river; dub, stagnant; stank, stagnant.
poor, adj., puir; ill-aff; sillerless: poor-house, n., puirs'-hous.
pop, v., n., pap: pop out, v., lowp.
Pope, n., Paip: popery, n., paperie: papist, adj., papish.
porcelain, adj., wallie: porcelain dish, n., wallie.
porch, n., entry; hallan; tae-faa.
porpoise, n., gairfish; sea-swine.
porridge, n., parritch: meal and water porridge, n., crowdie; cauld steirie: porridge with butter added, n., brose: porridge stick, n., spurkle.
port, n., harbourie.
portend, v., bode; spae; freit.
porter, n., caddie.
portion, n., blaud; feck, large; scart, small: share, n., faa.
portrait painter, n., limner.
position, n., bit; locus: alter position, v., flit.
positive, adj., gleg-shair.
possess, v., aucht; awn.
post, stake, n., stab; stang; tree.
postman, n., post: postage, n., post.
posterior, adj., hinder: the posterior, n., hin-en; dowp; bum; erse.
postpone, v., aff-pit.
posture, v., play-act; n., pouster; shape.
posy, n., bab.
pot, n., pat; pig; goblet: potted meat, n., potty-heid.
potato, n., tattie; spud: mashed potatoes, n., champit tatties: potato digger, n., tattie howker: potato leaf, n., shaw: potato pit, n., bing/clamp: potatoes and salt, n., tatties and dab: potatoes and onions stewed, n., stovies.
pot-bellied, adj., gutty.
potent, of liquor, adj., stark; steive.
pothole, n., trap; kettlehole, in bog.
potter about, v., fouter; plowter; doiter.
pottery, n., piggery: a pottery, n., pig-wark.
pouch, n., spung; spleuchan.
pound, of weight/money, n., pun.

pound, v., champ; chap; beetle: **pounding**, n., beetlin.

pour, v., blash; teem, trans. and intrans.: **pour out**, v., birl; fill.

pout, v., glunt; lat doun the lip; n., glunt; thraw.

poverty, n., puirtith; scant and want.

powder, v., n., pouther: **powdery**, adj., poutherie; fluffie.

power, n., pouer; docht: **powerful**, adj., buirdly; feckfu: **powerless**, adj., feckless.

practice, habitual, n., cast; gate: **sharp practice**, n., hokery-pokery.

praise ingratiatingly, v., phraise; rouse.

prance, v., stend.

prank, n., cantraip; pliskie; shavie.

prate/prattle, v., blether; claiver.

pray, v., incaa: **prayer**, n., incaain; be-thankit.

precarious, adj., kittle; unsiccar.

precede, v., forerin: **precedent**, n., prattick.

precipice, n., heuch; scaur: **precipitate**, adj., ramstam: **precipitately**, adv., ramstam.

precise, adj., perjink; pernickety: **precisely, quite so**, adv., juist that.

precocious, adj., auld-farrant.

predestined, adj., fey.

predicament, n., plicht; pliskie; snorl.

predict, v., spae; weird: **prediction**, n., spae; weird.

preen, v., straik.

prefer, v., choise: **preference**, n., prefairance.

pregnant, adj., in the wey; on the road: **make pregnant**, v., bairn.

prejudiced, adj., nerra-nebbit; tae-sided.

premature, adj., untimeous.

premier, adj., heidmaist.

premonition, n., forecast; foregang.

preoccupy, v., uptak.

prepare, v., busk; graith.

presage, v., n., bode; freit; spae.

prescience, n., moyen.

prescribe, v., stent: **prescription**, n., line.

present, v., gift; n., fairin.

present oneself, v., kythe; compear: **presentable**, adj., faisible.

present, at hand, adj., forrit.

preserve, v., hain.

press, v., birse: **press down**, v., clap; knidge: **pressure**, n., birse; thraw.

prestige, n., wind.

presume, v., tak: **I presume**, v., I'm thinkin: **presumptuous**, adj., brow-den.

pretend, v., fenyie; let on: **pretence**, n., pit on; wheetie-what: **pretentious**, adj., spawcious; nabby: **pretentious-ness**, n., fantoosherie.

pretext, n., aff-pit; whilly-wha.

pretty, adj., bonny; eesome; winsome.

prevail upon, v., weir roun: **be prevalent, of disease**, v., gae about.

prevaricate, v., flaunter; hum and hae.

prevent, v., kep; forfend.

previous, adj., umquhile: **previously**, adv., syne.

prey, n., fang; grab; spulyie.

price, fix price, v., strike: **lower/raise price**, v., lat doun/heicht.

prick, v., n., brog; jag: **prick out**, v., pyke out: **prickly**, adj., jaggy.

pride, n., concait; crouseness; skeich-ness.

prig, n., primp: **priggish**, adj., pensie; perjink.

prime, fill, v., fang.

primer, school primer, n., penny-buff.

primitive, adj., auld-farrant.

primrose, n., buckie-faulie; meyflouer.

principal, n., heid bummer/deister; adj., heich; heid.

print, v., prent: **impression**, n., steid.

prison, n., jyle; nick; tolbooth, old town jail.

private, adj., ain, personal; quait, secret: **privately**, adv., quaitly.

privet, n., privy.

privilege, n., fordel; fore.

privy, n., wee hous; shunkie.

prize, n., gree.

probable, adj., like: **probably**, adv., like as no; likely.

probe, v., gudge; prog: **investigate**, v., speir.

problem, n., kinch; set; tickler.

proceed, v., ongae; haud on: **procedure**, n., practick: **procession**, n., walk.

proclaim, v., annunce; lat ken.

procrastinate, v., aff-pit: **procrastina-tion**, n., aff-pittin.

procure, v., come by; filsh, by stealth.

prod, v., prog; brod; guddle, with hands.

prodigal, adj., spendrife; wasterfu: **prodigality,** n., fill and fesh mair.

product, n., outcome: **production,** n., throu-pit: **productive,** adj., berthy.

profane, v., fyle; adj., ill; sainless.

profess, v., ledge.

proficient, adj., profite; weill-seen: **proficiency,** n., profiteness.

profit, n., fore; win: **profit by,** v., mak on.

profligate, adj., ill-daein; wastrife.

profound, adj., fell.

profuse, adj., rowth: **profusion,** n., rowth.

progress, v., come speed; n., endwey; forder: **help in progress,** v., forrit.

prohibit, v., refuise; dischairge.

project, v., ledge: **scheme,** n., prattick; projeck: **projection,** n., ledgin.

prolific, adj., berthie; growthie.

prolong, v., twine out.

prominent, adj., kenspeckle; marked.

promiscuously, adv., throuither; frimple-frample.

promise, v., hecht; shore; n., hecht: **promising,** adj., likely.

promote, v., forrit; forder.

prompt, adj., gleg; slippy.

prong, n., tyne; stang; grain.

pronounce, a word v., name; sound: **pronouncement,** n., speak.

proof, n., prief.

prop, v., n., prap; stoup; stell; haud: **prop up,** v., shord up.

propel, v., steir; erse on: **propeller,** n., whurlie-birlie.

propensity, n., brou; inklin; mynd.

proper, seemly, adj., douce; mensefu; wycelike.

property, n., hae; aucht; haddin.

prophesy, v., spae; weird.

propitiate, v., cullie: **propitious,** adj., tiddy; fordersome, of weather.

propose for discussion, v., propone.

proprietor, n., guidman; laird.

propriety, n., mense.

prosecute, v., pursue: **prosecute to a conclusion,** v., thorough.

prospect, n., forelook; tae-look.

prosper, v., come speed; thrift: **prosperous,** adj., bien; weill-aff: **prosperity,** n., bienness; thrift; thrive.

prostitute, n., dunty; callet; hure; paikie; penny jo.

prostrate, v., flauchter; founder, with fatigue; adj., aval.

prosy, adj., dreich; dryward; fushionless.

protect, v., bield; hap; hain: **protection,** n., bield; hap.

protest, v., compleen; reclaim; n., plaint.

protract, v., lenthen: **protracted,** adj., langsome; dreich.

protrude, v., belge; boggle, of eyes.

proud, adj., concaity; heich-heidit; pauchtie; vaunty; vogie.

prove, v., prieve/pruve; pree.

proverb, n., say; auld word.

provide, v., plenish; sort wi: **provide for,** v., fend: **provided that,** conj., sae be.

provident, adj., foresichtie; gair.

provisions, n., meat; scran; vievers.

proviso, n., percunnance.

provoke, v., chaw; thraw: **provoking,** adj., angersome ("ng" as in "sing").

prow, n., neb.

prowl about, v., screenge; skive; spounge.

prudent, adj., canny; douce; tentie; wycelike.

prudish, adj., perskeet; mim.

prune, v., sned; cow.

pry, v., keek; snowk: **prying,** adj., lang-nebbit.

psalm, n., saum.

publish, v., blezzin; set out.

pudding, n., puddin.

puddle, v., guddle; n., dub; slush.

puff, v., n., pech; fuff: **puff out,** v., belge: **puff up,** v., flozen.

pugnacious, adj., fechty: **pugnacity,** n., fecht.

pull, v., pou; drug; harl; n., pou; drug.

pullet, n., pout; howdie.

pulley, n., whurlie; hing.

pullover, n., smoukie.

pulp, n., potterlow; glush.

pulpit, n., poupit: **canopy over pulpit,** n., soundin-box.

pulsate, v., thrab; gowp; dirl.

pulverise, v., crummle; murl: **pulverised, of soil,** adj., muildy.

pummel, v., beetle; nevel.

punch, v., nevel; punce; dowf; n.,

punce; breenge.

punctual, adj., timeous.

puncture, n., stug.

pungent, adj., fell; snell; nippy: **pungency**, n., nip; neb.

punish, v., pey/pey hame; sort: **punishment**, n., peys; serin; sortin.

puny, adj., shilpit; peely-wally; nirly.

pupil of eye, n., staur/starn o the ee.

puppet, n., dorrity.

puppy, n., whalp.

purchase, v., coff: **shop purchases**, n., messages; eerans.

pure, limpid, adj., skyre: **innocent**, adj., sackless: **purify**, v., blainch; ush.

purge, of medicine, v., scour; work: **purgative**, n., scour.

purple, n., purpie.

purpose, v., n., **purposeless**, adj., feckless; weirdless.

purr, v., thrum; murr.

purse, n., tocher: **purse the mouth**, v., thraw the mou.

pursue, v., hund; win efter.

pus, n., maitter; getherin; atter.

push, v., caa; dunch; shog: **push forward roughly**, v., breenge: "**push**", n., caa-throu; gurr: "**pushing**", adj., forritsome.

put, v., pit: **put past**, v., pit by: **put off**, v., aff-pit.

putrefy, v., moch; dow; spill: **putrid**, adj., mawkit; mochie.

putty, n., potty.

puzzle, v., bumbaze; dumfouner.

Quack, charlatan, n., gar-me-true.

quaff, v., waucht; sowff.

quagmire, n., souk; qua; lair.

quail, v., flaunter; staumer.

quaint, odd, adj., droll; freikit: **quaint-looking person**, n., ticket.

quake, v., dinnle; quak; trummle.

qualify, limit, v., stent: **qualified**, adj., habile.

quality, kind, n., kidney; set: **good qualities**, n., guid fores.

qualm of faintness, n., turn; soum: **of doubt**, n., drow.

quandary, n., swither.

quantity, large, n., feck; hantle; sicht: **small quantity**, n., tait; wee pickle.

quarrel, v., n., argie-bargie; cast out; tiff: **quarrelsome**, adj., thrawn-

gabbit.

quarry, n., delf; heuch: **quarrier**, n., craigman.

quarry, prey, n., fang; creagh.

quarter, lodge, v., ludge; howff; herbour: **quarters**, n., ludgins.

quaver, v., trummle.

quay, n., shipping; shore.

queer, adj., droll; unco.

quell, v., quall; daunton: **extinguish**, v., douse; smoor/smuir.

quench, v., slock/slocken; draik.

querulous, adj., girnie; tirrie; thrawn.

quest, n., reenge; fork.

question, v., speir at; n., speir.

quibble, v., cangle ("ng" as in "sing"); carble.

quick, adj., slippy; clever; swippert: **quickly**, adv., swythe: **quickness**, n., rake; snellness.

quicksand, n., flow; lair.

quiet, adj., quait; caum: **quietness**, n., caum; saucht: **quieten**, v., quaiten.

quilt, n., quitin/cweetin.

quirk, n., kink; skew: **quirky**, adj., joukie.

quit, v., quat; skail: **leave off**, v., deval; gie owre; stent.

quite, adv., fair; hale.

quiver, v., dirl; dinnle; quak; skimmer, in gleams.

quizz, v., backspeir.

quota, n., faa; dail.

Rabbit, n., mappie; kinnen; kippen; bawtie: **rabbit burrow**, n., clap.

rabble, n., raible; canailyie; clamjamfry.

race, n., kin; stryne.

race, v., skelp; scour.

rack, strain, v., rax.

rack, shelf, n., bink; heck, for fodder; skibbet, for letters.

racket, n., dirdum; rammy; stramash.

radiant, adj., skyre: **radiance**, n., skinkle: **radiate**, v., skinkle.

radish, n., rifart.

raffle, lottery, n., lucky-pock.

rafters, n., couples; bougars; kebars; trees.

rag, n., brat; clout; dud: **ragman**, n., candyman: **ragged**, adj., raggit; duddy.

ragamuffin, n., loun; skybal.

rage, v., feim; rampage; n., feim; rampage; tirrivee: **fly into a rage, v.,** flirr; fuff: **in a great rage, adj.,** dancin mad.

ragwort, n., dug flourish; tansy; benweed.

raid, n., rode; creagh; spreath.

railway buffers, n., dunchers: **railway points, n.,** snecks.

rain, n., weit; smir, drizzling: **downpour, n.,** onding: **spot of rain, n.,** spit: **rain heavily, v.,** teem; ding: **rain slightly, v.,** spit.

raise, v., heize; heist; heicht.

rake, v., harl; n., harl; drag-tae.

rake, **wanton person, n.,** loun; ne'er-dae-weill.

ram, n., tup/tip; v., stap; stech.

ramble, v., n., rammle; stravaig.

ramp, n., cant; ledge.

rampage, v., rant.

ramshackle, adj., ricklie; shauchlin: **ramshackle object, n.,** rickle.

rancid, adj., ranshy; tarf.

rancour, n., gaw; umrage.

random, adj., antrin.

range, v., reenge; raik.

rank, row, n., raw: **social rank, n.,** gree; rang: **of high/low rank, adj.,** muckle/semple.

rank in growth, adj., ruch; gosky: **rank in taste, adj.,** wild; strounge.

ransack, v., ranseck; rype.

ransom, v., borrow.

rant, v., flyte; bairge.

rap, v., n., knap; knoit: **rap at door, v., n.,** chap.

rapacious, adj., grippy; gair.

rape, v., herry.

rapid, adj., slippy; swippert: **rapidly, adv.,** swippert.

rare, adj., antrin; daimen; seenil: **rarely, adv.,** seenlins: **rarity, n.,** unco.

rascal, n., bleck; skellum; skybal: **rascally, adj.,** gallus; skybal.

rash on skin, n., fleesh; rush.

rash, adj., rackless; ramstam; raucle; gallus: **rash person, n.,** ramstam.

rasp, v., n., risp.

raspberry, n., rasp; hainberry.

rat, n., rattan/ratton.

rate, speed, n., courss; raik: **at any rate, adv.,** onieweys.

rate, tax, v., n., cess; stent.

rather, adv., raither: **rather than, conj.,** or.

ratify, v., upbear; sustain: **ratify a bargain, v.,** chap.

rational, adj., solid; wyce.

rattle, v., n., blatter; dirl: **wooden rattle, n.,** ricketie.

ravage, v., flae; herry; reive.

rave, v., raible; taiver: **raving mad, adj.,** rampin mad.

ravel, v., n., fank; fankle; snorl.

raven, n., corbie; croupie-craw.

ravine, n., gill; heuch; glack.

raw, of weather, adj., hullerie; oorlich: **raw-boned, adj.,** raucle-baned.

ray of light, n., blink; leam.

reach, v., rax: **arrive at, v.,** win to: **try to reach, v.,** ettle at.

read volubly, v., screed aff: **read indistinctly, v.,** bummle.

ready, **make ready, v.,** busk; buss; graith.

real, adj., rale.

realm, n., kinrik; ryke.

reap, v., shear; maw: **reaper, n.,** cutter; shearer.

rear, v., creddle; upbring.

reason, cause, n., raison; wey: **reasoning power, n.,** wit: **reasonable, adj.,** wyce.

rebel, v., reist.

rebound, v., n., stot; skite.

rebuke, v., tairge; speak a word to; n., flytin; throu-gaun.

recall, v., cry back: **bring to mind, v.,** think on.

recant, v., cock; resile.

recede, v., reteir.

recent, adj., new: **recently, adv.,** short syne.

recess, n., neuk: **room recess, n.,** bole; crannie.

recite, v., dirl aff; say owre; souch: **recitation, n.,** reading.

reckless, adj., rackless; gallus; raucle.

reckon, v., rackon; upcast, calculate: **the reckoning, n.,** the lawin.

recline, v., lig.

recluse, n., mowdiewort.

recognise, v., ken; tell; look the road o: **recognition, n.,** kennin.

recoil, v., resile; winch; n., winch.

recollect, v., mynd; think on: **recollec-**

tion, n., myndin.
recommend, v., moyen: recommendation, n., moyen.
reconcile, v., gree; sowther: become reconciled, v., gree; come tae.
record, n., back-leuk; wryte, written.
recount, v., tell owre.
recourse, have recourse to, v., betak.
recover, get back, v., recour: recover from bad turn/illness, v., come tae/ come throu: recovered from illness, adj., better.
recreant, n., backdrawer.
recruit, v., list.
rectangular, adj., fower-neukit.
rectify, v., mend; straight.
recuperate, v., mend; weir roun.
red, adj., rid/reid: redden, v., ridden.
redeem, v., outredd.
redress, v., n., remeid.
reduce, v., howe; slack, a debt; lowden, in intensity: reduction, n., howe.
reed, n., seg; sprot.
reef, n., skerrie; skir.
reel for thread, n., pirn.
reel, v., stot; stoiter; wintle: reel off, v., dirl/screed aff: reel, dance, n., spring; jorum.
reference book, n., direction book: with reference to, prep., anent.
referee, n., midman; thirdsman.
refine, v., blainch; ush: refined in manner, adj., sneith.
reflect, ponder, v., refleck; think on.
reflection, n., scairy: reflecting glass, n., shining-gless.
reform, v., mend: reformation of conduct, n., meniment.
refrain, n., owrecome; threne.
refrain, v., gae frae; haud by.
refresh, v., caller; brisken up: refreshing, adj., caller.
refrigerator, n., flaik-stand.
refuge, n., bield; hauld; girth: take refuge, v., bield; howff.
refuse, v., refuise: refusal, n., refuise.
refuse, n., fulyie; redd: refuse bin, n., fulyie-can: refuse dump, n., cowp.
regard, v., regaird; behaud; n., regaird: esteem, v., tender; n., tenderness.
region, n., kintra.
register, n., catalogue.
regret, n., efterstang; ilta.

regular, adj., reglar: regularly, adv., reglar.
rehearse, v., say owre.
reimburse, v., refound.
reins, n., rynes.
reiterate, v., threip; cuckoo.
reject, v., rejeck: rejected, adj., outcuissen: rejection, n., fling; kick.
rejoice, v., rejyce: rejoicing, n., gaudeamus.
relapse, n., backset; backturn.
relate, v., tell owre.
relate, pertain, v., effeir: related, adj., sib; tender: relative, n., frien; kin: relatives, n., nain-folk.
relax, v., sock, from work; swage, after meal: physically relaxed, adj., lither: period of relaxation, n., sockin-oor; speil.
release, v., lowse.
relentless, adj., dour; fell.
relieve, v., speil, at work; exoner, from burden: relief, n., easement.
relinquish, v., pass; quat.
relish, n., gou; gust; kitchen: give relish to, v., kitchen.
reluctant, adj., sweirt; laith; dour.
rely, v., lippen: reliance, n., lippenance: reliable, adj., sponsible; siccar.
remain, v., byde; stey; stop: remainder, n., lave.
remark, n., say; stang, witty: remarkable, adj., byous; unco: remarkably, adv., byous; uncommon.
remedy, v., n., remeid.
remember, v., mynd; think on.
remind, v., mynd; remember: reminiscence, n., myndin.
remnant, n., shaird: remnants, n., getherins.
remorse, n., efterstang; ilta: feel remorse, v., tak til anesel; tak the rue.
remote, adj., faur-awa; outland.
remove, v., flit; remuve: house removal, n., flittin.
rend, v., rent; rive.
rendezvous, n., tryst.
renegade, n., backdrawer.
renounce, v., owregie; renunce.
renovate, v., new.
renown, n., nameliheid.
rent, n., tack-duty: rent on lease, v., mail.

repair, v., sort; clout, pots etc.; n., sort: reparation, n., mends.

repay, v., repey: repayment, n., requitance.

repel, v., scunner; skeichen; rebat, snub.

repent, v., tak the rue: repentance, n., rue.

repetition, constant, n., threip; thrain: empty repetition, n., rat-rhyme.

replace, v., repone.

replenish, v., plenish; beit.

replete, adj., fou; sert: fill to repletion, v., ser.

replica, n., limn; parrymauk.

reply, v., repone; speak back; n., repone.

report, v., clype; n., word; din, scandalous: press reporter, n., newsbilly.

repose, v., lig; lay by; n., saucht.

repress, v., haud in about: repressed, adj., dounhauden.

reprimand, v., check; flyte; faut; n., flytin; tellin-aff; throu-gaun.

reprove, v., check; flyte: reproof, n., flytin; tellin-aff.

repudiate, v., rue; disherish.

repugnance, n., scunner; staw: repugnant, adj., scunnersome; stawsome.

repulse, v., n., rebut, snub: repulsive, adj., scunnersome; ugsome.

repute, n., record: of good repute, adj., namely: reputation, n., nameliheid.

request, v., speir; n., crave; asking.

require, v., requair: requirements, n., needfuls.

requite, v., pey hame; quat.

rescue, free, v., redd; lowse.

resemble, v., favour; tak aff: resemblance, n., swype; compare.

resent, v., tak ill out: resentment, n., ilta; ill-win.

reserved in manner, adj., bauch; fremmit; aff-staunin.

reservation, proviso, n., percunnance.

reservoir, n., pound.

reside, v., byde; stop; win; dwal: resident, n., indweller.

resign, v., demit; owregie.

resin, n., rozet.

resist, v., conter; stick up to.

resolute, adj., set; siccar; steive: resolution, n., siccarness.

resolve, v., conclude: solve, v., redd.

resort to, v., betak; rin to: place of resort, n., hauld; howff.

resound, v., dunner; dingle; stound.

resourceful, adj., fendie.

respect, v., n., respeck: respectable, adj., douce; honest; wycelike.

respite, n., blaw; baurley.

respond, v., speak back; repone: response, n., repone.

rest, the rest, n., the lave.

rest, v., lay by; lig; n., blaw; baurley; saucht: restless, adj., fidgin; steirin: restlessness, n., fyke: move restlessly, v., fidge; fyke.

restive, adj., skeerie; fliskie: be restive, v., fyke; flisk.

restitution, n., mends.

restrain, v., haud in about; kep; tether: restrained, adj., crubbit: unrestrained, adj., bandless: means of restraint, n., aweband.

restore, v., recour.

restrict, v., restrick; kep; stent: restricted, adj., scrimpit.

result, n., affcome; outcome; feck.

retail, v., broke: retailer, n., merchant.

retain, v., kep: retain vigour, v., weir.

retaliate, v., pey hame; play trumphabout.

retch, v., boke/bock; yesk.

reticent, adj., mim-moud.

retire, v., reteir.

retort, v., speak back; rejag; n., backcaa: settlin-brose, shattering.

retreat, v., reteir; skail: place of retreat, n., hauld; howff.

retribution, n., lawin.

retrieve, v., recour.

return, v., n., retour.

reveal, v., kythe; lat on, divulge: revelation, n., kythin.

revel, v., n., gilravage; splore; rant.

revenge, n., lawin; pennyworth: revenged on, adj., fitside wi.

reverberate, v., dirl; dunner: reverberation, n., dirl; dunner; stound.

reverie, n., dwam; sloum.

reverse, v., owreharl; n., backset; thraw.

review, v., scance; n., backleuk; scance.

revile, v., caa ill names; cry names.

revive, v., keckle/spunk up.

revolve, v., birl; trinnle: **cause to revolve**, v., birl; feeze.

reward, v., rewaird; quat; n., rewaird; fairin.

rheum, n., goor: **rheumatism**, n., rheumatics; cleiks.

rhyme, v., clink; mett; tell; n., clink; tronie.

rhythm, n., stot; lilt.

rich, adj., walthy; bien; weill-gethert.

rid, v., redd: **be rid of**, v., be shut/quat o; tyne.

riddle, n., guess.

riddle, sieve, n., shaker; ree; brander.

ride on wheeled vehicle, v., n., hurl.

ridge, n., rig; skift, broad: **ridged**, adj., runkled.

ridicule, v., scorn: **public ridicule**, n., sherrackin.

riff-raff, n., trashtrie; scruif.

rift, n., cleavin; rive.

right, adj., richt: **rightful**, adj., richtfu: **put to rights**, v., sort; tift.

rigid, adj., sterk; steive; strait.

rigorous, adj., dour; fell; snell.

rim, n., selvedge; laggin-gird.

rind, n., keel; huil; walt.

ringdove, n., cushat/cushie doo.

ring, of bell, v., n., jow; jing; ting: **give ringing sound**, v., dirl.

rinse, v., syne; sweil.

riot, v., n., splore; wap; gilravage.

rip, v., rive.

ripe, adj., maumie: **ripen**, v., haisle; maise.

ripple, v., n., lapper; pirl; wimple: **make rippling sound**, v., hushaweesh.

rise, v., heize; heave, above surface; prickle, erect: **rise hastily**, v., bang up.

risk, v., haizart: **risky**, adj., uncanny; wanchancy.

ritual, empty, n., fykemaleeries.

river, n., water: **rich land by river**, n., carse; merse: **river bank**, n., selvedge; brou: **river mouth**, n., inver: **river valley**, n., strath.

rivet, v., n., riv/ruive.

road, n., gang; gate: **direct road**, n., gain road: **steep road**, n., brae.

roam, v., stravaig; traik; reenge: **roamer**, n., traik; rinabout.

roan-coloured, adj., mirlie; grim.

roar, v., n., rair; gurl; gowl; buller;

rowt, of cattle.

roast, v., birsle; sotter; swee.

rob, v., herry; reive: **robber**, n., reiver: **robbery**, n., reiverie; stouth.

robe, n., manty.

robust, adj., hardy; stuffy; hale.

rock, n., clint; whin, hard crystalline: **rocky**, adj., clinty; craigy: **projecting mass of rock**, n., craig: **ridge of rock**, n., scaur.

rod, pliable, n., wand.

roe of fish, n., pelek; rawn.

rogue, n., hempie; loun; skellum; skybal: **roguery**, n., joukerie-pawkerie.

roll, register, n., catalogue.

roll, baked, n., rowe; bap.

roll, v., rowe; hurl; trowe: **roll up untidily**, v., bumphle.

romance, v., screed: **romancer**, n., fleggar.

romp, v., n., daff; jink; rant.

roof, n., ruif: **roof ridge**, n., riggin: **roof lining of wood**, n., sarkin.

rook, n., corbie; craw: **rookery**, n., craw-widdie.

room, space, n., waygate: **scope**, n., scouth: **room of house**, n., end: **sitting-room**, n., best room; spence: **outside/inside room**, n., but/ben: **roomy**, adj., scouthy; gutsy.

roost for hens, n., bauk; hen-laft.

root, n., ruit: **strike root**, v., tak: **deep-rooted**, adj., yirdfast.

rope, n., raip; hemp: **rope as cattle tether**, n., aweband.

rose arbour, n., roseir: **moss-rose**, n., foggy rose: **rock-rose**, n., solflouer: **rose hip**, n., dug-hip; buckie: **wild rose**, n., breer.

rot, v., foust; muilder: **rotten**, adj., draven, of meat; mozie, of fruit.

rotate/cause to rotate, v., birl; tirl: **rotation**, n., birl; tirl.

rough, adj., ruch/rouch; courss: **un-gentle**, adj., hashy; raucle.

round, adj., adv., prep., roun: **round-shouldered**, adj., roun-shouthert.

rouse, v., wauken; upsteir.

rout, v., skail; n., scatterment.

route, n., gate; road.

routine, n., hech-how; jundy; stot.

rove, v., stravaig; traik; reenge: **rover**, n., traik; rinabout.

row, line, n., raw; dreel.

row, noise, n., dirdum; rammy; stramash: quarrel, n., ruction; tiff.

row a boat, v., oar: rowlock, n., thowpin: rowing song, n., eeram.

rowan, n., rodden.

rowdy, adj., bousterous; outstrapalous: be rowdy, v., stramash.

royalty on books, n., lordship.

rub, v., dicht, to dry; feeze up, vigorously: graze, v., scuff: rub, n., dicht: chafe by rubbing, v., gaw.

rubber, n., gutty; cahoutchy.

rubbish, n., redd; trasherie: rubbish dump, n., cowp; tip.

rubble, n., ribble.

rudder, n., steerer.

ruddy of complexion, adj., rid-avised.

rude, adj., bardy; ill-moud; misleird.

ruffian, n., randy.

ruffle, v., runkle; tousle; n., bumphle; bord, frill: ruffled, adj., tousy.

rugged in manner, adj., raucle; ruch; courss: rocky, adj., clinty; scaury.

ruin, v., cowp; wrack; n., wrack; hership.

rule, have dominion over, v., ring: control, v., guide: govern, v., wald.

rumble, v., n., rummle; dunner.

rummage, v., reenge; screenge.

rumour, n., clatter; souch; wind.

rumple, v., bumphle; tousle: rumpled, adj., bumphly.

rumpus, n., dirdum; rammy; stramash.

run, v., rin; skelp; whid: run about wildly, v., startle: run away, v., fugie (fyoodjie): tak the gate: runaway, n., fugie.

rung of ladder, n., spaik.

rural, adj., landart; landward.

ruse, n., prattick.

rush, n., seg; thresh: rushy, adj., threshie.

rush, v., breenge; ramstam: rush about, v., flauchter: rush, of water, v., pish; scoosh: rush out, v., bang out: rush through air, v., wheich.

rust, v., roust; freit; n., roust: rusty, adj., rousty.

rustic, n., loun; geordie; jock; adj., hamespun; landart.

rustle, v., n., fissle; reesle.

rut, n., furr; chack; slunk.

Sack, dismiss, v., seck; pit awa: get the sack, v., get the road: sack, bag, n., seck: sackcloth, n., seckin; seckclaith.

sack, plunder, v., reive; rype; spulyie.

sad, adj., doolfu; dowf; waefu: sadlooking, adj., waelike: sadness, n., dolour.

saddle, v., n., saidle: saddle-girth, n., girdin.

safe, adj., sauf; hale; scart-free: safe to deal with, adj., chancy.

sag, v., saig: sagging, adj., howe.

sail of boat, n., cannas: of windmill, n., aw.

saint, n., saunt.

salad, n., sallet.

salary, n., screw.

sale, n., vent; rowp, by auction: put up for sale, v., rowp.

saliva, n., slaiver: salivate, v., slaiver; gush; slerp.

sallow, adj., din; wauchie.

salmon, n., saumon: salmon-fry, n., smelt.

salt, v., n., saut: salt cellar, n., saut dish/fat: saltless, adj., wairsh.

salute, v., halse; hat: salutation, n., hailzin.

salve, unguent, n., saw.

salver, n., server.

sample, v., pree; pruive; sey; n., blaud; preein; sey; swatch.

sanctify, v., sauntifee: sanctity, n., guidliheid.

sanction, v., approbate.

sanctuary, n., bield; girth; hauld; howff.

sand, n., saun: sandbank, n., air; sandstone, n., freestane: sandpiper, n., killieleepie.

sane, adj., solid; wyce: sanity, n., wit.

sanguine, adj., bluidy: ardent, adj., aiverie.

sap, n., bree.

sarcasm, n., saut; taird: sarcastic, adj., sauty; snell-gabbit; tuithy.

satiating, adj., fousome: satiety, n., staw.

satire, n., cockalane: satirical, adj., tuithie; snell-gabbit.

satisfy, v., satisfee; ser; suit: satisfied, adj., sert.

saturate, v., sowp; sype.

Saturday, n., Setterday.
sauce, n., kitchen: saucy, adj., dorty; pauchtie: saucepan, n., skellat.
saucer, n., flet.
saunter, v., dauner; toddle; n., dauner.
sausage, n., sassenger: sausages strung together, n., links.
savage, adj., gurly; wicket.
save, v., sauf; prep., binna: save up, v., pit by; hain: saving, frugal, adj., canny: savings, n., hainins; stocken; pose.
savour, v., n., goo; saur.
saw, proverb, n., auld word; freit; say.
saw, v., rip; shauve; n., shauve.
say by heart, v., tell: say on, v., say awa: say over and over, v., cuckoo.
saying, n., auld sang; say; word.
scab, n., scaur; scruif: scabbed, adj., scabbit.
scaffold, n., table: scaffolding, n., brandering.
scald, v., scad/scaud.
scales, n., wechts; wei-bauks; weis: public weighing machine, n., tron.
scale, flake, n., flaw.
scalp, n., scaup; pow.
scamp, n., bleck; loun; skellum.
scamper, v., scour; whid.
scan, v., scance; sicht.
scandal, n., clack; clash; clatter: talk scandal, v., clash; clatter.
scanty, adj., jimp; scrimpit; stintit: scantiness, n., scrimpitness.
scapegoat, n., wytesman.
scar, v., scaur; n., scaur; blane.
scaramouch, n., bangster; blouster; fleggar.
scarce, adj., jimp; scrimp; skimp: scarcely, adv., barelies; hardlies: scarcity, n., scant.
scare, v., scaur; fricht; fley; fleg: scarecrow, n., tattie-bogle.
scarf, n., gravat/grauvat; skerf.
scathe, v., skaith; brain, seriously; n., skaith; brain.
scatter, v., spairge; straw; skail: scatter liquid stuff, v., splairge: scatter-brained, adj., flea-luggit; maggoty-heidit.
scavenger, n., scaffie; fulyie-man.
scene, n., sain.
scent, n., fume: scent a smell, v., snowk; snifter.

sceptical, adj., doutsome.
schedule, n., inventar.
scheme, v., schame; n., schame; draucht; plottin: scheming, adj., drauchty.
scholar, n., buikman: scholarship, n., grammar; buik-leir.
school, n., schuil: schoolmaster, n., schuilmaister; dominie: infant school, n., wee schuil: school attendance officer, n., whupper-in.
scissors, n., shears.
scoff, v., flyre; geck at; lichtlie.
scold, v., flyte; bairge; channer; n., tairge: scolding, n., flytin; tellin-aff.
scoop, v., n., scuip: hollow out, v., howk.
scope, n., scouth: room, n., waygate.
scorch, v., birsle; scowther; sotter; n., scowther; sotter.
score, v., scart; claw: have the same score, v., be peils.
scorn, v., flyre; geck at; lichtlie.
scotfree, adj., halescart.
Scots, Lowland Scots tongue, n., Lallans: render into Scots, v., scotify.
scoundrel, n., bleck; skellum; skybal.
scour, v., screenge.
scourge, v., n., leish; tawse.
scowl, v., n., froun; glower; glunch.
scrabble, v., scraible.
scrag, lean creature, n., barebanes; rake: scraggy, adj., scranky.
scramble, v., n., scrammle; sprauchle; sprattle.
scrap, n., crum; haet: scraps, n., affaains; brock.
scrape, v., scart; claut; claw: scrape, dilemma, n., snorl; swither.
scrawl, v., scrape.
scream, v., n., skraich/skreich; skirl; yelloch.
scree, n., rattle; sclenter.
screech, v., skraich/skreich; skirl.
screen, n., sconce; hap.
screw, v., feeze; thraw: screw-driver, n., turn-screw: screw-key, n., runch.
scribble, v., scart.
scribe, n., scriever.
scrimmage, n., scrummage; tulyie; warsle.
script, n., scrieve; wryte.
scroll, n., skrow.

scrounge, v., mouch; scaff; sorn.

scrub, v., screenge; scrunt: **scrubber**, n., screenge.

scrub, brush-wood, n., scrogs.

scruff of neck, n., cuff; scriff.

scruple, v., n., stickle; tartle: **scrupulous in details**, adj., nick-nackity.

scrutinise, v., scance; sicht; vizzy: **scrutiny**, n., vizzy.

scud, v., whid.

scuff, v., scliff; shauchle.

scuffle, v., sprushle; tulyie; n., tulyie.

scum, n., sloum.

scurf, n., kell; scruif.

scurry, v., scutter; skelter; whid.

scythe, n., sythe; whittle.

sea, **arm of sea**, n., kyle: **sea floor**, n., grund: **sea fog**, n., rouk; haar: **seagull**, n., goo; maw: **seashore**, n., tide: **sea-spray**, n., spunedrift; stew: **sea swell**, n., draucht; upsouk: **seathrift**, n., sea daisy: **seaweed**, seaware/waur: **sea-worthy**, adj., seafierdy.

seal, sea mammal, n., selkie; tangie, brown.

seam, v., n., gaur: **seamed**, adj., fretten: **seamstress**, n., shewster.

sear, v., birsle; scowther; sotter.

search, v., reenge: **search out**, v., speir out: **search with hands**, v., graip.

season, n., saison; tid: **seasonable**, adj., tiddy.

season, v., saut; kitchen; gust: **seasoning**, n., kitchen.

seat, v., sait; bunker, outside; deas, stone/wood/turf; stoup, by the door.

second, adj., saicont.

secret, adj., saicret; dern: **secrecy**, n., dern: **secret place**, n., hidy-hole: **secretly**, adv., hidlins; stownlins: **secrete**, v., plank.

secretary, n., secretar; scriever.

section, n., pairt; dail: **slice**, n., sclice; shave; whang.

secure, v., mak siccar; ticht; adj., siccar: **become secure**, v., sevendle.

security, pledge, n., caution; wadset: **be security for**, v., staun guid for.

sedate, adj., douce; solid: **sedateness**, n., douceness.

sedge, n., seg; sour-grass.

sediment, n., gruns; settlins: **full of sediment**, adj., grummly; grunsie.

seduce, v., gow owre; draigle somebody's tails: **seductive**, adj., eesome.

see, v., fin, with senses: **seeing that**, conj., sae bein as; sith.

seed, run to seed, v., shoot: **seedling**, n., plantin.

seek, v., want; reenge for: **seek out**, v., speir out; snowk.

seemly, adj., mensefu; wycelike.

seep, v., seip; sype; sab.

seer, n., spaeman.

seesaw, v., swey; shog.

seethe, v., hotch; hotter.

segment, n., pairt; liff/lith of orange.

segregate, v., sinder; twin.

seize, v., cleik; grip/grup; nick; claucht, by violence.

seldom, adv., seenil; seenlins.

select, v., wale; choise; chap: **hand-selected**, adj., haun-waled: **selection of verses etc.**, n., blaud; swatch.

self, pron., sel: **self-conceited**, adj., concaity; pauchtie: **self-confident**, adj., crouse: **self-same**, adj., selsame: **self-willed**, adj., willyart.

selfish, adj., sellie; endie; inbigget.

sell, v., vent; rowp, by auction: **sell off stock** etc., v., displenish.

semblance, n., seem.

send, v., sen.

senior, adj., aulder: **seniors**, n., aulders.

sensation of pain/pleasure, n., gliff: **tingling sensation**, n., dinnle.

sense, good sense, n., gumption; mense; wit: **sensible**, adj., wycelike: **senseless**, adj., daft; glaikit; menseless.

sensitive, adj., nesh; kittle; saftskinned, to criticism.

sentiment, n., souch; plaister, fulsome: **sentimental**, adj., parritch-hertit.

sentry, n., gaird; weir.

separate, v., sinder; twin; adj., sindry.

septic, adj., mochie; sloumy.

sepulchre, n., urn.

sequel, n., pirlicue.

sequence, n., raik; tring.

serene, adj., lythe; lown; caum.

sergeant, n., sairgeant.

serious, adj., fell: **earnest**, adj., thochty; gargrugous.

serpent, n., sairpent.

serum, n., glit.

servant, n., sairvant; flunkie; girzie, female.

service, employment, n., servitude: helping hand, n., turn: serviceable, adj., lasty; feckfu.

servile, adj., souple-neckit; fuit-lickin; inhaudin: servile person, n., snool.

servitude, n., thirldom.

set, place, v., staun; stell: congeal, v., geal (jeel): set aside, v., lay by: set down, v., plank: set off, v., tak the gate.

set, coterie, n., fry; sect: complete series, n., stroud.

setback, n., thraw; tillielick.

settee, n., lang-settle.

settle, put in order, v., redd up; fettle: subside, v., swage: agree upon, v., gree: settlement, n., redd: provision, n., dounsit.

seven, n., adj., seiven.

sever, v., sinder; twin.

several, adj., sindry; a wheen.

severe, adj., dour; fell; sair: severe in manner, adj., dour; gargrugous.

sew, v., shew (shoo); stug, roughly: sew with loose stitches, v., baiss.

sewer, n., cundy; syver; syre.

sexual intercourse, illicit, n., hough-magandie: sexual desire, n., keist; string; rumplefyke: have sexual intercourse, v., lig; muddle; rummle.

shabby, adj., waff-like; taskit; riff-raff; orra.

shade, colour, n., gree; spraing.

shadow, n., sheddae; glaik, dancing.

shaft, n., tram, of barrow; shank; stang; stilt.

shaggy, adj., tousy; tawtit; feltered.

shake, v., n., shak; shog: move un-steadily, v., coggle; shoogle: tremble, v., dirl; quak; hotter, with cold/fear: shaky, adj., coggly; shooglie.

shall, v., sal; will: shall not, v., winna.

shallot, n., sybie.

shallow, adj., shalla; ebb: frivolous, adj., freevolous; glaikit.

sham, v. cod; let on; n., let on; flirdome; adj., fause.

shamble, v., shauchle; wauchle; n., shauchle: shambles, n., shamells.

shame, v., n., affront: intense shame, n., black-burnin shame: very ashamed, adj., black-affrontit. shameless, adj., baurdy; braisant.

shape, v., coll; feck; n., maik; set: out of shape, adj., gleyed; skew; squeegee (-jee): shapely, adj., ticht.

share, v., pairt; twin; n., faa; ettle-ment; dail: shared, adj., pairty.

sharp, adj., sherp; gleg: keen, adj., fell; snell: active, adj., gleg: sharp-tongued, adj., snell-gabbit: sharpen, v., sherpen; whittle.

shatter, v., wrack; stramash.

shave, v., scrape; skive; n., scrape: wood shaving, n., spail; chirl.

shawl, n., hap; shawlie, small.

sheaf, n., shaif: last harvest sheaf, n., clyack; maiden: erect sheaves to dry, v., stook: group of sheaves so erected, n., stook.

shear, v., share: act of shearing, n., shear.

shed, v., cast; skail: part, v., sinder; twin.

shed, n., shiel, for sheep; sconce, rough; strae-hous, for straw.

sheen, n., skinkle.

sheep, one-year-old, n., hog: young female/male sheep, n., ewe/tup hog: ram, n., tup: ewe, n., yowe: flock leader, n., belled wether: sheep-fold, n., bucht; fauld; fank: put in sheep-fold, v., bucht; fauld.

sheer, adj., sterk: downright, adj., evendoun.

shelf, n., bink; skelf.

shell, pod, n., shaup; swaup; huil: snail shell, n., buckie.

shelter, v., bield; n., bield; howff; hauld: sheltered, adj., bieldy; lown.

shepherd, v., weir; n., hird.

sheriff, n., shirra; stewart.

sherry, n., seck.

shield, v., bield; cour; hain; n., bield; hap.

shift, v., trans., intrans., steir; muive; moodge: effort, n., fend: shift of work, n., yokin.

shilling, n., shillin/shullin.

shilly-shally, v., waffle; wheegee.

shimmer, v., skimmer: shimmering air, n., landtide; simmer-cout.

shin of beef, n., skink: shin-bone, n., shank-bane; cuit.

shine, v., n., glint; sheen; skinkle; skyre: shine fitfully, v., flauchter: shiny, adj., glistery; glancy; skin

99

klin.

shingle, n., channel; stanners.

shinty, n., shimmy; carrick.

shipwreck, v., n., shipwrack: **shipwrecked**, adj., shipwracked; seabroken.

shirk, v., jouk; renaig.

shirt, n., sark.

shiver, v., chitter; trummle; grue, from fear/repulsion; n., grue; trummle: **shivery**, adj., chittery; oorie.

shoal of fish, n., drave; schuil/schule.

shock, v., n., gliff; shog; dunt; stamagast.

shoe, n., shae; bauchle, worn-out; broag, heavy: **fancy shoes**, n., smaa shune: **shoe-horn**, n., shae-spune: **shoemaker**, n., shaemaker; soutar.

shoot, v., shuit: **shoot of plant**, n., spirl; tiller, lateral.

shop stall, n., buith; crame: **shop selling cheap wares**, n., pennyrattler: **shop selling all kinds of small wares**, n., johnnie-aa-thing.

shore, n., tide; air: **sandy shore covered with bent-grass**, n., links.

shore up, v., shord up.

short, adj., jimp; cutty; scrimp; laich, in stature: **short-sighted**, adj., nearsichtit: **short-winded**, adj., pechie: **shorten**, v., dock; touk: **shortage**, n., shortcome: **a short time**, n., a wee; a blink.

shot, "go", n., crack; skelp; whup.

should, v., suid.

shoulder, n., shouther/shouder: **ride on another's shoulder**, v., ride cockiebreekie: **having sloping shoulders**, adj., hingin-shouthert.

shout, v., yelloch; skraich; goller.

shove, v., caa; dunch; shog; jundie.

shovel, n., shuil.

show, v., n., shaw: **sham**, n., flirdome: **show-off**, n., glancing-glass: **show at fair**, n., geggie: **showy**, adj., roarie; branky; fantoosh.

shower, n., shouer; onding, heavy; smeuchter, drizzling; thunderplump.

shred, n., shaird; thrum.

shrew, n., strae-mous; wuff: **ill-tempered woman**, n., randy; tairge.

shrewd, adj., able; canny; pawky.

shriek, v., n., skreich; skirl; skelloch.

shrill, adj., shill; snell: **shrill cry**, n., skelloch; skreich.

shrimp, n., arnet.

shrine, n., fertor.

shrink, v., gizzen; wizzen; cryne: **shrink from**, v., fugie (foodjie).

shrivel, v., gizzen; wizzen: **shrivelled**, adj., wizzent.

shroud, n., deid-claes; linens.

shrug, v., fidge; hotch; thring the shouther; n., fidge; hotch.

shudder, v., grue.

shuffle, v., shauchle; hauchle.

shun, v., eschew; jouk.

shut, of a door, v., gae tae; dirl tae, loudly: **shut door, eyes, etc.**, v., steik; fauld: **shut close**, v., shut tae: **shutter**, n., window-brod.

shuttle, n., spool: **shuttlecock**, n., feddery craw.

shy, adj., blate; bauch; ergh.

sick, adj., seik; badly: **become sick**, v., dwam: **sicken**, v., scunner; staw.

sickle, n., heuk; whittle: **sharpen a sickle**, v., straik.

side of anything, n., cheek: **sideboard**, n., by-table: **sideswipe**, n., skelp: **sidelong**, adj., sidelins: **sideways**, adv., sidyweys; agee (ajee): **side by side**, adv., cheek for jowl: **look/move sideways**, v., sklent.

sieve, n., sye; seil; brander.

sift, v., dicht.

sigh, v., n., sich; souch.

sight, n., sicht: **view**, n., shaw: **gunsight**, n., vizzy.

sign, n., shaw; whitter, emblem: **show signs of**, v., mak for: **give no sign**, v., gie nae inklin.

signal, n., waff; wag, beckoning.

signify, v., bode; bear.

silence, v., quait; whisht; n., quaitness; lown: **be silent**, v., haud ane's wheest; steik ane's gab.

silicosis, n., stourie lungs.

sill, n., sole.

silly, adj., daft; glaikit; fuil; menseless.

silt, n., sleik.

silver, n., adj., siller.

similar, adj., siclike: **similarly**, adv., siclike.

simmer, v., hotter; sotter; trottle.

simper, v., smudge.

simple, adj., semple; no richt, simple-minded: **simpleton**, n., gowk; cuif; sumph.

simulate, v., fenyie; let on.

since, adv., prep., conj., sin: **since then**, adv., sinsyne.

sincere, adj., aefauld; leal: **sincerity**, n., aefauldness.

sinew, n., sinnen; thow.

sing, v., lilt; cant; souch, softly; diddle, without words: **gracenote in singing**, n., twirl: **singing teacher**, n., sang-maister.

singe, v., birsle; scowther; sotter.

single, adj., aesome; free, unmarried: **single-minded**, adj., aefauld.

sinister, adj., weirdly.

sink in mire, v., lair: **sink**, n., jawbox; syver.

sip, v., sowp.

siren, n., whussle; bummer.

sirloin, n., backsey.

sister, n., titty.

sit, v., dowp doun: **sit close**, v., cuddle: **sit in crouching manner**, v., hunker.

site/situation, n., laroch; steid.

six, n., adj., sax: **sixth**, adj., saxt.

size, n., bouk: **size up**, v., swatch.

sizzle, v., skirl; papple.

skate, v., scutch: **skates**, n., scutchers.

skein, n., hank; bowt.

skeleton, n., gaishen; skelet: **walking skeleton**, n., rickle o banes.

skewer, n., prick; prod; spail.

skid, v., n., skite.

skiff, boat, n., currach; whillie.

skill, n., skeil; can; swick: **skilful**, adj., skeily; slee; knacky.

skillet, n., skellet; tillie-pan.

skim, v., skiff: **skim off**, v., scum; ream, of cream.

skin, v., flae; flype: **cuticle**, n., fell: **hide**, n., flae.

skip, v., lowp; hap: **omit**, v., owreleuk.

skirmish, v., n., scrummage; tulyie.

skirt, n., kirtle; coat: **tuck up skirt**, v., kilt; breek.

skit, n., cockalane.

skittish, adj., skeich; fliskie; starty, of horse.

skittle, n., kyle: **game of skittles**, n., kyles.

skulduggery, n., joukerie-pawkerie.

skulk, v., scouk; snoove.

skull, n., scaup; harn-pan: **skull-cap**, n., coul.

sky, n., lift: **skylark**, n., laverock: **clear sky on horizon**, n., wather-gleam.

slack, adj., lowss: **easy-going**, adj., easy-ozy; slaw.

slake, v., slock/slocken; draik.

slam, a door, v., dad; fling tae.

slander, v., sclander; skaive; n., sclander; ill-speakin.

slant, v., n., skew; sklent: **slanting**, adj., skew; sklent: **at a slant**, adv., skew; asklent.

slap, v., n., skelp; clowt; clash: **slap-dash**, adj., hashy; ramstam.

slash, v., n., sned; gully; whack.

slat, n., spaik.

slate, v., sclate; skaillie: **slate pencil**, n., slate-caum.

slattern, n., haurl; traillie-wallets: **slatternly**, adj., clarty; slaistery.

slaughter, v., fell; pit doun; slauchter; n., slauchter: **slaughter-house**, n., butch-hous; shammels/skemmels.

slaver, v., n., slever.

slavery, n., thirldom.

sledge, n., dreg; trail; caur, for peat: **sledgehammer**, n., forehammer.

sleek, adj., brent; feil; glaizie.

sleep, v., dover, lightly; sloum, restlessly; n., dover, light; sloum, unsettled: **fall asleep**, v., faa owre: **oversleep**, v., sleep in: **sleepy**, adj., noddy; dozent: **sleepless**, adj., wauk-rife.

sleet, v., n., slag.

sleight, n., slicht.

slender, adj., jimp; smaa.

slice, v., n., sclice; shave; whack; whang.

slick, adj., souple; weill-hung, of tongue: **adroit**, adj., feat; gleg.

slide, v., slidder: **slidy**, adj., sliddery; slippy.

slight, adj., slicht; smaa, in build.

slight, v., slicht; lichtlie.

slim, adj., jimp; spirlie.

slime, n., glit; slaich; slub: **slimy**, adj., glitty; clatty; slubbery.

sling, v., n., slung.

slink, v., scouk; snool; snoove: **one who slinks**, n., scouk; snool.

slip, v., n., slidder: **give the slip**, v., gie the geck/begunk: **slip away**, v., slee awa: **slippery**, adj., slidderie;

skytie; gleg, of ice.

slippers, n., baffs; bauchles; sclaffs, loose.

slipway, n., breist.

sliver, n., skelf; spail.

slobber, v., slever; slitter; slorp: **slobbery**, adj., slaichie.

sloe, n., slae.

slogan, n., ensenyie.

slop, v., n., skiddle; slabber: **slops**, n., slaps: **sloppy**, adj., slabbery.

slope, v., sklent; n., sklent; gair, grassy.

slot, n., sneck; snib.

sloth, n., slouth; sweirness: **slothful**, adj., slouthfu; sweir.

slouch, v., hirsel.

sloven, n., clart; hash; traillie-wallets: **slovenly**, adj., clarty; hashy.

slow, adj., slaw; ahin, of clock: **tedious**, adj., dreich: **slow down**, v., dackle.

slow-worm, n., slae-worm.

slug, n., torie-worm: **sluggard**, n., drool; lathron: **sluggish**, adj., mauchtless; smerghloss; thowless.

sluice, n., sluich; flush; clouse.

slump, v., clash; cloit.

slur, n., douncry; tash; ill.

slush, n., glush; glutter; goor; snawbree: **slushy**, adj., glushy.

slut, n., haurl; traillie-wallets: **sluttish**, adj., clarty; slaistery.

sly, adj., sleekit; slee; datchie: **slyness**, n., sleekitness; sleeness.

smack, v., n., scud; skelp; lick: **smacking**, n., lickin; skelpin.

small, adj., smaa; wee: **very small**, adj., tottie: **small thing**, n., smowt: **to a small extent**, adv., a wee bit.

smallholding, n., craft; taft; mailin.

smart, adj., smert; nait; snod; sprush; trig: **look smart, be quick**, v., look slippy: **smarten up**, v., sprush/tosh up.

smash, v., smush; stramash: **smash**, n., stramash.

smear, v., n., slaiger; slaister; sclatch; cleister.

smell, n., guff; goo; yowther; eem, fetid: **give off smell**, v., guff; stew: **smelly**, adj., guffie; fousome.

smile, v., n., smirk.

smirk, v., n., snirtle.

smite, v., clour; clowt; bash; bleach.

smithereens, n., potterskink.

smock, n., carseckie; wrapper.

smoke, v., n., reik; smeik: **smoky**, adj., reiky; smeiky.

smooth, adj., brent; feil; glaizie; gleg, of ice: **smooth-tongued**, adj., gleg-gabbit: **make smooth**, v., straucht; straik.

smother, v., smoor/smuir.

smudge, n., smitch; smad.

smug, adj., crouse.

smuggling, n., free trade; gentle traffic.

smut, n., smit; smitch; smad: **smutty**, adj., smitty; smouty.

snap, v., n., snack: **snap in two**, v., gae in twa: **snap with the teeth**, v., chack; gnap: **snappish**, adj., gurl; snell-gabbit.

snare, v., girn; fankle; snarl; n., girn; snarl.

snarl, v., n., gurl; gurr; wirr; girn.

snatch, v., claucht; cleik; nick.

sneak, v., scouk; snool; snoove.

sneer, v., n., snirtle; snicker; fleer/flyre.

sniff, v., n., snowk; snifter: **sniff contemptuously**, v., snaff.

snigger, v., snirtle; snicker.

snip, v., sneck; nick; whang.

snipe, n., earn/yern-bleater.

snippet, n., clippet.

snivel, v., bubble; sneevil; snotter; n., bubble; sneevil.

snobbish, adj., pridefu; upsticken; wally-close-gless-door.

snooper, n., teet-about.

snooze, v., dover; growf; swiff; n., dover.

snore, v., n., snocher; growf.

snort, v., n., snork; snirt; snifter.

snout, n., gruntle; grunzie; neb.

snow, v., n., snaw: **snow-ball**, n., snawbaa: **melted snow**, n., snaw-bree: **heavy/light snowfall**, n., oncome/skimmer: **bank of snow**, n., snaw-wreath: **snowflake**, n., flaucht: **snow-storm**, n., stour: **snow blown up from ground**, n., yird-drift: **snow driven by wind**, n., yowdendrift.

snub, v., snib; sneck.

snuff, n., sneishin: **snuff-box**, n., sneishin-mill: **take snuff**, v., sneish.

snug, adj., cosh; snod; ticht, of building: **snuggle down**, v., courie doun .

so, adv., sae; that, as in "that big": if it so happens, conj., sae-be.

soak, v., drouk; seip; sowp; sype: soak clothes in lye of urine, v., bouk; graith: soaked, adj., droukit.

soap, v., n., saip: soap-bubble, n., saip-bell: soap-suds, n., freith; sapples: wash with soapy liquid, v., sorple.

soar, v., tove.

sob, v., n., sab; greit.

sober, sedate, adj., douce; solid.

sociable, adj., couthie; sosh: social gathering, n., forgetherin; swarry; carrant.

society, neighbours' mutual benefit, n., manawdge.

sod, n., divot; turr; fail.

sodden, adj., steepit; water-drucken; daichie, of food.

soft, adj., saft; daichie, flabby; duffie, spongy; feil, smooth: soft and sticky, adj., claggy: soften, v., saften; souple.

soggy, adj., sottery; daichie, of food.

soil, v., fyle; clart.

soil, n., syle: crumbled soil, n., mool; muild.

solder, v., n., sowther.

sole of foot, n. howe o the fuit.

sole, Dover sole, n., rock sole: lemon sole, n., tobacco fleuk.

sole, adj., ae; yae: solely, adv., anerly.

solemn, adj., drummure; thochty.

solicit, v., fleich (fleetch): solicitous, adj., fain; fond; tentie.

solid, adj., sad, of baking: substantial, adj., sonsie: solidify, v., sturken.

solitary, adj., aesome; lane: solitude, n., aesomeness.

solve, v., redd up: difficult to solve, adj., kittle.

sombre, adj., drumly; mirk; wan.

somehow, adv., somehou; somewey: sometimes, adv., whyles: somewhat, adv., a bittie; a wee thing: somewhere, adv., someplace; somewey.

somersault, n., backfaa; simmerset: turn a somersault, v., birl the wulkies.

son, eldest, n., auld son: son-in-law, n., guid son.

song, n., sang; ballat; lilt; mane, mournful: song festival, n. sang-schaw.

soon, adv., belyve; in a wee; sune/shuin: sooner than, conj., or.

soot, n., suit; coom: dirty with soot, v., brouk: sooty, adj., coumy.

soothsayer, n., spaeman; spaewife; weirdman.

soothe, v., beit; dill.

sorcery, n., spae; warlockry: sorcerer/sorceress, n., warlock/gyre-carlin.

sore, n., sair; beilin; gaw; blain; adj., sair.

sorrel, n., sourock: wood sorrel, n., gowk's meat.

sorrow, n., dool; tein; wae: sorrowful, adj., waefu: sorry, adj., vext.

sort, kind, n., kinkind; teep; thing: sort out, v., redd; wale.

soul, n., saul; sowl.

sound, whole, adj., hale; ticht.

sound, n., clinkum-clank, ringing; clunk, of liquid from bottle; curmurrin, rumbling; grit, grating; whishie, barely audible; scliff-sclaff, of slippers on floor: make soundproof, v., deifen.

soup, n., bree; cockieleekie, leek and chicken; kail, colewort; tattie, potato: soup pot, n., kail-pat: watery soup, n., skinkin ware.

sour, adj., tairt; wairsh: sour-tempered, adj., crabbit; thrawn: soured, of milk, adj., thunnert: become sour, of butter, etc., chynge; wynt.

source, n., springheid.

southern, adj., suddron; southron: southerner, n., southron.

souvenir, n., myndin.

sow, n., sou.

sow, v., saw; cast: sown, adj., sawn; doun.

spa, n., wal.

space, room, n., waygate: spacious, adj., scouthy; gutsy, of house.

spade-depth, n., spadin: ledge on spade for foot, n., tramp.

span, v., n., spang.

spank, v., skelp; scud; lick.

spanner, n., wranch.

spar of wood, n., spaur; rung.

spare, extra, adj., lowss; orra: meagre, adj., jimp; stintit; scrimpit.

spark, n., sparkle; aizle; gleid.

sparkle, v., n., skinkle; sheen; glint.

sparrow, n., sparra.

sparse, adj., scrimpit; stintit.

spasm, n., grip; thraw; drow, of anxiety, etc.

spavin, of horses, n., spaivie.

spawn, v., n., redd: frog spawn, n., puddock-cruds; toadspue.

speak, v., blabber, indistinctly; blether, foolishly; gab, cheekily; haiver, foolishly; talk wee, softly; whurr, with a burr; yabble, confusedly; yammer, querulously; yap, affectedly; yatter, continuously.

spear, three-pronged for catching fish, n., leister.

special, adj., speecial; preceese: exceptional, adj., byous.

specimen, n., blaud; sey; swatch.

specious, adj., sleekit; mealy-moud.

speck, n., spark; flicht; smitch: specks in eyes, n., sleepy-mannies.

speckle, v., n., spreckle; sprainge.

spectacle, sight, n., meerical: spectacles, n., specks.

spectre, n., ghaist; bogle.

speculate, conjecture, v., ettle; jalouse.

speech, n., say; speak: language, n., leid: manner of speech, n., leid: long speech, n., screed; stour-o-words: speechless, adj., dumfounert.

speed, n., courss; raik; spinner, great: speedy, adj., clever; swith: speedily, adv., swith: at full speed, adv., at full (fu-ll) dreel.

speedwell, n., cat's een.

spell of magic, n., brief; cantraip: cast spell over, v., glaumerify; daumer.

spell, a turn, n., streitch: stretch of time, n., tift.

spelling, n., spell: spelling-book, n., spell-book.

spend, v., ware: spendthrift, n., wastrel; adj., throu-gaun.

sperm, n., melt.

spew, v., n., bock/boke; spue.

spices, n., kitchen.

spider, n., speeder; ettercap.

spigot, n., spicket.

spike, n., steug; carval nail.

spill, v., skail; drabble.

spin, v., wab: spin out, v., twine out: spinning factory, n., jeanie factory: spinning wheel, n., spinnie.

spin round, v., trowe; trinnle; doze, rapidly: cause to spin, v., trowe;

trinnle: spinning-top, n., peerie.

spindle, n., spinnle: spindly, adj., spirlie.

spine, n., rig: spineless, adj., thieveless; thowless.

spinster, n., towdie.

spire, n., prick: smoke spiral, n., tourock: rise spirally, v., spinner.

spirit, ghost, n., spreit; ghaist; bogle; doulie.

spirit, animation, n., smeddum; spunk; gurr: spirits, mood, n., wind: high spirits, n., kilter: low spirits, n., dauldrums: spirited, adj., spritty; skeich; birkie: spiritless, adj., feckless; fushionless.

spit, v., n., slauch; sloch: spit, of a cat, v., fuff.

spite, n., umrage; gaw: spiteful, adj., attery; ill-willie.

spittle, n., spittin; slauch.

splash, v., n., jaup; splounge: splash aimlessly, v., plowter; slitter: splash with mud, v., clart; splairge.

splay-footed, adj., deuk-fuitit.

splendid, adj., braw; grand; rare.

splice, v., skair; wup.

splint, n., spelk: splinter, n., skelf: splinters, n., flinders.

split, v., n., spleit; rive; gell.

splutter, v., splitter.

spoil, n., fang; sprecherie.

spoil, v., spyle; hash; bullox; connach; waste, with kindness.

spoke of wheel, n., spock; spog.

sponge, scrounge, v., mouch (mootch); skech; sorn; scaff; n., spounge: spongy, adj., fozie; duffie.

spontaneous, adj., aff-haun; aff-luif: spontaneously, adv., aff-haun; aff-luif.

spool, n., spule; pirn.

spoon, n., spune: horn spoon, n., gebbie.

sport, v., daff; jink; geck: sportive, adj., jinkin; glaikit.

spot, n., jaup; smitch; drab; spreckle: spotted, adj., spreckled.

spouse, n., fier; marrow.

spout, [v., stroan; n., stroup, of kettle.

sprain, v., n., rack; rax; stave; thraw: sprained joint, n., wrocht bane.

sprawl, v., sprauchle; squattle; spelder.

spray, v., spairge; n., spunedrift.

spread, v., spreid: spread about, v.,

104

skail; sparple: **spread out**, v., ted: **spread thickly, of jam, etc.**, v., slaiger.

sprig, n., spirl.

sprightly, adj., birkie; skeich; steirin; vieve.

spring of water, n., wal; spout; sype.

spring, the season, n., wair/ware.

spring, v., n., lowp; spang; stend: **spring forward, of horse**, v., breist.

sprinkle, v., spairge; strinkle: **a sprinkling**, n., a skimmerin.

sprocket-wheel, n., nicket-wheel.

sprout, v., breird; acherspyre; chun; n., chun.

spry, adj., spree; souple; swack.

spume, n., sea-bree; stour.

spur, v., n., brod.

spurious, adj., ill-come; ill-gotten.

spurn, v., misken; pit by the door.

spurt, v., scoot; stroan; n., jaw; stroan.

spy, v., keek; n., keeker.

squabble, v., argie-bargie; cast out; n., argie-bargie; collieshangie.

squad, n., core; curn.

squalid, adj., fousome; dichty.

squall, n., blaud; bluffart: **squally**, adj., blirty; flisty.

squander one's resources, v., gae throu; skail; splairge.

square, adj., fower-neukit.

squash, v., champ; squeesh; broozle.

squat, v., cour; hunker; squattle; adj., grulshy; stoushie.

squawk, v., squaich.

squeak, v., n., cheip; wheek.

squeal, v., n., skirl.

squeamish, adj., dainshoch; sweamish.

squeeze, v., chirt; thrummle; n., nip; thrummle.

squelch, v., plash; slush: **squelching sound**, n., slonk.

squint, v., adj., gley; sklent; n., gley; thraw.

squirm, v., wammle; thratch; twine.

squirrel, n., con.

squirt, v., n., scoosh; scoot.

stab, v., n., stick; prog: **stabbed**, adj., stickit.

stable, adj., siccar; steive.

stack of hay/corn, n., rick/ruck: **stackyard**, n., rickyaird.

staff, n., stave; tree; crummock, with crook for handle.

stage, stopping place, n., stance: **stage in progress**, n., stent.

stagger, v., n., staucher; stot; wintle.

stagnant pool, n., stank; dub: **stagnate**, v., stank.

staid, adj., douce; donsie.

stain, v., fyle; tash; sclatch; n., smitch; tash: **stained**, adj., broukit.

stair-top, n., stair-heid: **spiral staircase**, n., turnpike stair.

stake as support, n., stab.

stale, adj., dowd, of drink; muchty; wauch.

stalk of plant, n., shank; runt, hard; stock, hard.

stalk, v., stauk; strunt.

stall, n., staa; buiss, horse or cow: **merchant's stall**, n., buith; crame.

stallion, n., staig; cooser.

stalwart, adj., strappin; buirdly; wicht.

stamina, n., smeddum; fushion.

stammer, v., n., mant.

stamp, v., dird; ramp, with anger: **postage stamp**, n., heid.

stampede, v., n., startle.

stanchion, n., stanchel.

stand, v., staun: **endure**, v., thole; byde: **stand a drink**, be: **stand up to**, v., stick up to: **standstill**, n., stick.

standard, n., standart.

staple, n., steeple.

star, n., staur; starn: **evening star**, n., gloamin-staur: **shooting star**, n., fire-flaucht: **starlight**, n., staurlicht.

starboard, n., lineboard; faran.

starch, n., stairch; stiffenin.

stare, v., glower; gawk; geck; goave, stupidly; n., glower; gawk.

starfish, n., kelly.

stark, adj., sterk; skyre.

starling, n., stirlin; stuckie.

start, v., n., stert: **outset**, n., affgaun: **start with fright**, v., lowp.

startle, v., stertle: **easily startled**, adj., skeerie.

starve, v., sterve: **starving**, adj., hungert.

state, condition, n., case; fettle; tift: **state of affairs**, n., set.

stately, adj., michty; buirdly; gaucy.

state, declare, v., ledge: **statement**, n., speak.

station, v., n., stance.

statue, n., stookie: **statuesque**, adj.,

statuous.

stature, n., lenth.

status, n., rang.

staunch, adj., siccar; steive.

staunch, v., stench.

stave, n., stauf; tree: stave, break, v., brek: stave off, v., swee aff.

stay, support, n., prap; stell; stoup; haud.

stay, sojourn, v., stey; byde; n., stey.

steadfast, adj., siccar; steive; set.

steal, v., lift; nick; skech; reive; spulyie.

stealth, n., stouth: stealthy, adj., datchie; thiefty: stealthily, adv., hidlins.

steam, v., stove; stowf; n., oam; yowther: steamy, adj., smuchty.

steelyard, n., stalyard; trone; weis.

steep, adj., stey; steive.

steep, v., seip; sowp; bouk, in lye of urine.

steer, young ox, n., stirk; stot.

stem of plant, n., shank; runt; stock: stem of instrument, n., shank.

stench, n., guff; wheech; stew; yowther.

step, pace, n., stap; stot, springy: stage, n., degree; stent.

stepchild/mother/father, n., stap-bairn/ mither/faither.

sterile, adj., yeld/yell: sterile, of soil, adj., dour; deif; histy.

stern, adj., fell; stour; dour.

stern of boat, n., starn; tail: towards the stern, adv., eft.

stevedore, n., shore-humper.

stew, v., n., stove: odd bits of meat stewed up, n., staughies.

steward, n., stewart; factor, estate; bailie, farm.

stick, n., timmer, strong; rung, strong; spurtle, for stirring porridge.

stick, adhere, v., clag; grip to; lair, in mud: sticky, adj., claggy.

stiff, adj., stentit; steive; unbousome: formal, adj., primpit; sturken: make stiff, v., set; steive: stiffen, v., stiff; set.

stifle, v., smoor/smuir; stychle: stifling, adj., smoory; smochy.

stigma, brand, n., buist: reproach, n., affront; tash.

stiletto shoes, n., peerie heels.

still, adj., caum; lown; lythe; quait.

still for distilling, n., stell.

stilts, n., stilpers; stumps.

stimulus, n., kittle: stimulate, v., brisken/kittle up.

sting, v., n., stang; nip: stinging, adj., jaggy; nirly, of cold.

stink, n., guff; wheech; stew; yowder.

stint, v., scrimp; skimp; stent.

stir, v., steir; fissle; n., steir; adae: stir violently, v., rummle.

stirrup-cup, n., deoch-an-dorus.

stitch, v., n., steik: rough stitch, n., steug: dropped stitch, n., luppen-steik: stitch of pain, n., catch.

stob, n., stab; stuckin.

stock, breed, n., etion; swatch: farm stock, n., plenishin: of good stock, adj., weill-comed: furnish with stock, v., plenish.

stockade, n., peel.

stocking, single, n., stockin; hose: stocking with no foot, n., hushion: knitter of stockings, n., stockin weiver: stocking leg, n., shank.

stocky, adj., laich-set.

stodgy, adj., stechy.

stomach, n., stamack; wame; kyte; baggie: stomach and bowels, n., intimmers: stomach-ache, n., belly-thraw; mollygrubs.

stone, v., peeble; n., stane; peeble; chuckie: crushed stones, n., grush: heap of stones, n., cairn: square-hewn stone, n., aislar: stone-mason, dorbie: stony, adj., stany; clinty.

stook of corn, n., stookie, small.

stool, n., stuil; currie, small; creepie, small; sunkie, short-legged.

stoop, v., lout; hunker; jouk; n., lout; jouk.

stop, cease, v., deval; gie owre; quat, work: stop a moment, v., haud a wee: stop up, v., stap up; clag: stop-gap, n., pit-by: stoppage, n., stick: stopper, n., stapper: stopping-time, n., lowsin/skailin time.

store, v., hain; pit by: storehouse, n., girnel.

storey, n., flat/flet: storeyed, adj., lafted.

storm, n., wather; doister; stour: increasing storm, n., feedin storm: storm-stayed, adj., watherset: stormy, adj., hashy; courss; stourie:

between storms, adv., atween wathers.

story, n., scrieve, long; threne, short; flaw, exaggerated; lagamachie, discursive: **story-teller**, n., shenachy: **thread of story**, n., stot.

stout, adj., brosy; sonsy; gaucy: **strong**, adj., strappin; buirdly.

stove, n., grate.

straggle, v., straiggle; traik; vaig.

straight, adj., adv., straucht: **off the straight**, adv., skew; agley; asklent: **go off the straight**, v., skew: **straight ahead**, adv., straucht forrit: **straighten**, v., straucht/strauchten.

strain, v., rack; rax; n., stour; flocht: **sprain**, n., rax.

strain, stock, n., etion; swatch.

strain, v., sythe; syle; felter.

strait of water, n., kyle: **strait-laced**, adj., primsie; perjink.

strand of rope, n., faik; fauld; strawn.

strange, adj., ferlie; fremmit; unco: **stranger**, n., outland/unco body.

strangle, v., thrapple; worry.

strap, schoolmaster's, n., tawse; lochgelly, very heavy: **stroke with a strap**, n., luiffie; pawmie: **shoe-strap**, n., tag.

stratagem, n., prattick; fetch; pliskit.

stratum, n., lachter; leaf, of coal, etc.; seam, of coal, etc.

straw, n., strae: **bundle of straw**, n., wap: **straw rope**, n., wispin.

strawberry, n., straeberry.

stray, v., wauner; traik; stravaig.

streak, v., n., straik; sprainge: **streak of colour/light**, n., flake: **streak with dirt**, v., brouk: **streaky**, adj., fleckit.

stream, v., stroan; strin; n., burn; water, large, strin, of liquid.

streamer, n., spraing; pensil.

street, n., gate; loan; causey, cobbled: **crown of the street**, n., croun o the causey: **street-sweeper**, n., scaffie: **streetwalker**, n., paikie.

strength, n., docht; maucht; fushion: **strengthen**, v., cantle; sowther.

strenuous, adj., sair; hashie, of work.

stress, n., rack; stour.

stretch, v., streitch; rax: **stretch by pulling**, v., rax; straucht.

strew, v., straw; ted.

strict, adj., strick; nerra-nebbit; ticht; snar.

stride, v., leg; link; spang; n., spang.

strident, adj., stour; groff: **make a strident noise**, v., chirk.

strife, n., stour; sturt; wanpeace; pingle.

strike, v., clour; clowt; dad; bash; clash: **strike at**, v., lay at: **strike down**, v., founder: **strike, of clock**, v., chap: **strike up song**, v., dirl up.

strip off, v., tirl; tirr: **strip**, n., striffin.

stripe, v., n., sprainge; straik: **striped**, adj., strippit.

stripling, n., halflin; laddie-loun.

strive, v., warsle; tyauve; pingle.

stroke, rub, v., n., straik: **blow**, n., dunt; skelp; swype; beff: **stroke of work/stroke of clock**, n., chap.

stroll, v., n., dauner; dander; stravaig.

strong, adj., strang; wicht; feirdie; stour: **strong-tasted**, adj., wild.

struggle, v., n., warsle; fecht; tyauve: **struggle convulsively**, v., wark: **struggle forward**, v., warsle on.

strut, v., sturt; bairge; brank.

strut, prop, n., prap; tree; warpin.

stubble, n., stibble: **stubble-field**, n., stibble-rig/park.

stubborn, adj., dour; thrawn; thrawart: **stubbornness**, n., thraw.

stucco, n., stookie.

stud, n., stood; steethe.

student, n., collegianer: **arts student**, n., rid-goun.

study, v., vizzy, pore over; swat, assiduously.

stuff, v., stech; steek; stow: **stuff, material**, n., gear; graith; ware.

stuffy, of atmosphere, adj., mochie; stauchie.

stumble, v., stummle; stot; stacher/staucher; doiter; n., stacher; stot.

stump, v., stilp; dilp; n., runt; scrunt; **stumpy**, stump of pen.

stun, v., stoun; dumfouner; daiver.

stunt, v., nirl; scrunt; stint: **stunted**, adj., nirly; scrunty; wirly.

stupefy, v., stoun; dumfouner; daumer: **stupefied**, adj., donnert; doitit.

stupid, adj., stippit; daft; glaikit; diffy; donnert.

stupor, n., dwam; stoun; drow.

sturdy, adj., strang; wicht; feirdie.

stutter, v., n., mant.

107

sty for pigs, n., cray; cruive.
style, n., mak; souch; gang, of walking: stylish, adj., tippy.
suave, adj., fair-faced/spoken.
subdue, v., daunton; snool; cuddom; lowden.
subject to, v., thirl to: subject of gossip, n., speak.
subjugate, v., daunton; snool.
submit, v., hunker; cour; snool.
subscribe, v., subscrive.
substantial, adj., muckle-boukit; sonsie; stuggy, of meal.
substitute, v., chynge; n., by-pit; daenae-better.
subterfuge, n., prattick.
subtle, adj., airtie; drauchty.
subtract, v., deduce.
succeed, come after, v., come on: in succession, adv., efter ither.
success, n., speed; thrivance: be successful, v., come speed; win.
succinct, adj., cuttit.
succour, v., gie a lift; fend; n., fend.
succulent, adj., sappy.
such, adj., sic: suchlike, adj., siclike.
suck, v., n., souk: sucker, n., souker: suckling, n., soukin-bairn.
suction, n., indraucht: pump's capacity for suction, n., fang.
sudden, adj., suddent; swippert: suddenly, adv., swythe.
suds, n., sapples; freith.
suffer, v., thole; dree: suffering, n., byde; dool; dree.
suffice, v., ser: sufficiency, n., ser; serin.
suffocate, v., smoor/smuir; scomfish; stychle.
sugar, n., soukar; shugger.
suicide, commit suicide, v., mak wey o anesel.
suit, v., sort; fit; seem: suitable, adj., habile; wycelike.
suitor, n., wooster.
sulk, v., glunch; tak the dorts/dourles/drunt: sulky, adj., dorty; dour.
sullen, adj., dorty; dour.
sulphate of copper, n., bluestane: sulphur, n., brunstane.
sultry, adj., firy; glorgy.
sum, total, n., soum: large sum of money, n., bonny penny.
summer, n., simmer.

summit, n., tap; toupic.
summon, v., cry; warn: summons, n., cry; edict, to court.
sumptuous, adj., lordly.
sunbeam, n., sunblink/flaucht: sunset, n., dayset: sunrise, n., keek-o-day.
Sunday, n., Sawbath: Sunday clothes, n., Sunday braws.
sunder, v., sinder; twin.
sundry, adj., sindry; orra; dyverous.
sup, v., n., sowp: sup noisily, v., slairg
superb, adj., grand; rare.
supercilious, adj., pauchtie; upsettin; dorty; high-i-the-bend.
superficial, adj. ebb-mindit; glaikit.
superintend, v., owresee; grieve.
supernatural, adj., unyirdly; weirdfu: supernatural being, n., wicht: supernatural light, n., elf-candle: supernatural power, n., can; warlockry.
supersede, v., pit out somebody's ee; repone.
superstition, n., freit: superstitious, adj., freity; oorie.
supervise, v., owresee; grieve.
supple, adj., souple; swack: make supple, v., souple.
supplement, v., eik to; n., eik.
supply, v., plenish; sort wi: ample supply, n., rowth: short supply, n., scant.
support, v., n., prap; stoup; stell; haud: supporter, n., stoup; pairt-taker.
suppose, v., ettle; jalouse; tak.
suppress, v., daunton; snool; cuddom.
supreme, adj., bunemaist; heichmaist: supremacy, n., gree.
sure, adj., shair/shuir; siccar: sure-footed, adj., fittie.
surety, n., caution; wadset.
surf, n., landbrist; landbreach, heavy.
surface, n., face: rise to surface of a liquid, v., fleit.
surfeit, v., n., scunner; staw; stap: surfeiting, adj., fousome; stawsome.
surge, v., jow; walter; gurge: surge of waves, n., jow.
surly, adj., crabbit; thrawn; gurly.
surmise, v., ettle; jalouse; n., mump; wene.
surmount, v., surmunt; owretap.
surname, n., efter-name: additional surname, n., eik-name; to-name.

surpass, v., lick; cow; bang; ding: **surpass everything,** v., cow/ding aa.

surplus, n., the owremuckle; owreshot.

surprise, unpleasant, n., begunk; stammagast: **be surprised,** v., ferlie.

surrender, v., cour; hunker; snool.

surreptitiously, adv., hidlins; stownlins.

surround, v., rink.

survey, v., n., scance; sicht; vizzy: **surveyor,** n., metster.

survive, v., win/tyauve throu.

susceptible, adj., fey.

suspect, v., suspeck; dout; jalouse: **suspicion,** n., misdout.

suspense, n., tamtarrie; tig-tag.

swaddle, v., rowe; wap.

swagger, v., gester; prink; flore: **swaggerer,** n., gowster.

swallow, the bird, n., swalla.

swallow, v., swally; pit owre; gollop, hurriedly; slorp, noisily.

swamp, n., flow; lair; moss: **swampy,** adj., lairy.

swank, n., fantoosherie: **swanky,** adj., branky; dashy; fantoosh; vaunty.

swarm of bees, n., byke; cast: **swarm of creatures,** n., hatter; hotter; squatter: **swarm with,** v., hotch wi.

swarthy, adj., bleckit.

swathe, v., swarth; sweel.

sway, v., swee/swey; shog; wammle.

swear, v., sweir; ban: **swear words,** n., ill words.

sweat, v., n., sweit; feim.

sweep, v., n., soup: **quick sweep,** n., scutch: **street sweepings,** n., fulyie.

sweet. adj., maumie: **sweetness,** n., maumieness: **too sweet,** adj., fousome: **sweet, confection,** n., sweetie: **sweets,** n., sweeties; galshachs: **sweet jar,** n., sweetie-bottle: **sweet-seller,** n., sweetie-wife.

sweetheart, n., laud; lass; jo: **go sweethearting,** v., winch.

swell, v., swal; biggen; flozen; spate, of river: **swell of sea,** n., dumswaul; jow: **swelling,** n., swallin; beff, from a blow.

swelter, v., swelt; swither; leip.

swerve, v., n., sklent; swee/swey.

swift, adj., clever; slippy; swippert: **swiftly,** adv., swippert.

swill, v., sweil; syne.

swim, v., n., soum.

swindle, v., swick; n., swick; skin; shavie: **swindling,** n., cheatrie.

swing, v., n., swee/swey; shog; wammle.

swipe, v., scliff; wap; flisk; n., scliff; wap.

swirl, v., n., swurl; sweil; swither.

swish, v., n., sweesh; swoof, of bird in flight.

switch off, electric light, v., sneck aff.

swivel, v., sweevil; sweil; n., sweevil.

swoon, v., n., swound; fent; dwam.

swoop, v., swouff: **with a swoop,** adv., flaucht.

sword, n., swird; airn.

sycophant, n., aabody's body; kiss-ma-luif; fuit-licker; souk.

symbol, n., type; whitter; whurligig, involved.

sympathy, n., couthiness; innerliness: **express sympathy,** v., mane.

symptom, n., shaw.

syphilis. n., glengore.

syringe, n., spouter.

syrup, n., seerup.

Tab, n., tag.

tabby cat, n., roaned cat.

table, n., brod; buird: **side-table,** n., by-table: **table-cloth,** n., buird-claith: **table-mat,** n., bass: **take a seat at table,** v., draw tae; sit in.

taciturn, adj., dour; derf; allerish.

tack, direction, n., airt; cast; taik.

tackle, n., gear; graith.

tact, n., mense: **tactful,** adj., canny; gleg.

tadpole, n., beetle-heid.

tail, n., fud, of rabbit: **root of animal's tail,** n., runt.

tailor, n., tyler.

taint, v., fulyie; smit; n., smitch: **tainted,** adj., cassen; mocht.

take, v., tak: **take away,** v., wyse: **take heed,** v., tak tent.

tale-bearer, n., clype; clype-clash: **idle tales,** n., clash; claivers: **tell idle tales,** v., clash; clype.

talent, n., giftie; ingyne (injyne); genie (jee-nee).

talk, v., crack; caa the crack; clash; claiver; n., crack; speak; clash: **talk confidently,** v., craw crouse: **talk foolishly,** v., blether; haiver: **talk** incessantly, v., yap; yabble: **idle talk,** n., cleck; clishmaclaver: **silly talk,** n., blethers; haivers: **incessant talker,** n., yatter: **silly talker,** n., blether: **talkative,** adj., gabbie; tongue-deavin.

tall, adj., heich; lang; stalward, tall and strong.

tallow, n., tallie; tauch; glit; rind.

tally, n., nickstick.

talon, n., fang; gryfe.

tame, v., cuddom; cunjer; adj., cuddom.

tamper with, v., mell wi; prat wi.

tan, v., bark: **tanner,** n., barker: **tannery,** n., tanyaird.

tangle, v., n., fankle; snurl.

tangle, sea wrack, n., currack; burroe.

tankard, n., stowp; bicker.

tantrum, n., tirrivee; towt; funk.

tap, v., n., tig; chap.

tap, water tap, n., wal; cran; spicket.

tape, n., taip; stringin: **tape measure,** n., taip-line.

taper, v., dwimish; shirp; spear: **tapering,** adj., shirpit.

tar, n., taur: **tarry,** adj., taury.

tardy, adj., dreich; langsome.

target, n., mott; shooting-brod.

tarnish, v., fyle; tash; brouk.

tarry, v., hover; stey; dwadle.

tart, n., tairt.

tart, adj., sour; wairsh; sharrow.

task, n., speil; turn; handling.

tassel, n., bob; target; tourie.

taste, v., pree; try; cun; n., gust; saur; goo, bad: **a tasting,** n., a preein: **tasteless,** adj., saurless; wairsh; fushionless.

taunt, v., flyre; geck at; lichtlie.

taut, adj., stent; strait.

tavern, n., change; lawin-hous: **tavern-keeper,** n., change-keeper.

tawdry, adj., roarie; branky.

tax, n., cess; stent.

tea, n., stroup; wishie-washie, weak: **tea-leaf,** n., tea-blade: **teapot,** n., maskin-pot; trackie: **tea-party,** n., tea skiddle.

teach, v., learn; leir.

team, n., core: **plough team,** n., pleuch.

tear, v., n., teir; rive; rent: **tear off,** v., tirl; tirr.

tears, shed tears, v., bubble; blirt:

tear-stained, adj., broukit.

tease, v., bather; towt: **tease out,** v., taw; toust.

teat, n., tit.

tedious, adj., tedisome; dreich; dry-ward: **tedium,** n., dreichness.

teem, v., hotch; hatter.

teeth, uneven teeth, n., gam-teeth: **show teeth angrily,** v., girn.

teetotaller, n., cauld-water man.

telescope, n., faur-keeker.

tell, v., mou; let dab; clype: **tell tales about,** v., clype on.

temper, assuage, v., dave; lay; licht.

temper, mood, n., tid; tuin: **fit of temper,** n., birse; tirrivee; funk: **lose one's temper,** v., loss the heid: **bad-tempered,** adj., crabbit; thrawn.

temperament, n., strynd; kind; turn: **temperamental,** adj., stounie.

temperate, of climate, adj., merciful.

tempest, n., blouster; whusker.

temple, of features, n., haffet; forebrou.

tempt, v., tyze; wyse.

tenacious, adj., grippy; dour; thrawn.

tenant, n., mailer; tacksman: **tenancy,** n., tack.

tend, v., tent; see efter; work, animals: **be inclined to,** v., be/mak for.

tender, adj., nesh, of wound; douce, gentle; frush, fragile.

tender, offer for acceptance, v., put in for.

tendon, n., tenon.

tendrils, n., lingels.

tenement, n., land; staneland.

tenet, n., licht; lair.

tennis, n., cashepole.

tenon, v., tenor: **tenon-saw,** n., tanner-saw.

tense, adj., stentit; strait.

tenterhooks, be on, v., be on hecklepins.

tenth, n., adj., tent.

tenure, n., tack.

tepid, adj., luewarm; dowd.

term, limit, n., stent: **come to terms,** v., gree: **on good terms,** adj., faur ben.

terminate, v., mak throu wi.

terrible, adj., fearsome; eldritch; michty.

terrify, v., fricht; fley; fleg: **terrifying,** adj., frichtsome; flegsome.

terror, n., dreidour: **object of terror,** n., bogle; cow.

terse, adj., cuttit.

test, v., sey; skeil; n., prief: **test piece**, n., sey.

testament, n., settlement.

testicles, n., stanes; knackers; ballocks.

testify, v., testifee; depone, legal.

testimony, n., tint: **testimonial**, n., brief; testification.

testy/tetchy, adj., carnaptious; towty; attery.

tether, v., bind; n., binnen; langle.

text of sermon, n., grund: **large/small text**, n., big/smaa wryte.

texture, n., grist.

than, conj., nor.

that, adj., pron., thon; yon.

thatch, v., n., thack; theik.

thaw, v., thowe; lowse; n., thowe; saft.

theatrical road show, n., geggie.

theft, n., reiverie; stouth.

them, pron., thaim: **themselves**, pron., theirsels: **by themselves**, adv., their lane.

theme, n., owrecome; leid; speak.

thence, adv., therefrae.

thereabouts, adv., thereawa: **thereupon**, adv., syne.

these, pron., adj., thae; thir.

thick, adj., falloch; gutty; stuggy, of food: **thick and smooth, of liquid**, adj., maumie: **thicken, of food in cooking**, v., mak: **thickset**, adj., stoushie.

thicket, n., shaw; durk.

thief, n., taury-fingers; poucher: **thieve**, v., lift; nick; skech.

thigh, n., hoch, lower; hurkle, upper: **lame in the thighs**, adj., hippit.

thimble, n., thummle.

thin, adj., clappit; ill-thriven; scranky; spirlie.

thing, entity, n., article: **the very thing**, n., the very dab.

think, v., refleck; scance: **think about**, v., think on.

thirst, v., thrist; hae a drouth; n., drouth: **quench the thirst**, v., slocken: **thirsty**, adj., drouthy; gizzen, parched.

thirteen/thirty, n., therteen/therty.

thistle, n., thrissle: **thistle-down**, n., thrissle-tap.

thither, adv., theretil.

thong, n., whang.

thorn, n., jag; steug.

thorough, adj., throu-gaun: **thoroughly**, adv., richt; sair.

thoroughfare, n., gang; waygate.

those, pron., adj., thae; thon/yon.

though, conj., tho.

thought, n., thocht: **thoughtful**, adj., thochtfu: **thoughtless**, adj., tentless.

thousand, n., adj., thousan.

thraldom, n., thirldom.

thrash, v., leather; hammer; beetle: **thrashing**, n., beetlin; leatherin.

thread, n., threid: **ends of threads**, n., thrums: **threadbare**, adj., poukit.

threaten, v., boast; shore: **threat**, n., boast; mint.

three, n., adj., thrie: **three-ply**, adj., thrie-plet.

threshold, n., door-cheek/stane.

thrift, n., fendin; hainin: **thrifty**, adj., fendie: **thriftless**, adj., thieveless; weirdless.

thrill, v., n., thirl; stound.

thrive, v., come on; come speed; dae guid: **thriving**, adj., weill-daein.

throat, n., craig; hause; thrapple; weason.

throb, v., n., thrab; gowp; dirl; wallop.

throe, n., thraw.

throng, n., thrang; menyie; drave; steir.

throttle, v., thrapple; worry.

through, prep., throu; ben: **carry through to a finish**, v., throch.

throw, v., thraw; heave: **throw violently**, v., bung; fung.

thrush, n., mavis; feltie; thrisslecock.

thrust, v., n., thrist; dird; wap.

thud, v., n., dad; dunt; baff.

thug, n., randy.

thumb, n., thoum: **thumbscrew**, n., thumikins.

thump, v., n., dad; dunt; baff.

thunder, n., thunner: **thunderbolt**, n., fire-dairt: **thunderstorm**, n., thunderspate: **thundery**, adj., firy.

thwart, v., thraw; conter; thorter.

thyme, n., tae-girse.

tick, v., n., knap.

tick, buy on tick, v., forenail.

ticket, n., billy: **season ticket**, n., run ticket.

tickle, v., n., kittle: **ticklish**, adj., kittle;

fashious.

t ide season, n., tid: **sea-tide,** n., rin; string, strong: **ebb/flow of tide,** n., aff/in-souk: **tiderace,** n., tideheid; well.

tide over, v., pit by/owre.

tidy, adj., trig; nait; snod; sprush: **tidy up,** v., redd; snod; tosh up.

tidings, n., speirins; wittins.

tie, v., tether; tag; wap; n., twine; wap.

tier, v., fauld; ply; n., tire; fauld; ply.

tight, adj., ticht; jimp; strait: **tighten,** v., tichten; strait.

till, prep., or; conj., gin; or; while.

till, v., teil; work.

tiller, helm, n., tillie.

tilt, v., n., cowp; thraw: **full tilt,** adv., full (fuh-l) bung.

tilth, n., tilt.

timber, n., timmer; tree, material.

time, season, n., tid: **a long/short time,** n., a guid/wee while: **dismissal time,** n., skailin-time: **old times,** n., lang syne: **fix a time for,** v., tryst: **while away time,** v., pit by: **use up allotted time,** v., rin the gless: **well on time,** adv., weill tae: **before that time,** adv., aforesyne: **by the time,** conj., an; gin: **for some time past,** adv., this while back: **from the time that,** prep., frae: **in time,** adv., throu time.

timid, adj., chicken-hertit; bauch; ergh: **timid person,** n., feartie.

tin, article of tin, n., tin: **small tin mug,** n., tinnie: **tinplate,** n., white-airn: **tinsmith,** n., tin-tam.

tine, n., tae; grain.

tinge, n., teenge; gree.

tingle, v., dinnle; dirl; thirl: **cause to tingle,** v., dirl.

tinker, n., tink; tinkler; caird.

tinkle, v., n., ting; tink.

tint, v., n., spraing; lit.

tiny, adj., tottie; peerie.

tip, n., neb: **iron tip,** n., shod: **fit with iron tip,** v., shod.

tip, perquisite, n., fore: **tips,** n., chances: **tip,** v., creish the iuif.

tipple, v., dram; skink: **tippler,** n., drouth; skinker.

tipsy, adj., hauf-on; tozy.

tire, v., ding; trauchle: **tired,** adj., forfairn; forfochen; wabbit: **tired-**

ness, n., tiretness: **tiresome,** adj., dreich; tedisome.

tissue, n., tishie.

titbits, n., galshachs; sunkets.

tithe, n., teind.

titivate, v., sprush/tosh up.

title, n., teetle.

titter, v., n., keckle; snicher.

tittle-tattle, n., claivers; clash; gab.

to, prep., tae; til.

toad, n., puddock; taid: **toadstool,** n., puddock-stuil.

toast, v., n., scoll; toss: **toast bread,** v., birsle; roast, cheese.

tobacco, n., tibawkie: **tobacco pouch,** n., spleuchan.

today, adv., the day.

toddle, v., paidle; trottle: **toddler,** n., paidler.

toe, n., tae.

toffee, n., gundy; claggum; glessie, treacle.

together, adv., thegither.

toil, v., wark; swink.

token, n., taiken; arle-penny, pledge of service.

tolerate, v., thole; stamack; byde: **tolerable, passable,** adj., middlin.

toll, n., cess; teind.

toll, of bell, v., n., jow.

tombstone, n., heidstane; lairstane.

tomboy, n., gilpy.

tomfoolery, n., bitching; flumgummery.

tomorrow, n., the morn: **tomorrow afternoon,** n., the morn's efternune.

tone of voice, n., souch; tuin.

tongs, n., tangs; nippers.

tongue, speech, n., leid: **mother-tongue,** n., mither-leid: **hold one's tongue,** v., haud ane's wheesht: **tongue-tied,** adj., tongue-tackit.

tonight, adv., the nicht.

too, excessively, adv., owre; fou: **too much,** adv., overly.

tool, n., tuil; lume: **toolbox,** n., hurry.

tooth, n., tuith: **back tooth,** n., aizle-tuith: **toothless,** adj., teethless.

top, n., tap: **topmost,** adj., tapmaist; bunemaist: **topheavy,** adj., tappi-loorie: **top-hat,** n., lum/tyle hat: **top up,** v., eik up.

top, spinning-top, n., peerie; pirn, made with bobbin.

topic, n., speak; leid, favourite.

topple, v., cowp.

topsy-turvy, adv., heels-owre-gowdy; tapsalteerie.

torch, n., sownack, bog-fir; wisp, straw; reekie-mire, tow in kail-stock.

torment, v., n., rack; fash; pyne.

tornado, n., skailwind.

torrent, n., halewater; spate: **descend in torrents**, v., plash; daggle.

torrid, adj., scaudie.

tortoise shell, n., tortie shell.

torture, v., rack; pyne; ern; n., torter; mairtyrin: **instruments of torture**, n., bootikins; thumikins; branks; cashielaws.

toss, v., n., thraw; fung; wap: **toss the head**, v., geck; brank: **toss to and fro**, v., jow; heize.

total, n., the hale rickmatick: **total up**, v., fit.

totter, v., staucher; stot; wintle: **tottery**, adj., dodderie; staucherie.

touch lightly, v., tig; skiff: **touchy**, adj., carnaptious; attery.

tough, adj., teuch; tewed, with bad cooking: **make tough**, v., teuch; tew.

tour, v., jant; n., jant; outin.

tournament, n., bonspiel; rink: **tournament enclosure**, n., barras.

tow with tracehorse, v., theat; track: **tow-rope**, n., tether.

towards, prep., til; towarts.

towel, n., toul; haun/face-clout.

tower, v., tour; n., tour; bell-hous, church; peel, fortified border tower.

town, n., toun; brugh: **top/foot of town**, n., tounheid/fuit: **townhall**, n., toun-hous: **officer attending town provost**, n., toun officer.

toy, n., dye; tirly-whirly, spinning; whurligig, toy windmill.

trace, n., theat; train: **tracehorse**, n., theater.

trace, particle, n., haet; scart; perlicket.

track, trail, n., steid: **narrow track**, n., pad: **track down**, v., speir out.

tract, pamphlet, n., track.

trade, v., n., tred; traffick; troke; niffer.

tradition, n., wey; thrain.

trail, v., trauchle; traips: **trail in mud**, v., draigle: **trail, track**, n., steid: **trailing piece of material**, n.,

trailach.

train, v., upbring; cuddom: **instruct**, v., leir; wyse.

trait, n., particularity; swatch; ginkum.

traitor, n., fause loun.

tramcar, n., scoosh-caur.

trammel, v., n., hapshackle.

tramp, n., gangrel; tinkler: **tramp about in wet**, v., paidle: **tramp around**, v., traik; gallivant.

trample down, v., champ; dird: **trample on**, v., tramp.

trance, n., dwam; sloum.

tranquil, adj., lown; lythe.

transact, v., transack: **transactions**, n., traffick.

transcend, v., owretap; win owre: **transcendental**, adj., wanearthly.

transcribe, v., transcrieve.

transfer, v., have over.

transfigure, v., transmogrify.

transgress, v., lowp owre: **transgression**, n., ill-gate: **transgressor**, n., ill-doer.

transit, n., throu-gang.

translate into another language, v., owreset.

transparent, adj., skyre.

transport, v., flit; convoy: **transportation**, n., flittin: **transported in spirit**, adj., cairrit.

transverse, adj., thort: **transversely**, adv., thort.

trap, v., fankle; girn; n., girn; faa, for mice.

trappings, n., graithin.

trash, n., redd; trasherie; trumphery.

travel, v., n., trevel/traivel: **dust-stained traveller**, n., stourie-fuit.

traverse, v., reenge; stravaig.

treacherous, adj., uncanny; unsonsy.

treacle, n., trekkle.

tread, v., gae; gang; shank: **tread down**, v., tramp; paidle.

treadle of spinning-wheel, n., fuit-brod.

treason, n., traison.

treasure, n., traisir: **treasurer**, n., thesaurer: **treasury**, n., thesaury.

treat, v., n., trait: **behave towards**, v., ser: **treated badly/well**, adj., ill/weill-done-to.

treatise, n., screed.

treble, adj., treeple.

tree before house where guests were met,

n., covin tree: **clump of trees**, n., plantin; beltin; stell: **tree stump**, n., runt; scrog.

trefoil, n., triffle; craw-taes.

trellis, n., tirless.

tremble, v., trummle; chitter, with cold; dirl; n., trummle.

tremolo, adj., tirliewha.

tremendous, adj., awfu; terrible: **tremendously**, adv., awfu; terrible.

tremor, n., trummle; tirl.

trench, v., n., trinch; sheuch; cast.

trencher, n., truncher; troch.

trend, n., swee/swey.

trespass, v., n., owrelowp: **trespasser**, n., fence-lowper.

tress, n., flaucht.

trestle, n., cuddy; stuil.

trial, **try-out**, n., seyal: **suffering**, n., dool; byde; crook.

tribulation, n., pyne; fash.

tribute, n., stents.

trick, v., begeck/begowk; tak in; n., cantraip; prattick: **tricky**, adj., quirky: **difficult**, adj., fykie; kittle: **trickery**, n., joukerie-pawkerie.

trickle, v., driddle; trintle; sype; n., trintle; strinnle.

trifle, v., fouter; diddle: **worthless article**, n., fouter; wanworth: **small amount**, n., kennin: **the sweet**, n., whim-wham: **trifling**, adj., aff-pittin.

trigger, n., nail; stickle.

trill, v., lilt; n., tirlie/whirly-wha.

trim, v., fettle/sprush up; adj., nait; sprush; snod; dink: **trimmings**, n., fattrels; muntin.

trinket, n., dye; gee-gaw; wally; wheeram.

trip, **journey**, n., gate; vaige: **outing**, n., jant; outin.

trip, **move lightly**, v., link; fimmer: **stumble**, v., n., snapper; hyter.

tripe, n., painches.

triple, n., adj., treeple.

triumph, v., bear the gree; n., gree: **rejoice**, v., rejyce.

trivet, **bracket**, n., winter.

trivial, adj., fouterie; skittery: **trivial talk**, n., fyke-fack.

trolley, n., trowly.

trollop, n., haurl; traillie-wallets.

troll, n., trow: **trolls**, n., gray folk.

troop, n., core; curn.

trot, v., pad; troddle.

trouble, v., fash; steir; n., fash; fyke; adae: **greatly troubled in mind**, adj., distrackit: **troublesome**, adj., fashious; fykie.

trough, n., troch; baikie.

trounce, v., mell; lamp; whang.

trousers, n., breeks; trews, close-fitting tartan: **trouser braces**, n., gallowses; straps: **trouser flap**, n., ballop; shop-door.

trousseau, n., waddin-braws.

trout, **small**, n., finnock; pout.

trowel, n., trewan.

truant, n., truan; fugie (foodjie): **play truant**, v., fugie; play the plug.

truce, n., baurley: **ask for truce**, v., cry baurley-fummel.

truckle-bed, n., hurly-bed.

truculent, adj., farouchie; barritchfu; fell.

trudge, v., n., traik; trauchle; tramp: **trudge on**, v., dodge on.

true, adj., suithfast; leal; siccar: **truth**, n., truith; suith.

trump-card, n., trumph.

trumpet, n., bougil; touter: **sound of the trumpet**, n., tutti-tatti.

truncate, v., sned; stump.

truncheon, n., rung; cowt; souple.

trundle, v., trunnle; hurl.

trunk, **chest**, n., kist: **tree-trunk**, n., shank.

truss, v., n., turse.

trust, v., lippen; n., lippenance: **trust-worthy**, adj., suithfast; siccar.

try, **test**, v., pree; pruive; sey: **try, "shot"**, n., crack; skelp; whup.

tub, n., fat; kuiller; boyne/byne; bowie; washing.

tube, n., stroint.

tuck up, v., kilt; faik.

tuft, n., tift; tait; tourie.

tug, v., n., pouk; rug; harl.

tumble, v., n., tummle; cowp; whummle: **tumble, of building**, v., tolter.

tumour, n., girran; ingrowth (as in "now"); wind-gaw.

tumult, n., curfuffle; stramash; stushie; habble; dirdum.

tumulus, n., cairn.

tune, n., tuin: **bright tune**, n., lilt:

spring; rant: **slow tune**, n., drune; draunt: **strike up a tune**, v., lilt up; uptak.

unnel, n., tonnel; weem.

urbot, n., torbet; fleuk; gunner.

urbulent, adj., ramstam; raucle; throuither.

urf, a turf, n., turr; divot; fail: **turf fence**, n., truff dyke.

urkey, n., bubbly-jock, male; poullie.

urmoil, n., stramash; stushie; dirdum; fry.

urn, "shot", n., crack; skelp; whup.

urn, v., birl: **cause to turn**, v., birl; feeze: **turn inside out**, v., flype: **turn left/right**, v., haud tae/aff: **in turn**, adv., time about.

urnip, n., neip; tumshie; purple-tap, Swede: **sliced turnips**, n., hackit neips: **cut off turnip "shaws"**, v., shaw neips.

urnpike, n., toll.

urnstile, n., whurliegate.

urret, n., tappietourie; toupic: **turreted**, adj., tappietourie.

ussle, n., fecht; tyauve; warsle; pingle.

twaddle, n., blethers; haivers.

twang of a dialect, n., tuin; souch.

tweezers, n., pinchers.

twelve, n., adj., twal: **twelfth**, adj., twalt: **twelvemonth**, n., towmond.

twenty, n., adj., twinty: **twenty-first**, adj., twintieth and first.

twig, n., spirl; tiller: **dry twigs for burning**, n., sprots; browls.

twilight, n., gloamin; daurkenin: **last stage of twilight**, n., mirk.

twill, n., tweel.

twine, v., rowe; pirl; wimple.

twinge, n., rug; stound.

twinkle, v., skinkle; blinter; glint.

twist, v., n., tweest; thraw; birl; feeze; kink; snurl: **twisted**, adj., fanklet (fankle-t); thrawn; gleyed.

twitch, v., n., fidge; fyke; wicker, of eye: **pluck**, v., n., pouk; yank.

twitter, v., n., chirl; whitter.

two, n., adj., twa/twae: **two-faced**, adj., sleekit: **twopence**, n., tippence.

type, kind, n., swatch; thing: **typical**, adj., teepical.

tyrant, n., teeran; bangster.

Udder, n., edder; uther: **woman's breasts**, n., bubbies.

ugly, adj., ill-faured; ugsome.

ulcer, n., bealin; rinnin.

ultimate, adj., hinmaist: **untimately**, adv., at the hinner-end.

umbrage, n., umrage.

umpire, n., midman; thirdsman.

un-, prefix, **unabashed**, adj., braisant: **unaccommodating**, adj., stickin: **unappetising**, adj., wairsh; wauch: **unattractive**, adj., ill-faured: **unawares**, adv., unawaurs: **unbearable**, adj., untholeable: **unbecoming**, adj., menseless: **unbeknown**, adj., unbekent: **unbending**, adj., set; steive: **unblessed**, adj., unsained: **uncanny**, adj., eerie; eldritch; unco: **uncaring**, adj., tentless: **unceasing**, adj., undevalin: **uncertain**, adj., doutsome; whether-or-no; towtie, of temper: **be uncertain**, v., swither: **uncertainty**, n., swither; dackle: **uncivil**, adj., bardy; misleird: **uncomely**, adj., ill-faured: **uncommon**, adj., ferlie; unco: **uncompromising**, adj., throu-gaun: **unconscious, become unconscious**, v., blainch; taum: **unconsciously**, adv., unwittins: **unconventional**, adj., heronious: **uncouth**, adj., raucle; faur back: **uncultured**, adj., hill-run: **undeveloped**, adj., sitten: **undisciplined**, adj., misbehadden; willyart: **undo**, v., unsteik: **undress**, v., tirl; tirr: **unearthly**, adj., unyirdly; eldritch: **uneducated**, adj., unleired: **unequalled**, adj., unmarrowed: **uneven**, adj., crunkly; nurly: **unfamiliar**, adj., unkent; fremmit; unco: **unfasten**, v., lowse: **unfeeling**, adj., dowf: **unfortunate**, adj., unchancy; weirdless: **unfresh**, adj., dowd: **unfriendly**, adj., ill-willie: **ungainly**, adj., ill-set: **ungraceful**, adj., ill-faurd: **unharmed**, adj., hale; skaith-free: **unheard-of**, adj., unheard-tell-o: **unhealthy**, adj., unlifelike; poukit: **unimportant**, adj., frauchtless: **uninspired**, adj., dryward; fushionless: **uninvited**, adj., unsocht: **unique**, adj., lanerly: **unjust**, adj., iniquous; wrang: **unkempt**, adj., tousy; unkaimed; huddery: **unknown**, adj., unkent: **unlearned**, adj., leirless: **unlimited**, adj., stentless: **unload**, v., tuim: **unloose**, v., lowse: **unlucky**, adj., unchancy; weirdless: **unmanageable**, adj., unbiddable; camsteerie: **unmanly**, adj., lassie-like: **unmannerly**, adj., bardy; misleird: **unmarried**, adj., free: **unmatched**, adj., neibourless: **unmethodical**, adj., throuither: **unobserved**, adj., unbekent: **unpalatable**, adj., guffless; wairsh: **unploughed**, adj., lea: **unpopular**, adj., ill-likit: **unpractised**, adj., prentice: **unprincipled**, adj., waff: **unproductive**, adj., deif, of soil; yeld, of animals: **unpropitious**, adj., ill: **unprosperous**, adj., backgaun; weirdless: **unproved**, adj., unseyed: **unravel**, v., unfankle; tousle out: **unreliable**, adj., uncanny; slidderie: **unresourceful**, adj., feckless: **unresponsive**, adj., dowf; tapetless: **unrest**, n., wanrest: **unrestrained**, adj., ramstam; raucle: **unrestricted**, adj., unstint: **unruly**, adj., ramstam; throuither: **unsafe, of places**, etc., adj., fickle; unsiccar: **unsatisfactory**, adj., ill: **unscrew**, v., feeze aff: **unseasonable**, adj., unfordersome: **unseemly**, adj., menseless; misbehadden: **unsettled, of weather**, adj., unstowly; bladdy: **unshaven/unshorn**, adj., ruch: **unsightly**, adj., unbonny: **unskilful**, adj., uncanny; fouterin: **unsociable**, adj., stickin; ill-vanded: **unsophisticated**, adj., hamebred: **unspeakable**, adj., past aa: **unspoiled**, adj., unconnacht: **unsteady**, adj., coggly; immis; shooglie; tiltery: **unsuccessful**, adj., thriftless; stickit, in profession: **untidy**, adj., tousy; hashy; throuither: **untie**, v., lowse: **untimely**, adj., untimeous: **untold**, adj., untauld: **untoward**, adj., waywart: **untried**, adj., unseyed: **untrustworthy**, adj., slidderie; clem: **unusual**, adj., byornar; forby; unco: **unusually**, adv., byornar; unco: **unwell**, adj., no weill; badly: **unwieldly**, adj., unhanty; untowtherly: **unwilling**, adj., laith; sweirt; ergh: **unworthy**, adj., wanwordy: **unwrinkled**, adj., brent: **unyielding**, adj., dour; thrawn; willyart: **unyoke**, v., lowse.

under, adv., prep., ablow; aneath: **underclothing**, n., linens: **undercurrent**, n., undersouk: **underdeveloped**, adj., ill-thriven: **undergo**, v., thole; dree: **undergrown**, adj., ill-thriven: **underhand**, adj., foutie: **underhand dealings**, n., bent gates: **underhand person**, n., dykesider: **underlip**, n., faple: **undermost**, adj., neithmaist: **underneath**, adv., prep., neith: **undershirt**, n., semmit: **understand**, v., unnerstaun: pick up; uptak: **fail to understand**, v., misken: **understanding**, n., gumption; kennin: **have an understanding with**, v., collogue wi: **undertake**, v., tak on haun: **undertaking**, n., handling; ontakkin: **undervalue**, v., lichtlie.
unguent, n., gree; saw.
unite, v., sowther; wald: **unite in friendship**, v., eik.
university, n., college.
unleash, v., unkipple.
unless, conj., binna; without.
until, prep., or; conj., gin; or; while.
upbraid, v., get on to.
upland, n., heich; braes; adj., upthrou; hill-run.
uplift of the spirit, n., veem; gell.
upper, adj., buner: **uppermost**, adj., bunemaist; tapmaist.
upright, adj., aefauld; fairfurth; weill-cairryin, in bearing.
uproar, n., rammy; stramash; dirdum: **uproarious**, adj., rantin.
uproot, v., howk up.
upset, v., cowp; skail; whummle; n., cowp; whummle.
upside-down, adv., heels owre gowdy; tapsalteerie.
upstairs/up the road, adv., upby.
upstart, n., come-up; snirt.
upwards, adv., upwith.
urge, v., be at; eggle: **urge forward**, v., caa: **urgent**, adj., clamant.
urine, n., peeins; pish: **urinate**, v., pee; pish; stroan: **stale urine previously used for bleaching clothes**, n., graith; strang; wash.
use, v., yaise/uise: **useful**, adj., yuisfu: **useless**, adj., yuisless; thowless; fendless: **usage**, n., yaisage; prattick, precedent.
usher, v., convoy.

utensil, n., wark-lume.
utmost, adj., outmaist.
utter, adj., fair; sterk: **uttermost**, adj., yondmaist: **utterly**, adv., fair.
utter, v., mouth: **utter a word**, v., brak braith.

Vacant, adj., tuim: **vacate**, v., redd; vaik: **vacation**, n., vacancy.
vacillate, v., swither; flaunter; swee/swey.
vagabond, n., gangrel; tinkler; caird; waffie.
vagary, n., vaigrie; crankum; whig-maleerie.
vagrant, n., gangrel; waffie.
vague, **uncertain**, adj., doutsome: obscure, adj., drumly; mirk.
vain, **futile**, adj., knotless: **conceited**, adj., concaity; pauchty.
valet, n., chaumer chiel.
valiant, adj., bauld; wight; spritty: **valour**, n., manheid; spunk.
valley, n., hallie; strath, broad; glen, upper river; den, wooded; gill, narrow: **level land in valley**, n., howe; haugh.
value, v., n., vailue: **evaluate**, v., prize; size up: **value highly**, v., set by: **valuation**, n., prization.
valve, **in water or gas main**, n., toby.
vanish, v., vainish; saunt.
vanquish, v , lick; ding; bang; waur.
vapour, n., reik; stew; stife, choking: **emit vapour**, v., reik; stove.
variable, adj., kittle: **be at variance**, v., be at twa.
variegate, v., spreckle; strip: **variegated**, adj., fleckit; mirlie.
varnish, v., vernish.
vase, n., vawze; pig.
vast, adj., wappin.
vat, n., fat.
vault, v., n., pend: **leap**, v., n., lowp; hap; spang; stend.
vaunt, v., blaw; craw; bum.
veer, **of wind**, v., cast; flaunter, erratically: **veer, of boat**, v., var.
vegetables, n., greens.
vehement, adj., forcie; raucle.
veil for head, n., curch.
vein, n., condy.
velvety, adj., feil.
vendetta, n., feid.

venereal disease, n., glengore, syphilis; glim, gonorrhoea; sibbens.
vengeance, n., amends.
venom, n., venim; atter.
vent, n., bolehole: **ventilate**, v., haizer.
venture, v., venter; aunter; ettle; n., ploy; prattick.
veracious, adj., suithfast; leal.
verdant, adj., emerant.
verge, **edge**, n., selvedge; laggin: **limit**, n.. stent.
verity, n., truith; suith: **veritable**, adj., evendoun.
vermin, n., cattle.
vernacular, adj., hameart.
verse, **piece of verse**, n., screed: **doggerel verse**, n., crambo-clink: **selection of verse**, n., blaud: **writer of verse**, n., makar.
very, adv., awfu; geylies; michty; unco; verra: **very well**, adv., brawly.
vest, n., semmit; sarket.
vestige, n., haet; scart; perlicket.
veterinary surgeon, n., nowt-doctor; ferrier.
veto, n., interdict.
vex, v., chaw; fash; pit about; towt; sturt: **vexation**, n., vex; anger ("ng" as in "sing"); fash; sturt: **vexatious**, adj., angersome; fashious.
vibrate/cause to vibrate, v., thirl; dinnle; dirl: **vibration**, n., dirl.
vice, n., wicketness; backgate: **vicious**, adj., wicket; ill.
vice, the tool, n., clams.
vicissitude, n., chynge; twine.
victor, n., winner: **be victorious**, v., bear the gree.
vie, v., kemp; wrastle.
view, n., vizzy; swype; whuff, fleeting.
vigil over corpse, n., lykewake: **vigilant**, adj., waukrife.
vigour, n., virr; pith; smedduin: **vigorous**, adj., feckfu; wicht; stour.
vile, adj., laithsome; ugsome.
village, n., clachan; toun.
villain, n., bleck; loun; skellum.
vindicate, v., quat.
vindictive, adj., grudgefu.
violate, v., abuise; hash; wanuise.
violent, adj., teirin; wildrife; wud: **violence**, n., birr.
violin, n., fiddle: **violin strings**, n., thairms.

117

virago, n., tairge; randy; skelpy-limmer.

virgin, n., may: **virginity**, n., tap-pickle.

virile, adj., manfu; unlibbet.

virtue, n., vertue: **virtuous**, adj., gracie.

vision, n., sicht: **prophetic vision**, n., saicont sicht.

visit, v., veesit; cry in; n., veesit: **visitor**, n., veesitor; caa-er.

vital, full of life, adj., vieve.

vitriolic, adj., attery; hackit.

vivacious, adj., birkie; vieve; steirin.

vivid, adj., veevid; vieve.

vocabulary, n., vocables.

voice, n., vyce.

void, adj., tuim; boss; deif.

volatile, adj., skeerie.

vole, n., land-mous.

volley, n., stane-dunder: **volley of oaths**, n., plaister.

voluble, adj., glib-gabbit.

volume, bulk, n., bouk: **book**, n., buik.

volunteer, v., shore: **voluntary**, adj., free.

vomit, v., n., bock/boke; upthrow.

voracious, adj., gutsy; hungersome ("ng" as in "sing"); geenyoch.

vortex, n., swurl.

vouch, v., ledge; depone: **vouch for**, v., uphaud.

vow, v., vou; behecht; threip; n., vou.

voyage, n., vaige.

vulgar, adj., groff; hamebred; raucle.

Wadding, n., colfin.

waddle, v., toddle; daidle; waggle.

wade, v., paidle; plowter.

wag, wit, n., birkie: **waggish**, adj., aff-takkin.

wag, v., shoggle; walter.

wages, n., winnins; ettlins; penny-fee.

wager, v., n., wadger; wad.

waggon, n., wain.

waif, n., waff.

wail, v., n., walloch; skirl: **wailing**, n., wally-wallyin.

waist, n., middle: **waistcoat**, n., waiskit; fecket.

wait, v., byde; haud/hing on: **wait for**, v., stop/wait on: **wait a little**, v., byde a wee; hover a blink.

wake, v., wauk: **wake up**, v., wauken: **wakeful**, adj., waukrife.

walk, v., gae; gang; shank; link quickly; skelp, quickly; hirple lamely; slogger, aimlessly; stoiter unsteadily; trauchle, wearily; wauchle, laboriously; n., step; turn dander/dauner, slow; toddle leisurely.

wall, n., dyke: **common wall**, n., pairtisay waa: **turf wall**, n., fail/sod, cass'n dyke: **wall without mortar**, n., drystane dyke: **build a wall**, v., dyke: **let oneself down from wall with outstretched arms**, v., dreip a dyke.

wall-eyed, adj., ringit.

wallet, n., wallat; turkey: **beggar's wallet**, n., gaberlunzie.

wallow, v., swattle; wammle.

wan, adj., gash; peelie-wallie.

wand, n., wattle.

wander, v., wauner; traik; stravaig: **wanderlust**, n., gangin-fuit.

wane, v., n., dwyne.

wangle, v., n., pauchle.

want, v., seek: **want, privation**, n., puirtith; scant.

wanton, adj., keisty; cadgy.

war, n., weir: **warlike**, adj., weirlike.

warble, v., n., chirl; chirm.

ward off, v., kep; weir aff: **warder**, n., gaird; gokman.

wares, n., wallies; trokerie.

warm, v., beik; adj., het; cosh; tozy: **warm and moist, of weather**, adj., meith; mochie.

warn, v., wairn; tell: **warning**, n., tellin: **warning of doom**, n., weird.

warp, v., gizzen; kink; thraw.

warrant, n., warrandice; caption, for debtor's arrest.

warrior, n., weiriour; kemp.

wart, n., wrat.

wary, adj., canny; tentie; waur.

was, v., wis (wiz).

wash, v., sweil; syne, superficially; sapple, in soapy water: **superficial wash**, n., syne; cat's lick; caa-throu, of clothes: **wash-house**, n., washin-hous; steamie, public: **washing-tub**, n., boyne/byne.

wasp's nest, n., byke.

waste, v., waster; connach; n., wastrie: **waste away**, v., dwyne; dwinnle: **waste time**, v., daidle; trottle: **wasteful**, adj., wasterfu; wastrel.

watch, v., n., waik/wake: **watch over**, v., tent; leuk owre: **watchful**, adj., waukrife; tentie: **watchman**, n., gokman: **watchword**, n., ensenyie.

watch, old-fashioned pocket-watch, n., neip: **watchmaker**, n., lorimer.

water, v., n., watter: **foul water**, n., aidle; blouts: **low water**, n., grun ebb: **water barrel**, n., water-stand: **water beetle**, n., water clearer: **water closet**, n., shunkie: **water channel**, n., water-gang: **waterfall**, n., linn: ess; rin o water: **waterhole**, n., dub: **watering-can**, n., rooser: **watershed**, n., water-shear: **water wagtail**, n., water waggie: **water-wheel paddle**, n., ladle: **water-logged**, adj., sowpit; water-drucken: **dabble in water**, v., skiddle: slitter: **dash water over**, v., slounge.

wattle, n., wicker.

wave, v., waff; flaff: **wave about**, v., swee/swey: **wave of the sea**, n., water; swaw: **breaking wave**, n., bore: **breaking of waves**, n., brak; landbrist: **retreating wave**, n., backswaw: **surge of the waves**, n., caa.

waver, v., swither; flaunter; swee/swey.

wax, n., goor, ear; pick, cobbler's.

way, direction, n., wey; road; airt: manner, n., gate; wey: **lose one's way**, v., tyne the road: **make one's way**, v., win; wyse: **in any way**, adv., ochtlins: **in every way**, adv., aaweys: **in no way**, adv., nae-weys: **in the way**, adv., in the road: **wayside**, n., gateside.

wayward, adj., willyart; unbiddable; contermacious.

weak, adj., waik; silly; thowless; fushionless: **delicate**, adj., brashy: watery, adj., wishy-washy; wairsh: **weak in character**, adj., feckless; saft; thowless: **make weak/infirm**, v., craze; tak doun: **weakly**, adj., waikly; cranky; ill-thriven: **weakling**, n., wally-draigle.

weal, n., knurl.

wealth, n., walth; gear; graith: **wealthy**, adj., bien; weill-gethert.

wean, v., spean.

wear, v., n., weir: **wear out, tire**, v., weir doun; ding: **weary**, adj.,

wabbit; forfochen; forfairn.

weasel, n., wheasel; whitrat.

weather, n., wather: **bad weather**, n., wather: **wet weather**, n., saft wather; draik: **dry weather**, n., drouth: **change of weather**, n., turn.

weave, v., wab: **weaver**, n., wabster.

web, n., wab; mous-wab: **web-fingered**, adj., lucken-fingert ("ng" as in "sing").

wed, v., wad: **wedding**, n., waddin.

wedge, v., n., wadge; cog.

Wednesday, n., Wensday.

weeds, n., growth (as in "now"); wrack: **weedy**, adj., dirty.

weekday, n., ilka day.

weep, v., n., bubble; greit; sab: **fit of weepin**, n., roarin match.

weft, n., waft.

weigh, v., wei; wecht: **weight**, n., wecht: **heavy weight**, n., cairry: **weighing machine**, n., bauk; tron, public: **weightless**, adj., frauchtless.

weir, n., caul.

weird, adj., eerie; uncanny; unco.

welcome, v., n., walcome; adj., walcome; weill-come.

weld, v., wald; sowther.

welfare, n., weill.

well of water, n., wal; sunk: **well up**, v., wal; bowt.

well, adj., adv., weill; fine: **very well**, adv., fine; brawly: **well-behaved**, adj., weill-daein: **well-built**, adj., buirdly: **well-clothed**, adj., weill-pitten-on: **well-deserved**, adj., weill-wared: **well-fed looking**, adj., like ane's meat: **well-known**, adj., kent: **well-managed**, adj., weill-guidit: **well-preserved**, adj., weill-hained: **well-to-do**, adj., weill-gethert.

welt, n., walt; laggin.

welter, v., n., walter.

wench, v., winch; n., winch; callet; hizzie.

were, v., wur: **were not**, v., werena; wurna.

west, n., wast: **western**, adj., wastlin/westlin: **westwards**, adv., wastlins/westlins: **to the west of**, prep., wast; bewast.

wet, v., wat; weit; drouk, wet through; adj., wat; weit; saft, of weather: **soaking wet**, adj., droukit; sploungin (sploonjin).

whack, v., clowt; bash; clash; skelp; n., dad; dunt; bash; dirl.

whale, n., whaal/whaul; stourfish.

wharf, n., shipping; shore.

what, pron., whit: **what kind of**, adj., whatna/whitna.

wheedle, v., phraise; blaw i the lug; whillywha.

wheel, v., hurl; rowe; n., hurly; whurl, in machinery: **wheel rim**, n., tread: **wheelbarrow**, n., hurl-barra.

wheeze, v., wheezle; whaisk; clocher; n., wheezle; clocher.

whelk, n., wulk; buckie.

whelp, n., whalp.

when, adv., conj., whan.

where, adv., conj., whaur: **whereby**, adv., conj., whaurthrou.

whet, v., what; sherpen: **whetstone**, n., set-stane; sherpin-stane.

whether, conj., gif; gin; whither.

which, pron., whilk.

whiff, v., whuff; fuff; n., whuff; waff; fuff.

while, a little while, n., a wee: **a while ago**, adv., a while syne: **while away**, v., wyse awa.

whim, n., norie; bee; whigmaleerie: **whimsical**, adj., ebb-mindit; flea-luggit.

whimper, v., n., whumper; yammer; girn.

whin, bush and rock, n., whun.

whine, v., n., wheenge; sneevil; yammer; girn.

whinny, v., n., nicker.

whip, v., n., whup; leish: **whiplash**, n., whang.

whir, v., birr; snore; skirr; n., birr; snore.

whirl, v., n., whurl; birl; hurl: **whirligig**, n., whurlie: **whirlpool**, n., weil; souk: **whirlwind**, n., tourbillon.

whish, v., whush; souch: **whish**, interj., wheesht.

whisk, v., n., wheich; whusk.

whisker, n., whusker: **side-whiskers**, n., side-lichts.

whisky, n., baurley bree; usquebae: **a small whisky**, n., a wee hauf: **whisky still**, n., whisky pot.

whisper, v., whusper.

whistle, v., n., whussle: **whistle quietly**, v., souch: **whistle shrilly**, v., wheeple: **shrill whistle**, n., wheeple.

whit, n., haet; perlicket.

whitlow, n., whittle.

whizz, v., wheich; whinner; skirr; n., wheich; whinner.

who, rel., interr. pron., wha; whae: rel. pron., that: **whom**, rel. pron., wham; that: **whose**, rel., interr. pron., whase.

whole, adj., hale: **wholly**, adv., halelie; crap and ruit; stick and stow: **the whole lot**, n., the hale hypothec/ jingbang/rickmatick.

whooping-cough, n., kink cough/hoast.

whore, n., hure; dunty; paikie; racer.

why, interr. adv., conj., whit for; whit wey.

wick for lamp, n., raggin: **rush wick**, n., threshy-wick.

wicked, adj., wicket; guidless; ill-hertit.

wicker, n., wand.

wicket door, n., tirless.

wide, adj., braid: **roomy**, adj., gutsy; scouthy: **wide**, adv., abreid.

widow, n., weedae: **widower**, n., weedier.

width, n., boun.

wield, v., wag; swack.

wife, n., maik: **"wife"**, n., luckie; cummer/kimmer: **my wife**, n., the wife.

wiggle, v., n., weegle; wammle.

wild, unrestrained, adj., randy; gallus; wul: **wild, of weather**, adj., gurly.

wildfire, n., fireflaucht.

wilderness, n., wastage.

wile, n., cantraip; prattick: **wily**, adj., airty; drauchtie.

will, n., wull; list: **testament**, n., testment: **wilful**, adj., willyart; contermacious: **willing**, adj., fain; bousome: **will not**, v., winna/willna.

will-o'-the-wisp, n., spunkie; fireflaucht; deid-caunle.

willow, n., sauch: **weeping willow**, n., greitin sauch.

wilt, v., dwyne; sab.

win, v., bear the gree: **gain**, v., come by: **winning, attractive**, adj., gainin.

wince, v., flaunter; jouk.

winch, n., wranch.

wind, n., win/wun: **blast of wind**, n.,

blaud; skirl o wind: **strong wind,** n., whusker: **sound of the wind,** n., souch: **break wind,** v., pump; fart: **windmill,** n., whurlie-birlie: **windpipe,** n., thrapple; wizzen.

wind, of a river, v., wimple; twine: **wind up,** v., rowe up.

windlass, n., wranch.

window, n., windae; winnock: **bay window,** n., shot windae: **dormer window,** n., storm-heid windae: **recess window,** n., bole windae: **window aperture,** n., winnock-bole: **window curtain,** n., windae-claith: **window sash,** n., chess: **window seat,** n., winnock bunker: **window sill,** n., windae sole.

wink, v., n., blink.

winnow, v., dicht; rag, partially; wecht, with a tray called a wecht.

winsome, adj., gainin; lousome.

winter, n., deid o the year: **depth of winter,** n., howe o the winter: **winter pasture for cattle,** n., winterin.

wipe, v., n., dicht: **quick wipe,** n., scuff: **wipe off,** v., straik aff.

wise, adj., wyce; lang-heidit; auld i the horn: **wisdom,** n., mensedom.

wish, v., seek; wiss: **prefer,** v., list: **wishbone,** n., thocht-bane.

wisp, n., fuff, of smoke; knoost, of straw.

wistful, adj., pensefu; aiverie.

wit, n., wut: **wits,** n., harns: **collect one's wits,** v., gether anesel: **sharpen one's wits,** v., wauk ane's wits: **witless,** adj., stippit; diffy: **witty,** adj., concaity; auld-farrant: **witty remark,** n., affcome.

witch, n., wutch; carlin; galdragon: **witchcraft,** n., glamourie; spaedom.

with, prep., wi.

withdraw, v., reteir; resile, from agreement; hen, through cowardice.

wither, v., wally; dwyne; sab.

within, adv., ben; inby; prep., ben.

without, adv., outby; prep., athout; but: **do without,** v., dae wantin.

withstand, v., thraw; thorter; conter.

witness, n., sichter; deponent, legal.

wizard, n., warlock: **wizardry,** n., warlockry.

wobble, v., n., wabble; tolter.

woe, n., wae; dool; tein: **woeful,** adj., waefu: **woe betide,** interj., wae worth.

wolf, n., out; wowf: **wolfhound,** n., outdog.

woman, n., wumman; woman-body; wife; quean: **women,** n., weemen: **brawling woman,** n., maggie-rab: **loose woman,** n., limmer; racer: **old woman,** n., carlin: **peevish woman,** n., greitin Teenie: **perverse woman,** n., jaud: **silly dressy woman,** n., dally-doll: **slovenly woman,** n., haurl: **womanhood,** n., womanheid: **fully developed as woman,** adj., womanbig.

womb, n., wame.

wonder, v., wunner; ferlie: **a wonder,** n., ferlie; unco; meerical: **wonder at,** v., strange at: **wonderful,** adj., wunnerfu; byous.

won't, v., winna.

woo, v., gae wi; tryst: **wooer,** n., wooster.

wood, n., wuid; timmer; tree, material: **wood of trees,** n., wuid; plantin; shaw: **polished wood grain,** n., feather: **woodlouse,** n., slater: **wood-pigeon,** n., cushie-doo: **wooden leg,** n., pin leg.

woof, n., wuif.

wool, n., oo: **tuft of wool,** n., flaucht: **woollen,** adj., ooen: **tease wool for spinning,** v., taut: **gleaner of wool in fields,** n., oo-getherer.

word, n., vocable: **torrent of words,** n., blash; blatter.

work, v., n., wark; darg: **do dirty work,** v., scodge; clart; slaister: **set to work,** v., pit tae ane's haun: **stop work,** v., lowse: **work to little effect,** v., diddle; feist: **bungled work,** n., broggle: **end of day's work,** lowsin/quattin time: **hard heavy work,** n., trauchle: **person doing dirty work,** n., scodgie: **stroke of work,** n., haun's turn: **wet disagreeable piece of work,** n., plowter: **work done dirtily,** n., clatch; scutter: **fit for work,** adj., wark-fierdy: **hard-worked,** adj., hard-wrocht: **short of work,** adj., slack: **energetic worker,** n., hasher; raiker.

world, n., warld: **worldly wealth,** n., warld's gear.

121

worm for bait, n., brammel-worm, ringed; slick-worm.

wormwood, n., gall-wood.

worn, adj., tasht: worn-out, adj., forfochen; forjeskit.

worry, v., n., fash; fyke: tear to pieces, v., margullie.

worse, adj., warse; waur; iller.

worsted, n., wurset.

worth, n., adj., warth: worthless, adj., feckless; nochtless: worthless fellow, n., skellum; waff: worthless stuff, n., trumphery: worthy, adj., wordy; honest; dainty/denty.

would, v., wad/wid: wouldn't, v., wadna/widna.

wound, v., gulliegaw, with knife; mairtyr, severely; n., gulliegaw; stob.

wrack, sea wrack, n., burroe.

wraith, n., ghaist; bogle.

wrangle, v., argie-bargie; differ; n., argie-bargie; stushie; dirdum.

wrap, v., hap; rowe up; faik; wap.

wrath, n., sturt; tein; wirr.

wreak, v., wrack.

wreath, n., wraith.

wreck, v., n., wrack; stramash.

wren, n., cutty/jenny wran.

wrench, v., n., rack; rax; rive; wranch.

wrest, v., rive.

wrestle, v., wrastle; warsle; tyauve: wrestling match, n., shak; wap.

wretch, n., wratch; wolron, abusive: wretched, adj., sairie; wirmit (abusive).

wriggle, v., n., wammle; weegle: wriggling, adj., riggly.

wring, twist, v., thraw; wrythe.

wrinkle, v., n., runkle; crunkle; snurl.

wrist, n., reist; shackle: wrist bone, n., shackle-bane.

writ, n., brief; summons: writs, n., letters.

write, v., scrieve; clark, compose; scart, hurriedly: writer, n., scriever: writing, n., wryte; pen-wark: writing style, n., haun o wryte: a flourish in writing, n., squirl.

writhe, v., thratch; warsle; twine; wammle.

wrong, adj., wrang; wanricht; caur, morally: wrong-doing, n., ill-gates: go wrong, v., misgae; misfare; step aside, morally.

wry, adj., skewed; thrawn: make a wry face, v., shammle the chafts.

Yacht, n., yaucht.

yank, v., rive; yirk.

yard, n., yaird: covered yard for wintering cattle, n., ree.

yarn, tale, n., flawmont.

yarn, spun thread, n., yairn: hank of yarn, n., hesp: the thickness of yarn, n., grist: waste yarn, n., thrum yarn: yarn factory, n., twist mill.

yawl, n., yole; skift.

yawn, v., n., gant; gawp.

year, n., towmond; twalmonth.

yearn, v., grien: yearn for, v., hanker efter; weary on: full of yearning, adj., aiverie.

yeast, n., barm; quickenin.

yell, v., n., yall; yowl; skreich; skirl.

yellow, adj., yella/yalla: yellowish, adj., yallochie: yellowish-grey, adj., fauchie: yellow-hammer, n., yella-yite.

yelp, v., n., yalp; yap; yowl.

yes, adv., ay.

yesterday evening, n., yestreen.

yet, conj., still and on; yit.

yield, submit, v., cour; hunker; snool: yield, profit, n., outcome; win.

yoke, v., pit tae: shoulder yoke for water pails, n., neckbit; swee/swey.

yokel, n., jock; heather-lowper; neip.

yon, adj., thon: yonder, adj., adv., thonder: up yonder, adv., upby.

you, pron., ye: you are/shall/have/ would, v., ye're/ye'se/ye've/ye'd.

young, adj., smaa; wee; green: youngster, n., younker; shaver: lively youngster, n., cockie-dandie.

youth, n., halflin; laddie-loun: active youth, n., birkie; swankie: talented youth, n., lad o pairts: youthful, adj., halflin; green.

Zeal, n., birk; ettlin; instancy.

zest, n., gust: zestful, adj., gusty; fell: lacking zest, adj., wairsh.

zigzag, v., kink; sklent; jink, swiftly; n., kink; adj., strauchty-squinty; izzat; adv., wiggle-waggle.

zip, v., wheich; skirr; whinner.

zone, v., gird.

zoom, v., bizz; bum; souch.

122

ENGLISH-SCOTS VOCABULARY—SUPPLEMENT

Abate, v., slocken, of thirst/sorrow.

abdicate, v., owregie; renunce.

aberration, n., aff-faain.

abject, adj., snool-like; fuitlickin: abject person, n., fuitlicker; snool.

abrade, v., gaw; rase: abrasion, n., gaw.

abridge, v., dock.

absorbent, adj., souky; soukin.

abundant, adj., rowth: abundance, n., fouth.

abusive, adj., ill-scrapit.

accept, v., accep.

acoustics, test, v., soun.

acquaintance, n., acquantance.

acquiesce, v., gree; knuckle.

acrid, adj., sharrow.

acrimonious, adj., snell-gabbit; tuithy.

across, prep., atowre.

active, adj., linkin; yauld; snell: activity, n., birr: activate, v., rowt.

actuate, v., airt.

adage, n., freit; thrain; wey.

Adam's apple, n., knot o the craig.

addicted to drink, adj., drucken; drouthy.

adept, n., dab-haun; adj., skeely; slee; knacky.

adhere, v. clag; grip to: adhesive, adj., claggy; slairgie.

adjacent adj. nearhaun.

adjoin, v., mairch wi.

adjust, v., sort; sammer.

admonish, v., check; tell; speak a word to: admonition, n., tellin.

advantage, mean, n., backspang.

affix, v., lay til.

affray, n., fecht; rammy; ruction.

afoot, adv., on the steir.

aft, adv., eft.

agate, n., peeble.

agglomeration, n., hash.

aggregate, n., soum; tot.

agile, adj., linkin; swank; swippert.

agnail, n., anger-nail; wrattle.

agog, adj., cairrit.

aground, run, v., sand.

ahead, adv., aheid; forrit.

air, sprightly, n., spring; lilt.

akin, adj., sib.

alack, interj., ochone; wae's me.

alacrity, n., spryness; lichtsomeness.

alas, interj., ochone; wae's me.

albeit, conj., for aa that.

alder tree, n., aller.

algae, n., wrack: edible alga, n., slawk.

alien, n., outland body.

alight, set, v. spark.

alike, adj., adv., eeksie-peeksie.

alley, n., trance; vennel.

allude, v., mint.

alluvial soil, n., run soil; sleek.

ally, n., stoup.

aloft, adv., abune; alaft.

aloud, adv., out loud; abune the braith.

alter, of weather, v., turn.

altercate, v., argie-bargie; cangle: altercation, n., argie-bargie; tiff.

altitude, n., hicht; heichness.

alum, n., aum.

amalgam, n., jabble.

amanuensis, n., clerk.

amber, n., lammer.

ambiguous, adj., quisquous.

ambit, n., mairch; stent.

ambitious, adj., forritsome.

amble, v., dander; dauner; toddle.

amend, v., mend; mak a better o: amends, n., mends.

amenity, n., policy.

amicable, adj., frienly; great; thrang.

amid, prep., mang; amang.

amity, n., packness; thrangity.

amorous, adj., horny; keisty: amorous glance, n., love-blink.

amuse oneself, v., play oneself.

anaesthetic, adj., dissensing.

ancestors, n., aulders.

anger, n., birr: become angry, v., rouse.

angle-bar, n., swaip.

animated, adj., steirin.

animosity, n., ill-will.

annoy, v., bather: annoying, adj., wearisome: annoyance, n., bather; sorrow.

antagonist, n., fae.

antennae, n., gruppers.

anthrax, n., rid braxy.

anti-clockwise, adv., withergates.

antidote, n., conter-pizzen.

antipathy, n., scunner; staw; thraw

antirrhinum, n., mappie's mou.

antler branch, n., tin/tyne.

anxiety, n., thocht.

anywhere, adv., oniewey.

apathetic, adj., thieveless.
aperture, n., slap; jink.
apiary, n., bee-yaird.
apology, n., aff-come.
apostasy, n., backdrawin.
apparel, v., busk; graith; n., claes; cleidin; graithin.
appease, v., quaiten; slock.
apportion, v., lot; stent.
appraise, v., size up; prize.
apprise, v. avise.
appurtenance, n., pertinent; pendicle.
arch, n., airch.
area, n., aurea/aurrie.
are not, v., arena.
argument, n., splore; thraw.
arithmetic textbook, n., count book: arithmetician, n., counter.
armchair, n., bou-chair.
armistice, n., baurley.
armour, n., weir-harness.
arpeggio, n., pirl.
arraign, v. tak owre the coals.
arranged, badly, adj., throuither: arrangement, n., outset.
arrogant, adj., upsettin.
artful, adj., slee.
artichoke, n., worry-baldie.
artifice, n., prattick.
ash, n., aise: ash-box, n., aise-bucket.
ashlar, n., aisler.
a-social, adj., inbigget.
aspire after, v., weary on; hanker efter: aspire to, v., ettle at.
assent, v., knuckle.
asseverate, v., gie ane's aith.
assiduity, n., eydence: assiduous, adj., eydent.
associate with, v., troke wi.
assuage, v., lay; slocken.
astern, adv., astarn.
asthma, n., wheezles: asthmatic, adj., wheezly.
astringent, adj., strounge.
astute, adj., snell-nebbit.
asunder, adv., apairt; abreid.
as well as, adv., an aa.
at all, adv., at aa.
athletic, adj., swack; swankin.
atonement, n., mends.
atrophy, n., shak.
attest, v., testifee; depone.
attire, v., busk; cleid; n., claes; cleidin; graithin.

attractive, adj., luesome; trig; weill-faured: attractiveness, n., winsome-ness.
attune, v., sort; sammer.
audacious, adj., bauld; braisant.
august, adj., buirdly; michty.
Aurora Borealis, n., streamers.
author, n., talesman.
avarice, n., covetice: avaricious, adj., grabby; grippy: avaricious person, n., gled; skin-a-louse.
avenue to house, n., entry.
avuncular, adj., uncly.
award, n., ward.

Baa, cry of sheep, v., n., meh.
babel, n., habbleshow; gilgal.
baby's hip napkin, n., hippin.
bachelor, n., wanter; lad.
backwards, adv., backlins; erselins.
badinage, n., bantry; daffin.
bagpipe, n., pipes; drone.
baker, n., batchie.
balance beam, n., bauk.
bald-headed, adj., bauldy-heidit.
balderdash, n., blethers; haivers.
baleful, adj., ill-willie; uncanny.
ball game, n., baa-spiel.
ballast, n., ballage; stelling.
baloney, n., blethers; haivers.
bane, destruction, n., mischief; wrack.
bank, steep, n., heuch.
banshee, n., benshee.
bantam, n., buntin.
banter, n., daffin.
Baptist, n., dookit body.
barb, wicker; witter.
barely, adv., barelies.
bargain, v., prig: giveaway bargain, n., rug.
barley, n., baurley: beard of barley, n., yawin.
barnacle, n., claik.
barrister, n., advocate.
barrow-shaft, n., barra-stiel; barrow wheel, n., trinnle.
barrow, tumulus, n., Pecht's cairn.
barter, v., n., hooie.
basement, n., grun-hous.
basis, n., steid; grund, of discourse.
baste, stitch loosely, v., baiss.
batch of goods, n., raik.
batten, v., bat.
bawl, v., n., goller.

bayonet, n., bagnet.
beacon, n., balefire.
beagle, n., baigle.
bearable, adj., tholeable.
bearing, direction, n., airt: demeanour, n., cast.
beat, v., buff: a beating, n., laldie: outdo, v., bate: beat down in price, v., prig.
beau, n., macaroni; tip.
beckon, v., wag.
bed, get up out of, v., rise: bedridden person, n., beddal: woollen bedspread, n., bedmat.
bedaub, v., slaik; slaister; splatch.
bee's honey bag, n., blab.
befool, v., gowk; take the len o.
befoul, v., clart; fyle.
beg insistently, v., sorn: importunate beggar, n., sorner.
behead, v., heid.
behove, it behoves, v., it sets.
belabour, v., lay at; leather.
beldame, n., lucky; carlin; runt.
belfry, n., bell-heid; bell-hous.
bemuse, v., dumfouner; stoun.
bend, n., thraw; wimple, in road.
beneficent, adj., couthie; guidwillie: beneficence, n., couthieness.
berate, v., miscaa.
besides, adv., an aa.
beslobber, v., beslabber; slairie.
besmear/besmijch, v., slairg; slaik.
besom, n., bizzum.
bespangle, v., starn.
best, adj., prime.
bestride, v., striddle.
betimes, adv., timeously.
betoken, v., betaken.
betrayal, n., begeck.
betrothal, n., tryst.
bevel, v., cannel; wash doun.
bewildered, adj., taivert; wull.
bicker, v., n., tiff; tulzie.
bide, endure, v., dree; thole.
bifurcation of thighs, n., cleft; cleavin.
big and thriving, adj., wally: big with child, adj., baggit.
bigoted, adj., begottit; nippit.
bilberry, n., blivert.
bill, beak, n., neb.
billow, v., n., jow.
birthmark, n., strawberry.
bisect, v., half.

bitter, spiteful, adj., attery.
bizarre, adj., cowie; feenichin.
blab, v., blether; clype.
blackhead, n., shilcorn.
blandish, v., fleich; blaw up.
bleat, v., n., meh.
blemish, v., scaum.
blessed, adj., seilfu.
blister, n., blab.
blockhead, n., cuif; gomeril; gowk.
blood, n., bluid: bloodshot, adj., bluid-run: wet with blood, adj., rid-wat.
bloodhound, n., slow-hund; sleuth-dog.
blotch, v., n., splatch.
blow, n., wap; bat.
bludgeon, n., rung.
blurt, v., n., blirt.
blustery, adj., grumly.
bode, v., spae; weird.
bogie, n., bokie.
boil, v., byle.
boisterous, adj., bauld; gallus.
bollard, n., pall.
bold of door, n., slot.
bombast, n., stour-o-words.
booby, n., gawk; gowk; sumph.
book, engage, v., arle.
boon, adj., crouse: boon companion, n., crony.
boorish, adj., menseless.
Border tower, n., peel; tour-hous.
bore, male pig, n., brawn.
bosom, n., bosie.
bother, v., n., bather.
boundary, grass strip between farms, n., bauk: beyond the boundary of, prep., furth o.
bourgeois, n., half-knabs.
bout, spell, n., streitch; yokin, of work.
bow of ship, n., beuch.
bowl, n., caup.
bowl along, v., trintle.
boys and girls, n., louns and quines.
brace, v., n., stell: braces, n., straps.
brackish, adj., sauty.
brainstorm, n., wid-dreme.
brake, thicket, n., shaw.
brand, v., brend/bren.
brand, n., kenmark.
brandish, v., wag.
brash, adj., braisant; bardy.
bravado, n., blaw.
brawl, n., stishie; wap.
bray, v., n., rowt.

brazen-faced, adj., braisant.
brent-goose, n., clatter-goose.
brindled, adj., bawsent: brindled cow, n., branie.
brink, n., selvage; lip.
bristles, tuft of, n., birse.
broach a subject, v., mint.
broadcast, adj., roun-cast.
brook, n., burn.
broomstick, n., bizzum-stick.
brushwood, n., scrog.
bubble, soap, n., bell: bubbling full, adj., reamin.
buckler, n., target.
bucolic, adj., hamespun; raucle.
buffet, v., n., baff; blaud.
buffoonery, n., bitching.
bugle, n., bougil.
built-up area, n., biggit land.
bullrush, n., bull-seg.
bump, v., junner.
bumper of liquor, n., cauker.
bumpkin, n., dobbie; yochel; nowt.
bumptious, adj., concaity; pauchty.
bur, n., horse-thristle.
burden, n., lift; trauchle.
burgh, n., brugh (guttural).
business, do, v., traffick: business, n., traffick.
bustling, adj., stourie; thrang.
butterfly pupa, n., tammie-noddie-heid; willie-cock-up.

Cabbage, n., bow-kail.
cabinetmaker, n., cabinet-wricht.
cad, n., keelie.
cadaver, n., corp.
caddis-worm, n., creeper.
cajole, v., fleech; flether.
cakes, n., fine things.
calceolaria, n., fisherman's basket.
calipers, n., jennies.
calomel, n., calamy.
calumniate, v., caa ill names.
canal boat, n., track-boat.
cancel, v., elide.
candidates, list of, n., leet.
cannon in curling, n., wick.
canonise, v., besaunt.
capable, adj., likely.
capacity, ability, n., ingyne; fushion.
capitulate, v., owregie.
caprice, n., megrim; capricious, adj., hallickit.

captive, make, v., nick; jyle.
car steering column, n., stang.
caraway, n., carvie.
carnage, n., slauchter.
carpenter, n., square-wricht: carpentry, n., square-wark.
carriage and horses, n., yoke.
carrion, n., ket.
cascade, v., spout; n., jaw.
cash, n., siller; clink.
cashier, v., pit awa.
castigate, v., dicht; sort.
cast-iron, n., yetlin.
castrate, v., sned; snib.
catapult, n., slung.
catarrh, n., smucht.
catastrophe, n., mishanter; wanchance.
catch, v., kep.
cauldron, n., caudron.
caustic, adj., snell-gabbit.
cauterise, v., sneyster.
cave/cavern, n., cove.
cavil, v., cangle.
cavity, n., hallie; howe.
celebrate an undertaking, v., handsel.
cellar, n., dunny.
cerebral haemorrhage, n., shock.
chaffer, v., cangle.
chagrin, v., n., chaw.
chain, n., cheen.
chair, draw in, v., sit in.
chamfer, v., cannel; wash doun.
chandelier, n., gasolier.
chant, v., n., chaunt.
chap, crack, v., gaig: chapped, of skin, adj., hackit.
characteristic, n., particularity.
charitable donation, n., aumous.
charlatan, n., gar-me-true.
charm, talisman, n., lucky-stane.
chart, n., caird.
charwoman, n., hizzie; scodgie.
chary, adj., canny; tentie.
chaste, adj., weill-hained.
chatter, v., yabble; yatter: chatty, adj., gabby: chatterbox, n., yatter; rummlieguts.
cheerful, adj., gaucy; joco.
cheese-press, n., chessart.
chequered, adj., chackert.
chest for corn, n., ark.
chestnut, n., chaistain/cheston.
chicanery, n., joukerie-pawkerie.
chide, v., flyte; channer.

126

chief, adj., heich.

childish, adj., weanish.

chill, v., n., geal (jeel).

chimney cowl, n., whurlie; grannie: **chimney stack,** n., chimney stalk: **chimney-pot,** n., lum-can.

chin, double, n., choller ("ch" as in "chin").

chive, n., sithe.

choice, the choice, n., the wale.

choke, v., stap.

chops, jaws, n., chowks.

chortle, v., keckle.

chronic, adj., sitten-doun.

chrysalis of butterfly, n., tammie-noddie-heid; willie-cock-up.

chum, n., chim.

churl, n., carl; tyke.

cigarette end, n., dowp; dottle.

circuit, n., roun; roun-gang.

circumspect, adj., canny; tentie.

circumstances, prevailing, n., wather; wey.

cistern, n., cum (koom).

cite, v., warn.

claim, v., faa, with "canna"/"manna".

clamour, v., n., yammer.

clamp for fastening, n., glaun.

clap, gonorroea, n., glim.

clasp, v., n., clesp: **clasp-knife,** n., jocteleg.

classics, n., humanities.

cleft, n., clift; clivvie.

clement, adj., lythe; maumie.

click, v., chack.

climax, n., bit; spinnle-neb.

clinch a bargain, v., nail.

clod of turf, n., clat.

clot, v., barken: **clotted,** adj., clottert.

clothes, change, v., get shiftit: **clothes-horse,** n., winter-dykes.

clove, n., clow.

clump, v., clamp; clamper.

clutch of eggs, n., settin; lachter.

coating, n., scruif.

coax, v., fleich (fleetch).

cockade, n., heckle.

cock's crow, n., cockieleerie-law.

coddle, v., browden; dawt; waste.

coerce, v., gar.

coffer, n., kist.

cog of wheel, n., trinnle.

cogitate, v., refleck; scance.

cognate, adj., sib.

cognition, n., kennin.

cohere, v., grip to.

cold, be extremely, v., sterve: **cold in head,** n., snifters.

colewort, n., curly-kail.

collar, n., thrapple-girth: **collar-bone,** n., craig-bane.

collusion, n., collogue.

comatose, adj., sleepery.

comfortable, adj., snod; bien.

command, n., biddin.

commence, v., stert; faa tae.

commend, v., crack up.

comment, n., speak.

commonalty, n., semple.

commotion, n., stishie; stramash.

communal, adj., pairtisay.

companion, n., marrow.

compassion, n., peety; innerliness.

compensation for injury, n., assythment.

competent, adj., likely.

complain, v., molligrant; mump.

complex, adj., kittle; pernickety.

compliance, n., greeance; **compliant,** adj., bousome.

complicated, adj., fykie; ravelt.

composer, n., upmaker: **composition,** n., upmakin.

comprehend, v., pick up; uptak.

compress, v., sad; sadden.

comrade, n., billy; fier.

concave, adj., howe.

conceal, v., dern.

conceited, adj., vauntie: **conceited young fellow,** n., birkie.

concern, n., thocht.

conclave, n., forgetherin.

concord, n., greeance.

concourse, n., getherin.

condemn, blame, v., faut; doom, judicially.

condiments, n., kitchen.

conduct, v., allemand.

confront, v., tackle.

confuse, v., confaise: **confused,** adj., dumfounert: **confusedly,** adv., reel-rall; throuither.

congeal, v., sturken.

conglomeration, n., jummle; hatter.

congregate, v., forgether.

conquer, v., bang; ding; waur.

consequential, adj., big; pauchty; up-settin.

consort with, v., moup wi.

construe, infer, v., draw; gether.
continually, adv., aye; daily-day: continual, adj., uncessant.
contraband, n., gentle traffic.
contumacious, adj., camsteerie; dour.
contusion, n., brizz; breeze.
conundrum, n., quirk.
convene, v., forgether: convention, n., forgetherin.
convey in wheeled vehicle, v., hurl.
convoluted, adj., tirlie: convolution, n., wimple.
convulsion, n., thraw.
co-ordinate, v., kind; sammer.
copious, adj., rife; rowth; ruch.
copulate, v., muddle.
copy, draft, n., scroll copy.
coracle, n., currach.
cormorant, n., scart.
corpulent, adj., fodgel; gutty.
corridor, n., trance.
corrugate, v., runkle.
corrupt, adj., mankit.
corsets, n., steys.
cosset, v., browden; dawt.
cost, additional, n., oncost: costly, adj., saut.
coterie, n., clan; fry; set.
cotton-wool, n., wad.
couchgrass, n., quickens.
cough, v., hauch, to clear throat: hard cough, n., bark.
counterfeit, adj., ill, of coins.
courageous, adj., bauld; wicht.
court, v., winch.
covey, n., kivin.
cow stall, n., buiss; bizzie.
crab-apple, n., scrab/scribe; scrog.
craftsman, n., tredsman.
crafty, adj., slee.
cramp, n., croochie proochles.
crane, v., rax.
cranefly grub, n., torie-worm.
cranium, n., harnpan.
cranky, adj., carnaptious.
cranny, bore.
crash, v., raird; n., blaff; stramash.
crass, adj., daft; donnert; glaikit.
cravat, n., grauvat.
crave, v., weary on; hanker efter.
craven, adj., feart; n., feartie.
crawl, v., crowl.
creak, v., chirk.
cream, n., ream: cream jug, n., pourie.

crease, v., runkle; snurl.
creature, n., cratur; beast.
credit account book, n., tammy-book.
creditable, adj., suithfast.
creek, n., wick; gote.
creep, v., crowl; grue, of flesh.
crevice, n., bore; clift.
cringe, v., crei ge; snool.
criticise, v., scance: critical, adj., snell-gabbit.
crone, n., cailleach.
crop of fowl, n., crap; gebbie.
cross-eyed, adj., skellie.
crossroads, n., shedding.
cross-grained, adj., ill-set.
crowd, n., menyie; smacherie: crowded, adj., thrang.
crupper, n., curple.
crux, n., bit.
cuckoo spit, n., gowk spittles.
cudgel, n., rung.
cuff, v., n., fung.
cull, v., wale.
culmination, n., tap-rung.
cultivate, v., work; teil.
cup, shallow drinking, n., quaich.
cupola, n., toopick.
cure for drying or smoking, v., reest.
curio, n., unco.
curse, v., ban; sweir.
cut, deep, n., gulliegaw.
cypher, n., sieffer.

Daddy-longlegs, n., jenny-meggie.
dainty, adj., trig.
damage, v., mischieve: damages, n., skaith-dues: damaged, of fruit, adj., chippit.
dandruff, n., kell; luce.
dangerous, adj., uncanny.
darkness, overtaken by, adj., benichtit.
darning needle, n., stocken needle.
daub, v., n., clatch; slaiger.
deadweight, n., sod.
death rattle, n., daith-ruckle.
debar, v., baur out.
debauched, adj., ill-leevin; ruch.
debilitate, v., tak doun.
decapitate, v., heid.
deceit, n., cheatrie: deceitful, adj., fair-faced; sleekit; slidderie.
deck, v., busk; prink.
decompose, v., chynge.
decorum, n., mense.

128

decry, v., douncry.
deep, adj., howe: **deep-rooted**, adj., yirdfast.
deface, v., tash.
defame, v., bemean; black.
defecate, v., keech.
defile, n., slap.
definite, adj., stentit.
defoliate, v., blade.
deformed, adj., thrawn.
degenerate, adj., ill-leevin; gallus.
delay, n., aff-pittin.
deleterious, adj., skaithfu.
delight, n., delicht.
delinquent, n., ill-doer.
delirium, n., ravery.
depart, v., win awa.
dependable, adj., leal; lippenable.
depict, v., descrive.
deportment, n., effeir.
depreciate, v., cry doun; lichtlie.
depredate, v., herry; rook: **depredation**, n., spulyie; reiverie.
depressing, adj., waefu; weary.
deprived of, be, v., tyne.
deputy, n., depute.
deranged, adj., gyte; aff the heid.
derive, obtain, v., come by.
derogate, v., black; cry doun; lichtlie.
despoil, v., rook.
despondent, adj., dowie.
destruction, n., wrack; windrift.
deter, v., kep.
detest, v., hae a scunner at.
detract, v., cry doun; lichtlie.
deviate, v., step aside.
device, gadget, n., tirly-whirly.
devious, adj., slidderie; souple.
devour, v., scoff.
diamond-shaped figure, n., lozenge.
diarrhoea, n., hurlygush; spleiter.
dictum, n., say.
did not, v., didna.
diffuse, v., spairge.
digest, v., stamack.
digress, v., step aside.
dilate, v., biggen; swal.
diminutive, adj., peerie; tottie.
din, n., dirdum; bellum.
dingle, n., den.
dingy, adj., din.
direction, n., cast.
dirge, n., threne.
dirty, adj., bleck.

disadvantage, n., doundraucht.
disarrange/disarray, v., carfuffle.
disbelieve, v., misdout.
discoloured, adj., scaumed.
disconsolate, adj., dowie; waesome.
discourse, n., stour-o-words; clishma-claver.
discourteous, adj., bardy; ill-mould.
disdainful, adj., skeich.
disgrace, feel, v., think shame.
disinherit, v., disherish.
disinter, v., howk up.
disliked, adj., ill-likit.
dislocate, v., shammle.
disobliging, adj., stickin.
disordered, adj., tousy; ramfoozled.
disorganised, adj., throuither.
disparage, v., bemean; lichtlie.
disparity, n., odds.
dispirited, adj., dowie.
dispute, n., tiff; thraw; tulzie.
disrupt, v., affbrek.
dissect, v., disseck.
disseminate, v., skail; spairge.
dissimulate, v., jouk.
dissolve, v., smooler.
dissolute, adj., ruch; gallus.
distaste, n., scunner.
distillery, n., stell-hous.
distract, v., distrack: **state of distraction**, n., fash; fry.
district, n., kintra; pairt.
disturbance, n., rammy; stishie.
disunite, v., sinder; twin.
dither, v., waffle: **ditherer**, n., waffler.
ditty, n., sonnet.
diverge, v., twin.
diverse, adj., sindry.
dizziness, n., mirlygoes.
docile, adj., biddable.
doctrine, n., leir.
dogfish, n., sea-dog.
dogma, n., leir.
doldrums, n., dauldrums.
dole, v., dale.
dolour, n., dool; wae.
domicile, n., dwallin.
door knocker, n., chapper.
dormer window, n., stormont.
doughty, adj., bauld; wight.
downpour, n., thunner-plump.
drab, n., haurl; traillie-wallets.
dream, day-dream, n., dwam: **dreamy**, adj., dwamie.

dreary, adj., dreich.
dregs, n., sweilins; grummels.
drench, v., sowp: drenched, adj., sowpin-wat.
dried-up, adj., wizzent.
drill, the tool, n., wummle.
drinks, round of, n., service: drinking bout, n., bend.
drip, v., seip.
drive, "push", n., waygate.
droll, adj., unco.
drone of bagpipes, n., burden; bourdon.
drudgery, n., scodgie-wark.
drum, beat, v., ruff: drumbeat, n., ruff; touk.
drunk, very, adj., bleizin-fou.
duel, n., twasome fecht.
dumb., adj., tongue-tackit: dumb person, n., dummie.
dung, sheep, n., purls; trottles.
dupe, v., begunk.
duplicity, n., sleekitness.
durable, adj., steive.

Ear of grain, n., aicher/icker.
earnest, pledge, n., arles.
earnest, adj., thochty.
earth-bound, adj., yirdfast: earthly, adj., yirdie.
Easter, n., Pace/Paiss/Pess.
easy-going, adj., easy-osy.
eat dirtily, v., slork.
ebbtide, n., affsouk.
eccentric person, n., jeeger.
eel, n., yaw.
effeminate man, n., Jenny Wullock.
effort, n., fend; tizzie, great.
effrontery, n., impidence; hard neck.
eke, v., eik.
elapse, of time, v., weir in.
elated, adj., vogie.
elect, v., eleck.
elevate, v., heize; heichen.
elongate, v., rax.
exculpate, v., quat; assoilzie.
execrable, adj., enorm.
executioner, n., dempster.
exhalation, n., yowder.
exhaust, v., trauchle.
exotic, adj., fremmit.
expectation, n., lippenin.
expensive, adj., saut.
experienced, adj., skeelie.
expletive, n., aith; sweir.

explore, v., reenge.
explosion, gentle, n., pluff.
expropriate, v., herry out o.
extend, v., stent: extent, n., stent.
extinguished, be, v., whuff out.
extravagant, adj., wastrife.
extreme, adj., terrible.
eyebrows, n., briers.

Factory, stoppage of work at, n., steg.
fade, of colour, v., cast: faded, adj., scawed.
faithful, adj., aefauld.
fall heavily, v., play clyte.
familiar with, adj., acquant wi.
famous, adj., faur-kent.
fanatical, adj., wud.
farm animals, n., beasts.
farm, hill sheep farm, n., store ferm.
farseeing, adj., forehandit.
farrier, n., ferrier.
farthest, adj., yondmaist.
farthing, n., faurthen.
fashionable, adj., tippy.
fast-growing, adj., growthie.
fast, make, v., steik.
fateful, adj., weirdfu.
fatigued, adj., wabbit; forfairn.
faucet, n., stroup.
faulty, adj., wrang: fault-finder, n., pickfaut.
fawn, v., beinge.
feast, n., gaudeamus; foy, farewell.
feeble, adj., silly; thieveless.
felicity, n., blitheness; seil.
fence rail, n., spaur.
ferment, v., barm.
fern, n., brecken.
ferrous oxide, n., ure.
ferrule, n., virl.
ferryman, n., boatie.
fertile, of egg, adj., cocked.
fetid, adj., fousome; guffie.
fever, scarlet, n., rush fever.
few, a few, n., adj., twa-three; a wheen.
fib, n., whid; flaw.
fiction, piece of, n., upmak.
fidget, v., fitter; fidgety, adj., fykie.
fieldfare, n., stormcock.
fiend, n., fient.
fig, n., feg.
fight, n., faucht.
filch, v., pauchle; snick.
fillet, headband, n., snood.

130

filling, in cookery, n., stappin.
fillip, n., kittle.
filter, v., n., sey.
fine, adj., wallie; smaa, in texture.
finger-stall, n., steil.
fir cone, n., fir-yowe.
fishing-rod, n., wand.
fix in position, v., stell.
fixtures in property, n., standing graith.
flabbergast, v., dumfouner.
flaccid, adj., souple; mauchtless.
flange, n., ledge.
flat-footed, adj., sclaff-fittit.
flattery, n., whillywha.
flatulence, producing, adj., windisome.
fledgling, n., gorlin.
flicker, v., n., skimmer.
flimsy, adj., waff.
flounder, v., sprauchle; splacher, in mud.
flue, n., vent.
fluff out, v., pluff.
flunkey, n., flunkie.
flutter, v., flauchter; waff.
fly of trousers, n., ballop; shop-door.
foam, v., ream; n., sea-bree.
fob, n., spung.
fog, n., loom; thickness.
folly, n., daftness; gowketness.
fool, make fool of, v., tak the len o: foolish, adj., tuim-heidit.
forelock, n., swirl.
forget, v., disremember.
formal, adj., primpit; sturken.
former, adj., whilom: formerly, adv., umquhile; whilom.
fornication, n., sculdudry.
forsake, v., quat.
fortitude, n., smeddum; spunk.
fortune-teller, n., spaewife; weirdwife: fortune-telling, n., spaedom: tell one's fortune, v., spae ane's weird.
forward, rude, adj., forritsome.
foul water, n., aidle.
foundation, n., steid.
founder, v., founer.
fracas, n., rammy; stramash.
fragments, n., flinders.
frank, adj., aefauld.
frenzied, adj., raised.
friable, adj., frush.
friction, moving without, adj., glib.
friendly, adj., pack: friendliness, n., packness; thrangity.

fright, n., gliff: take fright, v., fleg
frighten, v., fleg; skeer.
fritter away, v., meisle.
frizzy, adj., swirly.
frowsy, adj., fousty; mochie.
frying-pan, n., skirlin-pan.
full, completely, adj., bung-fou.
furious, adj., feerious; wud.
furl, v., swift.
furtive, adj., datchie; skoukin: furtive look, n., scouk.
fuse of a shot, n., strum.
fuss, n., stramash: fussy, adj., fykie.

Gab, v., blether; claiver.
gad, v., trail; vaig: gadabout, n., raik; vaig.
gadget, n., tirly-whirly.
galosh, n., galash.
gander, n., ganner.
gannet, n., bass goose.
garbage bin, n., fulyie-can: garbage collector, n., fulyie-man; scaffie.
garden, ornamental, n., plantry.
gassy, of lemonade, adj., birky.
gaunt, adj., scranky.
gay, adj., vaunty.
gelatine, n., geal (jeel).
geld, v., sned; snib.
general dealer, n., Jenny/Johnnie-aa-thing.
genitals, n., wallies.
germane, adj., sib.
get in/out, v., win in/out.
gew-gaw, n., whigmaleerie.
gibber, v., gitter; yabble.
gibbet, n., dool-tree.
giddy, adj., hallickit.
gigantic, adj., wappin.
gimcrack, n., whigmaleerie.
gin, snare, n., girn.
gist, n., rinnin.
glance, v., n., gliff; scance.
gland, n., clyre.
gleam, v., n., glisk; glint.
glib-tongued, adj., tongue-ferdy, gash-gabbit.
glimmer, v., n., flichter; gleid, of fire.
glimpse, v., scance; n., whuff.
glitter, v., skimmer.
globules of fat, n., starns.
glutinous, adj., claggy.
gnarled, adj., swurly.
gnaw at, v., rug at.

131

goat, n., gait.
gobbet, n., mouthfu.
good-looking, adj., weill-faured.
gorge, ravine, n., gill; den; cleuch.
gormandise, v., lay into; worry.
gossip, v., yabble; n., speak.
grace note, n., tripling.
grain, particle, n., curn; quern.
grandchild, n., gran-wean.
grate, v., chirk; risp.
gratify, v., pleisure: gratified, adj., proud.
grating, n., stank.
gravestone, flat, n., throch-stane.
great, adj., awfu; terrible: greatcoat, n., tapcoat.
grievous, adj., sair; snell.
groomsman, n., best man.
grope, v., pawt.
grotesque, adj., cowie; feenichin.
ground, n., grun; yird: ground-nut, n., arnit.
grouse, v., girn; yammer.
grove, n., shaw.
growl, v., gurr; wirr.
gruff, adj., courss; ruch.
grumble, v. mump.
guilty, find not, v., assoilyie; quat: guiltless, adj., saikless.
guinea, n., geenie; Geordie.
gullet, n., weason.
gulp, n., gollop.
gums, n., gooms.
gust of wind, n., flaucht.
gusto, n., goo.
guts, n., puddins.
guttural, adj., howe.
guzzle, v., gollop.
gyrate, v., birl; whurl.

Habitable, adj., bigly.
haft, n., heft.
haggle, v., argie-bargie.
hailstone, n., hailstane; rattle-stane: hailstorm, n., blatter.
halter, n., tether-string; wuddie.
hammer, heavy stone-breaking, n., mash: mallet, n., mell.
hams, squat on, v., courie hunker.
handful, n., hantle.
handcuffs, n., shangies; snitchers.
handiwork, n., haun-darg.
handkerchief, n., neb-clout.
hang loosely, v., hudder.

hanky-panky, n., joukerie-pawkerie.
hapless, adj., donsy; weirdless.
happiness, n., seil.
harass, v., pursue; trauchle, with overwork.
harbinger, n., forerinner.
hard-pressed, adj., sair pitten til.
hard-worked, adj., sair wrocht: hard at work, adj., thrangsome.
hare, n., bawd; bawtie.
hare-brained, adj., bee-heidit; hallickit.
harlequin, n., galatian.
harm, n., mischief: harmful, adj., skaithfu: harmless, adj., saikless.
harum-scarum, adj., camsteerie.
harvest, v., win: harvester, n., shearer.
hash, hack, v., hag; chack.
hasp, n., hesp.
hat, top-hat, n., lum/tyle hat.
hate, v., hae an ill-will at.
haughty, adj., pauchty; upsettin.
haul, harl.
have, not to, v., want: cease to have, v., tyne.
hawker, n., treveller.
hay, spread to dry, v., ted: haycock, n., kyle.
hazardous, adj., uncanny; unchancy; cranky; insecure.
haze, n., oam.
head, n., pow.
headland, n., mull.
headway, n., waygate.
healthy, adj., stuffy.
heap, confused, n., hatter.
hearing, hard of, adj., dull o hearin.
heart-ache, n., hert-scaud.
hearth, n., fire-neuk.
heated twice, of food, adj., back-het.
heaven, n., heivin.
heed, v., n., tent: heedless, adj., tentless.
hefty, adj., swackin.
heinous, adj., wicket.
helpless, adj., silly.
herb, n., yirb.
heritable property, n., heritables.
hermaphrodite, n., scart; faizart.
hesitate, v., waffle.
hide, v., trans., intrans., scug.
high-born, adj., gentle.
hillock, n., tulloch; tummock.
hip-bone, n., heuk-bane: lame through stiffness in hips, adj., hippit.
hire-purchase, n., tryst-buy.

132

hiss, v., n., fuff.

hoarse, adj., roupit: **speak hoarsely**, v., crowp/croup.

hobbledehoy, n., halflin.

hobby-horse, n., habbie-horse.

hobgoblin, n., bokie; worricow.

hodge-podge, n., mixter-maxter.

honorarium, n., honorary.

hoodwink, v., cast stour i the een; draw the briers owre the een.

hooligan, n., randy.

hope, n., wan: **hopeful**, adj., wanlie.

hopscotch, n., peevers.

house-warming, n., hous-heatin.

howl, v., walloch.

hubbub, n., dirdum; rammy; stramash.

huckster, n., cadger; gaun body; packie.

hum, v., bummle: **humming beetle**, n., bumclock.

hum and haw, v., hum and hae; waffle.

humbug, n., wheetie-what.

hummock, n., humplock.

humour, bad/good, n., ill/guid tuin.

hunchback, n., humphy-back.

hunk, n., daud.

hurricane, n., skailwind.

hurry, v., n., chase.

hush child to sleep, v., baa/baw.

hussy, n., jaud.

hut, n., shiel.

hutch used in pit, n., tub.

hyacinth, wild, n., crawtae.

hydrangea, n., hyderange.

hypnotic, adj., sleepery.

hysterics, n., aixies: **fly into hysterics**, v., gang gyte.

Icicle, n., tangle.

identical, adj., sel-same; vivual.

ignite, v., kennle.

ill-disposed, adj., ill-gien; ill-hertit; ill-willie.

ill-matched in marriage, adj., ill-yokit.

ill-natured, adj., ill-set.

ill-nourished, adj., ill-thriven.

illegally, adj., wrangously.

illimitable, adj., stentless.

immaculate, adj., smitchless.

immediately, adv., affhaun; richt out.

immerse in hot water, v., plot.

immobile, adj., stane-still.

impassive, adj., dowf.

impecunious, adj., sillerless.

impediment, n., taiglement.

impertinent, adj., nebbie.

imperceptible, adj., insensible.

imperfect, adj., fauty.

imperious, adj., heich; pauchty.

implicate, involve, v., insnorl.

implore, v., prig.

imply, v., bear.

impolite, adj., misleird.

importune, v., threip at; pursue.

imprecation, n., aith; sweir.

impregnable, adj., unwinnable.

improper, adj., menseless; misbehadden.

improvident, adj., tentless; untentie.

impudent, adj., impident; braisant: **impudence**, n., impidence; backjaw; snash.

impure, adj., smitty.

inadequate, adj., scrimpit.

inarticulate, adj., mummlin; ravelled.

inaugurate with ceremony or gift, v., handsel.

inauspicious, adj., unchancy; uncanny.

incalculable, adj., unkennable.

incantation, n., cantraip.

incautious, adj., untentie.

incessant talker, n., yatter.

incise, v., sneck: **incisive**, adj., gleg.

incitement, n., provoke.

incivility, n., menselessness.

inclination, bent, n., inklin; turn.

income, constant good, n., dreipin roast.

incomparable, adj., maikless; marrowless.

incomprehensible, adj., unkennable.

inconsiderable, adj., frauchtless.

inconsiderate, adj., thochtless.

inconvenience, n., disconvenience.

incredible, adj., past aa.

indecisive person, n., waffler.

indecorous, adj., menseless; misbehadden.

indignation, n., tein; sturt.

indiscriminate(ly), adj., adv., throuither.

indisputable, adj., unquarrelable.

individual, adj., dividual.

indubitably, adv., sickerly.

indulge intemperately, v., gilravage.

inebriate, v., fill fou.

ineffective, adj., feckless; pauchlin.

inept, adj., thowless; weirdless.

inert, adj., dowf; smerghless.

133

inexperienced, adj., prentice.
infer, v., draw.
inferior in quality, adj., waff.
infirm, adj., crazed; dwaible; waik: make infirm, v., tak doun.
inflamed, of eyes, adj., bleert.
information, n., word; wittins.
infrequent(ly), adj., adv., seenil.
infused, become, v., draw.
ingenious, adj., auld-farrant.
ingenuous, adj., aefauld.
ingratiating, adj., slee; sleekit.
inhuman, adj., ill-set; ill-kindit.
inimical, adj., ill-willie.
iniquitous, adj., wrang; wrangous.
injunction, n., word.
innocent, adj., saikless.
innocuous, adj., ill-less; saikless.
innumerable, adj., undeemous; un-kennable.
inopportune, adj., untimeous.
inoffensive, adj., saikless.
inquietude, n., wanrest.
inrush of tlde, n., insouk.
insane, adj., aff the heid; wud.
insensitive, adj., dowf.
insinuate, v., mint: insinuating, adj., sleekit.
insincere, adj., pitten on: insincerity, n., pit-on.
insipid, adj., wishie-washie; waff: insipid drink, n., wabble.
insolvent, adj., broken,
instability, n., cockerieness.
insubordinate, adj., camsteerie.
intact, adj., hale.
inter, v., lair; yird.
intercessor, n., gang-atween.
interchange, v., n., giff-gaff.
intercourse with, have, v., forgether wi; troke wi.
interloper, n., incomer; sneckdrawer.
intermediary, lovers', n., blackfruit.
intermingle, v., mell.
internal organs, n., intimmers.
interpret, v., rede/redd.
interrogate, v., backspeir.
intertwine, v., warple.
interval, in the, adv., atweenwhiles.
intoxicate, v., fill fou: intoxicated, adj., fou: partially intoxicated, adj., hauf-on; tozy.
intractable, adj., set; stickin; thrawn.
intrigue, v., collogue; n., draucht.

introduce, v., inbring.
inure, v., yaise.
inveigh, v., caa ill names; cry names.
invert, v., whummle; cowp.
inveterate, adj., sitten-doun.
invincible, adj., unwinnable.
invitation, n., biddin.
involuntarily, adv., unwittins.
involve, v., insnorl; thrummle.
IOU, n., ticket.
irksome, adj., fashious.
irremediable, adj., ayont remeid.
irreparable, adj., unmendable.
irreproachable, adj., fautless.
irresolute, adj., feckless; wafflin.
irresponsible, adj., glaikit.
itinerant salesman, n., fleein merchant.

Jack in bowls, n., kittie.
jackpot, n., pubbie.
jaundice, n., gulsoch.
jeer, afftak.
jelly-fish, n., sculder.
jerk, jick.
jersey, n., gansey; mawsie.
jetsam, n., fores.
Jew's harp, n., trump.
jib, v., renaig.
jiffy, n., blink; crack.
jig, v., n., jeeg.
jocular, adj., couthy.
jocund, adj., canty; crouse; joco.
joiner, n., square-wright: joinery, n., square-wark.
jollification, n., foy.
jolt, v., n., junner.
jostle, v., shog; oxter.
jowls, n., chowks.
judgment, good, n., wut.
juniper, n., etnach; melmot.

Keel over, v., tirl owre.
keen, of weather, adj., snell.
keepsake, n., myndin.
kerchief, n., curch.
kernel/stone of fruit, n., paip.
key of door, n., check.
kid on, v., bum up.
kidney, n., kirnel.
kiss loudly, v., smack: loud kiss, n., smack.
kitchen garden, n., yaird; kailyaird.
kittiwake, n., tarrock.

knave, n., loun; skellum.
knick-knacks, n., wally-dyes.
knife, large clasp, n., jocteleg.
knitting needle, n., wire.
knobby, adj., nirlie; knaggie; wirlie.
knoll, n., bourock; humplock.
knot, n., snorl/snurl: knot in wood, n., knag.
knowing, adj., auld-farrant.

Labour, be in, v., shout.
laburnum, n., hoburn sauch.
lacerate, v., rive.
lackadaisical, adj., pinglin; thowless.
ladder, loft, n., trap lether.
lag, v., slogger.
lament, v., rair; threne.
laminated, adj., skelfy.
lance, n., prog.
lane, n., loan.
languid, adj., thowless; smerghless.
languish, v., dwyne.
large quantity, n., muckle.
lark, joke, n., tare.
lascivious, adj., radgie.
last, shoemaker's, n., deil's fuit.
latch, n., sneck.
late, to grow, v., weir on.
lattice, n., tirless.
laud, v., crack up; phraise.
layer, n., lachter.
lazy, adj., sweir.
league, be in league with, v., collogue.
leapfrog, n., cuddie-lowp-the-dyke.
learning, n., leir; grammar.
leash, n., shangie.
leaven, n., barm.
lees, n., grunds; settlins.
less, to grow, v., dwyne.
lethargic, adj., dowf; thowless; sleepery.
levity, n., glaikitness.
lewd, adj., horny; heisty.
lexicon, n., dictionar.
libidinous, adj., horny; keisty.
library, n., bibliotheck.
lice, n., cattle.
licence, permission, n., freedom.
lightning flash, n., flaucht.
likewise, adv., siclike.
lilac, n., lilyoak.
limber, adj., swack.
limestone, n., burnt shells.
limitless, adj., stentless.

limp, v., hilch.
limp, adj., yowden.
lineament, n., draucht; meith.
lissom, adj., souple; gleg.
list of persons at meeting, n., sederunt.
listless, adj., thieveless.
litter, stretcher, n., twa-haun barra.
livelihood, n., leevin.
livelong, adj., lee-lang.
lively, adj., sprack: lively young fellow, n., birkie.
living, alive, adj., quick.
loam, n., mool.
lock of hair, n., flaucht; tait.
loft, n., laft: loft ladder, n., trap lether.
lofty, adj., heich; pauchty, in manner.
loin, n., lunyie.
loll, v., sprauchle; squattle.
long for, v., weary on; hanker efter.
looking-glass, n., seein/keekin gless.
loot, n., scran.
loquacious, adj., gabbie; tongue-deavin.
lore, n., lair/leir.
loud, adj., roarie.
lower, v., lour.
lozenge, n., lozenger.
lucent, adj., skyrin.
lucrative, adj., gainfu.
ludicrous, adj., ridiclous.
luck, bad, n., ill-thrift: unlucky, adj., ill-weirdit.
lugubrious, adj., doolfu; dowf.
lull child to sleep, v., baa; baloo.
lullaby, n., baloo; lilly-loo; sleepsang.
lumber, rubbish, n., trashtrie.
lump sum, n., slump.
lust, n., keist; rumplefyke; yeuk: lustful, adj., radgie.
lymph, n., slubber.

Machination, n., draucht; plottin.
maggot, n., maith.
maintain in argument, v., uphaud.
majority, n., plurality.
makeshift, n., affpit; pit-owre.
malediction, n., ill-wish.
malevolent, adj., ill-gien.
malignant, adj., ill-hertit; ill-willie; uncanny, supernaturally.
malodorous, adj., fousome; guffie.
maltreat, v., demain.
manacles, n., shangies.
manger, n., crub.
manhood, grown to, adj., man-muckle.

135

mannerly, adj., menseful.
mansion-house, n., big hous.
mantle, n., manteel; rauchan.
maplewood, n., easer; ezar.
maraud, v., reive; spulyie.
marguerite, n., cairtwheel.
marigold, n., meadow gowan.
marrow, full of, adj., green.
marry, v., mairry: united in marriage, adj., yokit.
matchless, adj., marrowless.
material possessions, n., graith.
matted, adj., tawty.
matter in eyes, n., bleers.
mattress case, n., tike.
maudlin, adj., tozy.
maunder, v., haiver.
mayfly, n., scur.
meagre, adj., scranky.
mean, of low rank, adj., semple: stingy, adj., scrimp; moulie.
meander, v., wimple.
mediocre, adj., middlin.
medley, n., variorum.
meeting place, n., tryst.
mellow, adj., mervy.
memento, n., memorandum.
mend, v., sort.
mendicant, n., gaberlunzie; gaun body.
menial, n., ashypet.
mentally defective, adj., wantin; no richt.
mercury, n., deil's metal.
merrymaking, n., rant.
mess, liquid, n., skitter.
metal, fine metal worker, n., lorimer.
metamorphose, v., transmogrify; transmue.
metaphysical, adj., pneumatic.
meteor, n., shot staur.
methodical, adj., purposelike.
mettle, n., smeddum: mettlesome, adj., skeich; spunky.
midst, the, n., mid.
mien, n., vand.
mimulus, n., mappie's mou.
mince, v., n., minch: mincing in speech, adj., dockit.
mingle, v., mell; meng.
miracle, n., meerical.
mire, n., slabber: miry, adj., slabbery; slunky.
mirror, n., seein-gless.
misadventure, n., mishanter.

misapprehend, v., misunnerstaun.
misbegotten, adj., ill-cleckit.
misbehave, v., cairry on.
miscellaneous articles, n., trantles; trokes.
mischievous, adj., ill-deedie.
misdoubt, v., misdout; mislippen.
misguide, v., misleir: misguided, adj., wull.
mislay, v., tyne.
mismatched, adj., mismarrowed.
misshapen, adj., thrawn.
misspent, adj., ill-wared.
mistaken, adj., misleired.
mistimed, adj., untimeous.
mistrust, v., mislippen.
misty, adj., loomy.
mitigate, v., dave; sowther.
mixture, confused, n., clamjamfry.
mocking, adj., afftakin: mocking remark, n., afftak.
mode, n., gate; wey: modish, adj. tippy.
model, n., muild; swatch; set.
modicum, n., mention.
molar tooth, n., aisle-tuith.
mollify, v., saften: assuage, v., lay; quaiten.
moment, n., gliff.
mood, bad/good, n., ill/guid tuin.
mooring post, n., pall.
mope, v., peenge.
morass, n., flow; flowmoss; souk.
morning, n., mornin; very early morning, n., smaa oors.
morose, adj., dorty; thrawn.
mortal, adj., deadal.
mortgage, n., wadset.
mote in eye, n., sleepy-mannie.
motto, n., slogan.
moulder, v., muilder.
moult, v., mout.
mountebank, n., gar-me-true.
mouth, corner of, n., wick: mouth organ, n., mouthie.
move quickly, v., wheich: move unsteadily, v., habble.
much, very, adv., awfu.
mud, n., glabber; slabber: muddy, adj., jummly: plough through mud, v., slunk.
muff, bungle, v., bootch; fouter.
muffler, n., grauvat.
multi-storey building, n., multy.

munificent, adj., ruch-haundit.
mustard, n., mustart.
mutable, adj., sliddery.
myopic, adj., ner-sichtit.

Naive, adj., aefauld.
nape, n., cuff o the neck.
nark, v., bather; towt.
native of town, n., loun; gutterbluid.
natty, adj., tippy.
nauseate, v., staw; ug: nauseating,
    adj., scunnersome; ugsome.
navel, n. nyle.
navvy n., cley davie.
nearby, adj., adv., nearhaun.
neat, adj., tosh.
necromancy, n., spaedom.
negligible, adj., frauchtless.
nervous, adj., skeerie.
neutral, n., midman.
new, brand new, adj., split/spang new.
newspaper, local, n., the squeak.
newt, n., ask.
next, of time, adv., syne.
nick-nacks, n., trantles; trinkums.
niggardly, adj., nippit.
niggle, v., fouter.
nightjar, n., moch-hawk.
nimble, adj., swippert.
nincompoop, n., cuif; gowk.
nitwit, n., cuif; sumph.
nod repeatedly, v., nid-nod.
node, n., knot.
nominate, v., leet.
nondescript, n., kennawhat.
nonplus, v., bumbaze; dumfouner.
Norway, n., Norawa; Norroway.
nose, having long sharp, adj., whaup-
    nebbit: thumb the nose, v., dumb-
    sweir.
nostril, n., nostirl.
notch, v., n., natch.
notebook, n., scroll-book.
noteworthy, adj., namely.
Northern Lights, n., streamers.
notwithstanding, adv., still and on.
nought, n., nocht.
nourished, badly, adj., ill-thriven.
novel, n., novelle: novelty, n., unco.
noxious, adj., hurtsome; skaithfu.
nude, adj., nakit.
number, an indefinite, n., a wheen.
numbskull, n., cuif; gomeril.
numerous, adj., monie.

Obdurate, adj., dour; thrawn; stickin.
obedient, adj., tawie; biddable.
obese, adj., bouky.
oblique, adj., squint: obliquely, adv.,
    agley.
obloquy, n., fylement.
obnoxious smell, n., guff; wheech.
oboe, n., hoboy.
obsequious, adj., sleekit: be obsequious,
    v., snool.
observation, n., observe.
obsessed with, adj., no able to see past.
obsolete, adj., auld-farrant.
obstinate, adj., set; stickin; thrawart.
obtuse, adj., diffy; dowf.
occasionally, adv., whyles.
occupation, n., wey o daein.
oddness, n., onconess: odds and ends,
    n., trinkums; trokes.
oddity, n., whigmaleerie.
odious, adj., scunnersome; ugsome.
offensive, adj., fousome; scunnersome.
offhand, adv., affhaun.
official, n., adj., offeecial.
offset, n., set-aff.
old-fashioned, adj., auld-warld.
old, feeble person, n., bauchle.
omen, n., freit: ominous, adj., uncanny.
onslaught, n., oncome; onding.
opinion, n., mynd.
opposite, prep., anent.
oppressive, adj., sair.
orally, adv., aff the tongue.
orchid, wild, n., baldairie.
order, n., biddin: order beforehand, v.,
    speak for.
ordure, n., fulyie; keech.
orison, n., incaain.
ornamental, adj., wallie: ornamentation,
    n., flumgummery.
oscillate, v., swee; whummle.
osier, n., sauch.
ostentatious, adj., roarie; vaunty:
    ostentatious show, n., plaister;
    splairge.
ousel, n., heather blackie/cock.
oust, v., surplant.
outbreak, n., outbrak.
outclass, v., ding; lick; waur.
outcome, n., affcome.
outdistance, v., cappilow.
outdo, v. waur.
outdoor, adj., out-about.
outermost, adj., outmaist.

outgoing, adj., affgaun.
outing, n., jant.
outlandish, adj., feenichin; unco.
outlast, v., outlest.
outright, adj., evendoun; adv., richt out.
outstanding, adj., marked; kenspeckle.
outstrip, v., cappilow.
over, adv., prep., abune.
overcast, adj., lourdie.
overdressed, adj., fantoosh.
overdrive, v., hash.
overdue, adj., backhaun.
over-elaborate, adj., primpit.
over-fondness, n., glaikitness.
overhaul, thorough, n., throu-gaun.
overhead, adv., abune.
over-punctilious, adj., pea-splittin.
over-roast, v., scowder.
over-scrupulous, adj., pernickety.
over-shoe, n., galash.
over-time, n., by-oors.
overturn, v., whummle.
overweening, adj., high-i-the-bend; pauchty.
owe, v., aucht.
owl, barn, n., white houlet.
oxide, ferrous, n., ure.

Packed, hard-packed, adj., saddit.
pad, v., n., pluff.
painstaking, adj., pinglin.
pal, n., buttie.
palate, n., gab.
palpitate, v., gowp.
paltry, adj., waff.
pamper, v., spyle.
pan, shallow cooking, n., pingle.
pancreas, n., breids.
pang of pain, n., thraw.
pannier, n., currach.
panoply, n., effeir.
par, n., paur.
paraphernalia, n., graithin.
parlance, n., speak.
participate, v., tak pairt.
parturition, n., shoutin: time of parturition, n., time.
pass, mountain, n., balloch.
passion, n., birr: passionate, adj., birsie.
past, prep., by: get past, v., win by.
pasty-faced, adj., etten-and-spued.
patch for vegetables, n., taft.

patter, v., fitter.
pauper, n., bedesman.
payment before making bargain, n., arles.
peat bog, n., flowmoss: peat face, n., bink.
peculiarity, n., unconess.
peddle wares, v., cadge; trevel.
pedigree, n., hithercome.
peep, v., n., teet.
peevish, adj., birny.
peg, n., knag; dook, wooden peg in wall for nail.
pellets, lead, n., hail.
pendant, n., pendle.
pensive, adj., thochty.
penury, n., puirtith.
pepper, n., spice.
perdition, n., hership.
peregrine falcon, n., stock-hawk.
peremptory, adj., pauchty.
peritoneum, n., rim: rupture of peritoneum, n., rimburst.
perk, n., pruch.
pernicious, adj., hurtsome; skaithfu.
perquisites, n., pruch.
person, shortsighted, n., stymie.
personal, adj., ain.
pertain, v., effeir.
pertinacious, adj., stickin; thrawn.
perverse, adj., thrawart.
petrel, n., storm-finch; Peter's bird.
phantom, n., bogle; ghaist.
phenomenon, n., feck.
phosphorescence, n., water-burn.
photograph, n., caird.
phrase added to give time to think, n., crutch-phrase.
physic, n., feesick.
pickle, v., lay in saut.
pink, the flower, n., clow-gillieflouer.
pint, n., mutchkin.
pip of fruit, n., paip.
piping cry of bird, n., pleep.
pipit, n., titlin.
piquant, adj., pickant.
pit-a-pat, go, v., play whiltie-whaltie.
pity, v., n., peety.
plague, annoyance, n., sorrow.
plaintiff, n., complainer.
plate, n., flet.
plaster of paris, n., stookie.
plastic, adj., swack.
plausible, adj., slee; sleekit.

138

playful, adj., playsome.
pleased, adj., joco; suitit.
pleasure-ground, n., pleasance; policies.
pleat, v., n., plet; touk.
pledge, v., wage; wadge.
pliant, adj., swack; dwaible.
plight, n., plicht.
pluck, n., spunk: plucky, adj., stuffy.
plump, adj., fodgel; sappy.
plunder, v., rook; n., spulyie.
pod, n., huil/hool; shaup.
podgy, adj., bilshy.
poise on the wing, v., scove.
politic, adj., canny; lang-drauchtit.
poltroon, n., coucher.
polyanthus, n., spink.
pompom, n., tapitoorie.
pond, stagnant, n., stank.
ponderous, adj., wechty; unhanty, unweildy.
pool, n. waterhole; weil, deep.
pop-gun, n., billet gun.
poppy, n., sodger; thunnercup.
porous, adj., fozy.
porpoise, n., pellock.
porridge, n., poshie; drummock.
portfolio, n., blad.
portly, adj., gaucy.
portmanteau, n., portmanty.
pose, v., play-act.
poser, n., fizzer.
possession, n., aucht; graith.
poster, n., placad; placket.
postulate, v., ettle; tak.
potato, n., chat, small: seed potato, n., set; potato soup, n., tattie soup/ broth/bree: mechanical potato digger, n., grubber.
poultry, n., poutry.
powerless, adj., mauchtless.
practised, adj., skeily.
praise, v., crack up.
prate, v., yabble; yatter.
precipitous, adj., scaury.
precise, adj., preceese.
predicament, n., firrie.
predilection, n., prefairance.
preliminary, adj., forerinnin.
premeditation, without, adv., aff-luif.
premier, adj., heich.
prepare, v., dicht.
prepossessing, adj., winsome; settin.
presently, adv., belyve.
preserved, well, adj., weill-hained.

president, n., preses.
presumptuous, adj., upsettin.
pretentious, adj., fantoosh.
prim, adj., mim.
primula auricula, n., dusty miller.
prior, adj., umquhile.
privation, n., scant; want.
proclaim v. cry.
procreate, v., get.
prodding, keep, v., powter.
prodigal, adj., wastrife: prodigality, n., wastrie.
profit, n., rug, under-earned: profits, n., winnins.
progenitor, n., forebear: progeny, n., gets.
prognosticate, v., weird.
progress, n., waygate.
proletariat, n., hummelcorn.
promontory, n., ness; strone.
promulgate, n., scry.
prone, prostrate, adj., aval.
property, movable, n., gaun gear.
prophecy, n., weird: prophetic vision, n., saicont sicht.
propose to, a woman, v., seek.
prospect, view, n., vizzy.
prosperity, n., speed.
protuberance, n., knag; knurl.
proviso, n., percunnance.
provocation, n., provoke.
prowl about, v., smook; smool: prowler, n., skiver.
proximity, n., near-haunness.
pshaw, interj., tyach.
ptarmigan, n., tarmagan.
pubic bone, n., shear-bane.
pucker, n., bink.
puerile, adj., laddie-like.
puff, v., n., pluff; waff.
puffin, n., tammie-norrie; bass cock.
pull, v., n., rive; rug; yank, with a jerk.
pullover, n., mawsie.
pump, cold-water, n., wal.
punt boat, v., stang: punting pole, n., stang.
puny creature, n., wallydraigle: puny person, n., drochle.
purl, v., gurl: purling sound, n., gurl.
purloin, v., skech; smool.
purport, n., rinnin.
purse the mouth, v., crim the mou.
purulent, adj., attery.
pus, n., humour.

139

"push", n., waygate.
puzzle, v., bamboozle; wauchle.
pyre, n., balefire.

Quack, v., quaick.
quaint, adj., auld-farrant.
quantity, n., thrang.
quarter-day, n., term.
quartz, lump of, n., wally-stane.
quaver in music, n., quiver.
queasy, adj., wammlie.
query, v., speir.
quicklime, n., shells.
quicks, couch-grass, n., quickens.
quiet, interj., wheesht.
quietus, n., settlin.
quilt, v., twilt.
quiver, v., thirl.

Rabid, adj., rampin-mad; wud.
radiance, n., lowe.
ragamuffin, n., raggy-duds.
rage, mad with, adj., wud.
ragged, adj., raggit.
rail, fence, n., spaur.
rail, v., flyte; bairge.
railway pointsman, n., sneckshifter.
rain, downpour of, n., plump: **rainy**,
   adj., saft: **rainbow, incomplete**, n.,
   watergaw.
rally, v., gether anesel.
ram, castrated, n., wedder.
rampage, v., gilravage.
rank, of low, adj., little.
rankle, v., fash; fyke; vex.
rapscallion, n., skellum; rinagate.
rascal, n., limmer; rinagate.
rather, somewhat, adv., a bit; a wee.
raucous, adj., roupit; ruch.
ravish, herry.
rawhide, n., tug.
razor, n., rawzer.
rearing, n., upbringin.
rebuff, v., n., snib.
recalcitrant, adj., dour; thrawn.
**receive/reception of stolen goods for
   resale**, v., n., reset.
receipt, n., quittance.
reception, poor, n., hungry welcome.
recipe book, n., direction book.
reciprocity, n., giff-gaff.
reconsider, v., forthink.
rectify, v., mend; straight.
rectum, sparl.

red currant, n., rizzer.
redress, v., n., remeid.
reeds, n., bennels.
refractory, adj., dour; thrawn.
refulgent, adj., skyrie.
refurnish, v., replenish.
refuse, n., scran: **refuse collector**, n.,
   fulyie man; scaffie.
regard, n., respeck.
rehabilitate, v., repone.
reinstate, v., repone.
reject, v., ort: **rejects**, n., outwales.
reliable, adj., sponsible.
reliance, n., lippenance.
relic, n., relict.
religion, n., releegion.
reluctant, adj., sweir.
remainder, n., owreshot.
remarkable, adj., awfu.
remiss, adj., untentie.
remote, adj., out-o-the-wey.
remove quickly, v., wheich (guttural).
rend, v., teir.
rendezvous with, v., tryst wi.
reopen after holidays, n., tak up.
repair roughly, v., slap up.
repast, n., mail.
repeat monotonously, v., ryme on.
repellent, adj., fousome; scunnersome.
reprehend, v., faut; yoke on.
reproach, v., faut; flyte; cast up; n.,
   upcast.
reprove, v., yoke on.
repulsive, adj., fousome; unloesome.
request, v., n., requeest.
requisite, adj., necessar: **requisites**,
   n., necessars.
requital, n., requitance.
resident, n., residenter.
residue, n., lave.
resonance, lacking, adj., wairsh.
responsible, adj., sponsible: **respons-
   ibility for mistake**, n., wyte.
restless, adj., stourie; wanrestfu.
restive, adj., skeich.
restore to office, v., repone.
resuscitate, v., keckle up; spunk up.
retch, v., spue; reetch.
retinue, n., menyie.
retract, v., resile; hen.
room, sitting, n., ben room.
rope, n., tow.
rosary, n., bead.
rosette, n., bab.

rote, n., rat-rhyme.
roughcast, v., harl; sneckharl.
rounders, the game, n., bazies.
round of drinks, n., service.
row of houses, n., raw.
row, noise, n., stishie.
rowdy, adj., ruch.
rubbish, n., rubbage.
rump, n., curpin: **rump-bone**, n., rumple-bane.
runaway, n., rinawa.
runnel, n., burnie.
rupture, hernia, n., rimburst.
rush, n., rash: **rushy**, adj., sprettie.
rutty, adj., chacky.

Sacred, adj., halie; sanctly.
sad, adj., waesome; sairie.
saddle-girth, n., wame-gird.
sag, v., seg.
sage, adj., auld-farrant; lang-heidit.
said, v., quo.
sake, n., cause.
salacious, adj., randy; ree.
saline, adj., sauty.
sallow, willow, n., sauch.
salmon-curing shed, n., corf-hous.
salutary, adj., halesome.
sanction, permission, n., freedom.
sandstone, n., briestane: **sand shoes**, n., sannies.
sapwood, n., sapspail.
sarcastic, adj., tairdie.
sardonic, adj., seirie; sneisty.
sate, v., staw; stow.
saturate, v., sab; sapple.
saucy, adj., sneisty.
sausages strung together, n., slingers.
savings club, n., manawdge.
saw's width in cutting wood, n., carf.
scabbard, n., scabbert.
scabbed, adj., scaud.
scallop, n., scolp.
scamp, n., skemp; rinagate.
scamper, v., skelter.
scarlet fever, n., rush fever.
schism, n., aff-brak.
schooling, n., schuil-leir.
scorch, v., scaud.
scotch, frustrate, v., thraw.
scoundrel, n., scouneril.
scour, v., reenge.
scraggy, adj., poukit; shargie.
scramble, v., scrauchle.

scratch, v., n., scart; scrat.
scrawny, adj., scranky.
scream, v., scronach; skelloch; squeck.
scrofula, n., cruels.
scrotum, n., courage-bag.
scrounge, v., scran; skech; skive: **scrounger**, n., skiver.
scruffy, adj., scruiffy.
scurf, n., luce.
scuttle, v., skelter.
scythe shaft, n., sned.
sea, choppy, n., jabble.
seaweed, n., tangle; wrack.
sea inlet, n., wick.
search, v., ripe.
secluded, adj., out-o-the-wey.
sedate, adj., sad.
seed potato, n., set: **thin out seedlings**, v., single.
seep, v., sowp.
seesaw, v., showd.
self, by himself/herself, adv., his/her lane.
semi-detached house, n., half-hous.
seminary, n., seminar.
senile, adj., superannuate.
sentimentally, act, v., slorach.
separate, v., shed.
serenade, v., wake.
series, n., tring; strand; stroud.
sermon, n., preachin.
serried, adj., haffet-close.
servant, female, n., servin-lass.
serve, v., ser.
serviette, n., servit.
set of like objects, n., pair.
setback, n., backjar; backset.
settlement, n., reddance.
severe, adj., snell, of weather.
sexual intercourse, n., tail-toddle: **sexual desire**, n., yeuk: **sexually excited**, adj., yeuky.
sewage drain, n., lunkie-hole.
shabby, adj., scuffed.
shackles, n., shangies.
shake, v., wag; joogle.
shallow, adj., shaul.
shanty, n., cruive.
sheath, n., whittle-case, for knife.
sheep droppings, n., purls; trottles.
sheepish, adj., blate; bauch.
sheldrake, n., sly-goose.
shell peas, v., sheil.
shelter, v., n., scug.

141

Shetland pony, n., sheltie.
shiftless, adj., haunless; thowless.
shilly-shally, v., hum and hae.
shindy, n., sang; stramash.
shine brightly, v., beik.
shoal, shallow, n., shaul.
shoddy, adj., waff.
shoes, fit with, v., shod.
shooting star, n., shot staur.
shore, prop, n., stoup.
short-sighted person, n., stymie.
shoulder-blade, n., spaul-bane.
shoulder steak, n., foresey.
shower, n., scour; skiffle, slight; skite,
    short heavy.
shreds, n., deugs.
shrewdness, n., gumption.
shrewish, adj., thrawn-gabbit.
shrill, adj., skirly.
shrimp, n., sandclapper.
shrivelled, adj., shirpit.
shrunken, adj., wizzent.
shuffle, v., scliff.
shy, adj., strange; willyart.
sickness, n., trouble.
side-saddle, adv., sidelegs.
side-whiskers, n., side-lichts.
sieve, n., ree.
silence, interj., wheesht.
simple-hearted, adj., aefauld.
singular, adj., unco.
sinuous, adj., wimplin.
sip, n., sowp.
sitting-room, n., spence.
site, n., bit; stance.
sketch, outline, n., scantling.
skid, v., slidder.
skimmed milk, n., reamed milk.
skin eruption, n., hives.
skirting-board, n., skiftin-board.
skittish, adj., skeerie.
skua, Arctic, n., allan-hawk.
slab, thick slice, n., whang.
slander, v., miscaa.
slanting stroke, n., skite.
slap, v., n., yerk.
slat, n., spaur.
slaver, v., slabber; slorach.
sleazy, adj., clarty; slaistery.
sleeping cap, n., coorag.
sleeves, roll up, v., kilt.
slender, adj., spirlie.
slime, n., goor: slimy, adj., slairgie;
    slochy.

slink, v., smook; smool.
slippery, adj., slidy; slippy.
slipshod, adj., clarty; hashy.
slit, v., slyte.
slither, v., slidder; skite.
slobber, v., slabber; sloch.
sloppy, adj., slochy: sloppy mess, n.,
    slaister; slitter: slop basin, n.,
    slap-bowl.
slouch, v., n., slotch.
slough, n., flow; moss; slunk.
slovenly, adj., hudderie; sloggerie.
sludge, n., slink.
slush, n. slabber.
smack the bottom, v. skelp the bum,
small in build, adj., smaa-boukit: very
    small person, n., dot.
smallpox, n., pock.
smart, adj., gleg; spree: smarten up,
    v., trig up.
smart, v., soo; stang; stoun.
smear, v., n., slairie.
smirch, v., fyle.
smithy, n., smiddie.
smoked, of fish, adj., reistit.
smolt, n., smowt.
smooth-tongued, adj., slee-gabbit:
    smooth-running, adj., weill-gaun.
smoulder, v., smeuchter.
snack, n., by-bite; pick-an-dab.
snag, n., whaup-i-the-raip.
snail shell, n., buckie.
snapdragon, n., grannie mutch.
snatch, v., sneck.
sneak, n., snool.
snigger, v., n., snicker.
snook, n., dumb-sweir.
snore, v., sneer.
snort, v., n., sneer; snocher.
snot, n., snotter.
snow, half-melted, n., grue; blindrift,
    drifting; hogreik, driving: snowdrift,
    n., snaw-wreath: snowdrop, n., snaw-
    drap.
snuff-box, n., snuff-horn.
snub, n., snib.
snuffle, v., snocher.
soaked, adj., steepit: soaking-wet, adj.,
    seipin-wat.
sobriquet, n., by-name; tae-name.
social gathering, n., ploy; shine.
social standing, person of, n., knab.
socket, n., sock.
soil, v., tash.

soiree, n., suree; swarry.
sojourn, v., byde; dwal; stey.
soldier, n., sodger.
solicitor, n., agent; writer.
solid, adj., sad.
somnolent, adj., sleepery.
sopping, adj., seipin-wat; sploungin.
soporific, adj., sleepery.
sops, n., saps.
sorely, adv., sair.
sorrowful, adj., sairy; waesome: doomed to sorrow, adj., wae-weirdit.
sour look, n., glower; glunch.
southernwood, n., aippleringie.
souvenir, n., memorandum.
sow, n., grumphie; gilt, young.
Spanish, adj., Spainyie.
spanking, n., skelpit leatherin.
sparrow, n., speug; sprug.
spatter, v., spairge; spark.
spatula, n., spattle; spurtle.
spawn, n., melt.
species, n., speshie.
specific, adj., preceese.
speed, v., skelp; spank: at full speed, adv., full slap.
spell of work, n., yokin.
spells, book of, n., witch-book.
spendthrift, adj., wasterfu; wasterife.
sphagnum, n., white moss.
spill, v., skiddle.
spill for lighting, n., spail.
spin, v., sweil; trintle.
spine, n., rigbane.
spiraea, n., meadow queen.
spire, point of, n., pricket.
spiral staircase, n., turnpike stair: spiral staircase step, n., wheel step.
spiritless, adj., tapeless; waff.
splash, v., jaw; splairge: splash about, v., swatter.
splay-footed, adj., scash/splash-fittit.
splint, n., scob.
splinters, n., shivers.
split, v., speld.
splotch, v., fyle; sclatch.
spoil, n., scaff; spulyie.
spoke of wheel, n., spaik.
spongy, adj., fozie; soukin.
spoonful, n., sowp.
sprat, n., spirlin.
spree, n., splore; tare.
sprightly, adj., yauld.
spring onion, n., sybie.

sprinkling, n., strinklin.
sprint, v., sprent.
sprite, n., bogle; spreit.
spry, adj., swank.
spurt, v., spout.
spy-hole, n., vizzy-hole.
squabble, n., stramash.
squadron, n., squad; squadrone.
squally, adj., scourie.
squat, adj., stumpy; bilshy: squat person, n., stumpie.
squawk, v., n., squeck.
squeak, v., n., squeck.
squib, n., squeeb.
squint-eyed, adj., skellie.
stack, v., big, hay.
stagger, v., wauchle.
stake in marbles, n., stunk.
stammer, v., habber; stut.
stamp on, v., stramp.
staple, adj., heich.
stare, v., gowp.
starlight, n., staursheen.
stark mad, adj., rid-wud: stark naked, adj., mither-nakit.
start, outset, n., affset.
start upon, v., yoke/get yokit tae.
station-master, n., station agent.
staunch, adj., stench.
steak, shoulder, n., foresey.
steal, v., sneck.
steeple, n., toupick.
steer, v., airt.
stellar, adj., starny.
stem of tobacco pipe, n., stapple.
stepping-stones, n., stanner-stanes.
stethoscope, n., lughorn.
stick, beat with, v., timmer.
stickleback, n., bairdie.
stigmatise, v., douncry; tash.
stile, n., stiggy.
stingy, adj., moulie; nippit.
stint of work, n., yokin.
stocking, footless, n., hogger: stocking foot over shoes to prevent slipping, n., moggan.
stocky, adj., stoushie; stowfie.
stolid, adj., dowf.
stomach, n., bag: stomach-ache, n., sair belly.
stone, crush, v., breese: crushed stones, n., breese.
stoppage of work in factory, n., steg.
stormy, adj., gurly.

story, short, n., threne.
stow, v., pit by.
straddle, v., striddle.
straight, off the, adv., agee (ajee).
strainer, n., sye; syle; sythe.
strand of rope, n., ply.
stray, adj., waff; n., gangrel; waffie.
streaked, white-streaked, adj., bawsent.
stream that dries up in summer, n., syke.
street ballad, n., strowd: street arab, n., gutter-bairn.
strength, n., strenth.
stretch, v., n., streik; rack.
strew, v., skail; strinkle.
strike, v., yerk, with hand; slash, with wet cloth.
stroke, blow, n., bat: paralytic stroke, n., shock.
strong-tasted, adj., ramsh.
structure, n., work.
struggle, n., chauve; pauchle.
strumpet, n., duntie.
stubborn, adj., stickin.
stuffing, n., stappin.
stumble, n., v., snapper; wauchle.
stump, n., scrog; stock; stug.
stunted, adj., wanthriven: stunted creature, n., scrog.
stupefied, adj., ramfoozled.
stupid person, n., gowk; gomeril; sumph.
sturdy, adj., stoushie.
stutter, v., habber; stut.
subjoin, v., eik to.
sub-lease, v., sub-tack.
subside in mud, v., lair.
subsistence, n., leevin.
subterfuge, n., prattick.
sub-title, n., paratitle.
subway, n., weem.
suckle, v., souk.
suggest, v., mint; moot.
suit, v., set.
suitcase, n., walise.
sulk, v., tak the sturdies.
sullen, adj., thrawn: look sullen, v., glunch; glower.
sully, v., fyle; tash; brouk.
summary, n., adj., summar.
sundial gnomon, n., dial-cock.
sunken, adj., howe.
superabundance, n., galore.
superfluous, adj., orra.
superimpose, v., onlay.

supernumerary, adj., orra.
superscribe, v., superscrive.
supine, passive, adj., dowf.
supplant, v., pit somebody's ee out.
support, v., uphaud.
suppurate, v., beil.
supremacy, n., owrance.
surety, stand surety for, v., staun guid for.
surfeited, adj., stappit.
surplice, n., sark.
sustain, keep up, v., keep.
swaddle, v., sweel.
sward, n., swaird.
sweet, large chewy, n., gob-stopper/sticker: sweetshop, n., sweetie-shop: sweet-bag, n., sweetie-bag.
sweetheart, n., quean/quine.
swiftly, move, v., wheich; raik.
swig, n., waucht; sowp.
swill, v., slorp.
swindle, v., n., pauchle.
swing, v., n., showd.
switch, cane, v., wand.
swollen, adj., baggit.
swoon, v., swarf.
swop, v., swap.
symmetrical, adj., equal-aqual.
syringe, n., scooter.

Table-cloth, n., table-clout.
table jelly, n., trummlin/chitterin Tam.
tadpole, n., podlie; powheid.
talisman, n., lucky-stane.
talk idly, v., jauner: talk incessantly, v., yatter.
tambourine, n., wecht.
tang, prong, n., taing.
tangled, adj., tousy.
tanned, adj., barkent: tannery, n., tanyaird.
tantalise, v., grype.
tap, water-tap, n., stroup.
tape, n., knittin; trappin.
tarry, v., tarrow.
tart in speech, adj., birkie.
taste/smell, having bad, adj., wauch: strong-tasted, adj., wild.
tatters, n., duds; trollops.
tattle, v., n., clash; clatter.
taunt, cast up, v., upcast.
tea, high, n., tea-an-tilt: teapot, n., drawpot: tea urn, n., tea kitchen: tea party, n., tea skiddle.

144

tear-stained, adj., begrutten.
telescope, n., prospect-gless.
temerity, n., racklessness.
temper, bad/good, n., ill/guid tuin.
tender, ship's, n., yagger.
termagant, n., randy; tairge.
tern, n., pictarnie; sheartail.
terrier, n., tarrie.
test piece, n., sey-piece.
testy, adj., tuithy.
textile factory, n., claith-mill.
theatrical, adj., play-actin.
theodolite, n., oglet.
thick, of porridge/soup, adj., lithy:
    thickset, adj., stumpie: thickset
    person, n., stumpie.
thievery, n., theftdom.
thighs, bifurcation of, n., cleavin; clift.
thin, adj., poukit: thin-skinned, adj.,
    saft-skinned: very thin person, n.,
    skinnymalink: thin seedlings, v.,
    single.
thong, n., thang.
thorax, n., kist.
thrashing, get a, v., get laldie.
threadbare, adj., scuffed.
three-fold, adj., adv., thrie-fauld.
threshold, n., threshal.
thrift, the flower, n., sea-daisy.
thriving, adj., growthie; wally.
throb, v., stoun; soo: throbbing pain,
    n., sooin.
thronged, adj., thrang.
thrash, the ailment, n., sproo.
thud, interj., wham.
thump, v., n., wap.
thwart, v., thort.
tidings, n., word.
tidy, adj., tosh; spree.
tier, n., lachter.
tiff, n., cast-out; argie-bargie.
tiger, n., teeger.
timely, adj., timeous.
timorous, adj., timorsome.
tinder, n., tunder; tindle.
tingle, v., soo.
tinsel, adj., roarie.
tiny, adj., little wee.
tipple, v., taste; tout.
titillate, v., kittle.
tittle-tattle, v., n., clatter.
toady, n., fuit-licker; souk.
tobacco, thick black, n., bogie-rowe.
to-do, n., adae; sang; steir.

toil, v., warsle.
tolerable, adj., tholeable.
tone-deaf, adj., timmer.
tongue of shoe, n., bur.
toothache, n., tuithache; sair teeth.
toper, n., drouth; bender.
torpid, adj., dowf; tapetless.
torque, n., tork.
torrents, descend in, v., teem.
toss to and fro, v., rowe; whummle.
total, n., soum.
totter, v., teeter; fitter: tottery, adj.,
    shooglie.
tough, n., randie.
towel, hand, n., servat.
tower, n., broch, prehistoric; tourock,
    little.
town native, n., gutterbluid.
toy windmill, n., whurlie-birlie.
tractable, adj., tawie.
tramp, v., trail; n., vaig; waffie.
trample, v., stramp.
tranquillity, n., lown; saucht.
transfer, picture, n., dabbity.
transform, v., transmogrify.
transmute, v., transmogrify; transmue.
travel-stained, adj., traikit.
tread, v., tramp.
tremble, v., quack.
tremolo, adj., twirliwa.
tremulous motion, n., reemle.
trenchant, adj., gleg.
trepidation, n., fash; dreidour.
trestle, n., tress.
trick, n., shavie; swick.
trickle, v., n., trinkle.
trifle, v., didder: trifling, adj., skittery.
trigger, n., tricker.
trio, n., threesome.
triple, n., adj., threeple: triplets, n.,
    threeplets.
trouble, v., n., bather.
trousers waist-band, n., breik-band.
truant, play, v., plunk/troon the schuil.
truck, dealings, n., troke; niffer.
trudge, v., n., trail.
trumpery, n., trasherie.
trundle, v., trintle; whurl.
trustworthy, adj., leal; lippenable.
truth, n., sooth; suith.
tuck, n., touk.
tuft, n., tummock; taut, matted.
tug, v., n., yerk.
tumour, n., clunkart.

tuneless, adj., timmer.
turbid, adj., drumly; grumlie.
turbot, n., rawn.
turmoil, n., stour.
turn, n., birl; wimple, in road.
turnstile, n., tirless yett.
tussock, n., tait; tift; toog.
twang, n., plunk.
tweed mill, n., oo-mill.
twice, adv., twyst.
twine, length of, n., tow.
twirl, v., pirl; tirl.
twist, v., skew.
twitch, v., yerk.
two or three, adj., twa-thrie.

Umbilical cord, n., naelstring.
unaccustomed, adj., out o the wey o.
unaffected, adj., hamely.
unambitious, be, v., flee laich.
unattractive, adj., unluesome.
unbelievable, adj., undeemis.
unburied, adj., unhousened.
unchristian, adj., unkirsen.
uncomely, adj., ill-farrant.
uncommunicative, adj., inbigget.
uncompromising, adj., throu-gaun.
uncultivated/uncultured, adj., ruch.
unctuous, adj., slee; slidderie.
undamaged, adj., hale.
undecided, adj., waffly.
undernourished, adj., ill-thriven.
undersized, adj., scrimpit.
undervest, n., baiklet.
uodiluted, adj., untaen-doun.
undulate, v., swaw.
unearth, v., howk: unearthly, adj.,
    uncanny.
uneasiness, n., unease; wanrest.
unemployed, adj., lowss.
unfair, adj., iniquous.
unfamiliar with, adj., unacquant wi.
unfavourable, adj., thrawart.
unfit, adj., ill able: unfit for, adj.,
    unable for.
ungenerous, adj., scrimp; ill-hertit.
unhappy, adj., unseely; forfairn.
unheeding, adj., untentin.
unlatched, adj., aff the sneck.
unlike, adj., unalike.
unlucky, adj., uncanny.
unmannerly, adj., menseless.
unmelodious/unmusical, adj., timmer.
unobservant, adj., tentless.

unnoticed, adj., unbekent.
unoccupied, adj., tuim.
unpaid, adj., backlyin.
unpalatable, adj., fousome: make un-
    palatable, v., pizzen.
unpleasant, adj., scunnersome.
unpremeditated, adj., affhaun; aff-luif.
unprepossessing, adj., ill-farrant.
unreliable, adj., wanchancy.
unrestrained, adj., bandless.
unsalted, of butter, adj., sweet.
unscathed, adj., hale.
unseasonable, adj., untimeous.
unsound, adj., fauty.
unstable, adj., unsiccar; skeerie.
upbraid, v., bairge.
uproar, n., stishie; strooshie.
upshot, n., owrecome; upcome.
urge, have a strong, v., yeuk; urgency,
    n., clamancy.
usher, v., allemand.
usual, adj., yaisial.
utilise, v., yaise.
uvula, n., clap o the hause.

Vacant gaze, n., gype: gaze vacantly,
    v., gype.
vacillate, v., waffle: vacillating person,
    n., waffler.
vagrant, n., vaig; randy, ruffianly.
vain, adj., vaunty; vogie.
valance of bed, n., bed-pand.
valise, n., pockmantie; walise.
valour, n., gurr; manheid.
vanity, n., pridefuness.
variation in music, n., variorum.
various, adj., sindry.
vegetable juice, n., wuss.
velocity, n., raik; spinner.
verbiage, n., rift.
verruca, n., warrock.
versatile, adj., fendie.
vertigo, n., mirligoes.
very, adv., gey.
vestibule, n., trance.
vex, v., fyke.
vicious, adj., veecious.
victuals, n., vievers.
vigorous, adj., stuffy; yauld.
vilify, v., cry names; douncry.
virago, n., bessie.
viscera, n., harigals.
viscous, adj., claggy; slairgie.
vision, n., veesion.

vista, n., swype; vizzy.
vitiate, v., fulyie; thraw.
vitreous, adj., glazie.
vituperate, v., caa ill names; cry names.
vixen, virago, n., tairge.
vociferate, v., rowt; yelloch.
volubly, talk, v., yabble.
voraciously, eat, v., lay into; worry.
vote, v., n., voice.

Wadding, n., wad.
waddle, v., wauchle.
waft, v., souch.
wag, v., waff.
waggle, v., weegle.
wainscot, v., box: wainscotting, n., boxin.
wait at table, v., wait the table.
waken, v., wauken.
walk with shuffle, v., sclaff: walk heavily, v., lab: walking stick, n., staff; cummock.
wallow, v., walter.
wand, n., widdie.
wander, v., raik; vaig.
want, v., wiss: be in want, v., want.
warrant, v., n., warrand.
wart, n., warroch.
waste material, n., redd: waste away, v., wally: waste of time, n., affpit: wastrel, n., dae-nae-guid; waff.
water channel, n., watergate: waterhen, n., stankie.
waver, v., waffle.
wayward, adj., wull.
weapon, n., wappen.
wearisome, adj., tedisome.
weathercock, n., aircock.
web-footed, adj., wab-fuitit.
wedlock, n., wadlock.
weighty, adj., wechty.
well, very, adv., bravely: well-disposed, adj., weill-willie: well-educated, adj., weill-leared: well-off, adj., bien: well-spent, adj., weill-wared: as well, adv., an aa.
wheel, v., whurl; n., whurlie: wheelbarrow shaft, n., tram.
whim, n., megrim.
whimper, v., wheenge.
whine, v., peenge; yirm.
whir, v., n., whurr.
whirl, v., n., sweil; whummle.

whisky still, n., stell.
whisper, v., n., toot-moot.
whitewash, chalk used to, n., whitenin.
whizz, v., whidder.
whorl, n., thorl.
why not, interr. adv., what for no.
wicked, adj., illdeedie.
wickerwork basket, n., skep.
widgeon, n., whistlin deuk.
wig, n., gizz.
wight, n., wicht.
wild, adj., hallickit.
willow branch, n., sauch wan: willow cane, n., scob; widdie: willowy, adj., sauchen.
windlass, n., winnace.
window, dormer, n., stormont: window shutter, n., windae brod.
windpipe, n., hause-pipe; thrapple.
wise beyond one's years, adj., auldfarrant.
wishy-washy, adj., fushionless; wairsh.
wit, n., ingyne: witty, adj., gash; gleg.
wobbly, adj., cogglie; shooglie.
woebegone, adj., waebegane.
woman, n., frow, buxom; caileach, old; quine, young.
wonder, full of, adj., wondersome.
wont, habit, n., cast; gate.
wooden, adj., timmer: woody, adj., wuidie.
word, my, interj., my sang.
workhouse, n., puirshous: workshy, adj., sweirt.
worn, adj., scuffed.
worst, v., waur.
worst, adj., warst.
worthless, adj., wanworth.
worthwhile, adj., weill-wared.
wrap in clothes, v., sweel.
wriggle, v., wimple.
wring, v., thraw.
writing pad, n., scroll.
wrong, go, v., gang agley: wrongful, adj., wrangous.

Yap, v., yowl; yamph.
yellow-hammer, n., yorlin.
yes, adv., u-huh.
yokel, n., yochel.
youth, n., younker: youthful, adj., youngsome: state of youth, n., youth-heid.

Scots-English Vocabulary

Supplementary list begins on page 224.

---

* Words marked with an asterisk also appear in the alphabetical list of key words in the section on Scots Idiom (pages 19-28).

*Aa, n., adj., adv., all: **aabody**, pron., everybody: **aa-roads**, adv., everywhere: **aathegither**, adv., altogether: **aathing**, pron., everything.

abbacee, n., the alphabet.

abbreviate, n., abstract; summary.

abeich, adv., aloof; at a distance.

*able, adj., astute; clever.

ableize, adv., ablaze.

ablow, adv., prep., below; under.

abreid, adv., abroad; apart.

abreist, adv., abreast.

abuise, v., abuse.

abune, adv., prep., above; over.

accresce, v., accrue.

ach, interj., expressing impatience.

acherspyre, v., germinate; n., germination; sprout.

ack, v., n., act.

ackwart, adj., awkward.

acquant/acquent, v., acquaint; adj., acquainted.

adae, n., difficulty; fuss; ceremony.

advent, n., bank interest.

advocate, n., barrister.

ae/yae, adj., adv., one: **aefauld**, adj., artless; frank: **aesome**, adj., sole.

*aff, adv., off; prep., from: **affbrak**, n., schism: **affcome**, n., result; witty remark: **affgang/gate**, n., outlet for water/goods: **aff-haun**, adj., brusque; extempore; adv., immediately: **aff-lat**, n., outlet for water; display: **aff-luif**, adv., extempore: **aff-pit**, v., postpone; n., excuse: **aff-pittin**, adj., procrastinatory: **aff-set**, n., beginning; apology; stoppage: **aff-souk**, n., tide's ebb: **affstaunin**, adj., aloof: **aff-tak**, n., deduction; mocking remark: **aff-takkin**, adj., sarcastic.

affront, v., n., reproach; disgrace.

afore, adv., prep., conj., before: **afore-fit**, adv., promiscuously: **aforesyne**, adv., previously.

aft/aften, adv., often.

afuit, adv., afoot.

agate, adv., abroad; on the road.

agee (ajee), adv., askew; ajar.

agin, prep., against.

*aglee/agley, adv., askew; wrong; off the straight road.

agrun, adv., aground.

aheid, adv., ahead.

*ahin/ahint, adv., prep., behind: **ahin-haun**, adj., late.

aiblins, adv., perhaps.

aicher, n., ear of corn: **aichert**, adj., eared.

aicht/aucht, n., adj., eight: **aichty**, n., adj., eighty.

aidle, v., addle; n., ditchwater; adj., infertile, of eggs: **aidle-dub**, n., cesspool.

aik, n., oak: **aiknit**, n., acorn.

aiker, n., ripple caused by darting fish.

ain, adj., own; private; personal.

aince/ance/yince, adv., once.

aipple, n., apple: **aippleringie**, n., southernwood.

air, adj., adv., early: **air/ere-yestreen**, n., the night before last.

airm, n., arm.

airn, v., n., adj., iron: **airns**, n., horse shoes; shackles.

airt, v., direct; take the road to; instigate; n., direction; tack: **airt out**, v., detect: **airter**, n., instigator.

airt, n., art: **airty**, adj., accomplished: **airtist**, n., artist.

aise, n., ashes: **aise-midden**, n., ashpit.

aish, n., ash tree.

aislerwark, n., masonry.

aith, n., oath.

aither, pron., adj., conj., either.

aits, n., oats: **ait-bannock**, n., oatcake.

aiver, n., cart-horse.

aiverie, adj., desirous; fervent.

aix, n., axe.

aixtree, n., axle.

aizle, n., red-hot ash; spark.

148

alaft, adv., aloft.

alane, adj., alone: **lae/let alane**, v., leave undisturbed.

alang, adv., prep., along.

alicreish, n., licorice.

aller, n., alder tree.

allerish, adj., bleak, of weather; taciturn.

almichty, adj., almighty.

alowe, adv., afire.

alse, adv., also.

amang, prep., among.

amends, n., vengeance.

amna, v., am not.

__*an__, conj., and; if.

ane, pron., adj., one; n., a certain person.

aneath, adv., prep., below; under.

anent, prep., alongside; concerning.

anerly, adj., only; adv., only; solely.

anger ("ng" as in "sing"), n., vexation: **angersome**, adj., annoying.

anither, pron., adj., another.

anter/aunter, v., adventure: **aunterous**, adj., adventurous.

antrin, adj., chance; haphazard; rare.

apairt, adv., apart.

apen, v., adj., open.

apoplectick, n., apoplexy.

appearinly, adv., apparently.

approbate, v., approve; sanction.

Aprile, n., April.

argie, v., argue: **argie-bargie**, v., n., dispute.

ark, n., corn bin.

arles, n., payment, of arle-penny, on engagement of services; foretaste.

arnit, n., ground-nut.

arra, n., arrow.

arselins/erselins, adv., aback; backwards.

ashet, n., large meat-plate.

ashypet, n., menial servant.

aside, prep., beside.

ask, n., lizard.

asklent, adv., askance; askew.

aspar, adv., astride.

assoilyie, v., clear; discharge.

astarn, adv., astern.

asteir, adv., astir.

asthmaticks, n., asthma.

atemeat, n., parasite.

athort, adv., prep., across.

athout, prep., without.

athraw, adv., askew.

atowre, adv., prep., above; over; across.

atter, n., poison; pus: **attery**, adj., bitter; spiteful.

atween, prep., between: **atweenwhiles**, adv., in the interval.

atweill, adv., assuredly; indeed.

auchimuty, adj., trivial.

aucht, v., own; n., ownership; property.

aucht, v., owe: **auchtin**, adj., owing; due.

aucht, pron., aught.

auk, n., guillemot.

auld, adj., old: **auld auntie/uncle**, n., great-aunt/uncle: **auld-fangle**, adj., archaic: **auld-farrant**, adj., wise beyond one's years: **aulder**, senior: **aulders**, n., seniors.

aumous, n., alms.

aumrie, n., cabinet; chest; cupboard; pantry.

auntie, n., aunt; strumpet.

auntient, adj., ancient.

ava, adv., at all.

avail, n., wherewithal; value.

aval, adj., prostrate, as of sheep.

awa, adv., away: **awa wi't**, adj., done for.

awe, v., possess: **awner**, n., owner.

awe, v., owe: **awn**, adj., owing; due.

aweband, n., tether rope for cattle; curb.

awfu, adj., disgraceful; adv., very: **awesome**, adj., awe-inspiring.

awpron, n., apron.

ay, adv., yes.

aye (as in "mine"), adv., always.

ayont, adv., prep., beyond.

Baa, n., ball: **baa-spiel**, n., football match.

baa, v., hush to sleep.

baa-siller, n., coins thrown to children at a wedding.

bab, v., bob.

bab, n., bow; knot; posy.

babbin, n., bobbin.

babby-clouts, n., child's napkin.

babidoozler, n., very showy object.

__*back__, v., address a letter; n., back premises; adj., late, of crops: **back-about**, adj., isolated: **backart**, adj., backward: **backies / backiewards/ backlins**, adv., backwards: **backbane**, n., backbone: **backdrawer**, n., recreant: **backgaun**, n., retrogression; adj., unprosperous: **backhaud**, n., obstacle: **back-haun**, adj., overdue: **back-het**, adj., twice heated: **backin**, n., address of a letter: **backjar**, n., setback: **backjaw**, n., impudence: **back-leuk**, n., chronicle; flash-back: **back-lyin**, adj., unpaid: **backset**, n., setback: **backspeir**, v., analyse; interrogate: **backswaw**, n., retreating wave: **backturn**, n., relapse: **back-yett**, n., private gate.

bad, adv., badly: **badly**, adj., ill; in bad health.

baff, v., beat; thud; n., blow; thud.

baffs, n., slippers.

baffy, adj., plump.

bag, v., bulge; swell; n., small sack: **baggie**, n., belly: **baggit**, adj., swollen; big with child: **baggage**, n., worthless thing.

bah, v., bleat.

baigle, n., obnoxious person.

baikie, n., ashbox; coal bucket; trough.

baiklet, n., undershirt.

bailie/beylie, n., magistrate, equivalent of alderman; farm steward.

baird/beird, n., beard: **bairdie**, n., stickleback.

bairge, v., abuse; upbraid; walk in stilted, pretentious manner.

bairn, v., make pregnant; n., child: **bairnlike**, adj., childish: **bairn-time**, n., childhood.

baiss, v., stitch loosely.

baith, pron., adj., conj., both.

bake, v., knead; n., biscuit: **bakeboard**, n., board for kneading dough on.

balefire, n., beacon fire.

ballant/ballat, n., ballad; song.

balloch, n., pass between hills.

ballocks, n., testicles.

ballop, n., flap in front of trousers.

baloo, v., sing a lullaby; n., lullaby.

bamboozle, v., amaze; confuse.

ban, v., swear.

band, n., pledge; moral bond: **band-less**, adj., morally unrestrained.

bane, n., bone: **bany**, adj., bony: **bane idle**, adj., thoroughly idle.

bane, n., hatred; malice.

banefire, n., bonfire.

bang, v., excel; overcomesu;rpass.

bang out, v., rush out: **bang up**, v., rise hastily.

bannet, n., bonnet: **bannet laird**, n., one who works his own farm.

bannock, n., oatcake.

bany-stickle, n., stickleback.

bap, n., baker's roll.

bard, n., minstrel; poet: **bardy**, adj., brash; impudent; uncivil.

bare-fuit, adj., barefoot: **bare nakit/ scuddie**, adj., quite naked.

barelies, adv., hardly; scarcely.

barken, v., coagulate.

barm, v., ferment; n., yeast: **barmy**, adj., foolish; giddy.

barr, n., big hill.

barra, n., barrow: **barra-stiel**, n., barrow shaft.

barras, n., tournament enclosure.

base, n., bass singer.

***bash**, v., beat; bruise; n., blow; bruise: **bash hat**, n., soft hat.

basnet, n., steel helmet.

bass, n., door mat.

bastert, n., bastard: **bastardrie**, n., illegitimacy.

bat, v., batten; grow fat.

bat, n., blow; stroke.

bather, v., annoy; tease; n., annoyance.

bats, n., colic.

batter, n., book-board; paste.

bauch, adj., blunt-edged; insipid; timid: **bauchness**, n., bashfulness.

bauchle, v., shuffle; n., worn-out shoe; old, feeble person.

baudrons, n., cat.

bauk, n., cross beam; joist; hen roost; weighing machine.

bauk, n., boundary mark; hollow between corn rigs.

baukie bird, n., bat.

bauld, adj., brave; energetic; impetuous.

baun, n., choir; musical band.

baur, v., n., bar: **baur out**, v., exclude.

baurley, n., barley: **baurley bree**, n., whisky.

***baurley**, n., breathing space; respite; truce.

bausy, adj., big and fat.

bawbee, n., halfpenny: **bawbees**, n., money.

bawd, n., hare.

bawm, n., balm.

bawsent, adj., brindled; white-streaked, of animal's face.

baxter, n., baker.

be, v., stand a drink: **be at,** v., urge: **be for,** v., be inclined to.

beadle, n., church officer; town bell-man.

beal, v., see beil.

bear, n., see bere.

bear, v., denote; purport.

beast, n., creature: **beasts,** n., farm animals.

beatle, v., beat; pound; strike: **beatlin,** n., beating; thrashing.

***beck,** v., bend; bow; curtsy; n., curtsy; deferential bow.

beddy, adj., interfering; rude.

bedesman, n., pauper.

bedfast, adj., bedridden.

bed-plyde, n., blanket.

bedral, n., gravedigger and church officer.

bedunder, v., besot.

bee, n., whim: **bee-yaird,** n., apiary.

beet, v., see beit.

beek, v., see beik.

beetle, v., see beatle: **beetle-heid,** n., tadpole.

beezer, n., very big/good person or thing.

befaa, v., betide.

beff, v., beat; thud; n., blow; thud.

begeck/begowk, v., betray; deceive; n., betrayal; deceit.

beglaumer, v., enchant; bewitch.

begottit, adj., infatuated.

begrutten, adj., stained with tears.

begunk, v., betray; deceive; n., betrayal; deceit.

behauden, adj., indebted; obliged.

beheft, n., ship's stern.

beik, v., bask.

beil, v., fester; n., festering sore: **beilin,** n., boil; pus; ulcer.

beinge, v., fawn.

beir, v., bear; carry.

beird, n., see baird.

beit, v., instigate; kindle; replenish; soothe.

bejant, n., first-year student at university.

beld, adj., bald.

belike, adv., maybe; probably.

bell-heid, n., belfry: **bell-hous,** n., church tower.

bellises, n., bellows.

belloch, v., n., bellow; low.

bellum, n., momentum; noise.

belly-flaucht, adv., flat on belly: **belly-rive,** n., feast: **bellythraw,** n., stomach-ache: **belly-timber,** n., food.

belt, v., flog.

beltin, n., clump of trees.

belyve, adv., presently; soon; by and by.

bemean, v., abase; humiliate.

ben, n., inner part of house; adv., prep., inside; within: **benmaist,** adj., farthest in: **benmaist bore,** n., innermost recess.

ben, n., mountain.

bend, n., drinking bout: **bender,** n., toper.

bennels, n., reeds.

bense, v., walk energetically.

***bent,** n., long, wiry grass: **white bent,** n., mat-grass.

bentset, adj., determined.

benweed, n., ragwort.

bere, n., hardy variety of barley.

berthy, adj., productive.

besides, prep., compared with.

bessie, n., impudent woman.

bestial, n., cattle.

best maid, n., bridesmaid.

betak, v., have recourse to.

bethankit, n., grace after meal.

***better,** adj., healed; recovered from illness.

beuk, n., see buik.

bey, n., bay.

beylie, n., see bailie.

bicker, n., beaker; drinking bowl; tankard.

bicker, v., flicker; gleam; fight with stones; n., lunge; fight.

***bid,** v., invite: **biddable,** adj., obedient: **biddin,** n., invitation.

bide, v., see byde.

bield, v., shelter; take shelter; n., shelter: **bieldy,** adj., sheltered.

bien, adj., affluent; cosy; in good condition: **bienness,** n., affluence.

big, v., build: **biggin,** n., building; house; cottage.

big, adj., arrogant; elated: **big-coat,** n., greatcoat: **biggen,** v., augment.

151

bike, n., see byke.
bile, v., see byle.
bill, n., bull.
billie, n., brother; companion; fellow.
bilsh, n., squat person: bilshy, adj.,
squat.
binch, n., bench.
bind, v., tether: bindwood, n., ivy.
bing, v., n., heap.
bink, n., bench; chest; shelf; hob on
grate.
bink, n., fold; pucker.
binna, prep., except; conj., unless.
bird, n., girl: birdie-cock, n., cockerel.
birk, n., birch: birken, adj., of birch.
birk, n., fervour: birk up, v., cheer up:
birkie, adj., alert; animated; n., alert
youth.
birl, v., rotate; cause to rotate; carouse;
dance; n., dance; whirl: birlin, n.,
carouse; carnival.
birn, n., burden.
birn, n., ground with stubbly heather
stalks: birny, adj., dried up; peevish.
birr, v., whir; n., whir; animation;
force.
birse, v., n., bruise.
birse, v., bristle; n., bristle; fit of bad
temper: birsie, adj., irascible.
birsk, n., cartilage.
birsle, v., broil; roast; toast.
birst, n., brunt; stress.
*bit, n., climax; place; situation:
bittie/bittock, n., a little bit; a short
time/distance: a bittie, adv., somewhat.
bitching, n., tomfoolery.
bite, n., food.
bizz, v., n., bustle; buzz; hiss; zoom.
bizzum, n., broomstick; loose woman;
mischief-making female.
blab, v., stain; n., blob; blot; bubble;
drop.
blabber, v., jabber; babble.
black, adj., downright; thorough;
overcast; adv., thoroughly: black-
avised, adj., dark-skinned: blackfuit,
n., lovers' intermediary: black-neb,
n., person working during strike:
blackstrap, n., molasses; treacle.
blade, v., defoliate; n., cabbage leaf.
blae, adj., blue-grey: blaeberry, n.,
bilberry: blaes, n., blue-grey clay.
blaff, n., bang; blast.

blagyaird, n., blackguard.
blainch, v., purify; whiten; become
unconscious.
blane, n., omission; scar; score.
blash, v., pour; drench; n., deluge;
torrent of words: blashy, adj., wet
and windy.
blast, v., boast.
blastie, n., contemptible person; dwarf.
blate, adj., diffident; timid: blateness,
n., bashfulness.
blathrie, n., trumpery.
blatter, v., pelt with stones; rattle; n.,
hailstorm; torrent of words.
blaud, v., batter; deface; defame; n.,
blow; downpour.
blaud, n., sample; selection of verses.
blaw, v., blow; boast; n., blast; boast;
respite: blaw-out, n., feast.
blaw, v., n., bloom; flourish.
blawort, n., bluebell; cornflower.
bleach, v., beat; strike; n., blow:
bleachin, n., drubbing.
bleck, v., make dirty; defame; n.,
negro; rascal; soot; adj., black.
bleert, adj., dim, of eyes; stained with
weeping.
bleize, v., n., blaze: bleize out, v.,
declaim.
blellum, n., silly, talkative person.
blether, v., babble; chatter; speak
long and foolishly; n., babbler;
gossip: blethers, n., chatter; nonsense: bletherskite, n., silly talker.
blether, n., bladder; blister; buoy.
blin, v., blind; adj., blind; dense, of
fog.
blink, v., evade; ignore; look at fondly;
wink; n., beam of light; glimpse;
kindly glance; wink; instant:
blinker, n., pretty girl.
blinkit, adj., soured, of milk.
blinter, v., glimmer; glitter.
blirt, v., burst out crying; n., gust of
wind: blirtie, adj., squally.
blitter, n., sloppy mess.
block, n., fellow.
blouster, v., blow roughly; bluster; n.,
gale; scaramouch.
blue-bonnet, n., marauder; titmouse:
blue-goun, n., licensed beggar.
bluffart, n., blast of wind; squall; a
blow.
bluid, v., bleed; n., blood: bluid-friens,

n., kin: **bluid-hert**, n., red-breasted minnow: **bluidy**, adj., bloody.
bluiter, n., bittern; silly talker.
blume, v., n., flourish.
bluntie, adj., snivelling.
blush, v., blister: **blushin**, n., blister.
boakie, n., hardened nasal mucus.
boast, v., n., menace.
bob, v., dance; make obeisance; n., dance: **bobbit**, n., lady's obeisance.
bob, n., bunch of flowers; decorative knot or tassel.
bob, n., butt; mark.
bock/boke, v., gush forth; retch; n., retch: **bock-fou**, adj., chock-full.
bod, n., little man: **bodach**, n., old man.
boddle, n., small coin.
boddom, n., bottom: **boddomless**, adj., abysmal.
bode, v., foresee; presage: **bodeword**, n., augury; forecast.
bode, v., bid at an auction.
bodle, n., copper coin of little value.
body, n., human being; person.
boggle, v., protrude, of eyes.
bogle, n., ghost; object of terror; scarecrow.
bole, n., alcove; wall recess: **bole hole**, n., hole in wall for ventilation.
boll, n., dry measure.
bon accord, n., concord.
bonalie, n., farewell drink.
*__bonny__, adj., beautiful; considerable: **bonny wallies**, n., knick-knacks.
bonspiel, n., curling match.
bool, v., play bowls; n., bowl; marble: **bool-fuitit**, adj., club-footed.
boost, v., behoved; ought.
booze, v., drink hard; n., drink.
bootch, v., n., bungle; muddle.
bootikins, n., instrument of torture.
bord, n., hem; ruffle.
bore, n., crack; crevice; breaking wave.
borestane, n., flagstaff stone.
borrow, v., n., pledge.
boss, n., frame at haystack centre: **bossin**, n., vent hole in stack.
boss, adj., devoid; empty; hollow.
botch, n., tumour.
bothy, n., farm servants' quarters.
bottle, v., bundle hay/straw.
*__bou__, v., n., arch: **bou-backit**, adj., hump-backed: **bou-hocht**, adj., bandy-legged.

bouar, n., renter of dairy cows.
bougars, n., rafters.
bougil, n., trumpet.
bouk, v., dilate; swell; n., bulk; size; volume; carcase.
bouk, v., steep clothes in lye of urine: **boukin**, n., such a steeping.
boun, v., prepare.
boun, n., extent; latitude; width: **bouns**, n., district.
bountith, n., bounty; supplementary payment.
bour, n., bower.
bourach, v., heap; n., confused heap; hillock; hovel.
bourie, n., burrow; lair.
bourtree, n., shrub elder.
bousome, adj., willing.
bousterous, adj., boisterous; fierce; rowdy.
bout, n., swath.
bow, n., see **bou**.
bowder, n., storm of rain and wind.
bowf, v., n., bark.
bowie, n., barrel; bucket; cask; pail.
bow-kail, n., cabbage.
bowlie-leggit, adj., bandy-legged.
bowster, n., bolster: **bowster-cup**, n., nightcap.
bowt, v., bolt; spring; well up; n., bolt; spring.
bowt, n., skein.
box, v., butt; wainscot: **boxin**, n., wainscotting: **box-bed**, n., wall-bed.
boy, n., apprentice; smart fellow.
boyne/byne, n., milk container; washing-tub.
brace, n., fireplace; mantelshelf.
brae, n., hill; river bank; steep road: **brae-face**, n., hill-slope: **braeheid**, n., hilltop.
brag, v., n., challenge: **braggie**, adj., boastful.
braid, adj., broad; plain; downright: **braidness**, n., breadth.
braik, n., instrument for dressing flax.
brain, v., injure severely; n., severe injury.
brainch, n., branch.
braisant, adj., bold; insolent.
braith, n., breath; opinion: **brak braith**, v., utter a word.
brak/brek, v., break; n., break; breach; bankruptcy; breaking of

153

waves; hollow in hill: **brak-faith**, adj., perfidious.

brammel-worm, n., ringed worm used as fish-bait.

brammle, n., bramble.

brander, v., broil; grill; n., gridiron; grill; riddle; sieve.

brank, v., strut: **branksome**, adj., dashing: **branky**, adj., showy.

brank, v., bridle: **branks**, n., wooden horse curb; instrument of punishment.

brash, v., rush; n., attack of illness: **brashy**, adj., ailing.

brat, n., apron; bib: **brats**, n., clothing.

brattach, n., banner; ensign; flag.

brattice, n., partition wall.

brattle, v., advance quickly; n., hurry; short race; rattling noise.

bravely, adv., exceedingly well.

braw, adj., comely; pleasant; excellent; considerable: **braws**, n., best clothes: **brawly**, adv., very well: **braw and** ... adv., very ...

braxy, n., sheep with inflammation of stomach; flesh of such a sheep.

brecham, n., horse collar.

breckan, n., bracken.

bree, n., liquid; broth; gravy; juice.

*****bree**, n., brunt.

breek, v., tuck up skirt: **breeks**, n., trousers.

breenge, v., see **breinge**.

breer, n., briar; wild rose bush.

breeshle, v., n., hurry; rush.

breid, n., bread: **girdle breid**, n., oatcakes.

breid, n., breadth; adj., broad.

breif, n., see **brief**.

breinge, v., push forward impetuously; n., violent rush.

breird, v., germinate; sprout; n., sprout; a sprouting.

breist, v., spring forward, of a horse; n., breast; slipway.

brek, v., see **brak**.

bren, v., burn: **brent**, adj., smooth; steep: **brent-new**, adj., brand-new.

bricht, adj., bright: **brichten**, v., brighten.

brick, n., brick-shaped loaf.

bridie, n., meat pie.

brief, n., certificate; diploma; testimonial; spell.

brief, adj., apposite.

brig, n., bridge.

brisken up, v., freshen; stimulate; titillate.

brisket, n., breast.

britchin, n., strap over horse's loins.

brithal, n., bridal; marriage.

brither, v., find an equal; match; n., brother; equal.

broach, n., clasp; yarn spindle.

broag, n., heavy shoe.

broch, n., prehistoric tower.

broch, n., halo round moon.

brock, n., badger.

brock, n., kitchen food as refuse for pigs; leavings; scraps.

brod, v., n., poke; goad; spur.

brod, n., board; book board; lid; table.

brog, v., jab/pierce with sharp instrument; n., awl; gimlet; prick.

broggle, v., bungle; spoil; n., bungle; job badly done.

brogue, n., trick.

broken, adj., bankrupt: **broken man**, n., outlaw.

broo, n., see **bree/brou**.

broose, n., horse race at weddings.

broozle, v., crush; squash; squeeze.

brose, n., porridge made of meal, water, salt and butter.

brosy, adj., coarse in manner; stout: **brosy-faced**, adj., fat-faced.

brou, n., brow; brim; overhanging bank.

*****brou**, n., liking; propensity.

brough, n., see **brugh**.

brouk, v., streak with dirt: **broukie**, adj., smutty: **broukit**, adj., tear-stained.

broun, adj., brown.

brounkaties, n., bronchitis.

browden, v., indulge; pet: **browdent**, adj., petted; spoiled with kindness.

browls, n., dry twigs for burning.

browst, n., a brewing of ale: **browster**, n., brewer.

bruckle, adj., brittle; frail; friable, of soil.

brugh (guttural), n., burgh: **brughman**, n., burgher; citizen.

bruit, n., brute.

brulzie/brulyie, n., brawl; commotion; fight.

brume, n., broom, the plant.

brunstane, n., brimstone; sulphur.

brunt, adj., burnt.

brust, v., ebb; n., ebbtide.

bubbies, n., woman's breasts.

bubble, v., blubber; shed tears: **bubbly,** adj., tearful.

bubbly-jock, n., male turkey.

bucht, v., put sheep in fold; n., fold; pen; shelter.

buckie, n., mollusc shell; whelk; stubborn person; useless object.

buckie, n., rose hip.

buff, v., beat; flatten; n., muffled blow.

buff, n., irrelevant talk; fuss.

buik/beuk, n., book: **the Auld Buik,** n., the Bible: **buik-leir,** n., education: **buik-leired,** adj., educated: **buikman,** n., scholar.

buird, n., board; plank; table; committee: **buird-claith,** n., tablecloth.

buirdly, adj., powerful; stalwart; august; stately.

buiss, n., stall for horse or cow.

buist, v., had to; must.

buist, n., box; chest.

buist, n., brand; stigma.

buit, n., boot.

buith, n., booth; shop; stall.

bul, n., bull.

buller, v., gurgle; seethe; roar; n., gurgling sound; roar.

bullie (bul-ie), n., bullfinch.

bullox, v., make a mess of; spoil; n., mess.

bum, v., n., buzz; hum; zoom: **bumbee,** n., bumble-bee: **bumclock,** n., humming beetle: **bummer,** n., bluebottle; siren: **bummle,** n., idle fellow.

bum, n., backside.

bu-man, n., brownie.

bumbaze, v., abash; amaze; bewilder.

bummle, v., blunder; utter indistinctly: **bummler,** n., blunderer.

bumphle, v., roll up untidily: **bumphly,** adj., rumpled.

bunch, n., small plump girl.

bundle, v., cohabit; live with concubine.

bune, prep., above: **buner,** adj., upper: **bunemaist,** adj., highest; topmost.

bung, v., throw violently; n., violent throw.

bungie, adj., fuddled.

bunker, n., chest; seat.

bunsucken, adj., obliged to take corn for grinding to a certain mill.

bural, n., burial: **buryin,** n., funeral.

burd, n., bird: **burdie,** n., little bird; child.

burdalane, n., only remaining child of a family.

bure, v., did bear.

burn, n., brook; stream: **burngate,** n., water-channel.

burnewin, n., blacksmith.

burnist, adj., polished.

buroo, n., bureau; Labour Exchange.

burroe, n., sea wrack; tangle.

burr-thistle, n., spear thistle.

bursen, adj., panting from supreme effort.

burth, n., birth: **burth-brief,** n., birth certificate.

busk/buss, v., clothe; dress; make ready.

buss, n., bush; shelter: **bussie,** adj., bushy.

*****but,** n., outer part of house; adv., in the outer part of house.

but, prep., without: **but and,** conj., unless.

butch-hous, n., abattoir.

butt, n., starting point in race.

butter ark/crock, n., butter receptacle.

buttock-mail, n., church fine for fornication.

butty, n., friend.

by, adj., done for; adv., prep., past; conj., compared with: **by-bite,** n., snack: **bygane,** adj., past and gone: **by-hand,** adj., accidental: **by-oors,** n., leisure time: **by-job,** n., extra job: **by-ornar,** adj., abnormal; extraordinary; adv., abnormally: **by-pit,** n., stop-gap: **by-table,** n., side-table.

byde, v., dwell; remain; endure; n., pain: **byde by,** v., abide by.

byke, n., bee-hive; wasps' nest.

byle, v., boil: **byler,** n., boiler; kettle.

byle, n., a boil.

byne, n., see boyne.

byous, adj., exceptional; special; adv., exceptionally; specially.

byre, n., cattle-shed; cow-house.

*****Caa,** v., call; miscall; n., call; need: **caa in,** v., visit in passing.

*****caa,** v., knock; push; urge forward;

n., knock; push; surge of waves: **caa-through**, n., commotion; "push".

cabal, n., social group.

cabbrach, n., decayed flesh; adj., predatory.

caber, n., tree trunk; pole from fir tree trunk; clumsy staff.

cadden-nail, n., nail holding cart to axle.

caddie, n., public messenger; porter; ragamuffin.

caddis, n., fluff; shoddy; cotton-wool.

*****cadge**, v., carry loads; hawk; beg: **cadger**, n., pedlar; hawker.

cadgy, adj., avid; cheerful; sportive.

caff, n., chaff of cereals: **caff-bed**, n., chaff-filled mattress.

cahoutchy, n., india-rubber.

cailleach, n., crone; old woman.

caird, n., card; chart.

caird, n., gipsy; tinker; beggar.

cairn, n., heap of stones; monument.

cairry, v., carry; n., burden; borrowed ride: **cairriage**, n., carriage: **cairrit**, adj., elated: **cairry-on**, n., piece of bad behaviour.

cairt, n., cart: **cairtwheel**, n., marguerite.

cairts, n., playing cards.

calimanco, n., kind of cotton cloth.

callan, n., boy; lad.

caller, v., cool; adj., cool; fresh.

callet, n., wench; prostitute.

calshie, adj., fault-finding.

camrie, n., cambric.

camshach, adj., deformed; surly: **camshachle**, v., distort; twist.

camsteerie, adj., giddy; unruly; wild.

can, n., skill; witchcraft.

canailyie, n., riff-raff; rabble.

cangle ("ng" as in "sing"), v., cavil; quibble; n., disturbance.

canker, v., fret; n., bad temper: **cankert**, adj., irritable.

canna, v., cannot.

cannas, n., sail of a boat.

canny, adj., cautious; adroit; dexterous; favourable; gentle; gradual; pleasant; fortunate; tactful; wary.

cant, v., sing; tell a light-hearted story.

cant, n., ramp.

cantle, v., set up; strengthen: **cantle up**, v., trans., intrans., cheer up.

cantle, n., ledge of rock; projection.

cantraip, n., incantation; spell; prank trick.

canty, adj., contented; comfortable; buoyant; cordial; merry.

cap-ale, n., small beer.

capercailzie, n., very large species of grouse.

capernoitit, adj., perverse; sourtempered.

cap-stane, n., copestone.

cappilow, v., outdistance; outpace.

cappit, adj., peevish; short-tempered.

caption n., warrant for debtor's arrest.

caraff, n., crystal water-jug.

carble, v., carp; quibble.

cardoo, v., patch; mend.

careous (care-ous), adj., anxious; curious.

carkidge, n., carcase.

carl, n., boor; fellow; old man: **carlish**, adj., boorish; churlish.

carldoddie, n., ribwort.

carle, n., carol; joyful song.

carl-hemp, n., male, more vigorous, stalk of hemp.

carlin, n., crone; witch.

carnaptious, adj., crabbed; badtempered.

carrant, n., expedition; frolic; uproar.

carritch, v., catechise; n., catechism.

carse, n., rich flat land by river.

carseckie, n., light summer jacket; smock.

cartoush, n., woman's short jacket.

carvie, n., caraway.

case be, conj., lest.

cashepole, n., tennis.

cashielaws, n., instrument of torture.

cassen, adj., tainted.

cast, v., give birth to; shed; sow; trench; swarm, of bees: **cast out**, v., disagree: **cast up**, v., recall spitefully.

cast, v., veer, of wind; n., direction; tack.

cast, n., appearance; demeanour; habit; likeness.

castock, n., cabbage stem.

casual, adj., arbitrary.

catalogue, n., register.

catch, n., knack: **catch-the-plack**, n., search for wealth; self-interest.

cate, v., be in heat.

catlowp, n., short distance/time: cat-wuttit, adj., short-tempered.

cat's een, n., speedwell.

cattle, n., lice; vermin: cattle-beasts, n., livestock.

caudron, n., cauldron.

cauf, n., calf: cauf kintra, n., birth-place; native district.

cauk, n., chalk.

cauker, n., glass of liquor; poser.

caul, n., weir.

*cauld, n., dose of cold; adj., cold: cauldrife, adj., chilly: cauld steirie, n., oatmeal and cold water: cauld-wamed, adj., cold-blooded.

caum, adj., calm; quiet.

caumstane, n., pipeclay.

caunle, n., candle.

caup, n., cup.

caur, n., sledge for peat.

caur, adj., left-hand: caurry haun, n., left hand: caurry-haundit, adj., left-handed.

causey, v., pave; n., cobbled street: causey-stane, n., cobble.

caution, v., guarantee; go bail; n., guarantee; bail.

cavie, v., confine; coop up; n., hen-coop.

certes, adv., assuredly; certainly.

cess, n., levy; rate; tax.

chack, v., grab with teeth; hack; n., bite; snap; snack.

chack, n., rut: chackie, adj., rutty.

chack, v., n., click.

chackart, n., stonechat.

chaff, v., chafe; n., bad temper.

chaft, n., cheek; jaw: chaft-blade, n., cheekbone.

chaip, adj., cheap.

chaipel, n., chapel.

chairge, v., charge; n., charge; cost; expense.

challenge, v., find fault with; repri-mand.

champ, v., mash; pound; squash; trample down.

chancy, adj., lucky; propitious.

chandler-chaftit, adj., lantern-jawed.

change, n., patronage; tavern: change-keeper, n., landlord of a tavern.

channel/channer, n., gravel; shingle.

channer, v., complain; fret; scold; n., strife.

chanty, n., chamberpot.

chap, v., hammer; knock; strike, of clock; n., knock; stroke of clock.

chap, v., choose; ratify bargain: chaps me, interj., I claim.

chapman, n., packman; pedlar.

charnle-pins, n., hinge-pins.

charrit, n., gig.

chat, n., packed lunch; light meal: chattle, v., nibble.

chate, v., cheat.

chattie, n., boar.

chaumer, n., chamber; bedroom; sitting-room: chaumer-chiel, n., valet.

chaunt, v., chant.

chaw, v., provoke; vex; n., disappoint-ment; sharp rejoinder.

chaw, v., chew; n., something chewed in the mouth.

cheatrie, n., deceit; fraud; adj., fraudulent; spurious: cheatery-packery, n., fraud: cheat-the-wuddy, n., rogue.

check, n., door-key.

*cheek, n., the side of anything.

cheeny, n., china.

cheip, v., chirp; squeak; whisper; n., chirp; squeak; hint.

chess, n., window sash.

chicken-hertit, adj., cowardly; timid: chickenweed, n., chickweed.

chief, adj., friendly.

chiel, n., child; lad; man.

chimla, n., chimney; fireplace; hearth: chimla-lug, n., fireside.

chingle, n., coarse gravel; pebbles; shingle.

chirk, v., creak; grate; n., creaking or grating sound.

chirl, v., chirp; twitter; warble; n., chirp; warble.

chirl, n., wood shaving.

chirm, v., croon; warble; n., warble.

chirt, v., clench teeth; squeeze; n., embrace; squeeze.

chitter, v., shiver; tremble; flicker: chittery, adj., shivery.

choise, v., choose; prefer; select.

chollers ("ch" as in "chin"), n., fish gills.

chookie, n., chicken; hen.

chore, n., see core.

chork, v., make squelching sounds.

*chow, v., n., chew: **chows,** n., coal nuts.

chowk, n., cheek; jaw.

Christmas, n., Christmas present.

chucken, n., chicken: **chuckie,** n., brood hen.

chuckie, n., small pebble; marble, in game.

chuffy, adj., fat-faced.

chug, v., n., jerk.

chun, v., burgeon; sprout; n., sprout.

chyce, n., choice.

chynge, v., change; exchange; substitute; become sour; n., change; exchange; substitute; vicissitude: **chynge anesel,** v., change clothes.

clabber, n., mud: **clabbery punt,** n., dredger.

clabbydoo, n., large mussel.

clachan, n., hamlet; village.

clack, v., chatter; n., impudent talk; scandal.

*claes, n., clothes; garb: **claes-raip,** n., clothes-rope.

clag, v., clog; n., sticky lump: **claggum,** n., candy: **claggy,** adj., sticky.

claik, v., n., cackle; cluck; chatter.

claister, v., clog; bedaub; n., sticky substance.

claith, n., cloth: **claithe,** v., clothe.

claiver, v., chatter; gossip: **claivers,** n., chatter; tittle-tattle.

clamihewit, n., blow; calamity.

clamjamfry, n., crowd; mob; rabble.

clammersome, adj., bellicose.

clamper, v., clutter up.

clams, n., pincers for castrating animals; vice.

clan, n., clique; coterie.

clap, v., flop; pat; press down; n., blow; pat: **clap doun,** v., flatten.

clap, n., rabbit's burrow.

clapper-claps, n., mill clapper: **clapmill,** n., wooden clappers.

clappit, adj., shrunken; thin.

clark, v., write; compose creatively; n., clerk.

clarsach, n., harp.

clart, v., befoul; besmear; work in wet, dirty conditions; n., dirt; filth; mud; slovenly person: **clarty,** adj., dirty; messy; sticky.

clash, v., fall suddenly; slap; strike; n., slap: **clash-tae,** n., cohabitation.

clash, v., gossip; n., chatter; scandal: **clash market,** n., centre for scandal.

clat, n., clod; clot of dung: **clatty,** adj., slimy; muddy.

clatch, v., walk through mud; n., mass of mud: **clatchy,** adj., muddy.

clatch, n., bungler; slovenly person; slut.

clatter, v., gossip; talk scandal; n., gossip; scandal.

claucht, v., clutch; snatch; seize; n., clutch; grasp.

claut, v., claw; scrape; n., scraper.

claut, n., lump; mass of matter.

*claw, v., handle; scrape; scratch: **clawin-shell,** n., scallop-shell.

clean, adj., absolute; complete; adv., completely.

cleavin, n., fissure.

cleck, v., babble; talk idly; n., claptrap; insolence.

cleck, v., breed; hatch; invent: **cleckin,** n., brood; family; litter.

cleg, n., gadfly.

cleid, v., clothe; cover: **cleidin,** n., dress; garb.

*cleik, v., clutch; seize; gaff salmon; walk arm in arm; n., crook; hook; salmon gaff: **cleiks,** n., lumbago; rheumatism.

cleisher, n., large specimen.

clem, adj., sneaky; perfidious.

clep, n., gaff; pot-hook.

cless, n., class.

cleuch (cluch/clooch guttural), n., chasm; crag; glen; coal pit.

cleuk, v., claw; seize; n., claw; hand.

clever, v., hasten; adj., fast; fast-talking; eloquent.

cley, n., clay: **cleyie,** n., marble; adj., clayey: **cley davie,** n., navvy.

clinch, v., limp: **clincher,** n., cripple.

cling, v., contract; shrink with heat: **clung,** adj., shrunken.

clink, v., n., rivet; rhyme: **clinker,** n., large specimen.

clink, n., money.

clinkum, n., bellman: **clinkum bell,** n., church/town bell.

clint, n., flint rock; precipice: **clinty,** adj., flinty; stony.

clip, n., mischievous girl: **clippie,** n., talkative female; adj., sharp-tongued.

158

clippie, n., shorn sheep: **clippin**, n., sheep-shearing: **clips**, n., woolshears.

clish-clash, n., gossip; rumour.

clishmaclaver, n., gossip; long discourse.

clitter, n., wet, disgusting mess.

clocher, v., wheeze; n., wheeze; throat mucus.

clock, v., sit on eggs to hatch; sit lazily over fire; n., cluck of broody hen: **clocker**, n., broody hen.

clock, n., beetle: **clock-leddy**, n., ladybird.

clocks, n., dandelions in seed.

cloit, v., fall heavily; n., heavy fall.

cloiter, v., work dirtily: **cloitery**, adj., dirty; messy.

cloot, n., hoof: **Auld Clootie**, n., the devil.

clorach, n., disgusting mess.

close, n., alley; courtyard; passageway between houses.

clour, v., beat; bump; strike; n., blow; bump.

clout, v., mend; n., rag; garment; patch: **clouts**, n., clothes: **cloutie**, adj., patched: **cloutie dumplin**, n., dumpling wrapped in a "clout".

clow, n., clove: **clow-gillieflouer**, n., pink; carnation.

clowt, v., slap; strike; thrash; n., blow; slap.

clud, n., cloud.

clug, n., batten; log of wood: **clugs**, n., wooden shoes.

clunk, v., clank; walk heavily.

clunk, n., sound of liquid poured from bottle.

clure, v., see **clour**.

cluther, v., n., clutter.

clyack, n., last sheaf of harvest.

clype, v., blab; tell tales; n., idle tale: **clype/clype-clash**, n., tale-bearer.

clytach, v., talk unintelligibly; n., unintelligible conversation.

coachbell, n., earwig.

coal, n., glowing ember: **coal gum**, n., coal dust: **coal heuch/cleuch**, n., coal pit: **coal neuk**, n., coal cellar; **coallier**, n., miner.

coat, n., skirt.

coble, v., rock/cause to rock; seesaw; n., seesaw.

coble, n., flat-bottomed fishing-boat.

cocked, adj., fertile, of egg: **cockabendie/cockie-dandie**, n., small, lively person: **cockieleekie**, n., leek and chicken soup: **ride cockie-breekie**, v., ride on someone's shoulders: **cockieleerie**, n., cock: **cockieleerie-law**, n., crow of cock: **cock-laft**, n., church gallery: **cockstuil**, n., pillory: **cocks-and-hens**, n., trefoil.

cockalane, n., skit; satire.

cocker, v., walk unsteadily/with rocking step: **cockerie**, adj., unsteady.

cockernony, n., lock of hair tied with ribbon.

cockle up, v., revive.

cockle-heidit, adj., scatter-brained.

cod, v., hoax; sham; trick.

cod, n., cushion; pillow; penis; pod.

cod-bait, n., sea-worm.

coddle, v., cuddle.

coddled aipple, n., roasted apple.

coff, v., buy.

cog, v., n., wedge.

cog/coggie, n., bowl; wooden dish.

coggle, v., move unsteadily; rock/cause to rock: **coggly**, adj., unsteady.

cole, v., put up in stacks; n., haystack.

colleck, v., collect; think about.

collie, v., overrule.

collie, v., concede.

collieshangie, n., brawl; dispute; uproar; dogfight.

collogue, v., confer; conspire: **collogue wi**, v., associate with.

*****come**, v., become; expand: **come back on**, v., repeat, of food: **come by**, v., get; win: **come on**, v., improve: **come owre**, v., befall; happen to.

come, prep., by; by the time that.

comitee (com-i-tee), n., committee.

commanding, adj., rendering incapable.

compare, n., resemblance.

compear, v., present oneself.

compesce, v., repress; subdue.

complainer, n., plaintiff: **complaint**, n., ailment.

compliment, n., gift.

complouter, v., concur; co-operate; n., blend; mix-up.

concait, n., conceit; opinion: **concaity**, adj., conceited; apt; neat.

condescend upon, v., specify.

condy, n., vein.
confab., v., n., chat.
confeerin, adj., congruous: **conference,** n., correspondence; resemblance.
conform til, prep., in accordance with.
confoun, v., abash; perplex.
connach, v., mar; spoil.
connect, adj., logical.
considerin, adj., considerate; thoughtful.
conteen, v., contain; comprise.
conter, v., contravene; oppose; prep., against: **contermacious,** adj., self-willed; wayward.
contrack, v., n., contract.
contrair, adj., contrary; diametrically opposite.
convene, n., gathering; meeting.
conveniency, n., desirability.
convoy, v., accompany; transport; n., escort; transportation.
coof/cuif, n., lout.
cook, v., appear and vanish.
cookie, n., soft bun.
cool, n., woollen cap.
coom, n., see coum.
coomceiled, adj., having a sloping roof.
coont, v., see count.
coordie, v., see courdy.
coorie, v., see courie.
coorse, n., adj., course.
coort, v., see court.
cooser, n., stallion.
coot, n., see cuit.
corbie, n., raven; rook: **corbie steps,** n., steps on house gable-end.
cordiner, n., shoemaker.
core, n., choir; gang; group; team.
cork, n., overseer.
corkir, n., lichen producing purple dye.
corky, n., frivolous person.
corn, v., feed horse; n., grain; oats: **cornkister,** n., farmworkers' song: **corn-laft,** n., barn; granary.
coronach, n., dirge; lament.
corp, n., corpse: **corp-lifter,** n., body-snatcher: **corp-sheet,** n., shroud.
corrie, v., be intimate with: **corrie-neuchin,** pres. partic., chatting intimately.
corrie, n., hollow in hills.
corse, n., cross.
cosh, adj., comfortable; contented; amiable; friendly.

cottar, n., servant occupying farm cottage.
cou, n., cow.
coucher, n., coward; blow as challenge to fight.
coulter, n., iron cutter in front of ploughshare: **coulter-nebbit,** adj., sharp-nosed.
coum, v., begrime; n., coal dust; soot: **coumy,** adj., grimy; sooty.
counger (coonjer), v., overawe; intimidate.
count, v., count; do arithmetic: **counts,** n., arithmetic; sums: **count book,** n., account book: **keep counts,** v., do book-keeping.
country/kintra, n., country; district; region.
coup, v., see cowp.
couples, n., rafters.
cour, v., cower; squat; submit; protect.
courdy, v., put to shame; shrink: **courdy-lick,** n., challenging blow.
courie, v., bend; cower; cringe: **courie doun,** v., snuggle; nestle.
course, n., rate; speed.
courss, adj., badly-behaved; rough; stormy.
court, v., court; woo; n., court: **court-hous,** n., court-building.
couth/couthy, adj., congenial; pleasant; sympathetic: **couthiness,** n., graciousness; kindness.
covetice, n., greed.
covin tree, n., tree before house where laird met/parted with guest.
covine, n., compact; company of witches.
cow, v., cut; prune; n., haircut.
cow, v., outdo; surpass.
cow, n., goblin; apparition; object of terror: **cowie,** adj., bizarre.
cowan, n., drystane dyke builder.
cowd, n., rocking motion: **cowdie,** v., float.
cowk, v., n., vomit.
*cowp, v., capsize; tilt; n., tumble; upset; rubbish dump.
*cowp, v., bargain; exchange; n., bargain: **cowper,** n., broker; dealer.
cowt, n., colt; boor; clumsy fellow.
cowt, v., beat; n., strong stick; truncheon.

crab, v., become angry: **crabbit**, adj., crabbed; bad-tempered.

crack, v., n., chat; gossip: **cracky**, adj., sociable; chatty.

cradlie-baa, n., lullaby.

craft, n., croft: **craftland**, n., land constantly cropped.

craig, n., cliff; cape; headland: **craig-man**, n., quarrier.

craig, n., gullet; neck; throat.

craighle, v., cough; croak; n., croaking sound.

craik, v., n., creak; croak; grumble.

cramasie, n., crimson cloth; adj., crimson.

crambo-clink, n., doggerel.

crame, n., booth; stall.

crampet, n., spiked plate on curling shoes.

cran, n., herring measure.

cran, n., water-tap.

cran, n., crane; heron.

crank, v., grate; n., grating sound; adj., inharmonious.

crankie, adj., dangerous; insecure; weakly: **crankous**, adj., irritable.

crannie, n., room recess.

cranreuch, n., hoarfrost.

*crap, v., n., crop.

crap, v., stuff.

crap, n., top; boiled whey: **crapweeds**, n., surface weeds.

crap, n., breast; stomach.

cratur, n., creature: **the cratur**, n., whisky.

crave, n., desire; hankering; petition; request.

*craw, v., crow; boast; n., crow: **craw-bogle**, n., scarecrow: **craw-heid**, n., chimney-top: **craw-plantin**, n., rookery: **craw-road**, n., direct road: **craw-siller**, n., mica: **craw-steps**, n., steps on house gable.

cray, n., pen; hutch.

craze, v., enervate; make infirm: **crazed/crazy**, adj., dilapidated; rickety.

creagh (guttural), n., foray; prey; quarry.

creddle, v., rear a child; n., cradle.

creed, n., rebuke.

creekle, v., tremble with weakness.

creel, n., basket carried on back; lobster trap.

*creep in/thegither, v., shrink: **creepin-wheat-grass**, n., couchgrass.

creepie-stuil, n., three-legged stool; church footstool/stool of repentance.

*creish, v., grease; n., fat; grease; lard: **creishy**, adj., greasy: **creishy-mealie**, n., oatmeal fried with onions.

crib, v., restrain; n., coping; kerb; hencoop.

*cries, n., marriage banns.

criffins, interj., expressing amazement.

crine, v., see **cryne**.

croagh (guttural), v., strangle with rope.

crock, n., earthenware vessel; jar.

crockanition, n., smithereens.

crockie, n., stool with hole in middle of seat.

crog, n., paw.

crony, n., companion.

croodle, v., nestle.

crood/croodle, v., n., coo, of a dove.

croon, v., hum; lament; wail; whimper; n., mournful song; whimper.

croot, n., small, weakly person.

crose, v., speak ingratiatingly; n., flattery.

cross-speir, v., cross-examine.

crottle, n., lichen giving brown dye.

crottles, n., crumbs; morsels.

crouchie, adj., hump-backed.

croud, n., crowd.

croun, v., crown; n., crown; first furrow in ploughing.

croupie-craw, n., raven.

crouse, adj., cheerful; jaunty; confident: **crouseness**, n., cheerfulness.

crout, v., make a rumbling noise, of bowels; n., bur in speech.

crowder, v., frequent.

crowdie, n., oatmeal and water porridge: **crowdie-time**, n., mealtime.

crowl, v., crawl.

crowl, n., dwarf; adj., dwarfish.

crowp, n., hoarseness: **crowpy**, adj., hoarse.

crub, v., curb; n., crib: **crubbit**, adj., confined; restrained.

cruban, n., crab; pannier.

crud, n., curd; frogspawn: **cruddle**, v., coagulate.

crue, v., put sheep in fold; n., sheepfold.

cruik, v., bend; crook; n., crook; hook.

cruive, n., hut; pen; pigsty; wicker salmon trap.

crum, n., morsel; particle.

crummie, n., cow with crooked horns.

crummle, v., crumble: crummles, n., crumbs.

crummock, n., staff with crook for handle.

crump, v., crackle: crumpie, adj., crisp; crumbly.

crunkle, v., contract; wrinkle; n., wrinkle: crunkly, adj., wrinkled.

crunt, v., hit on the head; n., blow on the head.

cruzie, n., oil lamp.

*cry, v., n., call: cry back, v., recall: cry dool, v., lament: cry doun, v., disparage: cry in, v., visit in passing: cry names, v., revile.

cryne, v., shrink.

cuckoo, v., harp on; reiterate.

cud/cuid, v., could.

cuddie, n., ass; donkey; horse; trestle.

cuddle, v., fondle; sit close; squat.

cuddom, v., accustom; subdue; train; n., custom; habit.

cudiech, n., bonus; bribe; perquisite.

cuff o the neck, n., nape of the neck.

cuif/coof, n., fool; simpleton.

cuik, v., n., cook.

cuil, v., adj., cool.

cuinyie, n., coin.

cuit, n., ankle; fetlock; shinbone.

cuiter, v., put to rights; wheedle.

cuitikins, n., gaiters; leggings.

cuitle, v., caress; flatter; fondle; tickle.

culrach, n., security.

cum (koom), n., cistern.

cummer, n., girl; "wife"; woman.

cumseil/coomceil, n., attic ceiling.

cundy, n., conduit; culvert; drain; sewer.

cunjer, v., tame.

cunning, adj., expert: cunning man, n., connoisseur; expert.

cunyie, n., corner.

curch, n., kerchief; head-veil; wimple.

curdower, n., itinerant tailor.

curfuffle, v., disarrange; n., disagreement; disorder; excitement.

curfumish, v., smell badly.

curl, v., play the game of curling.

curldoddy, n., fir cone; plantain; scabious.

curlyfuffs, n., false hair.

curly kail, n., colewort.

curmurrin, n., murmur; stomach rumble.

curn, n., band of people; squad; troop.

curn, n., quern; handmill.

curpin/curple, n., buttocks; rump.

currach, n., coracle; pannier.

currack, n., sea-wrack.

curran, n., currant.

currie, n., small stool.

currie, n., river pool.

curriehunker, v., squat on hams: curriehunkers, n., hams of legs.

currie-wurrie, n., dispute; quarrel.

cushat/cushie doo, n., wood-pigeon.

cushle-mushle, n., muttering.

custock/castock, n., cabbage stem.

custron, n., rascal; rogue.

cut, v., castrate: cut aff, v., excommunicate: cuttit, adj., abrupt; terse.

cutherie, adj., cold; sensitive to cold.

cuttie, n., hare.

cuttie, adj., short; stumpy: cutty-stuil, n., stool of repentance.

cuttle, v., sharpen; whet.

cutty-wran, n., wren.

cutworm, n., cabbage-root grub.

Dab, v., peck; prick with sharp point; n., peck; prick with sharp point.

dab/dab-haun, n., expert.

dacker, v., loiter; wander idly; search carefully; n., careful search.

dackle, v., hesitate; n., uncertainty: dacklin, adj., dilatory.

dad, v., bang; beat; drive, of wind; slam; n., bang; jolt; knock; thud.

dae, v., do: be daein wi, v., put up with: daeless, adj., helpless: dae-nae-better, n., substitute: dae-nae-guid, n., ne'er-do-well.

daff, v., play; sport: daffery/daffin, n., gaiety; dallying; frolic.

*daft, adj., crazed; doting; foolish; gay; thoughtless: daftlike, adj., absurd; preposterous: daftie, n., imbecile.

dag, v., fall as half-mist, half-rain; n., mist: daggy, adj., misty.

daggle, v., rain heavily.

daicent, adj., decent.

daich, n., dough: daichie, adj., flabby, of food; soggy.

daidle, v., dawdle; idle; waste time.
daidle, n., bib; apron: **daidlie,** n., pinafore.
daik, v., smooth the hair.
daiken, n., decade.
daiker, v., decorate; dress; jog along.
dail/dale, v., deal; dispense; distribute; n., section; segment; share.
daimen, adj., occasional; rare.
dainshoch, adj., fussy; squeamish.
daintice, n., delicacy.
dainty, adj., attractive; pleasant; worthy; considerable.
dairt, v., n., dart.
daise, v., rot; stun.
daith, n., death: **strae daith,** n., natural death.
daiver, v., benumb; bewilder; stun: **daivert,** adj., bewildered.
dall, n., doll: **dally-doll,** n., painted image; dressy woman.
dalt, n., foster-child.
dam, n., mill-pond.
damage, n., cost; outlay.
dammish, v., damage.
dams, n., draughts, the game: **dambrod,** n., draughtboard.
dander/dauner, v., stroll; wander; n., leisurely walk.
dander, n., cinder; clinker: **danders,** n., slag.
dander, n., anger.
dandilly, n., spoilt woman.
dang, v., bang.
dare, v., see **daur.**
darg, n., labour; day's labour: **dargsman,** n., casual labourer.
darn, v., thread one's way.
dash, v., dismay; expunge.
dashy, adj., gaudy; swanky.
dask, n., desk; pew.
dass, n., layer; stratum; ledge of rock.
datchie, adj., hidden; sly; observant.
daud, n., lump of material.
daumer, v., besot; bemuse; stun.
dauner, v., see **dander.**
dauntingly, adv., bravely.
daunton, v., appal; discourage; intimidate; overawe.
daur, v., abash; dare; intimidate: **daur upon,** v., affect.
daurk, n., adj., dark: **daurken,** v., darken: **daurkenin,** n., dusk: **daurk-**

avised, adj., dark-skinned: **daurklins,** adv., in the dark.
daurlin, n., darling.
dave, v., alleviate; allay; temper.
daw/dawin, n., dawn.
daw, n., slattern.
dawk, v., moisten; drizzle; n., fog: **dawkie,** adj., damp; wet.
dawt, v., caress; dote; indulge; pet: **dawtie,** n., pet; sweetheart.
*daylicht, n., daylight: **dayset,** n., nightfall: **the day,** adv., today.
deacon, n., adept; master of incorporated company.
dearmeal, n., time of famine.
dearth, n., expense: **dearthfu,** adj., expensive.
deas, n., stone/turf/wooden seat.
deave, v., deafen; bore; weary.
debosh, v., over-indulge; n., waste.
decern, v., decree.
decorement, n., adornment.
deduce, v., subtract.
*dee, v., die: **deid,** adj., dead; n., death: **deid-bell,** n., passing bell: **deidcaunle,** n., will-o'-the-wisp: **deidclaes,** n., shroud: **deid-hous,** n., mortuary: **deid-kist,** n., coffin: **deidman's-bells/flourish,** n., foxglove/meadow-sweet: **deid mirk,** n., pitch dark: **deid-thraws,** n., death-throes.
deif, adj., deaf; barren; void: **deifen,** v., deafen: **deifie,** n., deaf person.
*deil/deevil, n., devil: **deil's picturcairds,** n., playing-cards.
delate, v., accuse; denounce.
deleerit, adj., delirious; mad: **deleeritness,** n., delirium; mania.
delf, n., footprint.
dell, v., delve; dig.
delt, v., indulge; pet.
demaim, v., injure.
demember, v., amputate.
dempster/doomster, n., court official who pronounced death sentence.
den, n., dale; wooded valley.
denner, v., dine; n., dinner: **dennerpiece,** n., packed lunch.
dentice, n., rarity.
denty, adj., see **dainty.**
denum, v., benumb.
deoch-an-dorus, n., stirrup cup; parting drink.
depairt, v., depart.

depone, v., vouch; testify: **deponent,** n., witness.

depute, n., adj., deputy.

deray, n., noisy mirth.

derf, adj., daring; taciturn.

dern, v., hide oneself; adj., secret; blurred; vague; n., secrecy.

dern, v., n., darn.

descrive, v., define; depict; describe.

destinate, v., appoint; assign; ordain.

detfall, adj., owing.

deuk, n., duck: **deuk-dub,** n., duck-pond: **deuk's faul,** n., quandary.

deval, v., cease; quit; n., cessation.

devel, n., blow.

deviltry, n., devilry; mischief; evil.

dey, n., dairymaid; dairyman.

diceboard, n., board with chequer pattern in game of draughts/chess.

dichel, n., dilemma: **dichlin,** n., thrashing.

dicht, v., clean; wipe; wash superficially; winnow; chastise; n., rub; wipe: **dichtin,** n., drubbing: **dichtins,** n., leavings.

dichty, adj., foul; squalid: **dichty water,** n., cant.

diddle, v., dandle; tap with feet; hum; trifle; n., bright tune.

die, n., see **dye.**

diet, n., meal of food: **diet hour,** n., mealtime.

diet-book, n., diary.

differ, v., n., dispute.

diffy, adj., dull; stupid.

dight, v., see **dicht.**

dill, v., be calm; soothe.

din, adj., dark-complexioned; sallow; mouse-coloured.

din, n., rumour; scandal.

ding, v., dash down; surpass; defeat; drive; weary; rain heavily.

dingle, v., resound.

dink/dinkie, adj., neat; dandified.

dinna, v., do not.

dinnle, v., quiver; tingle; vibrate; n., tremor; vibration.

dint, n., opportunity; regard.

dird, v., bang; bump; n., bump: **dirder,** n., caretaker, of animals.

dirdum, n., fuss; uproar; scolding tantrum; squabble.

direck, v., adj., direct: **direction book,** n., reference book.

dirk/dirken, v., eavesdrop; slink.

dirl, v., clatter; pierce; reverberate; throb; n., blow; vibration: **dirl aff,** v., reel off: **dirl by,** v., pass swiftly, of time: **dirl up,** v., strike up, a song: **dirlie-bane,** n., funny-bone.

dirr, v., alleviate pain; adj., dull; having no feeling.

dirten, adj., filthy; mean: **dirtrie,** n., riff-raff: **dirty,** adj., weedy.

dischairge, v., acquit; ban; forbid.

discomfish, v., balk; get the better of.

discover, v., expose.

discreet, adj., affable; mannerly: **discretion,** n., politeness.

dishaunt, v., abandon: **dishauntit,** adj., derelict.

dish-clout, n., dish-cloth.

disherish, v., repudiate.

disherten, v., dishearten: **dishertsome,** adj., disheartening.

dishilago, n., coltsfoot.

disjaskit, adj., wearied; downcast.

disna, v., does not.

displeasure, v., displease.

displenish, v., sell off farm stock.

dispone, v., assign: **disposition,** n., assignation of property.

disrespeckit, adj., ignored.

dist, n., dust: **disty melder,** n., last meal from crop.

distan, v., discern: **distance,** n., distinction.

dit, v., shut up; stop speaking.

dite, v., compose; create.

divert, n., diversion; entertainment.

divider, n., ladle.

dividual, adj., individual; distinct.

divot, v., thatch with turf; n., sod; turf.

dizzen, n., dozen.

dobbie, n., lout; stupid person.

docher, n., strain; stress.

docht, n., deed; exploit; strength: **dochty,** adj., brave; powerful.

dochter, n., daughter.

dock, n., backside; buttocks.

dock, v., abbreviate; abridge; cut: **dockit,** adj., abrupt of speech.

docken, n., dock, the plant: **docken grub,** n., fat, white grub for bait.

doctor, v., slay.

dod, interj., expressing surprise.

doddie, n., hornless cow.

doddles, n., male genitals.

dodge on, v., jog/plod on: **dodge**, n., steady pace.

doer, n., agent; factotum.

doggerlone, n., destruction; ruin.

doilt, adj., unhinged; half-witted; fatigued.

doingless, adj., indolent.

doister, n., storm of wind.

doit, n., small coin.

doit, n., sot: **doitit**, adj., absent-minded; crazed; stupefied.

doiter, v., potter about; stumble.

dominie, n., schoolmaster.

donnert, adj., stupefied; stupid.

donsie, adj., unlucky; ill-tempered; restive.

doo, n., dove: **dooket**, n., dovecot: **doo-lander/doo-derter**, n., man's skipped cap.

doodle, v., dandle.

dook, n., bung of barrel; wooden peg in wall to take nail.

dook, v., see **douk**.

dool, n., grief; misery: **doolfu**, adj., sad: **dool-tree**, n., gallows.

dool, n., see **dull**.

dooms, adv., exceedingly; very.

doon, adj., see **doun**.

door-cheek, n., doorpost; doorway: **doorstane**, n., threshold.

doosht, v., n., thud.

dorbie, n., mason; initiate in Free-masonry.

dordermeat, n., light repast.

dorrity, n., puppet.

dort, v., sulk: **dorty**, adj., sulky; haughty; ailing: **dorts**, n., ill-humour.

doss, v., tidy up; n., bow; knot of a ribbon.

dotter, v., reel; stagger.

dottle, n., jot; particle; half-smoked plug of tobacco.

dottle, adj., feeble-minded: **dottle-trot**, n., old man's step.

douce, adj., decorous; grave; sedate; tidy: **douceness**, n., sedateness.

douk, v., n., bathe; dip: **douker**, n., little grebe: **sour douk**, n., sour milk.

*****doun**, adv., prep., down; adj., sown: **doun-by**, adv., down the road: **doun-come**, n., collapse; hernia: **douncry**, v., n., slur: **doundraucht**, n., handicap: **dounhauden**, adj., repressed:

dounheid, n., dislike: **dounleukin**, adj., haughty: **dounmaist**, adj., lowest: **dounset**, n., settlement.

doup, n., see **dowp**.

dour, adj., obstinate; austere; severe: sulky; barren; humourless; arduous: **dourness**, n., obstinacy.

douse, v., extinguish; quell.

dout, v., doubt; suspect; n., doubt: **doutfu**, adj., doubtful: **doutsome**, adj., apprehensive; sceptical; vague.

douth, adj., solid; substantial.

dove/dover, v., doze; drowze; n., doze: **dover owre**, v., doze off.

dow, v., avail; can; have the courage to: **dowless**, adj., feeble; lazy.

dow, v., decay; putrefy: **dowd**, adj., flat, of drink; unfresh.

dowf, adj., gloomy; inactive; spiritless: **dowfness**, n., dejection.

dowie, adj., ailing; dejected: **dowiness**, n., dejection.

dowp, n., buttocks; cigarette end: **dowp doun**, v., sit down.

doxy, n., mistress; concubine; wench.

doze, v., spin round rapidly: **dozer**, n., fast-spinning top.

dozent, adj., bewildered; stupefied; impotent.

drab, v., n., spot; stain: **drabble**, v., spill; besmear.

drag, n., harrow: **drag-tae**, n., rake.

draigle, v., bedraggle; spatter: **draigle a woman's tails**, v., seduce.

draigon, n., kite.

draik, v., quench; slake; n., wet weather.

*****dram**, v., tipple; n., drink of liquor.

drap, v., n., drop: **drappie**, n., small amount of liquor.

draucht, n., freight; feature; heavy breathing; photograph; plan; plot; sea-swell: **drauchty**, adj., artful; scheming.

draunt, v., drawl; n., drawl; slow tune.

drave, n., drove of cattle; shoal of fish; throng of people.

*****draw**, v., milk a cow; smoke a pipe; beach/launch a boat; deduce.

draw-moss, n., bog-cotton.

dredgie, n., dirge; funeral feast.

*****dree**, v., endure; last out; n., suffering: **dreefu**, adj., sad.

dreel, v., drill, in all its senses; n., line; row.

dreel, v., hustle; scold: dreel o wind, n., gale; hurricane.

dreep, v., see dreip.

dreg, v., n., dredge.

dreich, adj., dull; monotonous; tardy; desolate: dreichness, n., tedium.

dreid/dreidour, n., fear: dreidfu, adj., dreadful; fearful.

*dreip, v., n., drip; n., drizzling rain; soft, spiritless person.

dreiple, v., n., trickle.

dress, v., iron clothes; geld.

drib, v., drub.

drib/dribble, n., drop: dribs, n., dregs: dribble, v., tipple.

driddle, v., dribble; urinate; trifle; saunter; strum.

drieshach (dreeshach), n., glowing fire.

driffle, n., light rain.

drift, n., drove; herd; flock.

dring, v., dawdle; linger.

drochle, v., walk slowly; n., puny person: drochlin, adj., dilatory; puny.

drocht, n., drought; dry weather.

droddum, n., backside; hindquarters.

drodge, v., drudge; slave.

drog, n., drug.

droll, adj., eccentric; quaint; strange.

droshach, n., disgusting liquid food.

drouk, v., drench; soak: droukit, adj., soaked: droukin, n., soaking.

*droun, v., drown.

drouth, n., drought; thirst; heavy drinker: drouthy, adj., dry; thirsty.

drow, v., drizzle; n., drizzle; mist; sea fog.

drow, n., attack of illness; swoon; spasm; qualm of anxiety.

drow, n., sound of lamenting.

drug, v., n., drag; tug.

drugget-scone, n., potato scone with oatmeal.

drum-major, n., hussy; domineering woman.

drummle, v., make muddy: drummly, adj., muddy; gloomy; vague.

drummock, n., meal and water porridge.

drummure, adj., earnest; sad-looking.

drune, v., slow tune.

drunt/tak the drunt, v., sulk: drunts, n., huff; ill-humour.

drush, n., peat dust; powdered refuse.

druther, v., hesitate; n., awe.

dry-farrand, adj., distant in manner: drysome / dryward, adj., insipid; prosy.

dub, n., bog; pond; stagnant pool: dub-skelper, n., reckless person.

dud, n., dull, lifeless person: dudderon, n., slut.

duds, n., clothes; rags: duddy, adj., ragged; tattered.

due, be due, v., owe.

duffie, adj., wet and soft; spongy.

dug, n., dog: dug-flourish, n., ragwort: dug-hip, n., rose hip.

duke-ma-lordie, n., aristocrat.

dull/dull o hearin, adj., deaf.

dull/dule, n., goal; boundary.

dult, n., dullard; dunce.

dumb-sweir, n., snook.

dumfouner, v., amaze; stun: dumfounert, adj., amazed: dumfounerment, n., amazement.

dump, v., beat; bump; set down with a bump; deject; n., bump.

dun, n., fort on a hill.

dunch, v., n., bump; butt; jolt; push: dunchers, n., buffers.

dung, adj., overwhelmed.

dunk, n., adj., damp.

dunner, v., clatter; reverberate; n., clatter; reverberation.

dunny, n., basement.

dunt, v., bump; dent; knock; palpitate; n., blow; bump; knock; throb.

dunty, n., prostitute.

durk, n., claspknife; dirk.

durk, n., thickset person: durky, adj., thickset.

dursy, adj., stubborn.

dush, v., butt; thrust: dusht, adj., overcome.

dusty/disty-fuit, n., pedlar; traveller.

dusty miller, n., bumblebee; primula auricula.

dwadle, v., tarry.

dwaible, n., tall, weakly person; adj., pliable; shaky; weak.

dwall, v., dwell: dwallin, n., abode.

dwam, v., faint; become sick; n., stupor; trance: dwamminess, n., sickness.

dwinnle, v., dwindle; waste away.

dwyne, v., decline in health; dwindle; wane; n., decline: **dwyny**, adj., sickly.

dye, n., gew-gaw; child's toy.

dyke, v., build wall; n., wall: **dyke-lowper**, n., immoral person: **dyke-lowpin**, adj., immoral: **fail/cass'n/sod/taft dyke**, n., turf wall.

dyverous, adj., sundry.

dyvour, v., n., bankrupt.

Eard, n., see **yird**.

earn, v., clot; curdle.

earn, n., eagle: **earn-bleater**, n., snipe.

ease, v., abate: **easedom/easement**, n., relief from pain.

easin, n., eaves; horizon: **easin-butt**, n., barrel to catch eavesdrops.

eastart, adj., adv., eastward: **eastlin**, adj., eastern: **eastlins**, adv., eastwards: **eastie-wastie**, n., person of no firm convictions.

eattocks, n., confections.

ebb, n., space between high and low water; adj., shallow.

echt, n., adj., see **aicht**.

edder, n., adder.

edder, n., udder.

edict, n., court summons.

*****ee**, n., eye: **ee-brou**, n., eyebrow: **ee-sicht**, n., eyesight.

eelie/uilie, n., oil.

eelist, n., deformity; flaw.

eemis, adj., see **immis**.

eemock, n., ant: **eemock-pile**, n., ant-hill.

een/eenin, n., evening.

een, n., eyes; globules of fat on soup.

eend-on, adj., incessant; adv., incessantly.

eeram, n., rowing song.

*****eeran**, n., errand; shop purchase.

eerie, adj., afraid of supernatural; ghostly; strange; weird.

eeriorums, n., details.

ee-some/ee-sweet, adj., attractive; seductive.

eetim, n., article; item.

effeir, v., appertain; be appropriate; n., deportment; pomp.

efter, adv., prep., after: **eftername**, n., surname: **efternune**, n., afternoon: **efterstang**, n., contrition: **efter ten**, adv., past ten o'clock.

*****egg-dowpit**, adj., big-bottomed.

eggle, v., exhort; urge to mischief.

eidence, n., see **eydence**.

eik, v., add; augment; n., addition; extension: **eik-name**, n., cognomen.

eild, n., age; old age: **eildins**, n., equals in age.

eild, adj., see **yeld**.

eisin, v., be sexually desirous: **eisenin**, n., sexual desire.

eith, adj., easy: **eithly**, adv., easily.

elba/elbuck, n., elbow.

eldern, adj., elderly.

eldin, n., firewood; fuel.

eldritch, adj., frightful; hideous; unearthly, of sound.

eleiven, n., adj., eleven.

elf-caunle, n., ghostly light: **elfin**, n., elfland: **elf-ring**, n., fairy ring.

elide, v., abrogate; erase; rescind.

elshin, n., awl.

elt, v., begrime.

emerant, adj., green; verdant.

emmledeug, n., scrap meat: **emmlins**, n., giblets; leftovers.

*****en/end**, n., end; apartment; portion: **endlang**, adv., lengthwise: **endwey**, n., progress.

eneuch, n., adj., enough.

engrage, v., annoy; anger.

enlichten, v., enlighten; light up.

enorm, adj., atrocious; outrageous.

enow, n., adj., enough, of number.

ensenyie, n., motto; slogan; watchword.

enterteen, v., amuse.

entry, n., alley; avenue to house; porch; lobby.

equals-aquals, adv., alike; equally.

ergh (guttural), v., be timid; n., timidity; adj., timid; reluctant.

ern, n., see **airn**.

erse, n., backside: **erse on**, v., urge: **erselins**, adv., backwards.

esk, v., see **yesk**.

ess, n., ace; s-shaped pot-hook.

essart, adj., stubborn.

etin, n., giant; monster.

etion, (aishan), n., breed; stock; strain.

ettercap, n., spider; hot-tempered person.

ettersome, adj., aggressive; bitterly cold: **ettery**, adj., hot-tempered.

ettle, v., intend; conjecture; expect;

attempt; direct a missile; n., intention; supposition; attempt; ambition: **ettle at**, v., aim at: **ettle efter**, v., hanker for: **ettlin**, adj., ambitious: **ettlins**, n., wages.

even, v., compare; demean; attribute: **evens**, n., quits: **evendoun**, adj., absolute; frank: **evendounness**, n., honesty: **evenly**, adj., level; even.

ever and on, adv., continually.

evident, n., evidence.

evite, v., evade.

excaise, v., excuse; condone; n., excuse.

exem, v., examine.

exemp, v., exempt; n., exemption.

exerce, v., carry out official duties.

exoner, v., exonerate.

expawtiate, v., expatiate.

expede, v., expedite.

expensive, adj., extravagant.

expound, v., explain; interpret.

eydence, n., diligence; industry: **eydent**, adj., diligent; industrious.

eyntment, n., ointment.

eyst, v., covet; envy.

ezlar, n., ashlar.

ezzat, adj., zigzag.

*****Faa**, v., fall; happen; deserve; n., fall; hollow in ground; mousetrap; share; fate: **canna faa**, v., cannot claim: **faa out**, v., quarrel: **faa owre**, v., fall asleep: **faa tae**, v., begin; set to.

face, n., surface: **face-clout**, n., face towel.

factor, n., agent; estate steward.

faddom, v., fathom; measure; n., fathom.

fadge, n., rich, thick loaf.

fae, n., foe.

fae/frae, prep., from.

faem, v., n., foam.

faggot, n., flabby person; slut.

faik, v., tuck up; wrap; n., fold.

faik, v., excuse; let go with impunity.

faik, n., strand of rope.

fail, n., sod; turf.

fail, v., decline in health: **failed**, adj., impaired in health.

failyie, v., fail; default; n., failure; default.

faimish, v., famish.

fain, adj., glad; fond; willing; adv., gladly: **fainness**, n., affection: **fidgin fain**, adj., anxiously eager: **be fain o**, v., be fond of.

fair, v., stop raining; adj., dry, of weather; complete; adv., quite; absolutely: **fair-avised**, adj., blond: **fair-caain** / **fair-faced** / **fair-farrand**, adj., bland; specious; plausible: **fair-hornie**, n., fair play: **fair faa**, interj., good luck to.

fair, v., treat at a fair: **fairin**, n., gift bought at fair; deserts.

faird, v., bustle; n., bustle; impetuous act.

fairfurth, adj., explicit; honest; outspoken.

faisible, adj., presentable; tidy.

fait, n., accomplishment.

faither, n., father.

faizart, n., hermaphrodite fowl; mollycoddle.

faize, v., annoy; fray; n., annoyance.

falderal, n., bauble; excuse; whim.

falloch, adj., thick.

fane, n., fairy.

fanerel, n., tatter hanging from dress.

fang, v., grip; fill with water; prime; n., grip; bundle; talon; plunder.

fank, v., coil; ravel; catch in noose; n., coil.

fank, n., sheepfold.

fankle, v., entangle; ravel; trap; fumble; n., muddle; tangle.

fantoosh, adj., pretentious; showy: **fantoosherie**, n., pretentiousness.

faple, n., lower lip.

fard, v., decorate; gloss over.

fardel, n., large slice; parcel.

farin, n., food.

fareweill, v., n., farewell.

farl, n., oatcake; flour scone.

farlin, n., container used at herring gutting.

farouchie, adj., savage; truculent.

farrach, n., knack; flair.

fash, v., disturb; trouble; fret; annoy: **fash/fashery**, n., trouble; annoyance; vexation: **fashious**, adj., annoying; fractious; troublesome.

Fastern's Een, n., Shrove Tuesday.

fat, n., vat.

fat, adj., flourishing; fertile.

fattrels, n., loose pieces of trimming; embellishments.

fauch, v., n., adj., fallow: **fauchie,** adj., pale; yellowish-grey.

fauchentulie, n., squabble.

faucht, n., exertion; trouble; fight.

faul, n., ring of light round moon.

fauld, v., bend; fold; shut; n., fold; strand of rope; tier.

fauld, v., put sheep in fold; n., sheep-fold; milking.

faur, adj., adv., far: **faurest,** adj., farthest: **faur-awa,** adj., remote: **faur back,** adj., ignorant; uncouth; adv., long ago: **faur ben,** adj., very friendly: **faur-keeker,** n., telescope: **faur-kent,** adj., famous: **faur-seen,** adj., skilled: **faur throu,** adj., dangerously ill.

faurthen, n., farthing.

fause, adj., false; sham: **fause-face,** n., mask: **faus-loun,** n., recreant.

faut, v., fault; reprimand; n., fault; need: **fauty,** adj., defective.

fawsont, adj., decent; seemly.

feal, adj., steadfast; loyal.

fear, v., frighten; n., fright: **fear-fangit,** adj., apprehensive: **fearsome,** adj., frightful; timid: **feart,** adj., afraid: **feartie,** n., coward.

feat, adj., neat; attractive; apt; expedient; slick.

feather, v., fledge; grow feathers.

feather, n., polished wood grain.

Februar, n., February.

fechie-lechie, n., flat; savourless.

fecht, n., battle; struggle: **fechty,** adj., brave: **bonny fechter,** n., good fighter.

feck, v., contrive; shape.

feck, n., abundance; large number/portion; majority; worth: **feckfu,** adj., efficient; dynamic; serviceable: **feckless,** adj., footling; incompetent; weakly; worthless: **fecklins/feckly,** adv., mostly.

fecket, n., woollen undervest; under-waistcoat.

fedder, n., feather; plume: **feddery craw,** n., shuttlecock.

fee, v., n., engage/engagement as a servant: **fee wi,** v., hire oneself out to: **in fee,** adj., hired as servant:

feeing-fair, n., fair for hiring servants.

feegarie, n., frippery.

feenichin, adj., grotesque.

feerach, n., mental agitation.

feesick, n., medicine; physic.

feeze, v., twist; screw; n., twist: **feeze up,** v., rub vigorously.

feg, n., flick of finger.

fegs, interj., expressing surprise.

feid, n., feud; vendetta: **feidfu,** adj., hostile.

feil, adj., smooth; velvety.

feim, n., rage; sweat.

feinyie, v., fabricate; sham.

feir, n., array; host; crowd.

feir, adj., healthy: **feirdy,** adj., able-bodied; competent; stalwart.

feiroch, n., ability; adj., able; clever.

feist, v., fuss/toil with little result.

feith, n., salmon net staked across river.

fell, v., strike down; manhandle; slaughter.

fell, n., cuticle.

fell, adj., keen; astute; harsh; cruel; profound; severe; appetising.

felt, n., couch-grass; mass of fibrous matter: **feltered,** adj., matted.

felter, v., filter.

feltie, n., fieldfare; missel-thrush.

fen/fend, v., defend; succour; scrape an existence; n., effort; food; succour: **fendfu/fendie,** adj., capable; resourceful: **fending,** n., thrift.

fence-lowper, n., trespasser; wild, uncontrollable person.

fenester, n., window-frame; casement.

fent, v., n., faint.

ferlie, v., marvel; be surprised; n., marvel; novelty; monstrous creature; adj., wonderful; strange.

ferm, v., n., farm: **fermer,** n., farmer: **fermyaird,** n., farmyard.

fern, n., bracken: **fernie-tickles,** n., freckles: **fern-owl,** n., nightjar.

fern-year, n., last year: **auld fernyears,** n., stories of long ago.

ferrier, n., farrier; veterinary surgeon.

ferry, n., litter of pigs.

fertor, n., shrine.

fesh, v., fetch: **fesh up,** v., nurture.

fest, adj., adv., fast.

festen, v., attach; fasten.

fetch, v., aim a blow; attain; gasp; pant.

*fettle, v., set in order; n., strength; state of mind: fettle up, v., tidy up.

feu, n., land held on payment of "feu" duty; building site.

feugle, v., manipulate.

fey, adj., accursed; betwitched; doomed; predestined; susceptible.

fickle, adj., difficult; insecure; unsafe, of foothold.

fidder, v., hover, like hawk.

*fidge, v., fidget; itch; jerk; n., restless person: fidgin, adj., fidgety.

fient, n., devil, as in fient haet, devil a thing.

fier, n., companion; consort; match; spouse.

fift, n., adj., fifth.

figur/feegur, v., count; do arithmetic; n., figure.

fike, v., see fyke.

file, v., see fyle.

fill, v., pour out: fill fou, v., inebriate: filler, n., funnel for pouring.

filsh, v., filch; procure by stealth.

filsh, adj., faint with hunger.

fimmer, v., trip with light steps.

fin/find, v., find; grope; be conscious of; n., awareness; feeling.

fin, n., humour; mood.

fine, adj., comfortable; pleasant; well; adv., nicely; very well: fine and, adv., exceedingly: fine things, n., dainties; delicacies.

fingerfu, n., small amount: fingerneb, n., finger-tip.

finnock, n., immature trout.

fir-fecket/goun, n., coffin.

fire, n., fuel; a light: fire-dairt, n., thunderbolt: fire-en, n., fireside: fire-fangit, adj., scorched with over-fermentation: fire-flaucht, n., lightning; shooting star: firespang, n., volatile person: fire-stane, n., hearthstone: firy, adj., sultry: firy-tangs, n., lobster.

firlot, n., grain measure.

firrie, n., predicament.

firstlins, adv., firstly.

fish currie, n., fish "lie" in river: fish gowries, n., fish refuse.

fiss, v., fizz.

fissle, v., rustle; stir; rummage; n., rustle; stir.

fit, v., please; serve satisfactorily; suit; adj., able; inclined.

fit, v., total up.

fit, n., air; tune; habit.

fit, n., see fuit.

fitch, v., budge; handle.

fitter, v., dodder; fidget with feet.

fittie, adj., agile; sure-footed; expeditious.

fittie-lan, n., rear left-hand horse in plough team.

fittock, n., stocking foot worn as shoe.

fivver, n., fever: fivvert, adj., fevered.

fizz, v., fuss; bustle; n., excitement; fuss: fizzin drink, n., showy person.

flackie, n., straw draught screen.

flae, v., pare; skin; pillage.

flae, n., flea.

flaff, v., blow fitfully; flutter; flap; explode; n., flutter; flurry of wind: flaffer, n., fan.

flagarie, n., showy ornament; piece of frivolity; overdressed person.

flaiper, n., foolish, dressy person.

flair, n., floor.

flairdie, n., insincerity; wheedling person.

flane, n., arrow.

flannen, n., adj., flannel.

flap, v., n., flop.

flat/flet, n., storey: flatlins, adv., horizontally; at full length.

flaucht, v., fall in flakes; intertwine; strip off skin; n., lightning flash; gleam; gust of wind; lock of hair; snowflake.

flaucht, n., flight of birds; adv., in a spreadeagled manner.

flauchter, v., flap; flutter; shine fitfully; n., flutter; brood of young birds.

flauchter, v., pare off turf: flauchter-spade, n., turf-paring spade.

flauchter, v., lay flat on ground.

flaunter, v., blench; waver; veer erratically; equivocate.

flaunty, adj., flighty; gaudy.

flaw, n., falsehood: flawmont, n., anecdote; tale.

flaw, v., come off in flakes; pare; n., flake; scale.

flea-luggit, adj., capricious; eccentric; whimsical.

fleach, n., flea.

fleckit, adj., dappled; pied; streaky; variegated.

*****flee**, v., n., fly: **flee-about**, n., flighty person: **flee up**, v., take offence; n., quick-tempered person.

fleech, v., see fleich.

fleem, v., banish; chase; expel.

fleem, n., phlegm.

fleer, v., n., sneer.

fleesh, n., fleece; skin rash.

fleeter, n., bumper of liquor.

fleg, v., kick; n., blow; kick.

fleg, v., scare; dash about; n., scare: **flegsome**, adj., terrifying.

fleg, n., lie: **fleggar**, n., liar; romancer.

fleich (**fleetch**), v., flatter; solicit; importune: **fleichin**, adj., deceitful.

fleit, v., float; flow; inundate: **fleit owre**, v., overflow.

flench, v., flinch; blanch.

flesh, n., butcher-meat: **flesher**, n., butcher.

flet, n., flat; flat surface; saucer; adj., flat.

flether, v., flatter; be obsequious: **flethers**, n., flattering words.

fleuk, n., flounder; turbot: **fleuk-moud**, adj., crooked-mouthed.

fley, v., appal; drive off; frighten; take fright; n., fright.

flicher, v., flutter; fly unsteadily.

flicht, v., flee; perturb; n., flight: **flichtfu**, adj., fitful.

flicht, n., mote; speck.

flichter, v., flutter; glimmer; palpitate; n., flutter; glimmer: **flichtery**, adj., unstable; flighty: **flichter-lichtie**, n., unstable person.

flick/flake, n., streak of colour or light.

flim-flae, n., flattery.

flinder, v., smash: **flinders**, n., broken pieces; splinters.

fling, v., caper; dance; go off in pet; kick, of a horse; n., caper; dance; flounce; rejection; repulse: **fling to**, v., slam.

flingin-tree, n., flail.

flird, v., flaunt; move about impatiently: **flirdoch**, n., flirt.

flirr, v., flare up; intrude abruptly; n., flurry.

flisk, v., n., caper; flick; frisk; swipe: **flisky**, adj., frisky.

flist, v., explode; flare up with anger; flash: **flisty**, adj., passionate.

flister, v., flurry; hustle: **flistert**, adj., flurried.

flit, v., move from place to place; transport: **flittin**, n., house removal.

flitter, v., n., flutter.

flocht, v., excite; n., strain; stress: **flochty**, adj., excitable.

flochter, v., flutter; dart about.

flodge, n., fat, slovenly person.

floichan, n., snowflake.

flouer, n., flower; bouquet: **flouerin**, n., embroidery.

flourish, v., bloom; embroider; n., bloom.

flow, n., morass; quicksand: **flow-moss**, n., quaking bog.

flozen, v., bloat; puff up; swell.

fluffer, v., perturb; n., emotion; perturbation.

flumgummery, n., tomfoolery.

flunkie, n., lackey; male servant.

flush, n., marsh; sluice.

flype, v., strip off skin; turn inside out; n., flap of garment; shred of skin.

flyre, v., leer; mock; ogle; n., scornful laugh.

flyte, v., scold: **flytin**, n., scolding.

fodgel, n., fat, jolly person; adj., fat; buxom.

fog, n., lichen; moss: **foggie**, adj., mossy: **foggy rose**, n., moss rose.

foggage, n., rank grass not eaten in summer.

foggie, n., old, out-of-date person.

fogie-bee, n., wild bee.

follieshat, n., jellyfish.

follow, v., accompany.

foolyie, n., leaf foil.

foonge, v., be obsequious; show exaggerated respect for.

foorich, n., agitation; confusion.

foost/foosht, v., see **foust**.

footer, v., see **fouter**.

foppery, n., hallucination.

for, prep., in the direction of; to the advantage of: **for aa that**, adv., nevertheless: **be for**, v., incline to.

forby, adj., better; unusual; adv., besides; prep., as well as; except.

force, n., importance: **forcie**, adj., dynamic; impetuous; helpful to crops.

fordel, n., advantage; profit; progress.

forder, v., thrive; promote: **fordersome,** adj., adventurous; propitious.

fore, n., advantage; profit.

fore-, prefix, **forebreist,** n., forefront: **forebrou,** n., temple: **forecast,** n., forewarning: **fore-end,** n., beginning: **forefowk,** n., ancestors: **foregang,** n., premonition: **forehammer,** n., sledgehammer: **forehandit,** adj., foreseeing; prudent: **foreheid,** n., defiance: **foremaist,** adj., foremost: **forenail,** v., buy on tick: **forenent,** prep., facing; in front of; opposite: **forenuin,** n., forenoon: **forenuin bite,** n., forenoon snack: **forerin,** v., outpace; precede: **forerinner,** n., harbinger: **foresicht,** n., foresight: **foresichtie,** adj., provident: **foreside,** n., front of anything: **foresman,** n., foreman: **forespaul,** n., foreleg: **forespeak,** v., bespeak: **forestair,** n., open outside stair: **forestaw,** v., forestall.

forfairn, adj., decrepit; destitute; exhausted.

forfend, v., prevent.

forfluther, v., agitate; n., agitation.

forfochen, adj., exhausted.

forget, n., omission through absent-mindedness.

forgether/forgaither, v., meet together: **forgether wi,** v., associate with; encounter: **forgetherin,** n., meeting; social gathering.

forgie, v., forgive; condone; pardon.

forhoo, v., abandon, of a bird its nest.

forjeskit, adj., exhausted.

fork, v., n., hunt; search.

forlaithie, v., detest.

forleit, v., forget; forsake.

forrit, v., foster; promote; adj., fast, of clock; present; well advanced; adv., ahead; at hand: **win forrit,** v., advance: **forritsome,** adj., bold.

forsay, v., gainsay.

forslitting, n., chastisement.

fother, v., feed cattle; n., fodder.

fou, v., fill; load; n., full load; adj., full; drunk; adv., too; very: **fill fou,** v., make drunk: **fou hous,** n., house with ever-open door.

foumart, n., polecat.

found, v., lay the foundation of; n., foundation; reserve of money.

founder, v., collapse; prostrate with fatigue; shock; strike down.

fousome, adj., cloying; fulsome.

fousome, adj., filthy; smelly; squalid.

foust, v., n., decay; mildew; mould: **fousty,** adj., fusty; mouldy.

fouter, v., botch; fuss with little effect; potter about; n., bungler; muddle; trifle: **fouterie,** adj., paltry: **fouterin,** adj., fussy; unskilled.

fouth, n., plenty: **fouthie,** adj., plentiful; affluent.

foutie, adj., abject; mean; insidious; underhand.

fow, v., toss hay/straw; n., pitchfork.

fower, n., adj., four: **fowersome,** n., company of four: **fower-neukit,** adj., rectangular: **fower-weys,** n., crossroads.

fowk, n., folk; human beings; employees; inhabitants.

foy, n., leave-taking feast.

fozie, adj., flabby; spongy; hazy; frayed.

fraca, n., brawl; fuss; palaver.

frack, adj., eager; able-bodied.

frae/fae, prep., from; conj., from the time that.

fraik, v., mollycoddle; wheedle; malinger; n., freak; whim.

frainishin, n., passion; rage.

frank, adj., eager; without restraint.

frap, v., undermine; ruin.

fraucht, v., load; hire a boat; n., burden; freight: **frauchtless,** adj., trivial; weightless.

freck, adj., brash; hale and hearty.

free, adj., frank; cordial; generous; crumbly, of soil/pastry: **freestane,** easily worked sandstone: **free trade,** n., contraband.

freff, adj., cold in manner.

freir, n., friar.

freisk, v., rub vigorously.

freit, n., augury; superstition; whim: **freity,** adj., superstitious.

freit, v., chafe; eat into; rust: **freiting,** n., discontent.

freith, v., n., foam; lather.

fremmit, adj., alien; foreign; strange; aloof; unfriendly.

frenzy, v., enrage.

fresh, v., n., thaw.

fretten, adj., pitted; seamed.

fricht, v., frighten; n., fright: frichtit, adj., afraid: frichtsome, adj., frightful.

frien, n., friend; relative: frienly, adj., friendly.

frimple-frample, adv., indiscriminately.

frizzel, n., gun hammer.

front, n., front of house; front garden: fronty, adj., bold.

froun, v., n., frown.

frow, n., buxom woman.

frump/frumple, v., rumple.

frush, adj., decayed, of material; frail; friable; tender.

fry, n., coterie; group.

fry, n., state of distraction; tumult.

fud, n., rabbit's tail; buttocks.

fudder, n., blast of wind.

fuff, v., blow gently; explode; hiss; pant; n., explosion; hiss; puff; whiff: fuff up, v., explode with rage: fuffers, n., bellows.

fuffle, v., disorder; ruffle; n., great effort.

fugie (foodjie), v., flee; play truant; n., absentee; fugitive.

fuil, n., fool; adj., foolish: mak a fuil o, v., make a laughing-stock of.

fuird, n., ford.

*fuit, v., set on end; n., foot; footstep: fuitbrod, n., spinning-wheel treadle: fuitin, n., footing: fuitless, adj., tottery: fuit-licker, n., toady: fuitmaist, adj., lowest: fuitpad, n., footpath: fuit-shakin, n., dance: fuitsteid, n., footmark: deil's fuit, n., shoemaker's last: fuit the flair, v., dance: howe o the fuit, n., sole of the foot.

full (fuh-l), v., fill; adj., mature, of herring: full bang, adv., full tilt.

fulyerie, n., foliage.

fulyie, v., pollute; n., refuse: fulyie-can, n., refuse bin.

fume, n., perfume.

fummle, v., be clumsy; fumble; grope; be sexually impotent.

funder, v., founder.

fun egg, n., addled egg.

fung, v., cuff; fling; kick; pitch; toss; n., cuff; kick.

funk, n., resentment; tantrum: funky adj., easily offended.

funny, adj., curious; n., game of marbles where winnings returned, cf. keepy.

furdersome, adj., see fordersome.

furious, adj., insane.

furl, v., whirl.

furlie, n., see whurly.

furm, n., form; bench.

furr, n., drill; furrow: furr up, v., earth up, potatoes, etc.

furth, n., open-air; adv., forth; abroad: prep., from; outside: furth o, prep., beyond the boundaries of.

furthie, adj., affable; frank; energetic: furthiness, n., frankness.

furthsetter, n., publisher.

fush, v., n., fish.

fushion, n., ability; energy; nourishment: fushionless, adj., dull; tasteless.

fushloch, n., straw/rubbish lying around.

futrat/whitrat, n., weasel.

fuzzie, adj., effervescent.

fyauchled, adj., overworked.

fyke, v., fidget; fuss; aggrieve; vex; n., fuss; worry; exacting person: fykie, adj., exacting; fussy: fykesome, adj., fractious: fyke wi, v., dally with: mak a fyke, v., make a fuss: fykerie, n., fussiness.

fyke-fack, n., trivial talk: fyke-facks, n., chores.

fykemaleeries, n., empty ritual.

fyle, v., befoul; deface; desecrate: fylement, n., moral filth; obloquy.

Gaa, n., mock sun; parhelion.

gaa, n., see gaw.

gab, v., chatter; n., chatter; mouth; voluble speaker: gabber, v., gabble: haud ane's gab, v., shut one's mouth: gabbie, adj., chatty.

gaberlunzie, n., beggar's wallet: gaberlunzieman, n., licensed beggar.

gabbet, n., gobbet.

gad, n., goad: gadsman, n., the man who drove plough horses with a goad.

gadge, v., order off-handedly.

gadger, n., gauger; exciseman.

*gae, v., go; walk: gae back, v.,

deteriorate: **gae by anesel**, v., go mad: **gae in**, v., assemble; contract: **gae in wi**, v., accede to: **gae tae**, v., close, of door: **gae thegither**, v., amalgamate: **gae throu**, v., squander.

gaff/gaffaw, v., n., guffaw.

gaig, v., crack, of dry wood; n., crack in wood.

gaily, adj., healthy; adv., fairly.

gain, adj., straight; direct: **gain road**, n., direct road.

gainfu, adj., lucrative: **gainin**, adj., winsome.

gainter, v., pose; give oneself airs.

gair, n., grassy slope; gusset.

gair, n., avarice; adj.; avaricious.

gaird, v., guard; n., sentinel; warder.

gairfish, n., dolphin; porpoise.

gairten, n., garter.

gairy, adj., gaudy; many-coloured.

gaishen, n., person wasting away; walking skeleton.

gaislin, n., gosling.

gaitberry, n., brambleberry.

galatian, n., mumming play.

galdragon, n., witch.

gall (as in "ran"), n., bog myrtle.

gallant, v., flirt; gad about flirtatiously.

gallimaufry, n., hodge-podge.

gallivant, v., gad about; flirt.

gallowses, n., trouser braces.

gallus/gallows, adj., daring; rash; wild.

gallwood, n., wormwood.

galore, n., plenty; adv., in plenty.

galshochs, n., sweets; titbits.

gam, v., overlap, of teeth.

gamaleerie, n., lout; adj., loutish.

gambade, v., caper; strut.

gamf/gamph, v., gape; snap greedily.

gamf, v., act the buffoon; n., buffoon.

gammle, v., gamble.

gamphered, adj., embroidered.

*****gang**, v., go; walk; n., gait; journey; path; water channel: **gang gyte**, v., go out of one's mind: **gangable**, adj., passable, of road; negotiable, of currency: **gangrel**, adj., itinerant: **gangrel body**, n., vagrant.

gansh, v., bite by snapping; gnash teeth; stammer; n., stammer.

gant, v., n., yawn: **gant-at-the-door**, n., lounger.

gar, v., cause; compel; constrain.

gardevine, n., two-quart bottle.

gardymang, n., meatsafe.

gargrugous, adj., grave; severe.

gar-me-true, n., impostor; quack.

garron, n., sturdy hill horse.

garth, v., enclose; n., enclosure.

gash, v., chatter; talk animatedly; n., chatter; adj., animated; clever: **gash-gabbit**, adj., glib-tongued: **gashy**, adj., august.

gash, adj., ashen; hideous.

gast, n., unpleasant surprise: **gastrous**, adj., gruesome; macabre.

*****gate**, n., manner; way; knack.

*****gate**, n., street; journey: **gate-end**, n., locality: **gate-farrant**, adj., presentable: **gatelins**, adv., straight: **gate-side**, n., wayside.

gatty, adj., failing in body.

gaucy, adj., plump; cheerful; big and jolly; showy.

gaud/gad, n., goad; iron bar.

gaudeamus, n., carnival; rejoicing.

gaun, adj., busy.

gaur, v., n., seam.

gaut, n., castrated boar.

gaval, v., feast: **gavalling**, n., revelry.

gaw, v., abrade; chafe; harass; n., abrasion; bile; blemish; setback: **gaw-i-the-back**, n., grievance: **gaw-bursen**, adj., short-winded.

gaw, n., water-drain.

gawk, v., act foolishly; stare open-mouthed; n., lout: **gawkie**, n., fool; simpleton; adj., clumsy; stupid.

gawp, v., gape; yawn: **gawpus**, n., big-mouthed person.

geal (jeel), v., coagulate; freeze; n., ice; gelatine.

gean (gee-an), n., wild cherry.

gear, n., effects; equipment; money: **gear-getherer**, n., miser.

geck, v., mock; scorn; toss head derisively.

ged, n., pike.

gee (jee), v., stir; turn away; n., caprice; mood; whim.

gee-gaw, n., gew-gaw; cheap ornament.

geenyoch, adj., greedy.

geg, v., n., hoax; trick.

geggie, n., show at fair; travelling theatre show.

gell, v., throb; crack; split.

gell, n., inspiration; strong wind.

gemm, n., game.

174

gemm, adj., deformed: **gemm-leggit**, adj., lame.

gemmie, n., gamekeeper.

genie (jee-nee), n., aptitude; bent; faculty; talent.

gentie, adj., courteous; genteel; high-born: **gentiness**, n., grace.

gentle, adj., high-born: **gentle traffic**, n., smuggling.

gentrice, n., gentility; good breeding; magnanimity.

geordie, n., country bumpkin.

gester, v., n., gesture.

*get, v., be allowed; beget; find; n., bastard; offspring: **gets**, n., progeny.

gether, v., gather; save money: **getherin**, n., gathering; pus: **getherin-coal**, n., big coal to keep fire in overnight: **weill gethert**, adj., wealthy.

gey, adj., big; adv., very: **geylies**, adv., rather: **geylike**, adj., strange.

ghaist, n., ghost.

giddack, n., sand eel.

gie, v., give: **gie owre**, v., abandon; stop; quit: **gien**, adj., gifted.

gif, conj., if; whether.

giff-gaff, v., exchange, words, etc.; n., give and take; mutual aid.

gift, n., second sight: **giftie**, n., ability; talent.

gig, n., contrivance; trick.

gig-trot, n., routine.

gilgal, n., babel.

gill, n., gully; narrow valley.

gillygawkie, n., booby; silly, clumsy person.

gilpin, n., big fat child/fellow.

gilpy, n., mischievous boy/girl; tom-boy.

gilravage, v., act riotously; rampage; n., orgy; riot; uproar.

gilreverie, n., riotous feasting.

gilt, n., young spayed sow.

gimmer, n., ewe in its second year; woman.

gin, prep., before; by, of time; conj., if; whether; by the time that.

ginge (jinj), n., ginger: **gingebreid**, n., gingerbread; adj., showy.

ginger, n., aerated waters.

ginkums, n., mannerisms; traits.

gip (jip), v., gut herring; n., herring guts.

gird, v., strike; impel; n., blow; push; blast of wind.

gird, v., encircle; zone: **gird/girr**, n., hoop.

girdle, n., griddle; iron plate for baking scones and oatcakes.

girn, v., complain; fret; snarl; n., grumbler; snarl: **girnie**, adj., peev-ish.

girn, v., catch in a snare; n., snare; trap.

girnel, n., granary; meal bin.

girr, n., see **gird**.

girran, n., pustule; tumour; pimple.

girran, n., sturdy hill horse.

girse, v., graze; n., grass: **girse-lowper**, n., grasshopper.

girsle, n., gristle.

girt, n., girth.

girth, n., asylum; sanctuary.

girzie, n., house-maid.

gitter, v., gabble; jabber; n., silly talker.

gizz, n., wig.

gizzen, n., throat.

gizzen, v., become leaky; parch; shrink; warp; adj., dry; leaky.

glack, n., gully; ravine.

glaik, v., dazzle; flirt; frolic; n., gleam; prank: **glaikery**, n., silly conduct: **glaikit**, adj., foolish; giddy; super-ficial: **glaikitness**, n., ineptitude: **glaiky**, adj., enchanting.

glairy, adj., dazzling; glaring.

glaizie, adj., glassy; smooth.

glamour, v., dazzle; enamour: **glamourie**, n., enchantment.

glancy, adj., shiny: **glancing-glass**, n., flashy, superficial person.

glaum, v., eat greedily; grip; n., grip: **glaum at**, v., grasp at.

glaur, n., mud; slime: **glaury**, adj., muddy.

glazie, adj., vitreous.

gled, n., hawk; kite; greedy person: **blue gled**, n., peregrine falcon.

gledge, v., glance; n., glance; sideways look.

gleesh, v., burn brightly; n., large, bright flame.

gleg, adj., alert; nimble; dexterous; intelligent; sharp; smooth: **glegness**, n., acumen: **gleg-shair**, adj., positive.

gleib, n., glebe; plot of land.

gleid, n., ember; spark; glowing fire.
glendergane, adj., in poor condition.
glengore, n., syphilis.
glennie, n., safety lamp.
glent, v., shine; glance; n., sparkle; peep; sideways glance.
gless, n., glass: **glessie,** n., glass marble; treacle candy.
gley, v., go astray; squint; n., squint; anomaly; adj., adv., awry: **gleyed,** adj., off the straight: **gley-moud,** adj., crooked-mouthed.
glibby/glib-gabbit, adj., glib-tongued; eloquent.
gliff, v., scare; shock; n., scare; impulse; instant; feeling of pain/ pleasure.
gliff, v., n., flash; gleam; glimpse.
glim, n., gonorrhoea.
glime, v., n., squint.
glint, v., n., glance; gleam; peep.
glisk, v., glimpse; look cursorily; peep; n., flash; glance; glimpse.
glit, n., slime; phlegm; serum: **glitty,** adj., slimy; greasy.
gloam, v., grow dark: **gloamin,** n., dusk: **gloamin-staur,** n., evening star.
glock, v., n., gurgle.
glocken/gloff, v., boggle.
gloggie, adj., artificial; guttural.
glore, n., majesty: **glorious,** adj., hilariously drunk.
glorgy, adj., oppressive; stifling.
glotten, v., thaw slowly.
glower, v., n., frown; stare; gleam, of stars: **gloweret,** adj., lurid, of sky.
glugger, v., gulp down noisily; gurgle; n., gurgle.
glumph, v., look sullen; n., sullen person.
glumsh, v., sulk; n., sulky mood; adj., sulky-looking.
glunch, v., frown; sulk; n., frown; sulky look.
glunder, v., look sulky: **glunners,** n., sulks.
glunt, v., look sour; n., scowl: **the glunts,** n., the sulks.
glush, n., slush: **glushy,** adj., slushy.
glyde, n., ageing horse.
gnap, v., gnaw; snap with teeth.
goam, v., greet; notice; recognise: **goamless,** adj., stupid.

goave, v., stare stupidly; n., empty gaze.
gob/gab/gub, n., mouth: **gob-stopper,** n., chewy candy.
goblet, n., iron pot with bellying sides.
gokman, n., guard; warder.
golach, n., beetle: **forkie/hornie golach,** n., earwig.
goldie, n., goldfinch.
goller, v., n., bawl; howl; roar; shout.
gollop, v., gulp down; n., gulp.
gomeril, n., stupid person.
goo, n., sea-gull.
goo, n., savour; smell; disgust.
goon, n., see **goun.**
goor, n., half-melted snow; stagnant water; rheum; ear wax.
gorb/gorlin, n., fledgling; infant.
gorcock, n., moorcock; red grouse male.
gormaw, n., cormorant; greedy person.
gorsk, n., patchy dark-green grass: **gorsky,** adj., rank in growth.
gospel kail, n., Calvinistic preaching.
goss, n., companion; friend.
gote, n., gutter; marsh; sea inlet.
gotherlisch, adj., hypocritical.
goun, n., gown: **goun-alane,** adj., dowerless: **lang goun,** n., advocate.
gouster, v., bluster; bully; n., bully.
govie-dick, interj., expressing surprise.
gow owre, v., seduce.
gowan, n., daisy.
gowd, n., gold: **gowdie,** n., treasurer: **gowdspink,** n., goldfinch.
gowf, v., strike; n., stroke; golf: **gowfin stick,** n., golf club.
gowk, v., play the fool; n., cuckoo; dunce; fool: **gowkit,** adj., foolish: **gowk's eeran,** n., fool's errand: **gowk-storm,** n., spring storm.
gowl, v., n., bellow; growl; howl.
gowp, v., throb; pulsate; n., throb; ache.
gowp, v., gaze foolishly; gulp.
gowpen, n., double handful.
gowries, n., fish leavings.
gowsty, adj., desolate.
grab, n., booty; bargain: **grabby,** adj., acquisitive; greedy.
grace, n., virtue: **gracie,** adj., virtuous: **gracious,** adj., amiable.
graddan, n., refuse ground to powder; home-made snuff.

graff, n., ditch; grave.

graidly, adj., orderly, seemly.

grain, n., prong; arm of river/sea.

graip, v., grope; search with hand.

graip, n., manure fork.

graith, v., array; fit out; bleach clothes in lye of urine; n., commodities; equipment; harness; stale urine for bleaching; lather: **graithin**, n., dress; harness; furnishing.

gralloch, v., disembowel; n., entrails of deer.

gramashes, n., leggings.

grammar, n., learning; scholarship.

grampus, n., ignoramus.

gran/grand, adj., excellent; splendid: **grandsher**, n., old man.

grane, v., groan.

grannie, n., grandmother; chimney cowl: **grannie mutch**, n., columbine.

grass, v., pasture; **grassing**, n., pasturage.

grate, n., grating; stove.

gravat/grauvat, n., cravat; scarf; hangman's noose.

grave, v., bury: **grave-howker**, n., gravedigger.

grawl, n., grilse.

gray, v., dawn; adj., grey; dismal; sad: **gray-back**, n., hooded crow: **gray-baird**, n., earthenware liquor jug: **gray-daurk**, n., dusk: **gray duck**, n., mallard: **grayfish**, n., saith: **gray folk**, n., gnomes; trolls: **gray horse**, n., louse: **gray licht**, n., dawn.

great, adj., bulky; pregnant; intimate; in flood.

gree, n., ointment; unguent; dye.

gree, n., prize; social rank; fame: **bear the gree**, v., excel; win.

gree, v., agree; conciliate: **greeable**, adj., agreeable: **greement**, n., agreement.

green, n., lawn; adj., callow; youthful; fresh, of milk; immature, of manure: **green brees**, n., slimy water: **green kail**, n., borecole: **green lintie**, n., greenfinch: **greens**, n., vegetables in general.

greeshoch, n., glowing fire; enthusiasm; fervour.

greit, v., weep; sob: **greitin cheese**, n., oily cheese: **greitin-faced**, adj., sour-faced: **greitin Teenie**, n., peevish woman.

gress, v., pasture; n., grass.

grien, v., desire ardently; yearn.

grieve, v., act as overseer; n., farm bailiff; steward.

grip/grup, v., grasp; seize; n., grasp; spasm of pain: **grips**, n., fetters: **grippers**, n., antennae: **grippy**, adj., greedy; miserly: **catch grip o**, v., lay hold of: **grip to**, v., hold fast to.

grist, n., girth; fabric; grain of wood; texture.

grit, v., gnash the teeth; n., grating sound.

groff, adj., gross; coarse in texture; harsh; vulgar.

groozle, v., breathe heavily.

grouf, v., lie face downwards.

grout, n., evil-smelling stuff.

growf, v., sleep restlessly; snore.

growk, v., regard suspiciously.

growe, v., grow.

growth (as in "now"), n., growth; weeds: **growthie**, adj., fast-growing; fertile; thriving: **growthiness**, n., lushness.

grozet, n., gooseberry.

grub, v., seize greedily.

grubber, n., harrower.

grudge, n., complaint.

grue, v., shiver from aversion; creep, of flesh; n., grimace; shiver: **gruesome**, adj., abhorrent; ghastly; repulsive.

grue, n., half-melted snow.

gruggle, v., disfigure; n., angle.

grugous, adj., ghastly; horrible; ugly.

gruip, n., ditch; cowshed gutter.

grulsh, n., short, stout person.

grummel, n., dregs; sediment: **grummly**, adj., full of sediment.

grummle, v., grumble; find fault; n., grumble.

grumph, v., n., grunt: **grumphie**, n., sow: **grumphy**, adj., ill-natured.

grun/grund, n., ground; grave; sea floor; root of a matter: **grund-ebb**, n., lower foreshore: **grun hous**, n., basement cellar: **grun-nit**, n., earth nut: **grunstane**, n., foundation stone: **grunwark**, n., groundwork.

gruns, n., grout; sediment; lees: **grunsie**, adj., full of sediment.

grunsel, n., groundsel.

gruntle, v., grunt; n., grunt; pig's snout.

grunzie, n., face, contemptuous; nose and mouth like pig's snout.

grup, v., n., grip.

grush, v., grind; squeeze; n., gravel; grit.

grushie, adj., fast-growing; thriving; lush.

gryce, n., young pig.

gryfe, n., talon.

gub/gob/gab, n., mouth.

guddle, v., grope with hands for fish; do dirty work; muddle; n., muddle.

gudge, v., n., gouge.

guess, n., enigma; riddle.

guff, v., give off smell; n., odour; taste: **guffie**, adj., smelly.

guid, n., God; adj., good: **guidbrither**, n., brother-in-law: **guid-gaun**, adj., in good working order: **guid-leevin**, adj., pious: **guidless**, adj., wicked: **guidliheid**, n., honour; sanctity: **guidman**, n., head man; husband: **guidwife**, n., landlady; mistress of house: **guidwill**, n., gratuity: **guid-willie**, adj., cordial: **guid few**, n., considerable number: **guid folk**, n., fairies: **guid fores**, n., good qualities: **a guid's blessin**, n., a mercy: **guid word**, n., prayer: **dae guid**, v., thrive: **the unco guid**, n., self-righteous people.

guide, v., advise; handle: **guidal**, n., control: **guider**, n., director.

guise, v., masquerade; dissemble; n., masquerade: **guiser**, n., mummer.

gullie, v., knife; n., large knife: **gulliegaw**, v., gash; n., deep cut.

gulsoch, n., jaundice; satiety.

gum, v., film with moisture; n., film of moisture; coal dross.

gumph/gumphie, n., booby.

gumption, n., intelligence; self-confidence: **gumptious**, adj., pretentious.

gun, n., briar pipe.

gundy, n., toffee.

gunner, v., talk volubly; n., chatterer.

gunner, n., turbot.

gurl, v., n., growl; snarl; gurgle; adj., snappish: **gurly**, adj., inclement.

gurr, v., n., growl; snarl.

gurr, n., bravery; drive; spirit.

gurry, n., bustle; noisy quarrel.

gurthie, adj., stout; heavy.

guse, n., flat-iron.

guse, n., goose.

gushet, n., gusset; triangular ground between two properties.

gussie, n., young pig.

gust, v., n., flavour; relish: **gustless**, adj., tasteless: **gusty**, adj., tasty.

gutcher, n., grandfather.

guts, n., stomach; glutton: **gutsy/gutty**, adj., big-bellied; gluttonous; roomy: **gutsiness**, n., greed: **gutscraper**, n., fiddler.

guttie, n., rubber: **gutties**, n., gym shoes.

guzzle, v., n., debauch.

gype, v., gaze vacantly; n., booby; vacant stare.

gyre/gyre-carle, n., monster; evil spirit: **gyre-carlin**, n., witch.

gyrie (jyrie), n., artifice; trick.

gyte, adj., crazed; mad with desire: **gang gyte**, v., go off one's head.

Haa, n., hall; farmhouse; mansion house: **haa-bible**, n., family Bible.

haar, n., sea fog; huskiness: **haary**, adj., misty and cold.

habber, v., stammer.

habble, v., limp; perplex; n., confusion; difficulty: **habbleshow**, n., babel.

habile, adj., able; eligible; expedient; congruous.

habnab, v., hobnob; fraternise.

hack, n., chunk; adze.

haddie, n., haddock: **Finnan haddie**, n., smoked haddock.

haddin, n., abode; estate; property.

hae, v., have; believe; n., possession.

*haet, n., iota; particle; whit.

haffers, n., half-shares.

haffet, n., temple, of features.

hag, v., hack; fell; n., hack; undergrowth: **haggit**, adj., worn-out.

hag, n., peat-hole.

haggis, n., paunch; pudding of onions, oatmeal, sheep's lung, heart, liver.

haggle, v., cut unevenly; struggle forward.

haik, v., loiter; scrounge; n., loiterer.

hail line, n., goal line.

hain, v., save; enclose; protect: **hainin**, n., enclosure: **hainins**, n., savings.

hainberry, n., raspberry.

178

hainch, v., hobble; limp; n., haunch.

hairm/herm, v., n., harm.

hairse, adj., hoarse.

hairst, v., harvest; n., harvest; autumn.

haiser/haisle, v., dry off in sun: **haisert,** adj., half dried off.

haister, v., speak/act confusedly; n., person who so speaks/acts.

haiveless, adj., careless; meaningless.

haiver, v., talk nonsense: **haivers,** n., nonsense: **haiverel,** adj., nonsensical.

*****hale,** v., heal; n., health; adj., whole; sound; unharmed; adv., completely: **halelie,** adv., completely: **halescart,** adj., scotfree: **halesome,** adj., wholesome: **halewater,** n., torrent: **hale and fier,** adj., strong and well.

half, v., halve; n., one of two unequal parts: **halflin,** n., adolescent; apprentice; adj., adolescent; amateur: **halflins,** adv., partly.

halie, adj., holy: **haliday,** n., holiday.

hallan, n., cottage; dividing wall; draught-screen; porch; turf seat: **hallan-stane,** n., threshold.

hallickit/hallirackit, adj., capricious; whimsical.

hallie, n., hollow; valley.

hallion, n., buffoon.

halse, v., greet with an embrace.

halta dance, n., shimmering air; haze.

hame, n., home: **hameart,** adj., homemade; vernacular: **hame-bred,** adj., unsophisticated: **hamely,** adj., domestic; simple: **hame-drauchtit,** adj., fond of home: **hamespun,** adj., bucolic; crude: **hamewith,** adv., homewards.

hammer, v., drub; thrash.

hanch, v., gobble up; annex.

handfast, n., trial marriage.

handling, n., task; undertaking.

handsel, v., celebrate with a gift; n., such a gift.

handy, adj., adaptable; dexterous; moderately priced.

hand-wryte, n., handwriting.

hank, v., loop; n., loop; skein; cord.

hanker efter, v., desire; yearn for.

hanky, n., handkerchief.

hannie, n., ladle; milk pail.

hantle, n., great deal; handful; a number/quantity/volume of.

hap, v., n., cover; wrap; blanket; shawl; screen: **happin,** n., garment.

hap, v., hop; bob; jump; skip.

hap, n., strange occurrence: **happen,** v., happen to.

happer, n., mill hopper.

happity, adj., hobbling; lame.

hapshackle, v., n., fetter; hobble; trammel.

harbourie, n., accommodation; lodging; seaport.

hard, adj., strong, of drink: **hardlies,** adv., scarcely: **hard fish,** n., dried fish: **hard neck,** n., impudence: **hard-wrocht,** adj., hard-worked.

harigals, n., entrails.

hark at, v., hearken to.

harl, v., n., drag; haul; rake; tug.

harn, n., course linen.

harns, n., brains; intelligence.

hash, n., blockhead.

hash, v., abuse; harass; mangle; spoil; n., mess: **hasher,** n., energetic, rough worker: **hashy,** adj., rough; untidy; strenuous; stormy.

haskie, adj., husky; hazy.

hasp, v., n., latch.

hat, v., raise hat: **lum/tyle hat,** n., top-hat.

hatter, v., jumble; obstruct; swarm; n., swarm.

hauchle, v., limp; shuffle.

*****haud,** v., n., hold; prop: **haud at,** v., persist: **haud awa frae,** v., go away from: **haud for/to,** v., aim at: **haud on,** v., carry on; wait: **haud tae,** v., persist: **haud tae/aff ye,** v., turn left/right.

hauf, adj., adv., half: **hauf-fou,** adj., half-drunk: **hauf-hung-tae,** adj., semi-qualified: **wee hauf,** n., small whisky.

haugh (guttural), n., flat ground by river.

hauld, n., resort; sanctuary; shelter.

*****haun,** n., hand: **haun-clout,** n., hand towel: **haunle,** n., handle: **haunless,** adj,. handless; incompetent: **haun o wryte,** n., handwriting: **haun-waled,** adj., selected by hand: **haun-wryte,** n., autograph.

haunt, v., fraternise with.

haurdly/haurly, adv., hardly; scarcely.

haurl, n., slattern; slut.

hause, n., gullet; neck; throat: **clap o the hause**, n., uvula.

haver-meal, n., oatmeal.

havings, n., etiquette; good manners.

haw, n., hawthorn; berry of hawthorn.

hawkie, n., cow with white face; general pet name for cow.

hazelraw, n., kind of lichen.

hear til, v., heed: **hear tell o**, v., get news of.

heather-heidit, adj., bucolic: **heather-lowper**, n., countryman; yokel: **tak to the heather**, v., become an outlaw.

*heave, v., rise above surface; throw effortlessly.

hech ay, interj., expressing weariness.

hech-how, n., habit; routine: adj., humdrum.

hecht, v., n., forecast; offer; promise.

heck, n., fodder rack; manger.

heckle, n., cock's neck feather; cockade.

heckle, n., flax-dressing comb: **heckle-board**, n., flax-dressing board: **heckle-pins**, n., heckle prongs: **heckler**, n., flax-dresser.

heels-owre-gowdie/heid, adv., topsy-turvy; upside-down.

heft, n., pasture.

heft, n., haft; handle.

heh, interj., here.

*heich, adj., high; tall; arrogant; hilarious: **heich-heidit**, adj., arrogant: **heich-kiltit**, adj., immodest: **heichmaist**, adj., highest: **heichness**, n., height: **heicht**, v., heighten; exhalt; exhilarate; increase charges.

*heid, n., head; adj., principal: **heidie**, adj., impetuous: **heidlins**, adv., precipitately: **heidmaist**, adj., chief: **heid bummer/deister/yin**, n., boss; manager: **heidmaister**, n., headmaster: **heidstane**, n., gravestone.

heize/heist, v., hoist; rise; heave; exhilarate; n., hoist; exhilaration: **gie a heize**, v., encourage: **heizin**, n., encouragement.

help, v., mend: **help ma bob**, interj., expressing surprise.

hemp, n., cord; rope: **hempie**, n., gallows bird; rogue.

hen, v., withdraw through cowardice.

hen, n., affectionate term for female: **hen-laft**, n., hen roost: **hen-pen**, n.,

hen droppings: **hen-taed**, adj., in-toed.

herbour, v., lodge; shelter; n., harbour: shelter.

hereanent, adv., about this; **hereawa**, adv., hereabouts; hither.

heronious, adj., outrageous; unconventional.

herry, v., rob; rape: **herryment**, n., robbery: **herry out o**, v., dispossess.

hersel/himsel, n., mistress/master of household; pron., herself/himself: **her/his lane**, adv., by herself/himself.

hership, n., famine; ruin.

*hert, n., heart: **hertie**, adj., convivial: **hert-hungry**, adj., yearning: **hert-rug**, n., emotion: **hert-sair**, adj., heartsore.

hesp, n., brooch; clasp.

het, adj., hot.

heuch, n., cleft; crag; gully; coal pit; quarry.

heuk, v., hook; n., hook; sickle; anchor.

hey, n., hay: **hey-ruck**, n., hay-rick.

hicht, n., height: **hichten**, v., heighten.

hick, v., n., hiccup.

hidlins, adj., secret; adv., secretly.

hielan, adj., awkward.

high-gate, n., highway: **high-style**, adj., pretentious; florid: **high-bendit**, adj., ambitious.

hilch, v., n., halt.

hill-man, n., hill shepherd: **hill-run**, adj., boorish; uncultured.

hin-end, n., backside.

*hing, v., hang; n., knack; burden: **hing in**, v., persevere: **hingin-like**, adj., sickly-looking: **hingin-lock**, n., padlock: **hing/wait on**, v., linger.

hinmaist, adj., final; hindmost; ultimate.

hinner, adj., latter: **hinnerly/at the hinner-end**, adv., eventually.

hinner, v., hinder.

hinnie, n., honey; darling: **hinniesickle**, n., honeysuckle.

hinside, n., rear.

hippertie-tippertie, adj., overpunctilious.

hippit, adj., lamed through strain in the thighs.

hird, v., n., herd.

hirple, v., n., hobble.

hirsel, v., hustle; move clumsily; shuffle; slouch.

hirsel, n., flock of sheep.

his-sel, pron., himself.

histie, adj., dry; sterile.

hither and yont, adv., backwards and forwards.

hithercome, n., arrival; genealogy.

hizzie, n., charwoman; hussy; wench.

hoast, v., n., cough.

hoch, n., lower thigh; joint of beef from hind leg.

hoch ay, interj., expressing resignation.

hochle, v., walk clumsily; n., gawk: **hochlin**, adj., clumsy.

hodden, n., homespun undyed cloth.

hodge, v., barge.

hog, n., yearling sheep not yet shorn.

hogget, n., hogshead.

Hogmanay, n., New Year's Eve.

hokery-pokery, n., sculduggery.

hollin bush, n., holly bush.

honest, adj., decent; worthy: **honesty**, n., decency.

hoo, v., hoot; howl: **houlety-hoo**, n., owl hoot.

hooch, interj., expressing exhilaration.

hoodie/huidie-craw, n., hooded crow.

hoodock, adj., moneygrabbing.

hool, n., see **huil**.

hoolie, adv., slowly; cautiously.

hooloch, n., avalanche.

hoomet, n., cap; nightcap.

hoot awa, interj., expressing incredulity.

hope, n., bay; inlet.

hornshottle, v., slack, of tooth.

horny, adj., lascivious; salacious.

horse-cowper, n., horse-dealer.

hose, n., a stocking.

hotch, v., fidget; shrug; teem; n., shrug: **hotch up**, v., hitch up.

hotter, v., totter; shake; boil up; seethe; n., seething mass; swarm.

hou, adv., conj., how.

houghmagandie (guttural), n., whoring.

houlet, n., owl: **houlety-hoo**, n., owl hoot: **white houlet**, n., barn owl.

hous, n., house: **black hous**, n., dry-stone and turf house: **hous steid**, n., house site.

hove, v., distend; expand.

*hover, v., pause; tarry.

howd, v., n., pitch, of a boat: **howder**, v., move with rocking motion.

howdie, n., pullet; midwife.

howdle, v., swarm; n., mass of wriggling creatures.

howe, v., hollow; deplete; n., hollow; plain by river; boat hull; adj., hollow: **howe/howe-dumb-deid**, n., depth of night, winter.

howe, v., n., hoe.

howff, v., visit regularly; shelter; take refuge; n., haunt; sanctuary.

howk, v., dig; burrow; excavate; n., excavation: **howk up**, v., uproot.

howlet, n., see **houlet**.

howm, n., holm; piece of flat ground by river.

howtowdie, n., pullet.

hoy, v., urge.

hoyte, v., dawdle in an ungainly manner.

hud, n., builder's hod.

huddery, adj., unkempt.

huid, n., hood: **huidie**, adj., hooded.

huil, v., encase; shell peas; n., pod; shell; rind.

hull, n., hill.

hullerie, adj., wet and cold, of weather.

hum and hae, v., prevaricate.

humlie, n., cow without horns; mitten.

hummle, adj., humble.

hummlecorn, n., adj., proletariat.

*humph, n., hump: **humphie-backit**, adj., hump-backed.

humplock, n., hummock; small heap.

hund, v., n., hound.

hunder/hunner, n., adj., hundred.

*hunger, v., cause to starve: **hungersome**, adj., hungry.

hunker, v., squat: **hunkers**, n., haunches: **hunker doun**, v., abase oneself.

hunt-the-gowk, n., April fool; the cry set up on his being deceived.

hurcheon, n., hedgehog.

hurdies, n., haunches; buttocks: **hurdy gig**, n., pony trap.

hure, n., whore.

hurkle, v., crouch; n., upper thigh: **hurkle-bane**, n., hip-bone.

hurl, v., bowl along; wheel; n., forward surge; vehicle ride: **hurl-barra**, n., wheelbarrow: **hurly**, n., hutch: **hurly-bed**, n., truckle-bed.

hurlygush, n., rush of water; sound of rushing water.

hurry, n., wooden tool box.
hushie, v., hush to sleep: hush-a-baa, n., lullaby.
hushion, n., stocking with foot worn away.
hush-mush, n., rumour.
hyne, n., harbour.
hyne/hyne-awa, adv., to a distance; away.
hypothec, the hale hypothec, n., the whole lot/affair.
hyter, v., stumble; totter; trip; n., stumble.
hyte-styte, n., rack and ruin.

I, prep., in.
ice-hill, n., iceberg; icicle.
icker, n., ear of corn.
ieroe, n., great-grandchild.
ile, n., oil: ilie, adj., oily: iliecoat, n., oilskin.
ilk/ilka, adj., each; every: ilkane, pron., everybody: ilka body's body, n., sail-trimmer: ilka-day, adj., weekday: ilk ither, pron., each other.
ill, n., evil; harm; disease; adj., evil; difficult; malign; adv., badly: iller/illest, adj., worse/worst: ill-aff, adj., hard-up: ill breath, n., ill-feeling: ill chance, n., bad luck: ill-come, adj., illegitimate: ill-daein, adj., profligate: ill-dune-tae, adj., badly treated: ill-faured, adj., ugly: ill-gate, n., transgression: ill-less, adj., harmless: ill mou, n., abusive tongue: ill-scrapit, adj., abusive; sardonic: ill-spent, adj., misspent: ill-taen, adj., taken amiss: ill-thriven, adj., undergrown: ill-vandit, adj., unsociable: ill-wared, adj., wasted: ill-weirdit, adj., ill-fated: ill-will, n., dislike: ill-willie, adj., hostile: hae an ill-will at, v., dislike: tak ill, v., become ill.
immis/eemis, adj., ill-poised; unsteady.
impruive, v., improve.
in, adj., alert: no in, adj., absent-minded.
inbearing, adj., meddlesome.
inbigget, adj., introspective; self-seeking.
inby, adv., indoors; inside; within.
incaain, n., invocation; prayer.
inch, n., island; low land by river mouth.

income, n., arrival; ulcer: incomin, adj., following: incomer, n., intruder.
indite, v., convoke.
indwaller, n., inhabitant; resident.
ingan, n., onion.
ingang, n., access; entrance; entry.
ingate, n., access.
ingether, v., collect.
ingine, n., engine.
ingle, n., room fire: ingle-cheek, n., fireside.
ingrowth (as in "now"), n., abscess; tumour.
ingyne (injyne), n., ability; acumen; intellect; genius.
inhaudin, adj., abject; obsequious; frugal.
inklin, n., allusion; hint; rumour; propensity: gie nae inklin, v., give no sign.
innerlie, adj., low-lying; sympathetic.
inpit, v., give occupancy to tenant; insert; n., contribution.
insense, v., convince.
insnorl, v., embroil; implicate.
insouk, n., inrush of tide.
instancy, n., fervour.
insteid, adv., instead.
intae/intil, prep., into.
intimmers, n., internal organs; stomach and bowels; mechanism.
inventar, n., inventory; schedule.
inver, n., river mouth.
irk, n., pain.
I'se, v., I shall.
isna, v., is not.
ither, adj., other: ithergates, adv., elsewhere; otherwise.
itsel, pron., itself: its lane, adv., by itself.

Jabble, v., undulate; n., undulation.
jad/jaud, n., jade; perverse woman: play the jaud, v., wanton.
jag, v., prick; n., prick; thorn: jaggy, adj., prickly.
jaiket, n., jacket.
jalouse, v., conjecture; imagine; suspect.
jamb, n., buttress.
janitor, n., school caretaker.
jant, v., go on an outing; n., outing; tour.
Janwar, n., January.

jauner, v., go about/talk aimlessly.

jaup, v., dash, of water; splash; sprinkle; n., drop; spot.

jaur, n., jar.

jaurie, n., large clay marble.

jaw, v., n., rush, of water.

jawbox, n., kitchen sink: jawhole, n., sewage pool.

jeanie factory, n., spinning factory.

jeck-easy, adj., indifferent; offhand.

jeedge, v., adjudicate; judge.

jee/gee, v., move to and fro; swerve; n., swerve.

jeeg, v., n., jig.

jeelie, n., jelly; jam: jeelie-jaur, n., jampot.

jeist, n., joist.

jenny-hunder-feet, n., centipede: jenny-lang-legs/jennie-meggie, n., cranefly.

jenny-wran, n., wren.

jessie, n., effeminate man; mollycoddle.

jicker about, v., flit about.

jillet, n., flighty female.

jilp, v., dash water; n., thin, insipid liquid.

jimp, v., shorten; adj., close-fitting; short; slender; neat.

jink, v., n., dodge; frolic; zigzag: jinker, n., sprightly girl; libertine.

jirg, v., make a squelching sound.

jirt, v., squirt.

jist, adv., see juist.

jo, n., lover; sweetheart.

jock, n., rustic; yokel.

jocteleg, n., pocket or kitchen knife.

joggle, v., n., lurch.

johnnie-aa-thing, n., small general merchant.

joogle, v., juggle; rock.

jordan, n., chamberpot.

jorum, n., reel, the dance.

joug, n., jug; mug: jougs, n., collar-like instrument of punishment.

jouk, v., duck; elude; swerve; dissemble; n., swerve; stoop: joukie, adj., elusive: joukerie, n., evasion: joukerie-pawkerie, n., roguery; trickery.

jow, v., trans., intrans., n., ring; toll.

jow, v., move with rocking motion; surge; n., surge; swell.

jowl, v., n., toll.

juist, adv., just: juist that, adv., precisely; quite so.

jummle, v., n., jumble.

jumpin-jaik, n., kind of toy; unreliable person: jumpin-rope, n., skipping-rope.

jundie, v., n., jog; jolt; push.

jurmummle, v., mix up.

jute/joot, n., poor, sour liquor.

jyle, n., jail; prison.

jyne, v., join: jyner, n., joiner: jynerin, n., carpentry.

Kae, n., jackdaw.

kail, n., colewort; soup made from colewort: kail-pat, n., soup-pot: kail runt, n., cabbage stalk: kail-seller, n., greengrocer.

*kaim, n., comb.

kane, n., rent paid in kind.

katie-beirdie, n., woman with beard: katie-wran, n., wren.

kebars, n., rafters.

kebbuck, n., a cheese.

keckle, v., n., cackle; giggle; titter: keckle up, v., perk up.

keech, v., defecate; n., excrement; filth.

keek, v., n., glance; peep: keeker, n., spy: keek-hole, n., peep-hole: keekin-gless, n., mirror: keek-o-day, n., dawn.

keelie, n., kestrel or other hawk; town rough.

keelivine, n., pencil.

*keep, n., board and lodging.

keil, n., ruddle; red ochre.

keist, n., eroticism: keisty, adj., erotic; wanton.

kell, n., dandruff.

kelpie, n., water-sprite.

kelter, v., undulate.

kemp, n., combat; contest; warrior: kempy, adj., intrepid.

*ken, v., know; recognise; n., knowledge: kennin, n., knowledge; understanding; a little bit: kennawhat, n., person not easily described.

kennle, v., kindle.

kenspeckle, adj., prominent; remarkable.

kep, v., keep; prevent; ward off.

kerse, n., cress: kerses, n., lady's smock.

ket, n., clump of matted material; fleece.

183

kettle-hole, n., pothole in bog.
kill, n., kiln: **killogie,** n., kiln fireplace.
killieleepie, n., sandpiper.
kilt, v., tuck up.
kilter, n., high spirits.
kiltie, n., wearer of the kilt.
kimmer, n., intimate; midwife; loose woman.
kin, n., kind; lineage: **kindly,** adj., aboriginal; indigenous.
kinch, n., loop; noose; problem.
kind, v., arrange; classify: **kinkind,** n., category; sort.
kindness, n., attachment; affection.
kink, v., twist; zigzag; choke convulsively; n., bend; twist; quirk.
kinrik, n., kingdom; realm.
kipple, v., n., couple.
kirk, n., church: **kirk-gaun claes,** n., Sunday clothes: **kirkyaird,** n., cemetery.
kirn, v., n., churn.
kirn, v., entice: **kirn wi;** v., mollycoddle; show too much respect for.
kirn, n., grain of corn; harvest home: **kirn supper,** n., harvest home feast.
kirnel, n., kernel.
kirsen, v., christen.
kirtle, n., skirt.
kiss-ma-luif, n., flatterer; sycophant.
*kist, v., put in box/coffin; n., box; coffin; corn bin; thorax.
kitchen, v., season; give relish to; n., appetiser; sauce.
kittle, v., itch; tickle; poke a fire; n., itch; tickle; stimulus; adj., difficult; abstruse; changeable; precarious: **kittlie,** adj., easily tickled: **kittle-leggit,** adj., nimble: **kittle up,** v., stimulate.
kittlin, n., kitten.
kittock, n., giddy girl.
kivin, n., group of people; bevy.
kizzen, n., cousin.
knab, n., bigwig; swell: **knabbery,** n., gentry.
knack, v., n., click: **knacky,** adj., adroit; deft; skilful.
knackers, n., testicles.
knag, n., knob; lump; small cask: **knaggit,** adj., jagged.
*knap, v., n., knock; tap: **knapper,** n., mallet.
knap, n., knob; knot in wood; knee-cap; matted clump: **knap-bane,** n.' knee-bone.
knar, n., knotted piece of wood: **knarly,** adj., knotty.
knicht, n., knight.
knick-knackets, n., knick-knacks.
knoit, v., n., rap.
knoit, n., protuberance; hunk.
knotless, adj., aimless; futile.
knowe, n., incline; small hill: **knowe-heid,** n., hilltop.
knurl, n., knot; cyst; knuckle; weal.
kuiller, n., tub.
kurchie, v., n., curtsy.
kyle, n., arm of sea; strait of water.
kyle, n., ninepin; skittle: **kyles,** n., game of ninepins.
kyte, n., abdomen; stomach.
kythe, v., make manifest; present oneself: **kythin,** n., manifestation.

Lab, v., pitch; clash; walk with long, heavy step.
lachter, n., layer; stratum.
*laddie, n., boy: **laddie-loun,** n., youth.
lade, v., n., load.
lade, n., water channel.
ladle, n., water-wheel paddle; church collection box.
lae, v., leave.
laft, n., loft; attic; gallery: **laftit,** adj., storeyed.
lagamachie, n., discursive story.
laggin, n., edge; welt: **laggin-gird,** n., circumference; rim.
laich, adj., low; small of build: **laich-set,** adj., stocky: **laichen,** v., lower.
laiglen, n., milk-pail.
lair, v., sink in mud; n., bog; swamp: **lairy,** adj., marshy.
lair, v., bury; n., grave: **lair-stane,** n., tombstone.
laird, n., landowner; lord: **bunnet laird,** n., small landowner.
lairge, adj., lavish; numerous; plentiful.
laithe, v., abhor; loathe: **laith,** n., loathing; adj., loath: **laithfu,** adj., loath; timid: **laithsome,** adj., loathsome; abhorrent.
lallan, adj., lowland: **Lallans,** n., Lowland Scots tongue.
Lammas, n., term beginning 1st August.

lammer, n., amber.

lamp, v., trounce.

lampit, n., limpet.

lan, n., land; tenement building: **lanafore**, n., foremost horse in plough: **landart**, adj., uncouth: **landbreach/brist**, n., surf: **landlowper**, n., vagabond: **landimere**, n., town boundary: **landmeith**, n., boundary stone: **landmous**, n., vole: **landtide**, n., shimmering air: **landward**, adj., rural.

lane, adj., isolated; solitary; **lanesome**, adj., lonely.

lanerly, adj., special; unique.

***lang**, adj., long; tall: **lang-drauchtit**, adj., scheming: **lang-gabbit**, adj., boring; prolix: **lang-goun**, n., judge: **lang-heidit**, adj., sagacious: **langnebbit**, adj., nosy: **lang oor**, n., midnight: **lang-settle**, n., settee: **langsome**, adj., lengthy; boring: **langsyne**, n., days of long ago; adv., long ago.

langle, n., tether.

lanstell, n., parapet.

lapper, v., coagulate; curdle: **lappert milk**, n., curdled milk.

lapper, v., lap; ripple

larick, n., larch.

laroch, n., foundation; site.

lashins, n., plentiful supply.

lass, n., girl; sweetheart: **lassie days**, n., girlhood: **lassie-like**, adj., effeminate.

lasty, adj., long-lasting.

lat, v., let: **lat be**, v., let alone: **lat flee**, v., hurl: **lat ken/wit**, v., announce: **lat on**, v., divulge: **lat see**, v., show.

latch, n., loop.

lathron, n., lounger.

lauch, v., n., laugh.

laud, n., lad; boy friend; sweetheart.

lave, n., the rest; the residue.

laverock, n., lark.

law, n., rounded hill.

lawin, n., reckoning; retribution.

lay, v., allay; temper.

lay aff, v., hold forth: **lay at**, v., strike at: **lay by**, v., rest: **lay into**, v., attack vigorously: **lay past**, v., save: **lay the brains asteep**, v., meditate.

lazy, **bone/horn lazy**, adj., very lazy.

lea, adj., unploughed: **lea rig**, n., ridge of unploughed grass.

leal, adj., faithful; true; accurate; chaste: **lealty**, n., loyalty.

leam, v., gleam; n., gleam; ray of light.

learn, v., instruct; teach; **learnin**, n., instruction.

leather, v., beat; flog; hurry: **leatherin**, n., flogging.

leave, v., let; allow.

leddy, n., lady.

ledge, v., project; jut out; n., flange; ramp: **ledgin**, n., projection.

ledge, v., declare; profess; vouch.

lee, n., lie: **leear**, n., liar: **lee-buik**, n., novel: **leefu**, adj., fictional.

leed, n., lead, the metal; pendulum.

leed, n., see **leid**.

lee-lang, adj., livelong.

leerie, n., lamplighter.

leesome, adj., see **lousome**.

leet, v., make list of candidates; n., list of candidates.

leeve, v., live: **leevin**, n., living.

leg, v., stride: **leggins**, n., leggings: **pin leg**, n., wooden leg.

legate, v., give a legacy.

leglin, n., wooden milk-pail with upright handle.

leid, n., dialect; language; topic: **mither-leid**, n., mother tongue.

leip, v., scorch; scald; swelter.

leir, v., learn; teach; n., learning; belief: **buik-leared**, adj., learned.

leish, v., lash; scourge; whip: **leishin**, adj., full of drive.

leister, n., three-pronged fish spear; trident.

leme, v., n., glow; shine.

***len**, v., n., loan.

lenth, n., length; stature: **lenthen**, v., lengthen: **the lenth o**, prep., as far as.

lest, v., last.

let, n., abatement; lull.

let, v., see **lat**: **let aff**, v., break wind: **let bug**, v., disclose: **let on**, v., divulge; sham.

lether, n., ladder.

leuk/luik, v., look: **leuk near**, v., visit: **leuk owre**, v., watch over: **leuk the road o**, v., recognise: **leuk to/til**, v., look at; observe.

levin, n., lightning: **levin-bolt**, n., thunderbolt.

ley, n., see lea.

lib, v., castrate; geld: libbert, n., eunuch.

libbard, n., leopard.

libel, v., indict; n., indictment.

licht, v., light; n., light; doctrine; adj., light; bright; pale: lichten, v., illuminate; alleviate: licht-heidit, adj., dizzy: lichtsome, adj., agile; gay.

lichtlie, v., belittle; despise; mock; n., slight.

lichtnin, n., lightning.

*lick, v., thrash; defeat; surpass: lickin/licks, n., thrashing.

lick-ma-luif, adj., obsequious.

lie owre, v., remain unpaid.

liff/lith, n., orange segment; slice.

lift, v., gather potato crop; apprehend; steal; n., burden; help.

lift, n., sky.

lig, v., lie; rest: lig wi, v., consort with: ligger, n., newly spawned salmon.

like, adj., likely; adv., probably: like as no, adv., probably.

lilt, v., sing softly; trill; n., rhythm; bright tune: lilt up, v., strike up a tune.

lime, n., cement; mortar: limewark, n., limekiln.

limmer, n., jade; loose woman; undisciplined girl.

line, n., certificate; diploma; prescription; written authorisation.

linens, n., shroud; underclothes: twal/ seiventeen hunner linen, n., fine/very fine linen.

lingel, n., tag; thong: lingels, n., tendrils.

link, v., stride; trip lightly: link at, v., act energetically towards.

links, n., sandy, bent-covered shore; sausages strung together.

linn, n., cliff over which water falls; waterfall.

linset, n., linseed.

lint, n., flax: lint mill, n., linen factory: lint threid, n., linen thread.

lintie, n., linnet.

lip, n., brim; edge: lippin fou, adj., full to the brim.

lippen, v., trust; confide; anticipate: lippenance, n., trust.

lippen, v., lick; come across; find.

lirk, v., n., crease; rumple.

list, v., prefer; wish; n., appetite; choice; will.

list, v., enlist; recruit.

lit, n., tint.

lith, n., hinge; segment of orange.

lithe, adj., see lythe.

*loaf, cutting loaf, n., loaf baked yesterday: pan loaf, n., loaf baked in tin.

loan/loaning, n., lane; milking-place; paddock.

loch, n., lake: loch lily, n., water lily.

lochgelly, n., schoolmaster's heavy leather strap.

lodesman, n., pilot.

loof, n., see luif.

loom, n., haze; mist.

loonie, n., lunatic: loonie-hous, n., mental asylum.

lordly, adj., sumptuous: lordship, n., royalty on books, etc.

lorimer, n., watchmaker.

losh, interj., expressing surprise.

*loss, v., lose.

lou, v., love: lousome, adj., affectionate; delightful; lovable.

louance, n., pension.

loun, n., fellow; rascal; rustic.

loup, v., see lowp.

lour, v., become overcast; lurk; n., ambush: lourdie, adj., overcast.

lous, n., louse.

lout, v., stoop; curtsy; demean oneself.

love-bairn, n., bastard: love blink, n., affectionate glance.

lowden, v., becalm; reduce intensity of; subdue.

lowe, v., blaze; n., flame; fire; radiance: tak lowe, v., catch fire.

lown, n., calm; peace; adj., calm; peaceful; sheltered; unassuming.

lowp, v., n., leap; start; throb: lowpen steik, n., lapse.

lowse, v., loosen; release; detach; say grace for: lowss, adj., loose; slack; spare: lowsin time, n., end of day's work.

lozen, v., glaze; n., pane of glass; lens.

lucken, adj., webbed: lucken-fingert/taed, adj., web-fingered/toed.

luckie, n., landlady; "wife"; hag.

lucky bag, n., paper bag with sherbet sucked through licorice tube; raffle: lucky box, n., penny bank.

ludge, v., lodge: **ludgins,** n., lodgings: **dry ludgins,** n., lodgings with no board.

lue, v., see **lou.**

luewarm, adj., lukewarm.

*****lug,** n., ear: **luggie,** n., bowl/dish/pail with "lug": **lug-horn,** n., hearing aid: stethoscope.

*****luif,** n., palm of hand; paw: **luiffiie,** n., stroke with a strap.

lum, n., chimney; **lum-can/heid,** n., chimney-pot/top: **lum-hat,** n., top-hat.

lume, n., loom; tool.

lunt, v., kindle; blaze; smoke a pipe; n., match.

luve, v., n., love.

lyart, adj., grizzled; grey.

lyke, n., corpse: **lyke-hous,** n., mortuary: **lykewake,** n., vigil over corpse.

lythe, n., peace; lee side; adj., calm; gentle; sheltered; mild-tempered.

Machair, n., low land by shore covered with bent-grass.

machine, n., carriage; trap: **machinery,** n., factory.

macklike, adj., neat; suitable.

mad, adj., angry: **dancin/fleein mad,** adj., in a great rage.

mae, v., n., bleat.

mae, adj., more; extra.

mag, n., big hand; paw.

maggie-rab., n., brawling woman.

maggoty-heidit, adj., eccentric; scatter-brained.

magirkie, n., woollen helmet; large clumsy object.

maiden, n., guillotine; last sheaf of harvest.

maik, n., halfpenny.

maik, n., companion; equal; image; likeness; mate: **maikless,** adj., match-less.

mail, n., a meal.

mail, v., rent; n., duty; tax: **mailin,** n., smallholding: **mail gairdener,** n., market gardener.

mainner, n., manner: **mainners,** n., manners.

mains, n., home farm.

mair, adj., extra; more.

mairch, v., fix boundaries; n., boundary: **mairch dyke,** n., boundary wall.

mairriage, n., marriage: **mairriage lines,** n., marriage certificate.

mairt, n., salted beef.

mairtyr, v., afflict; n., martyr: **mairtyrin,** n., agony; torture.

maise, v., ripen.

maisic, n., music.

maist, adj., most; adv., almost: **maistly,** adv., mostly.

maister, n., master: **maister and mair,** n., aristocrat.

*****mait,** n., meat; food.

maitter, n., matter; affair; pus.

*****mak,** v., make; create; mature, of manure; thicken, of porridge; n., make; design: **mak o,** v., profit by: **mak on,** v., pretend: **mak up on,** v., overtake: **makar,** n., bard; composer: **makdom,** n., idiosyncrasy.

malchance, n., accident.

mammy, n., mother: **mammy's big tumfie,** n., spoiled child.

man, n., husband: **the man,** n., man in authority: **man-body,** n., male adult: **manheid,** n., manhood; bravery: **mannie,** n., little man.

mane, v., cry; complain; n., complaint; lament: **manerife,** adj., plaintive.

mang, v., mutilate.

mang, prep., among.

manna, v., may not.

manner, v., ape; mimic.

mant, v., have impediment in speech; n., stammer.

manty, n., loose outer garment; robe.

mapamound, n., atlas.

mappie, n., rabbit: **mappie's mou,** n., antirrhinum.

mar, v., maim; obstruct.

margullie, v., debase; tear to pieces.

mark, v., note down: **marked,** adj., distinguished; illustrious.

marl, v., n., mottle.

marrow, v., match; n., match; mate; friend: **marrowless,** adj., incomparable.

mart, n., building for livestock auction; market.

mashle, n., mixture; mix-up: **mashlum,** n., mixture of beans, oats, peas.

mask, v., brew; infuse: **maskin-pot,** n., teapot.

maucht, n., energy; power: **mauchtless,** adj., limp; helpless.

maukin, n., see mawkin.

maumie, adj., calm; mild; luscious; ripe; sweet: mauminess, n., sweetness.

maun, v., must: maundae, n., necessity.

maut, n., mault; ale: maut-dub, n., pond for steeping malt.

maw, n., mother.

maw, n., common gull.

maw, v., mow; reap.

mawk, n., maggot: mawkit, adj., infested with maggots; putrid.

mawkin, n., hare: mawkin-mad, adj., frenzied.

mawmet, n., effigy; idol.

mawn, n., small basket.

maze, n., astonishment.

meal ark/girnel/kist, n., oatmeal chest: mealy-moud, adj., plausible.

meat, v., cater; feed; n., food; nourishment.

meedie, n., meadow; piece of marshy grassland.

meenit, n., minute: a wee meenit, n., a short time.

meer, n., see meir.

meerical, n., spectacle; wonder.

meet in wi, v., encounter.

meikle, adj., much.

meir, n., mare.

meith, n., landmark; clue; distinguishing feature.

meith, adj., mild; warm and damp.

melder, n., amount of corn treated at the one grinding.

mell, v., mix: mell wi, v., tamper with.

mell, v., drub; maul; trounce; n., mallet.

melt, n., sperm.

melvie, v., soil.

memorandum, n., epitaph.

men/mend, v., mend; improve upon; recuperate: mends, n., compensation; penance.

meng, v., blend; merge; amalgamate.

mennen, n., minnow.

mense, v., honour with one's presence; n., commonsense; courtesy; amenity; respect; propriety: mense-fu, adj., polite; discreet; respectable: menseless, adj., foolish; ill-bred; unbecoming.

mention, n., modicum.

menzie/menyie n., crowd; medley; retinue; noisy festive gathering.

mercat, n., market; market transaction.

merchant, n., retailer: merchandie, n., merchandise.

merciful, adj., temperate, of weather; propitious.

merle, n., blackbird.

merse, n., flat rich ground by river; fertile hollow in hills.

messages, n., shop purchases: go the messages, v., do one's shopping.

messan, n., cur; mongrel.

mett, v., measure.

Mey, n., month of May.

micht, n., might; power: michty, adj., mighty; majestic; adv., very.

midden, n., dunghill; refuse dump: midden creel, n., pannier for manure: midden dub, n., pool for dunghill effluent.

middlin, adj., fair to medium; moderate: middlins, adv., moderately.

midge, n., gnat.

midman, n., referee; umpire.

milk-hous, n., dairy: milk-sye, n., milk sieve.

mill, n., factory; pipe organ: mill haun, n., factory worker.

mill-lade, n., mill-race.

mim/mim-moud, adj., prim; affected in manner/speech: mimp, v., talk affectedly.

mind, v., see mynd.

mint, v., hint; threaten; n., hint; cue.

mirk, v., darken; blur; n., darkness; adj., dark; gloomy: mirken, v., grow dark: mirkness, n., gloom: mirk-daurk, adj., pitch-dark.

mirlie, adj., mottled; variegated; roan-coloured.

mirligo, n., dizziness; delusion.

misbehadden, adj., unseemly; undisciplined.

miscaa, v., miscall; mispronounce; denounce.

mishanter, n., accident; calamity; mischance.

mischieve, v., damage; aggrieve.

misdout, v., doubt; mistrust; n., mistrust; suspicion.

misgae, v., go awry, of plan; fail.

misgate, n., wrong course of action.

mish-mash, n., mix-up.
misk, n., grassy moorland.
misken, v., misunderstand; spurn: misken anesel, v., give oneself airs.
misleir, v., misguide; misinform: misleird, adj., rude.
mislippen, v., mistrust; overlook; betray.
miss, v., fail to accomplish/happen.
mis-sweir, v., commit perjury.
mistak, v., n., mistake: mistak a fuit, v., stumble: mistak anesel, v., err.
mistent, v., ignore; n., error.
mistrystit, adj., left in the lurch.
mither, n., mother.
mittens, n., knuckle gloves.
mixter, n.,. blend: mixter-maxter, n., confusion; adj., chaotic: mixtie-maxtie, n., confused mixture; jumble; adj., motley; jumbled.
moch, n., moth: moch-hawk, n., nightjar.
moch, n., warm, moist air: mochie, adj., clammy; rotting: mocht, adj., tainted.
mockrife, adj., mocking.
moger, v., bungle; dabble in messy stuff; n., bungle; mess.
moggan, n., stocking.
molligrant, v., n., grumble; lament; whine.
mollygrubs, n., belly-ache.
*monie, adj., many.
mooch, v., see mouch.
moodge, v., budge/cause to budge; shift.
mool, n., ground; soil: mools, n., earth; grave.
moop, v., see moup.
morn, the morn, n., tomorrow: the morn's efternune, n., tomorrow afternoon.
morsel, n., a little to eat.
mortal, adv., exceedingly.
mort-claith, n., pall.
moss, n., bog; marsh; peat.
mott, n., target.
mou, v., utter; n., mouth; speech: mou-frauchty, adj., palatable.
mouch, v., idle around: moucher, n., idler.
mouler, v., moulder: moulie, adj., mouldy; decayed; stingy.

mountain dew, n., whisky.
moup, v., nibble; graze.
mous, n., mouse: mous-wab, n., spider's web; gossamer.
mow, v., copulate.
mowdie/mowdiewort, n., mole; short-sighted person: mowdie-hill, n., molehill.
moyen, v., recommend; n., recommendation; prescience.
muck, n., clean out a byre; n., dirt; mud; dung: mucky, adj., dirty; muddy: muck creel, n., dung basket: muck-flee, n., bluebottle.
muckle, n., a great deal; adj., big; much; adv., much: muckle-boukit, adj., bulky.
muddle, v., have sexual intercourse.
muild, n., mould; frame; pattern.
muild, n., pulverised soil: muildy, adj., decayed: muilder, v., decay.
muir, n., moor: muircock/hen, n., male/female red grouse.
muist, n., musk.
muith, v., oppress with heat; n., close, damp heat; adj., oppressive.
muive, v., move.
mull, n., mill.
muller, v., crumble.
mulsie, n., milk strainer.
mummle, v., mumble.
mump, v., mope; mumble; n., surmise.
mune, n., moon: munelicht flittin, n., removal by night to escape creditors.
munt, v., ascend; mount; n., low, tree-covered hill.
muntin, n., trimmings.
murl, v., reduce to fragments; n., fragment: murly, adj., crumbly.
murn, v., mourn.
murr, v., purr.
murther, v., bedevil; torment.
murther, v., n., murder.
musardrie, n., poetry.
mush, n., mash: mushy, adj., mashy.
muslin-kail, n., thin broth.
mutch, n., woman's cap.
mutchkin, n., pint measure.
mynd, v., call to mind; evoke; look after; n., mind; opinion: myndin, n., memento; souvenir: keep mynd o v., bear in mind.
myow, v., n., mew.

Nab, n., pretentious person: **nabby**, adj., pretentious.

***nae**, adj., no: **naebody**, n., nobody: **nane**, pron., none: **naethin**, n., nothing.

naig, n., nag; stallion: **naigie**, n., pony.

nail, v., clinch a bargain; n., trigger.

nailhorn, n., finger-nail.

nainfolk, n., associates; relatives.

naipkin, n., handkerchief.

nait, adj., neat; smart.

***naither**, pron., adj., conj., neither.

naitur, n., nature: **naitral**, n., halfwit; adj., natural; normal.

nakit/bare-nakit, adj., naked/quite naked.

name, v., pronounce: **namely**, adj., reputable: **nameliheid**, n., reputation; glory.

nane, pron., none.

nap, v., hammer; blow with hammer.

nappy, n., ale; beer.

na-say, v., deny; n., denial.

natter, v., nag; wrangle.

near, adv., nearly: **near-haun**, adv., close at hand: **nearmaist**, adj., nearest: **near-sichtit**, adj., myopic: **near-the-bit**, adj., miserly.

neb, n., beak; nose; tip; prow; strong taste: **nebby**, adj., inquisitive.

necessar, n., necessity; requisite; adj., essential; intrinsic.

neckbit, n., yoke on shoulder for carrying water pails.

ned, n., stupid person: **neddy**, n., donkey.

need-be, n., necessity: **needfu**, adj., needy: **needfuls**, n., requirements.

neeger, n., nigger.

ne'er, adv., never: **ne'er-dae-weill**, n., rake; adj., profligate.

neibour, v., be situated near; n., neighbour: **neibourless**, adj., not matching.

neip, n., turnip; pocket watch: **neip-green**, adj., callow: **neipheid**, n., stupid person: **shaw neips**, v., cut off turnip leaves.

neist, adj., adv., prep., next.

neith, adv., prep., underneath: **neithmaist**, adj., undermost.

nerra, adj., narrow: **nerra-nebbit**, adj., bigoted; prejudiced.

nesh, adj., sensitive; tender, of wound.

nesty, adj., nasty; offensive.

nethermaist, adj., undermost.

neuk/nuik, n., corner; nook; alcove; recess.

nevel, v., pummel; punch.

new, v., renovate; adj., recent; adv., newly: **new-fangle**, n., innovation: **new-fanglt**, adj., novel: **news**, n., newspaper: **news-billy**, n., reporter.

newin, n., yeast.

nicht, v., pass the night; n., night: **the nicht**, adv., tonight: **nichtgoun**, n., nightgown; dressing-gown: **nichthawk**, n., large moth.

nick, v., grab; steal; snip; imprison; n., groove; jail.

nicker, v., n., whinny.

nick-nackity, adj., scrupulously careful about details.

nicks, n., knuckles.

nidge, v., nudge.

nid-nod, v., nod repeatedly.

nieve, v., clench fist; n., fist: **nieves**, n., boxing: **dry nieves**, n., bare-fist punching: **nieve-shakin**, n., golden handshake.

niffer, v., bargain; exchange; trade; n., exchange; trade.

niff-naff, v., be punctilious over details; n., detail.

nip, v., nibble; sting; steal; n., sharpness; squeeze; small piece: **nippit**, adj., stingy: **nippy**, adj., biting, of wind: **nippers**, n., forceps.

nirl, v., gnaw; nip; stunt; n., morsel; puny person: **nirly**, adj., puny.

nit, n., nut: **deif nit**, n., nut with no kernel.

nit, n., louse egg.

nither, v., lay low; undervalue.

nizzart, n., sharp-faced person.

no, adv., not: **no in**, adj., inattentive: **no that**, adv., not very: **no weill**, adj., ill.

nocht, n., nothing: **nochtie/nochtless** adj., insignificant; worthless.

nock, n., clock.

noddy, adj., sleepy.

nog/nag, n., peg.

nor, conj., than.

norie, n., caprice; fad; freak; whim.

norie, n., puffin.

norlan, adj., northern: **northart**, adj., northward.

notandums, n., notes.

notion, n., affection; liking.

nou, adv., now: **the nou,** adv., just now.

nowt, n., cattle; oxen: **nowt doctor,** n., veterinary surgeon.

nummer, v., n., number.

nune, n., noon.

nurice, n., nurse.

nurl, v., become lumpy: **nurly,** adj., lumpy; uneven.

nyabble, adj., ignoble; narrow-minded.

nyaff, n., contemptible person; trifle.

nyarr, v., n., snarl.

O, prep., of; about: **oh ay,** adv., oh yes.

oam, n., current of warm air; heat haze; condensation; aroma.

oar, v., row.

obleege, v., oblige: **obleegement,** n., obligement.

observe, n., remark.

ochone, interj., expressing sorrow.

ocht, v., ought.

ocht, pron., aught: **ocht o the twa,** pron., either of the two: **ochtlins,** adv., in any way.

odds, n., difference; disparity; inequality.

oe, n., grandson.

oen, n., oven.

offer, n., gesture.

officiar, n., officer.

offish, adj., frigid in manner: **offishness,** n., reticence.

offran-stane, n., altar.

on, prep., about; regarding.

oncome, n., approach; onset; shower.

oncost, n., outlay.

onding, n., downpour; onset; aggression.

ongauns, n., happenings; antics; carry-on; bad behaviour.

onie, adj., pron., any: **oniegate,** adv., anyhow; anywhere: **oniething,** n., anything: **oniewey,** adv., anyhow: **oniewhaur,** adv., anywhere.

ontak, n., big job; palaver: **ontakkin,** n., undertaking.

oo, n., wool: **ooen,** adj., woollen: **ooie,** adj., woolly: **oo-mull,** n., tweed mill.

oobit, n., hairy caterpillar.

oon, adj., addled, of egg.

oor, n., hour.

oorie, adj., eerie; shivery; superstitious.

oorlich, adj., raw, of weather.

ooss, n., carpet sweepings; fluff.

*or, prep., until; conj., lest; rather than; until.

ordinar/ornar, adj., ordinary.

orra, adj., abnormal; peculiar; occasional; miscellaneous; supernumerary; shabby; vagrant: **orra body,** n., vagrant: **orra duddies,** n., shabby clothes; **orra-man,** n., odd-job man: **orras,** n., odds and ends.

ort, v., reject.

out, n., wolf: **outdog,** n., wolfhound.

*out, v., turn out; eject; adj., finished, of a meeting: **out about,** adv., outside: **outbrak,** n., outburst; eruption: **outby,** adj., outlying; adv., outside: **outcasten/outcuissen,** adj., rejected: **outcome,** n., product; profit; yield: **outgaein,** n., ebbing: **outgang,** n., outlay: **outgate,** n., exit: **outin,** n., excursion; jaunt: **out-kneed,** adj., bandy-legged: **outland,** adj., outlying: **outland body,** n., outcast; stranger: **outlers,** n., cattle wintered in fields: **outmaist,** adj., maximum; utmost: **outpit,** n., expenditure: **outredd,** v., redeem; put in order: **outrig,** v., equip; fit out; n., costume: equipment: **outset,** n., exhibition; publication: **outsettin,** n., lay-out: **outstrapalous,** adj., rowdy: **out-the-road,** adj., remote: **outwales,** n., rejects: **outwith,** adv., prep., beyond; adj., adv., outward.

overly, adj., excessive; adv., excessively.

own, v., identify as one's own.

owrance, n., supremacy.

owre, adv., above; too; prep., over: **owrecome,** n., aphorism; chorus; theme: **owrecowp,** v., upset: **owrefret,** adj., embroidered: **owregae,** v., exceed; master; oppress with heat; infest: **owregang,** v., overgrow: **owregie,** v., capitulate; resign: **owreheid,** adj., average; adv., on an average: **owrehing,** v., impend: **owreleuk,** v., overlook: **owrelip,** v., overflow: **owrelowp,** v., overleap; trespass: **owrerax,** v., overreach; overstrain: **owrerin,** v., overrun:

owreset, v., translate from one language to another: **owreshot**, n., remainder: **owresman**, n., foreman: **owretap**, v., transcend: **owrethraw**, v., overthrow: **owretree**, n., lintel.

owse, n., ox: owsen, n., oxen.

oxter, v., take by the arm; elbow; embrace; n., armpit; embrace.

Pack, n., pact; adj., intimate.

packie, n., packman.

paction, n., agreement; understanding.

pad, v., travel on foot; trot; n., narrow track; path.

paidle, v., paddle; toddle; tramp down: **paidler**, n., toddler.

paikie, n., street-walker; whore.

painch, n., paunch; stomach: **painches**, n., bowels; entrails; tripe.

Paip, n., Pope: **paiperie**, n., popery.

paip, n., fruit stone.

pairt, v., part; share; n., district; part; share: **pairtisay waa**, n., common wall: **pairt-taker**, n., partisan: **pairty**, adj., party; common.

Paiss, n., Easter.

paiter, v., chatter; indulge in monologue.

paitrick, n., partridge.

palin, n., fence: **palin stab**, n., fence post.

pandomie, n., chaos.

pang, v., pack full; cram.

*pan scone, n., pancake.

panse, v., contemplate.

pantry, n., larder.

papingo, n., parrot; popinjay.

paper, n., newspaper.

papple, v., bubble; sizzle; sputter.

paraffle, n., pomp; sham.

paraphernally, n., show; turnout.

paratitle, n., subtitle.

parkie, n., public park attendant.

parpane, n., partition.

parritch, n., porridge; breakfast: **parritch-hertitness**, n., sentimentality.

parrymauk, n., replica.

partan, n., crab.

particlar (parteeclar), adj., noteworthy; quaint: **particularities**, n., characteristics; traits.

partlet, n., ruff.

pass, v., relinquish: **pass water**, v., leak.

past, adj., done with: **past aa**, adj., beyond belief.

pat, n., pot.

patent, adj., accessible; available.

pauchle, v., embezzle; wangle; manipulate; contend.

pauchtie, adj., arrogant; conceited: **pauchtiness**, n., arrogance; conceit.

paulie, adj., weak; paralysed.

pawkie, n., mitten.

pawkie, adj., astute; guileful: **pawkiness**, n., guile.

pawm, v., foist; n., palm of hand: **pawmie**, n., stroke with strap.

pawns, n., curtains for wall bed.

pawt, v., finger; paw; grope.

peacod tree, n., laburnum.

peakit, adj., gaunt; thin.

*pease-brose, n., porridge of ground pea flour: **pease-meal**, n., ground pea flour.

pech, v., n., gasp; pant; puff: **pechie**, adj., asthmatic; short-winded.

pechan, n., stomach; crop.

Pecht, n., Pict.

pee, v., piddle: **peeins**, n., urine: **pee-the-bed**, n., dandelion.

peeble, v., pelt with stones; n., pebble.

peel, n., border tower; palisade; stockade.

peel, n., pill.

peel, v., see peil.

peelie/peelie-wallie, adj., delicate; sickly: **peelie-wersh**, adj., nondescript.

peen, n., pin.

peenie, n., pinafore.

peenie-rose, n., peony.

peerie, n., spinning-top.

peerie/peerie-weerie, adj., tiny/minute: **peerie-heels**, n., stiletto heels: **peerie-winkie**, n., little finger/toe.

peesie/peessweep, n., peewit; lapwing.

peevers, n., hopscotch.

peil, v., n., equal: **be peils**, v., have the same score.

peir, n., pear.

pelfry, n., fripperies.

pen, n., feather; plume.

pend, n., arch; vault.

pendicle, n., accessory; adjunct.

pendle, n., pendulum: **pendle shank**, n., pendulum rod.

192

penny-buff, n., school primer: **penny-chap**, n., dominoes: **penny fee**, n., wages: **penny jo**, n., prostitute: **penny-rattler**, n., shop selling cheap wares: **penny wheep**, n., weak ale: **pennyworth**, n., bargain; revenge.

pense, n., study; thought: **pensefu**, adj., thoughtful: **pensie**, adj., affected; priggish: **pensieness**, n., pomposity.

pent, v., n., paint.

penwark, n., writing.

percunnance, n., proviso; reservation.

perempt, adj., unequivocal.

perfite, adj., consummate; expert: **perfiteness**, n., perfection.

perish, v., destroy; dissipate; exterminate.

perjink, n., nicety; fastidious person; adj., fastidious; precise; prim.

perk, v., n., perch.

perlicket, n., iota; scrap; trace; whit.

perlin, n., lace.

pernickety, n., detail; trifle; adj., fastidious; dainty; complex.

perqueer, adj., precise; elaborate.

pertinent, n., accessory; adjunct; appendage.

pest, v., trouble; plague; n., epidemic disease.

pettle, n., spade for cleaning plough.

pettle, v., pet; cherish.

peuchlin, adj., ineffective.

pey, v., pay; punish; n., pay: **peys**, n., punishment: **pey in**, v., subscribe.

peyzart, n., miser.

philabeg, n., kilt.

phizz, n., beard.

phraise, v., flatter; wheedle; n., flattery: **phraisy**, adj., fulsome.

pick, v., eat little; tap; n., bite of food; grudge: **pick up**, v., understand.

pick, n., bitumen; pitch.

pickelty, n., plight.

pickie, adj., trifling: **pickit**, adj., scant.

pickle, n., indefinite amount; a little: **wee pickle**, n., small amount.

pictarnie, n., oyster-catcher; tern.

piece, n., snack: **the piece**, adv., apiece.

pie-eyed, adj., squint-eyed.

pig, n., earthenware bowl/pot; pitcher: **piggery**, n., pottery.

pinch, n., lever: **pinchers**, n., pincers; pliers.

pin, n., skewer.

pine, n., pain; uneasiness.

pingle, n., small pan.

pingle, v., strive; compete; n., struggle; contest.

pinion, n., pivot.

pinkie, n., little finger.

pinnet, n., pennant.

pint-stoup, n., pint measure.

pirl, v., n., ripple; purl; twine.

pirlicue, n., flourish in writing; mannerism; summary: **pirlicues**, n., peculiarities.

pirn, n., bobbin; spool; top made with a bobbin.

pish, v., rush, of water; urinate; n., urine: **pishminnie**, n., ant.

pit, v., put: **pit about**, v., disconcert; vex; inconvenience: **pit awa**, v., dismiss: **pit by**, v., hoard; tide over; n., expedient; light meal: **pit doun**, v., kill an animal; plant: **pit in for**, v., apply for: **pit on**, v., pretend; n., pretence: **pit tae**, v., subject to; yoke: **pit tae ane's haun**, v., lend a hand; set to work: **pit up to**, v., entice; incite.

pizzel, n., penis.

pizzen, n., poison.

placket, n., bill on public display; public announcement.

plack, n., small copper coin: **plackless**, adj., penniless.

plain, adj., level: **plainstane**, n., paving stone: **plainstanes**, n., pavement.

plaister, v., plaster; n., plaster; showy person; sentimentality.

plait, v., pleat; fold; pucker.

plank, v., deposit; dump; n., cache; dump.

plantin, n., plantation; wood; seedling.

plapper, v., bubble.

plash, v., cascade; fall in torrents; squelch.

*play, v., perpetrate; n., country festival; pastime; sport: **play-act**, v., posture: **play-actin**, adj., theatrical: **play-fier/marrow**, n., playmate: **play trumph-about**, v., retaliate: **play whiltie-whaltie**, v., go pit-a-pat.

plea, n., lawsuit.

pleep, v., chirp.

pleisure, v., please; n., pleasure.

plenish, v., furnish; stock: **plenishin**.

n., furnishing: **plenishment**, n., farm stock.

plet, v., see **plait**.

pleuch, v., n., plough; n., plough team: **pleuch-land**, n., arable land.

plicht, n., predicament.

plisky, n., prank; wild idea: **pliskit**, n., stratagem.

ploo, v., see **pleuch/plou**.

plook, n., see **plouk**.

plot, v., be very hot; foment with hot water; n., immersion in hot water.

plottin, n., plot; stratagem.

plou, v., n., plough: **plou-stilts**, n., plough handles.

plouk, n., pimple; pustule; blotch: **ploukie**, adj., pimply.

ploum, n., plum.

plowp, v., n., plop.

plowter, v., potter/splash about aimlessly; n., muddle; ill-prepared food.

ploy, n., escapade; joke; undertaking; social gathering.

pluff, v., puff; n., puff; squib.

plump, v., make plopping sound; n., sudden downpour.

plumper, n., plunger, the instrument.

plunk, v., propel marble from thumb and forefinger.

plunk, v., be absent: **plunk the schuil**, v., be absent from school without leave.

plyde, n., plaid.

po, n., chamberpot.

poach, v., reduce to mush.

poachie, n., poacher.

poind, v., seize in lieu of rent.

poke/pock, n., bag.

polis, n., policeman.

poortith, n., see **puirtith**.

port, n., gateway.

pose, v., n., hoard; cache.

post, n., mail; postage; postman.

pot-metal, n., cast-iron.

potterlow, n., pulp; ruin: **potterskink**, n., chaos; smithereens.

potty, n., putty.

potty-heid, n., potted meat.

pou, v., n., pull.

*****pouch**, n., pocket: **poucher**, n., thief.

pouer, n., power; control; large number.

pouk, v., n., pluck; twitch; moult: **poukit**, adj., pinched; emaciated.

poupit, n., pulpit.

pourie, n., cream jug; oil can.

pousion, n., see **pizzen**.

poussie-baudrons, n., cat: **poussie-willow**, n., catkin.

pouster, n., posture.

pout/powt, n., pullet: **poutry**, n., poultry.

pout, n., small trout.

poutiier, v., n., powder.

pow, n., head; scalp.

pownie, n., pony.

powsowdie, n., mush.

powter, v., work aimlessly: **powterin**, adj., officious.

prap, v., n., prop; stay.

prattick, n., practice; habit; artifice; daring feat; project; stratagem.

prat wi, v., tamper with.

preceese, adj., precise; special.

precent, v., conduct church singing: **precentor**, n., conductor of singing.

preclair, adj., pre-eminent.

pree, v., sample; taste; prove: **preein**, n., a tasting: **pree the lips**, v., kiss.

preen, n., pin: **preen-cod**, n., pin-cushion.

prejudge, v., prejudice.

prent, v., n., print.

prentice, v., n., apprentice; adj., inexpert: **prentice-haun**, n., novice.

preses (pree-ses), n., chairman; president.

press, n., cupboard.

pretty, adj., dainty; cultured; elegant.

prick, v., stampede, of cattle; n., arrowhead; skewer.

prickle, v., rise erect.

prickmadentie, n., affected person; adj., mincing in manner.

pridefu, adj., self-respecting; snobbish: **pridefulness**, n., vanity.

prief, n., proof; test: **prieve/pruve**, v., prove; sample.

prig, v., beg; bargain contentiously; insist: **prig at**, v., importune.

prime, adj., best.

primp, v., act priggishly; n., prig: **primpit**, adj., stiff; formal.

primsy, adj., demure; priggish; strait-laced.

prink, v., swagger: **prinkie**, adj., dandified.

privy, n., privet.

prize, v., evaluate: **prization**, n., valuation.

profite, adj., proficient.

prog, v., poke; goad; stab; n., thorn.

proochy-lady, interject., used in calling a cow.

propine, v., propitiate; propose for discussion.

proud, adj., gratified.

pruve, v., see **prieve**.

puddin, n., pudding.

puddock, n., frog: **puddock-cruds**, n., frog spawn: **puddock-stuil**, n., toadstool.

puggie, n., bank; "kitty".

puggy, n., monkey: **puggy-nit**, n., peanut.

puil, n., pool.

puir, adj., poor: **puir face**, n., pathetic expression: **puirtith**, n., poverty: **puirs'-hous**, n., poorhouse.

pump, v., break wind from anus.

pun/pund, n., pound, weight or sterling.

purchase, n., love affair.

purge, v., absolve.

purpie, n., adj., purple.

purpose, n., efficiency: **purposefu**, adj., efficient; methodical.

put on, n., rig-out.

pyat, n., magpie: **pyatie**, adj., multicoloured; piebald.

pyke, v., pick, all senses; impale; n., pick-axe: **pykerie**, n., theft.

pyle, n., single grain of corn.

pyne, v., torment; torture; n., affliction; pain; tribulation.

pynt, v., n., point.

Qua, n., quagmire.

quaich, n., drinking-cup.

quair, n., literary work.

quait, v., quieten; adj., quiet; calm; private: **quaitly**, adv., privately.

quak, v., quake; quiver: **quakin aish**, n., aspen: **quakin bog**, n., shifting bog.

quall, v., quell; be quelled.

quarrel, v., challenge the truth of; contest a fact.

quat, v., quit; acquit; desist; cease work; leave; reward: **quattin time**, n., end of day's work.

quean, n., girl; hussy; woman.

queer, adj., amusing: **queerlike**, adj., strange-looking.

quern, n., granule; mill grinding stone: **querny**, adj., granulated.

quey, n., heifer; young cow.

quicken, v., ferment: **quickenin**, n., yeast.

quirky, adj., tricky.

quitin/cweetin, n., quilt; coverlet.

quittance, n., riddance.

quyne, n., see **quean**.

Racer, n., loose woman; whore.

rack, v., sprain; wrench; worry; n., sprain; worry: **rackless**, adj., careless.

rack/rackon, v., reckon; suppose.

rack, n., sparred frame on wall for crockery.

rae, n., roe-deer.

rag, v., winnow partially.

raggie, n., ragman: **ragabash**, n., motley crowd.

raggin, n., lamp wick.

ragnail, n., torn skin at base of fingernail.

raible, v., rave; n., mob; rabble.

raik, v., range over; n., journey; speed; wanderer: **raiker**, n., hard worker.

raik, n., batch of manufactured goods.

****raip**, n., rope.

rair, v., n., roar.

raird, n., outcry.

raise, v., rouse; alarm; infuriate; leaven.

****raither**, adv., rather.

raivel, v., dishevel; entangle; n., tangle.

rale, adj., actual; authentic; genuine.

ramfoozle, v., muddle.

ramgunshoch, adj., bluff in manner; boorish.

rammish, adj., wanton.

rammy, n., disturbance; uproar.

ramp/rampage, v., rage; stamp in anger; n., rage: **rampin mad**, adj., raving mad.

rampler cratur, n., wanderer.

ramscooter, v., throw into panic.

ramsh, v., munch.

ramsh, adj., strong-tasted; unpalatable.

ramstam, v., rush headlong; n., headstrong person; adj., headstrong; rash.

ramsteegerous, adj., boisterous.

ramstoorie, adj., slapdash.

rance, v., n., brace.

randy, n., brawling woman; shrew; thug; adj., dissipated; obscene; wild.

rane, v., rhyme; n., rhyme; story in rhyme.

rang, n., social rank; status.

ranshy, adj., rancid.

rant, v., rampage; revel; n., noisy revel; romp; sprightly tune; wild frolic: **rantin**, adj., boisterous; uproarious.

ranter, n., serge.

rape, n., see **raip**.

raploch, n., coarse homespun cloth; adj., crude.

rapt, n., rape; robbery.

rapture, n., paroxysm.

rare, adj., grand; exquisite; superb.

rase, n., paper guillotine.

rash, n., rush, the plant.

rasp, n., raspberry.

ratch, v., lacerate.

ratch, n., gun barrel.

rat-rhyme, n., doggerel; meaningless repetition; rote.

rattan, n., rat.

rattle, n., scree: **rattle-skull**, n., stupid person: **rattle-shot**, n., salvo.

rattlin, adj., boisterous.

raucle, adj., bluff; coarse; impetuous; unruly: **raucle-baned**, adj., rawboned.

ravel, v., tangle; outwit; ramble in speech; n., tangle; confused speech.

ravel, v., fit with handrail; n., handrail.

ravery, n., insane anger.

raw, v., align; n., line; row.

rawn, n., fish roe.

rax, v., extend; stretch by pulling; sprain; wrench: **raxing**, n., hanging: **rax anesel** v., exert oneself: **rax for**, v., reach for.

ray, v., array; n., arrangement; order.

reading, n., recitation.

ream, v., foam; effervesce; n., foam; cream: **reamin fou**, adj., brimful.

rebat, v., repel; snub.

reck, v., see **rack**.

record, n., account; repute; value.

recour, v., recover; retrieve.

redd, v., clean up; set in order; dis-
entangle; judge; rebuke: n., a settlement: **reddance**, n., riddance: **redd o**, adj., rid of.

redd, v., n., spawn.

rede, v., advise; deliberate; explain a riddle.

ree, n., covered yard for wintering cattle; inner harbour; small dock.

ree, v., n., riddle.

ree, adj., frenzied; salacious.

reef, adj., see **rife**.

reek, n., see **reik**.

reel-rall, adv., in a disordered manner.

reemle, v., move tremulously; n., tremulous motion.

reenge, v., range; rummage; search; n., quest; rank; row.

reesle/reeshle, v., n., rustle; crackle.

reest, v., see **reist**.

refound, v., refund.

refuise, v., abnegate; forbid; refuse; n., refusal.

reglar, adj., regular; adv., regularly.

rehable, v., rehabilitate.

reif, n., loot.

reik, v., smoke; n., smoke; vapour: **reikie**, adj., misty; smoky: **reikit**, adj., acrid: **reikie-mire**, n., kail stock filled with tow, used as torch.

reist, v., jib; rebel.

reistit, adj., stunted; cured, of fish.

reive, v., grab; plunder; rob: **reiver**, n., robber; cattle raider.

rejyce, v., rejoice; triumph.

remeid, n., redress; remedy.

remember, v., remind.

remuve, v., remove.

renaig, v., shirk.

render, v., melt dripping, etc.

rent, v., rend.

renunce, v., renounce; abdicate.

repone, v., replace; supersede.

resile, v., recoil; recant; withdraw from agreement.

rest, n., vehicle park.

resume, v., summarise.

resurrector, n., body-snatcher.

reteir, v., retire; withdraw.

retour, v., return; n., return journey.

rhyme, v., repeat over and over: **rhymeless**, adj., meaningless.

rib, n., fire bar.

ribble, n., rubble.

richt, adj., right; adv., exceedingly:

richtfu, adj., rightful: **richt-like,** adj., equitable; just: **no richt,** adj., abnormal; simple-minded.

rick/ruck, n., stack of hay/corn: **rickle,** n., small stack of corn.

ricketie, n., wooden rattle.

rickle, v., build badly; n., dilapidated building; loose pile: **ricklie,** adj., ramshackle: **rickle o banes,** n., living skeleton.

rickmatick, n., affair; business.

rid/reid, adj., red: **rid-avised,** adj., ruddy of complexion: **rid-cock,** n., arson.

ridiclous (rideeklus), adj., absurd.

rifart, n., radish.

rift, v., make wind: **rifty,** adj., verbose.

rig, n., ridge of land between furrows; spine: **rigbane,** n., backbone: **riggin,** n., roof ridge/rafters; roof.

rigwiddie, adj., lean; tough and bony-looking; good-for-nothing.

rile, v., aggravate; anger; irritate.

rimburst, n., rupture.

*****rin,** v., run; melt; n., current; tide: **rinagate,** n., rascal; scamp: **rin ahin,** v., be in arrears: **rin out,** v., leak: **rin to,** v., resort to.

rind, n., melted tallow.

ring, v., n., rule.

ringit, adj., wall-eyed.

rink, n., arena; tournament; demarcation line.

rinnin, n., ulcer; gist; main point.

rip, v., saw; n., tatter hanging from dress.

rip, n., handful of corn.

ripple, n., back-ache.

ripplin-kaim, n., flax-dressing instrument.

rise, n., hoax: **tak a rise out o,** v., hoax.

rise, v., repeat, of food.

risk, v., grate.

risp, v., file; grate; grind; n., file; grating noise.

rit, v., n., scratch.

rive, v., rend; rip; wrench; burst; grapple; n., tear; split; wrench.

*****road,** n., direction; route; method.

roarie, adj., garish; noisy: **roarin fou,** adj., very drunk: **roarin gemm,** n., game of curling.

rock, n., distaff; bundle of flax on distaff.

rodden-tree, n., rowan tree; mountain ash.

roke/rouk, n., fog: **roukie,** adj., foggy.

rone, n., air funnel; gutter for drawing off water.

roon, n., shred; selvage of woollen cloth.

roon, prep., see **roun.**

roose, v., see **rouse.**

roost, v., see **roust.**

roseir, n., rose arbour.

rouch, adj., see **ruch.**

roun, adv., prep., around: **get roun,** v., achieve: **roun-shouthert,** adj., round-shouldered.

roup, v., croak; n., huskiness in throat.

rouse, v., flatter: **rousing,** n., boisterous merrymaking.

roust, v., n., rust: **rousty,** adj., rusty.

routh, n., see **rowth.**

rowe, v., roll; enfold; twine; n., roll: **rowe up,** v., enwrap; wind up.

rowp, v., sell by auction; n., auction sale: **cry a rowp,** v., proclaim an auction.

rowt, v., n., bawl; low; roar.

rowth, n., abundance; adj., abundant: **rowthness,** n., profusion; generosity.

rozet, n., resin.

rubbin-stane, n., pipe-clay.

rubbins, n., embrocation.

ruch/rouch, adj., rough; hoarse; unshaven; abundant; affluent: **ruch-handit,** adj., aggressive; generous: **ruchsome,** adj., uncouth: **ruchness,** n., hoarseness.

ruck, n., see **rick.**

ruction, n., brawl; riot; quarrel.

rue, v., repudiate; n., repentance: **rue on,** v., pity: **tak the rue,** v., regret.

ruffle, v., affront.

rug, v., drag; tug; n., tug; twinge.

ruif, n., ceiling; roof: **ruif-tree,** n., roof ridge.

ruit, n., root.

ruive, v., n., rivet.

rummle, v., rumble; shake up violently; n., rumble; concoction; clumsy person: **rummlin,** adj., slap-dash; unrestrained.

rump, v., clip; make bankrupt.

rumple-fyke, n., itch on bottom; sexual appetite.

run/rin, v., distil whisky.

runch, v., crunch: **runchie,** adj., crunchy.

runch, n., screw-key.

rung, v., bludgeon; n., cudgel; spar of wood: **tap rung,** n., acme.

runkle, v., n., wrinkle; crease; ruffle: **runkled,** adj., ridged.

run-metal, n., cast iron: **run-ticket,** n., season ticket.

runt, n., rump; stump of plant; tail; dwarfish person; hag.

rush, n., dysentery; skin rash: **rush-fever,** n., scarlet fever.

ryke, n., dominion; empire; realm.

ryke, v., reach.

rynes, n., reins.

rype, v., ransack; poke; plunder; n., search: **rype-pouch,** n., pickpocket.

Sab, v., sob; weep; drip; seep.

sab, v., subside; wilt.

sackless, adj., see **saikless.**

sad/sadden, v., solidify by hammering/ tramping down: **sad,** adj., firm; solid.

saddle-iron, n., stirrup.

sae, n., state of affairs; adv., so; conj., in order that: **sae be,** conj., if it so happens: **sae bein that,** conj., seeing that: **sae-say,** n., report.

sae, v., see **sey.**

saft, n., thaw; adj., soft; rainy; weak of character: **saften,** v., soften: **saftie,** n., stupid, weak-willed person: **saft-skinned,** adj., sensitive.

saicont, adj., second.

saicret, adj., secret.

saig, v., sag.

saikless/sackless, adj., guiltless; harmless; feeble.

sail, v., be awash: **sailfish,** n., basking shark.

saim, n., fat; lard.

sain, v., bless; hallow; protect from evil; n., blessing; benediction.

saip, n., soap: **saip bells,** n., soap bubbles: **saip blots/sapples,** n., soap suds.

sair, n., sore; adj., sore; dire; severe; grief-stricken; adv., badly; greatly: **sair dung,** adj., hard pressed: **sair heid,** n., headache.

sairie, adj., sorrowful; wretched; needy.

sairin/serin, n., deserts; helping of food; punishment.

sait, n., chair; seat.

saitin, n., satin.

sal, v., shall.

sallet, n., salad.

samen, adj., same: **the samen,** n., the same.

sammer, v., adapt; adjust; attune; classify.

sanctly, adj., holy.

sandlin, n., sand-eel.

sandy mill, n., sand castle: **sandy piper,** n., sandpiper.

sang, n., song: fuss: **auld sang,** n., old story: **sang-maister,** n., singing-master: **sangschaw,** n., music festival: **sang-schuil,** n., music school.

sapple, v., steep in soapy water: **sapples,** n., soap-suds.

sappy, adj., moist; juicy; unctuous: **sappy-heidit,** adj., simple-minded.

saps, n., sops: **sapsy,** adj., effeminate; sloppy.

sark, n., shirt; woman's shift: **sarket,** n., woollen vest: **sarkin,** n., wood roof lining.

sassenger, n., sausage.

sauch, n., willow: **greitin sauch,** n., weeping willow: **sauch creel,** n., osier basket: **sauchen,** v., make pliable; adj., made of willow.

saucht, n., ease; quietness.

sauf, v., save; adj., safe.

saul, n., soul.

saum, n., psalm.

saumon, n., salmon.

saun, n., sand: **sauny,** adj., sandy.

saunt, v., disappear; spirit away.

saunt, n., saint: **sauntifee,** v., sanctify.

saut, v., salt; season; n., salt; sarcasm; adj., expensive: **sauty,** adj., salty: **saut dish,** n., salt-cellar: **lay in saut,** v., pickle.

saw, v., sow.

saw, n., ointment.

sax, n., adj., six: **saxt,** adj., sixth.

say, n., remark; speech; aphorism: **say owre,** v., recite: **say thegither,** v., concur.

scabbert, n., scabbard.

scad, n., faint colouring.

scad, v., n., burn; scald; scorch.

scaff, v., scrounge; n., booty from scrounging: **scaffie**, n., scavenger.

scairy, n., reflection; metaphor.

scaith, n., see **skaith**.

scance, v., scan; ponder; criticise; review; n., review; rough estimate.

scant, n., scarcity; poverty: **scantlins**, adv., scarcely.

scantling, n., rough outline/sketch.

scart, v., scratch; scrape; engrave; write hurriedly; n., scratch; particle.

scart, n., cormorant; hermaphrodite.

scaud, v., scald; inflame with rubbing; n., scald: **scaudie**, adj., torrid.

scauld, v., scold.

scaum, v., blight; burn; film over; n., red glow in sky: **scaumed**, adj., discoloured.

scaup, n., scalp; skull.

scaup, v., pare; scrape.

scaur, v., gash; scar; n., scar; cliff.

scaurie, n., young gull with brown-speckled feathers.

scawt, adj., scruffy; scabbed.

schenachy, n., bard.

schuil/schule, n., school; shoal of fish: **wee schuil**, n., infant school.

sclaff, v., slap; walk flat-footedly; n., loosely-fitting shoe/slipper: **sclaffert**, n., stroke; slipper: **sclaffie**, adj., untidy.

sclander, v., n., slander.

sclatch, v., n., smear; stain.

sclate, n., slate.

sclent, v., see **sklent**.

sclenter, n., scree.

sclice, n., slice.

scliff, v., scuff feet on ground in walking; n., blow with hand; swipe: **scliff-sclaff**, n., sound of slippers on floor; adv., with shuffling gait.

sclim, v., n., climb.

scob, v., baste, in sewing; n., splint.

scodge, v., drudge; **scodgie**, n,, kitchen menial: **scodgies**, n., chores.

scog, v., n., shelter.

scoggie, n., apron.

scoll, v., drink a health; toast.

scolp, v., scallop.

scomfish, v., choke; stifle.

sconce, v., screen; n., partition; rough shed.

scoor, v., see **scour**.

scoosh, v., rush, of water; squirt; n., rush of water; aerated waters: **scoosh-caur**, n., tramcar.

scoot, v., gush forth; spurt; hurry off; n., squirt; diarrhoea.

scorn, v., make fun of.

scotify/scoticise, v., render into Scots.

scouk, v., lurk; move stealthily; n., sneak.

scouneril, n., scoundrel.

scour, v., clean out; purge; n., diarrhoea; laxative: **scourie**, adj., shabby.

scour, v., n., race; scamper; rush.

scouth/scowth, n., room; scope; freedom: **scouthy**, adj., capacious; spacious.

scowder/scowther, v., blight; scorch; n., scorch; singe.

scowder, n., thin covering of snow.

scrab, n., withered stump of plant/tree.

scraich, v., see **screich**.

scrammle, v., n., scramble.

scran, v., scrape together; cadge; scrounge; n., provisions; loot.

scranky, adj., lean; gaunt; scrawny; scrawling, of writing.

scrape, v., n., scrawl; shave: **scrape o the pen**, n., a letter.

screed, n., harangue; letter; treatise: **screed aff**, v., reel off.

screenge, v., glean; scour vigorously: **screengins**, n., gleanings.

screich, v., n., shriek; scream.

screw, n., salary.

scrieve/screive, v., write; n., letter; script: **scriever**, n., writer; secretary.

scrieve, v., career; glissade; skid.

scriff, n., scruff of neck.

scriff, n., see **scruif**.

scriffin, n., crust.

scrift, n., long passage of prose/verse read off.

scrim, n., coarse cloth.

scrimpit, adj., frugal; undersized: **scrimpitness**, n., scantiness.

scrog, n., stunted creature/tree: **scroggie**, adj., gnarled; stunted.

scronach, v., make an outcry; n., outcry.

scruif, v., cover/become covered with thin layer; n., crust; film; dandruff.

scrummage, v., n., scrimmage.

scrunt, v., make harsh sound; scrape.

scrunt, n., puny person; miser: **scruntit,** adj., meagre: **scrunty,** adj., stunted.

scud, v., beat; move quickly; n., smack: **bare scuddie,** adj., naked.

scuff, v., graze; rub; wipe quickly; n., quick wipe.

scug, v., lurk; move surreptitiously; n., shelter; shade.

sculdudry, n., unchasteness; obscene language; adj., unchaste.

scum, v., remove surface floating matter from.

scunner, v., cause/get feeling of aversion; n., surfeit; aversion; loathing; nausea; nuisance: **scunnersome,** adj., abhorrent; disgusting; surfeiting.

scurdy, n., resting-place.

scutch, v., hoe; skate; beat; sweep perfunctorily; n., perfunctory sweep.

scutter, v., work dirtily; n., dirty, slovenly working.

sea-bree, n., foam; spume: **sea-broken,** adj., shipwrecked: **sea-sock,** n., puffin: **sea-craw,** n., cormorant: **sea-fierdy,** adj., seaworthy: **sea-gled,** n., osprey: **sea-hen,** n., guillemot: **sea-swine,** n., porpoise.

seal-skitter, n., jellyfish.

seck, v., dismiss from job; n., sack: **seckclaith/seckin,** n., sackcloth.

see after, v., attend to; tend: **see at,** v., consult: **see awa,** v., outlive: **see me,** v., give me.

seek, v., search for; invite; wish.

seel, n., see **seil.**

seem, v., suit; n., appearance.

seenil, adj., rare; adv., seldom: **seenlins,** adv., rarely.

seep, v., see **seip.**

seeth, v., boil up.

seg/sag, n., iris; reed; sedge.

seik, adj., sick.

seil, n., bliss; happiness: **seilfu/seily,** adj., happy; propitious.

seil, n., sieve.

seip, v., ooze; percolate; leak: **seip in,** v., imbibe.

seirie, adj., sardonic.

seiven, n., adj., seven.

sel, pron., self: **ainsel,** pron., self, emphatic: **sel-same,** adj., self-same.

selkie, n., seal: **selkie wife,** n., mermaid.

sellat, n., lidded cooking pan.

selvedge, v., fringe; form a margin; n., border; edge; parapet.

semmit, n., undershirt; vest.

semple, n., common people; adj., low-born.

sen, v., send; n., message; messenger.

sennicht, n., week.

sensible, adj., obvious.

ser., v., serve; suit; satisfy; pass muster; fit, of clothing: **sert,** adj., replete; sated: **ser out,** v., suffice.

server, n., salver.

serviette, n., table napkin.

session saint, n., church elder.

set, v., congeal; mature; incline one's opinion; lease; n., check in cloth; physique; quality; seed potato; adj., resolute: **set aff,** v., display; fob off; n., offset: **set on,** v., attack; adj., devoted to: **set out,** v., publish: **set tae,** v., begin; n., quarrel: **set-stane,** n., hone: **settin,** n., set of eggs for hatching: **it sets,** v., it behoves; it suits.

settlement, n., testament.

settlins, n., sediment.

sevendle, adj., steadfast; secure.

sey, v., n., assay; sample; test.

sey, n., sirloin.

sey, v., strain milk; n., milk strainer; milk pail.

sgian-dhu, n., dirk.

shackle, v., hobble; cripple; n., ankle; wrist: **shackle-bane,** n., wrist bone.

shae, v., n., shoe: **shae-spune,** n., shoehorn: **smaa shune,** n., fancy shoes.

shair/shuir, adj., sure; certain.

shaird, n., shred; remnant; contemptible person.

shairn, n., cow dung.

shairp, adj., see **sherp.**

shaivle, v., see **shevel.**

shak, v., shake; n., atrophy; wrestling match: **shak a fuit/leg,** v., dance.

shalla, adj., shallow.

shamed, be ashamed, v., think shame: **black-burnin shame,** n., deep shame.

shamells/skemmels, n., shambles; abattoir: **shammle-shankit,** adj., bandy-legged.

shan-gabbit, adj., lantern-jawed.

shangan, n., cleft stick.

shangie, adj., gaunt.

shangies, n., manacles.

shank, v., walk; n., leg; handle; shaft; stem: **shank-bane**, n., shin-bone.

shape, v., intend; n., posture.

shargan, n., thin, shrivelled person: **shargie**, adj., lean; scraggy.

sharrow, adj., acid; bitter; sour.

shauchle, v., shuffle; shamble; n., shamble; tumbledown object: **shauchled**, adj., misshapen: **shauchlin**, adj., mean; ramshackle.

shaul/shall, n., shallow; shoal.

shaup, v., shell peas; n., peapod.

***shave**, v., cut in slices; n., slice; segment.

shaver, n., a wag.

shavie, n., prank; trick; swindle.

shaw, v., show; n., show; sign; symptom; view.

shaw, n., coppice; grove; turnip/potato leaf.

shawlie, n., small shawl.

shear, v., reap; n., a shearing; guillotine blade: **shears**, n., scissors.

shear-bane, n., pubic bone.

shed, v., divide; part hair; n., slice; parting of hair: **shedding**, n., parting of ways: **shed wi**, v., separate oneself from.

sheddae, n., shadow.

sheen, v., n., gleam; glitter; shine.

***sheepie-meh**, n., child's name for sheep: **sheepshank**, n., useless person.

shell out, v., pay out.

shells, n., unslaked burnt limestone.

shenachy, n., story-teller.

sherp/shairp, adj., sharp; frosty: **sherpen**, v., sharpen: **sherpin-stane**, n., whetstone.

sheuch, v., trench; n., ditch; gutter; trench.

shevel, v., disarrange; distort; screw up face.

shew (shoo), v., sew: **shewin**, n., sewing: **shewster**, n., seamstress.

shiel, n., hut; shelter: **shieling**, n., temporary summer abode, for shepherd.

shilfa, n., chaffinch.

shill, n., see **shuil**.

shill, adj., shrill.

shilpit, adj., emaciated; puny; shrunken.

shimmy, n., shinty.

shine, n., social gathering.

shipping, n., pier; quay; wharf.

shirra, n., sheriff.

shirp, v., contract; taper: **shirpit**, adj., tapering.

shit/shite, v., void excrement; n., excrement: **shitten**, adj., contemptible.

shock, n., stroke of paralysis.

shod, v., fit with shoes; n., heel/toe protector for shoes.

shog, v., n., nudge; push; jolt; shake: **shoggie-bog**, n., moving quagmire.

shoggle, v., wag; jog along.

shoogle, v., dangle; quake; swing; n., swing: **shooglie**, adj., unsteady.

shool, n., see **shuil**.

shoot, v., run to seed.

shop-door, n., trouser flap.

shore, v., n., offer; promise; menace.

shore, n., harbour; wharf: **shore-humper**, n., stevedore.

short, v., offend; n., jiffy: **short syne**, adv., recently.

shot, n., shuttered casement.

shot brae, n., steep bank; avalanche.

shouer, n., shower; paroxysm.

shouder / shouther, n., shoulder: **shouderie**, n., pickaback.

shouting, n., childbirth.

shugger, n., sugar.

shuil, n., shovel.

shuit, v., shoot.

shunkie, n., latrine; privy.

shurl, n., glissade of snow from roof.

shut tae, v., shut close: **shut o**, adj., rid of.

shy, adj. disinclined.

sib, n., kin; adj., akin; related; intimate: **sibness**, n., kinship.

sic, adj., such; adv., so: **sicca/sicna**, adj., such a: **siclike**, adj., suchlike.

siccar/sicker, v., fix firmly; adj., sure; staunch; true; loyal; resolute: **mak siccar**, v., ascertain: **siccarness**, n., firmness; resolution.

sich, v., n., sigh.

sicht, v., scan; inspect; n., scrutiny; considerable number/quantity: **a guid sicht**, adv., far: **saicont sicht**, n., prophetic vision.

sidelins, adj., indirect; oblique; adv., indirectly; sideways: **side-lichts**, n., sidewhiskers: **sidesman**, n., arbiter: **sidyweys**, adv., sideways.

sile, n., see syle.

siller, n., silver; money: **sillerless,** adj., penniless: **dry siller,** n., ready money.

silly, adj., flimsy; frail; hapless; innocent.

simmer, n., summer: **simmer cout,** n., haze; shimmering air.

simple, adj., see semple.

simulate, adj., artificial.

sin, adv., prep., conj., since.

sin, n., sun; son.

sinacle, v., vestige.

sinder, v., sunder; separate; single, of seedlings: **sindry,** adj., sundry.

sine, v., see syne.

sing smaa, v., defer; "pipe down".

single, v., thin out seedlings: **single-end,** n., one-apartment house.

sink, v., dig a pit shaft; n., pit shaft.

sinsyne, adv., since then.

sirken, adj., punctilious in paying.

sirs (sirce) me, interj., expressing surprise.

sit in, v., take seat at table: **sit still,** interj., sit at peace: **sit upon,** v., fit: **sittin,** n., position: **sitten doun,** adj., persistent, of cold, etc.

skaigh, v., see skech.

skail, v., disperse; scatter; spill; upset: **skailin,** n., departure; dispersal: **skailin time,** n., stopping time: **skail-win,** n., tornado.

skaillie, n., slate: **skaillie-brod,** n., writing slate: **skaillie-pen,** n., slate pencil.

skair, v., make a joint, as with fishing rod; n., such a joint.

skaith, v., n., hurt; damage: **skaithfree,** adj., unharmed: **skaithfu,** adj., injurious: **skaith-mail,** n., blackmail: **skaithie,** n., draught screen.

skaive, v., slander.

skech, v., cadge; pilfer; purloin; steal.

skeelie, adj., see skeilie.

skeelie, n., gruel.

skeer, adj., nervous: **skeerie,** adj., flighty; restive.

skeich, adj., gay; frisky; arrogant: **skeichness,** n., pride; skittishness.

skeil, v., test; n., skill; test: **skeilie,** adj., capable; shrewd; skilful.

skeldrake, n., oyster-catcher.

skelf, n., sliver; splinter: **skelfy,** adj., arranged in layers.

skellat, n., handbell.

skellet, n., saucepan.

skellie, v., go off the straight; adj., lop-sided; squint-eyed.

skelloch, v., n., shriek; scream.

skellum, n., rogue; worthless fellow.

skelp, v., beat with flat weapon; slap; throb; n., slap; sideswipe: **skelpin,** n., thrashing.

skelp, v., hurry; race; dash about.

skelpie-limmer, n., hussy; virago.

skelter, v., scurry; scuttle.

skemmel, n., lanky person: **skemmlie,** adj., lanky.

skeoch, n., rock fissure; small cave.

skep, n., bee-hive.

skep, v., go/put to bed: **get skeppit,** v., go to bed.

skew, v., go off the straight; move sideways; distort; n., twist; quirk; adj., oblique; adv., askew; aslant; awry.

skiddle, v., dabble in water; n., slop: **skiddlie,** adj., insignificant.

skiff, v., skim; glide; graze; n., slight shower.

skift, v., skim; n., yawl.

skimmer, v., shimmer; glide swiftly; n., glimmer; light snowfall.

skin-a-lous, n., miser: **skin-claes,** n., waterproof clothing.

skink, v., pour liquor into another container; tipple; n., liquor.

skink, n., shin of beef; small portion: **skinkin ware,** n., watery soup.

skinkle, v., gleam; shine; glitter; n., lustre; radiance.

skip, n., peak of cap: **skippit bannet,** n., peaked cap.

skir, n., reef.

skirl, v., n., shriek; scream; yell: **skirler,** n., gale: **skirlcrake,** n., corncrake.

skirl, v., frizzle; fry; sizzle: **skirl-i-the-pan,** n., oatmeal-onion fry.

skirr, v., whir; whizz.

skite, v., fly off obliquely; ricochet; skid, n., rebound: **skitie,** adj., slippery.

skitter, v., have diarrhoea; n., watery excrement: **skittery,** adj., trivial.

skive, v., move swiftly; prowl about.

sklent, v., slant; glance/move sideways; swerve; zigzag; n., obliqueness;

slant; bias; adj., oblique: **sklentit**, adj., sloped; angled.

skleut, v., walk with heavy step.

skliff, v., see scliff.

skliff, n., slice; layer.

sklute, n., soft, wet mass of material; slovenly person.

sklyter, v., slop; n., mass of slops.

skraich/skreich, v., see **screich**.

skrow, n., scroll.

skybal, n., contemptible person; ragamuffin; old horse; adj., rascally.

skyme, v., flash; catch a glimpse of; n., flash.

skyre, v., shine brightly; adj., bright; limpid; stark: **skyrin**, adj., garish.

skyte, n., duffer; merry frolic.

slab up, v., lap up.

slabber, v., dribble; slaver; n., slop; slush: **slabbery**, adj., sloppy.

slack, v., slacken; pause; n., gap in clouds; hollow; adj., short of work.

sladge, n., slovenly woman.

slae, n., sloe.

slag, v., sleet; n., sleet; marsh.

slaich, v., smear; n., slime: **slaichie**, adj., slimy; slobbery.

slaiger, v., besmear; spread thickly; n., smear; wet mass; sloppy food.

slaik, v., blotch; lick; n., blotch; lick; slobbering kiss.

slairg, v., besmear; sup noisily; n., smear: **slairgie**, adj., sticky.

slairie, v., beslobber; smear; splash with mud.

slaister, v., bedaub; do messy work; n., sloppy mess; work done dirtily.

slaiver, v., dribble; slobber; talk nonsense; n., saliva.

slap, n., gap in wall; pass between hills; gate; nick.

slaps, n., slops.

slash, v., splash; n., torrent of rain; clash.

slate-band, n., schist: **slate-caum**, n., slate pencil.

slater, n., woodlouse.

slauch, v., n., spit.

slauchter, v., n., slaughter.

slaver, v., see slaiver.

slaw, adj., slow; easy-ozy.

slee, adj., sly; deft: **slee at**, v., peer at: **slee awa**; v., slip away.

sleekit, adj., hypocritical; unctuous: **sleekitness**, n., guile; slyness.

sleep, v., go numb; lapse: **sleep in**, v., oversleep: **sleepy-mannies**, n., specks in eyes.

sleik, n., silt.

slicht, v., slight; jilt; n., slight; adj., slight; still, of sea.

slicht, n., sleight.

slickworm, n., mud-worm used as fish-bait.

slidder, v., slide; slither: **slidderie**, adj., slippery; smooth-tongued.

slight, v., fritter away one's time.

slink, v., deceive; n., despicable person.

slip, n., youngster; slim person.

slip awa, v., die: **slippy**, adj., slippery; speedy: **slippit**, adj., aborted.

slitter, v., splash aimlessly in water, n., sloppy mess; slovenly person.

sloch, v., spit out phlegm; n., phlegm: **slocher**, v., breathe asthmatically.

slock, v., slake; abate: **slocken**, v., quench.

slogger, v., dawdle; walk in slovenly manner; n., such a walker.

slonk, n., muddy drain; bog; squelching sound.

sloom, v., see **sloum**.

sloonge, v., see **slounge**.

slorach, v., beslobber; behave sentimentally; n., sloppy mess.

slork, v., make squelching sound.

slorp, v., eat dirtily; swallow noisily; n., messy food.

slotter, v., eat noisily; n., wet, disgusting mass.

sloum, v., sleep restlessly; n., unsettled sleep; trance; reverie.

sloum, n., scum: **sloumy**, adj., septic.

slounge, v., drench; splash; plunge; n., drenching; downpour of rain.

slouth, n., sloth: **slouth/slouthfu**, adj., idle; slothful.

slouster, n., messy person.

slub, n., slime: **slubber**, v., slobber; n., overboiled food: **slubbery**, adj., overboiled.

slug, n., overall.

sluich, n., flood of water: **sluich-buird**, n., sluice-gate.

slump, v., sink in mud; n., bog; swamp.

slung, v., n., sling.

slunk, v., plough through mud; n., marsh; rut in road.

slush, v., squelch; n., melting snow; thin, insipid liquid.

slype, v., peel off; fall over; n., lout.

*smaa/smaa-boukit, adj., small/small in stature: smaa drink, n., nonentity.

smacher, v., huddle: smacher/smacherie, n., crowd of small objects.

smad, v., stain; n., smut.

smairg, v., smear.

smairt, adj., see smert.

smeddum, n., pith; vigour; animation; drive; spirit.

smeik/smuik, v., smoke; n., smoke; fumes; odour: smeiky, adj., smoky.

smelt, n., salmon-fry.

smelterin, adj., raging, of flames.

smergh, n., marrow; spirit: smerghless, adj., lethargic.

smert, v., smart; smarten; adj., smart.

smeuch/smeuchter, v., n., smoke; drizzle.

smiddy, n., smithy.

smirr, v., n., drizzle.

smirk, v., n., smile.

smirtle, v., see snirtle.

smit, v., infect; taint; n., contagion: smittle, adj., contagious; infectious.

smit/smitch, n., smut; stain; taint: smitty, adj., smutty.

smithereens, n., small fragments.

smoochter, v., see smeuchter.

smool, v., purloin; slink: smooler, v., dissolve.

smoor/smuir, v., choke for air; extinguish; obscure; stifle; n., drizzling rain; stifling atmosphere: smoory, adj., stifling; suffocating.

smoorich, v., kiss stealthily; n., stolen kiss.

smowt, n., young salmon; anything small: smowty, adj., small; trifling.

smuchty, adj., fuggy; steamy.

smush, v., smash; grind small; n., grime; leavings.

smytrie, n., crowd of small creatures.

snab, n., incline.

snack, v., snap; gobble up; n., snap.

snaff, v., sniff contemptuously.

snag, n., knob.

snagger, v., n., snore.

snapper, v., fall by tripping; n., stumble; mischance; moral lapse.

snar, adj., strict; ill-tempered.

snash, v., insult; sneer; speak impertinently; n., abuse; impertinence.

snaw, n., snow: snaw-bree, n., slush: snaw-wreath, n., snowdrift.

sneck, v., n., bolt; latch: sneck-drawin, adj., stealthy; underhand.

sneck, v., cut; snip: sneck aff, v., switch off: sneck-harl, v., roughcast.

sned, v., chop off; prune; castrate.

sneer, v., n., hiss.

sneevil, v., n., snivel; whine.

sneish, v., take snuff: sneishin, n., snuff: sneishin-mill, n., snuffbox.

sneisty, adj., sardonic.

sneith, adj., smooth; cultured.

snell, adj., cold; biting, of wind; acrid; sharp: snelly, adj., chilly: snell-gabbit, adj., sharp-tongued: snell-nebbit, adj., astute.

snib, v., bolt; snub; restrain; n., door catch; snub.

snick, v., pilfer.

snicker, v., n., sneer; titter.

snift, n., scent: snifter, v., sniff; smell; inhale; n., sniff; smell.

snirt, v., n., snort.

snirt/snirtle, v., n., sneer; snigger.

snocher, v., n., snort; snore.

snod, v., trim; tidy up; adj., trim; tidy: snod aff, v., finish off.

snood, v., hold in hair with headband; n., hair ribbon; hair net.

snool, v., cringe; intimidate; n., sneaky person: snool-like, adj., sneaky.

snoove/snuive, v., glide; lurk; slink.

snore, v., n., drone; whir.

snork, v., n., snort.

snotter, v., snivel: snotters, n., nasal mucus: snottery, adj., slimy with mucus.

snout, n., headland; peak of cap.

snowk, v., scent; sniff; pry; n., sniff.

snurl, v., twist; crease; wrinkle; n., tangle; dilemma.

socher, v., be over-fastidious about one's health.

sock, n., supporting frame; ploughshare.

sock, v., relax: sockin-oor, n., after-work period of relaxation.

sod, n., very heavy weight or person.

sodger, n., soldier.

sodie, n., soda: **sodie scone,** n., soda scone.

sole, n., sill.

solid, adj., sound; sensible; sedate.

somehou, adv., somehow: **someplace,** adv., somewhere: **somewey,** adv., somehow.

sonnet, n., ditty; song.

sonse, n., good fortune; success: **sonsy,** adj., plump; capacious; lucky; hearty.

sook, v., see **souk.**

soom, v., see **soum.**

soop, v., see **soup.**

soor, adj., see **sour.**

sooth/suith, n., truth: **soothfast,** adj., authentic; true; faithful.

sorn, v., cadge; forage; live parasitically: **sorner,** n., parasite.

sorple, v., wash with soapy liquid.

sorrow/sorra, n., grief; plague; troublesome person.

sort, v., repair; heal; adapt; chastise: **sort wi,** v., supply with.

sosh, adj., frank; sociable; n., co-operative store: **sosherie,** n., sociability.

sot ("o" as in "not"), adv., so, in **it is sot.**

sotter, v., roast; scorch; simmer; n., scorch.

sotter, v., make soggy; work dirtily; n., loafer: **sottery,** adj., soggy.

sou, n., sow: **sou-cruive,** n., pigsty.

*****souch,** v., sigh; hum; sing/whistle softly; n., sigh; moan; opinion; tune.

*****souk,** v., suck; dry up; lap; n., suck; quagmire; whirlpool; sycophant: **souker,** n., horse leech; plant sucker: **soukies,** n., clover flowers.

soum, v., swim; float; turn giddy; n., swim; attack of faintness.

soun, v., n., sound; adj., sound; sleeping deeply: **soundin-box,** n., pulpit canopy.

soup, v., sweep: **souper,** n., brush.

souple, v., make supple; n., truncheon; adj., supple; limp; glib; slick; tractable: **soupleness,** n., nimbleness: **souple-neckit,** adj., servile.

sour, adj., acid; bitter; forbidding: **sour douk,** n., buttermilk: **sour-faced,** adj., surly: **sour-grass,** n., sedge: **sourock,** n., sorrel.

soutar, n., cobbler; shoemaker.

southron, n., southerner; the English language; adj., southern.

sowdie, n., pudding containing many mixed ingredients.

sowens, n., flummery; oats steeped and boiled into a pudding.

sowff, v., see **souch.**

sowff, v., quaff.

sowl, n., soul.

sownack, n., bog-fir torch.

sowp, v., sup; drink; n., sup; draught of liquor.

sowp, v., soak: **sowpit,** adj., waterlogged.

sowse, v., douse in water.

sowth, v., try over a tune with a low whistle.

sowther, v., solder; weld; strengthen; reconcile; n., solder.

spadin, n., spade-depth.

spae, v., predict; tell fortunes; n., prediction: **spaedom,** n., witchcraft.

spaik, n., batten; slat; rung of ladder; perch.

spail, n., lath; splinter; shaving; skewer: **spail basket,** n., basket of interwoven "spails".

spainial, n., spaniel.

spairge, v., spray; scatter; make public.

spaivie/spavie, n., swelling on horse's hock.

spang, v., leap; stride; flick; measure by pacing; n., leap; stride.

spang-new, adj., quite new.

spank, v., move nimbly: **spankie,** n., energetic person.

spar/spaur, n., perch; axle linchpin.

spark, v., spatter; n., speck: **sparkles,** n., flying sparks.

sparple, v., strew.

sparra, n., sparrow.

spate, v., swell, of a river; n., torrent.

spatril, n., musical note: **spatrils,** n., gaiters.

spattle, n., spoon-shaped blade.

spaul, n., leg; limb.

spave, v., remove the ovaries.

spavie, n., see **spaivie.**

spawcious, adj., pretentious; spacious.

speak, v., bespeak; n., speech; pronouncement; topic: **speak a word to,** v., advise; rebuke: **speak back,** v., retort: **speak for,** v., engage as servant.

spean, v., wean: **spean frae,** v., separate oneself from another.

specks, n., spectacles.

speed, n., success: **come speed,** v., make progress.

speeder, n., spider.

speil, v., climb; mount; relieve at work; n., job; period of rest.

speir, v., ask; investigate; ask in marriage; n., inquiry; investigation: **speir at,** v., inquire of: **speir for,** v., ask after: **speir into,** v., investigate: **speir out,** v., seek out; track down: **speirins,** n., tidings.

speld, v., slice/tear open: **speldin,** n., gutted and dried fish; kipper.

spelder, v., sprawl; stretch oneself out.

spelk, v., set in splints; n., splint.

spell, v., recount; interpret; n., spelling.

spence, n., parlour; sitting room.

spendrife, adj., spendthrift; extravagant; lavish.

speug, n., sparrow.

spice, v., n., pepper.

spicket, n., spigot; bung of barrel; water tap.

spiel, v., play; n., game; match.

spill, v., putrefy: **spilt man,** n., leper.

spink, n., pink; carnation.

spinner, v., move speedily; rise spirally; n., great speed.

spinnle, n., spindle: **spinnle-shanks,** n., long thin legs.

spirl, n., twig: **spirlie,** n., smoke spiral; adj., thin; slender.

spirlin, n., sprat; young herring.

*****spit,** v., rain slightly; n., spot of rain: **spittin,** n., spittle.

spit, n., image; likeness: **the spitten image,** n., the exact likeness.

spital, n., hospice; hospital.

spite, v., spurn: **spitten,** adj., mean.

splacher, v., flounder.

splairge, v., besmear; splash; scatter liquid stuff; squander; n., display.

splash-fuit, n., splay foot.

splatch, v., n., blotch.

splatter, v., n., splash.

spleit, v., split.

spleuchan, n., purse; tobacco pouch.

splirt, v., discharge water or other liquid.

splitter, v., splutter; n., splutter; fuss.

splore, v., frolic; riot; n., carouse; prank; exploit; outing.

splounge, v., splash about in water: **sploungin,** adj., soaking wet.

spoatch, v., poach; scrounge; n., scrounger.

sponsible, adj., reliable: **sponsibility,** n., reliability.

spool, n., shuttle.

spounge, v., n., sponge, in all its senses.

spout, v., n., cascade; spurt.

sprack, adj., alert; lively; smart.

spraing/sprainge, v., speckle; streak; stripe; n., streak; tint.

sprattle, v., scramble.

sprauchle/sprachle, v., sprawl; flounder; struggle; n., sprawl; struggle.

sprecherie, n., plunder; perquisites.

spreckle, v., n., speckle; spot; freckle; mottle.

spree, v., make merry; be in heat; n., carouse; frolic.

spreid, v., spread.

spreit, n., spirit.

sprent, v., sprint; intersperse.

spring, n., cheerful tune; reel.

spritty, adj., mettlesome.

sprots, n., dry twigs for burning.

sprung, adj., drunk.

sprush, v., smarten; tidy up; adj., dapper; tidy: **sprush new,** adj., quite new.

spud, n., potato.

spue, v., n., spew; retch.

spulyie, v., plunder; desolate; n., booty; jetsam.

spune, n., spoon.

spung, v., thieve; n., pouch; purse; watch pocket.

spunk, n., animation; bravery; a match: **spunkie,** adj., mettlesome; frisky.

spurtle, n., porridge stick.

spyle, v., indulge; pamper; spoil.

squaich, v., squawk.

square-wricht, n., carpenter.

squatter (squa-ter), v., sprawl; flutter in water; n., crowd; swarm.

squattle (squa-tle), v., squat; nest.
squeef, n., male flirt.
squeegee (squeejee), adv., out of shape.
squeesh, v., squash; n., the gushing forth of water.
squirl, n., flounce of dress; fancy flourish.
staa, n., stall.
*stab, n., stob; pole; stake; stem of plant: stabby, adj., jagged.
stacher, v., stagger; stumble: stacherie, adj., tottery.
staidel, n., foundation of haystack.
staig, n., stallion; gelding; colt: staigchiel, n., groom.
staig, v., walk in dignified manner; n., dignified step.
stainch/stench, v., staunch; adj., staunch.
staincheon/stanchel, n., window bar.
staing, n., pole; shaft; boat mast; prong.
stamack, v., tolerate; n., stomach: fyle the stamack, v., upset the stomach.
stamagast, v., bewilder; disgust; shock; n., disgust; shock.
stamp-airn, n., branding-iron.
stance, v., station; n., station; bushalt; street trader's pitch.
standart, n., standard; stature.
stander, v., support with pillars; n., pillar.
stane, n., stone: stany, adj., stony: stanechack, n., stonechat: staneland, n., large stone tenement: staneraw, n., lichen giving purple dye.
stang, n., see staing.
stang, v., sting; n., sting; shooting pain.
stank, v., stagnate; n., ditch; stagnant pool.
stanners, n., shingle: stanner-stanes, n., stepping-stones.
stap, v., n., stop; step.
stap, v., stop; block; cram; n., surfeit: stapper/stapple, n., stopper; plug: stap-fou, adj., chock-full: stap out, v., gouge out.
stap/step-bairn, n., stepchild: stapmither, n., stepmother.
stark, adj., very strong, of liquor.
starn, n., blob of fat; point of needle.
starn, n., ship's stern.

starn, n., star; pupil of eye: starnwatcher, n., astronomer.
startle, v., n., stampede, of cattle.
starty, adj., easily startled.
statute, v., enact.
staucher, v., see stacher.
stauchie, adj., close; muggy.
staughies, n., odd bits of meat stewed.
stauk, v., stalk.
staumer, v., blunder: staumrel, n., blunderer; stupid person.
*staun, v., stand; last; afford; n., goods stall: staunin graith, n., fixtures.
staup, v., stride heavy-footedly.
staur, n., star: staur-glint, n., meteor: staur o the ee, n., pupil of eye.
stave, v., n., bruise; sprain: stave on, v., barge on.
staver, v., stumble.
staw, v., cloy; nauseate; disgust; bore; n., nausea; disgust: stawed, adj., sated: stawsome, adj., cloying; tiresome.
stead, v., see steid.
steading, n., farm building, with or without farmhouse.
steamie, n., public wash-house.
stech, v., cram; stuff: stechie, adj., stiff; stodgy: stechin, n., hearty meal.
stech, v., n., gasp; stink.
steek, v., see steik.
steeple, n., staple.
steer, v., see steir.
steeve, adj., see steive.
steid/sted, v., lay the foundation of; n., foundation; site; print; track.
*steik, v., sew; stitch; close; n., stitch: lowpen-steik, n., dropped stitch.
steil, n., finger-stall; handle.
steir, v., stir; disturb; propel; n., stir; fuss; disturbance: steirin, adj., active; mischievous: steirless, adj., lifeless.
steive, adj., firm; stiff; steep; staunch; inflexible.
stell, v., set up; prop; n., prop: stellnet, n., salmon net on stakes.
stell, n., still for distillation.
sten/stend, v., leap; cascade; n., leap; striding step.
stench, v., allay hunger/thirst; n., surfeit; adj., staunch; rigid.

stend, v., stretch; spring; rear, of horse: **stends,** n., dimensions.

stent, v., stretch; n., extent; limit; adj., taut: **stentit,** adj., tense: **stentless,** adj., infinite.

stent, v., assess; rate; tax; n., assessment; tax: **stents,** n., tribute.

stent, v., stint; leave off; allocate; appoint; prescribe; n., bound; stage; set task; term.

step, n., walk: **step aside,** v., err morally; n., misdemeanour.

sterk, adj., stark; rigorous; sheer; utter; adv., utterly.

stert, v., n., start.

stertle, v., startle.

sterve, v., starve; n., bout of abstinence.

steug, v., stab; prick; stitch roughly; n., prickly object; spike; thorn.

stew, v., give off smell; n., smell; vapour.

stew, n., mental agitation.

stewart, n., steward.

stey, v., steep.

stey, v., dwell; remain; n., sojourn.

stibble, v., stubble: **stibbler,** n., gleaner: **stibble park,** n., stubble field.

stichle, v., n., rustle.

***stick,** v., fail; n., stoppage: **stickin,** adj., unaccommodating; unsocial.

stick, v., gore; stab: **stickit,** adj., stabbed.

stick in, v., persist: **stick into,** v., concentrate on: **stick up to,** v., stand up to.

sticks, n., furniture: **stick and stow,** adv., wholly.

stickle, v., n., scruple.

stiddie, n., blacksmith's anvil; forge.

stieve, adj., see **steive.**

stife, n., choking atmosphere.

stiff, v., become/make stiff: **stiffen,** v., treat clothes with starch.

stiggy, n., stile.

still, n., lull in wind.

still and on, adv., notwithstanding; yet.

stilp, v., stride; stump: **stilpers,** n., stilts.

stilt, v., walk stiffly/pompously; n., crutch: **stiltie,** n., redshank.

stimpart, n., dry measure.

sting, v., punt a boat; n., punting pole.

stinkin nettle, n., dead-nettle.

stint, v., droop; stunt: **stintit,** adj., scanty; short.

stippit, adj., stupid.

stirk, n., bullock; castrated young ox.

stirlin, n., starling.

stirrup-dram, n., parting drink.

stishie, n., turmoil.

stite, n., see **styte.**

stith, adj., unshakable; taut.

stivven, v., go numb; freeze to death.

stob, v., stab; n., pointed instrument; stab.

stock, v., invest money: **stocken,** n., hoard; savings.

stock, v., cramp; stiffen; n., plant stalk; tree stump.

stockin, n., stocking: **stockin needle,** n., darning needle.

stodge, n., heavy, fat person; substantial, quick-filling food.

stoich, n., suffocating atmosphere.

stoit/stoiter, v., reel; stagger.

stoo, v., see **stou.**

stook, v., erect sheaves to dry; n., group of sheaves set up to dry.

stookie, n., stucco; pipe-clay: **stookie man,** n., effigy; plaster statue.

stoon, v., see **stoun.**

stoop, n., see **stowp.**

stoor, n., see **stour.**

stop, v., dwell; remain: **stop on,** v., wait for: **stop wi,** v., live with.

stormcock, n., fieldfare; misselthrush: **stormfinch,** n., petrel.

stot, n., bullock; castrated male ox.

stot, v., bounce; rebound; stagger; n., bounce; stagger; rhythm: **stottin bits,** n., scraps of meat: **stotter,** v., move unsteadily.

stou, v., graze; nibble; nip off.

stoun, v., stun; clang; n., clang; heavy blow.

stoun, v., n., ache; throb; thrill: **stounie,** adj., moody; temperamental.

stoup, n., see **stowp.**

***stoup,** v., prop; n., prop; pillar; support.

stour, n., dust; blizzard; spume; stress; bustle; battle; adj., grim; stubborn; hoarse: **stour about,** v., rush about: **stour o words,** n., bombast: **stourie,** adj., dusty; stormy: **stourie-fuit,** n., stranger.

stoushie/stoussie, adj., stoutly-built.

stouth, n., thievery; stealth: **stouthrie,** n., larceny.

stove, v., steam; stew; n., stew: **stovies,** n., potatoes stewed with onions.

stow, v., cram; gorge; stuff.

stowf, v., steam; n., fine powder.

stowff, v., stump along: **stowfie,** adj., stocky.

stownlins, adv., secretly; stealthily.

stowp, n., jug; mug; tankard; flagon.

stracht, adj., see **straucht.**

strae, n., straw: **strae daith,** n., natural death: **strae-hous,** n., straw shed: **strae-mous,** n., shrew: **strae-wisp,** n., weak-minded person.

straiggle, v., straggle: **straiggly,** adj., scattered.

straight, v., rectify; adv., candidly.

straik, v., streak; caress; preen; smooth; n., streak; caress; stroke of pen.

stramash, v., smash; n., fuss; squabble; brawl.

strand, n., stream; gutter.

strang, adj., strong.

strang, n., stale urine for bleaching clothes.

strange at, v., wonder at.

strap, v., tie in a bunch; n., bunch; lath: **straps,** n., braces.

strappin, adj., burly; stalwart.

strath, n., broad river valley.

straucht/stracht, v., straighten; smooth out; n., straight line; want; adj., straight; adv., at once: **strauchtforrit,** adj., straightforward.

stravaig, v., gad; ramble; stroll; wander; n., ramble.

straw, v., scatter; strew.

straw basher/tap, n., straw hat.

strawn, n., strand of rope.

streenge, v., whip.

street-hous, n., flat on ground floor.

streik, v., extend from one point to another; stretch; n., stretch.

streind, v., n., sprain.

streitch, v., stretch; n., distance; extent; spell; turn.

strenth, n., strength.

stress, v., overwork; stretch to capacity; n., great exertion.

strick, adj., strict: **stricks,** n., strict terms.

striddle, v., straddle; stride: **striddle-leggit,** adv., straddle-wise.

striffin, n., membrane; narrow strip.

strike, v., be hooked, of fish: fix a price.

strin, v., see **stroan.**

string, n., sexual desire; strong tide.

stringin, n., ornamental lace; tape.

strinkle, v., sprinkle: **strinklin,** n., sprinkling.

strinnle, v., n., trickle.

strip, v., variegate: **strippit,** adj., striped.

strippins, n., last milk from cow.

stroan, v., spout; spurt; piddle: n., spurt.

strone, n., headland.

stroop, n., see **stroup**

strooshie, n., turmoil; uproar.

stroud/strood, n., complete series; set.

strounge, adj., astringent; rank-tasting.

stroup, n., spout; faucet; tea: **stroupie** n., teapot.

strum, n., fuse of a shot, in mining.

strunt, n., toddy.

strunt, v., strut; sulk; offend; n., pique: **strunty,** adj., sulky.

strynd/stryne, n., disposition; lineage.

stuckie, n., starling.

stuck up, adj., conceited.

stuff, n., material; baggage; possessions: **stuffrie,** n., material.

stuffy, adj., hardy; healthy; robust.

stug, v., n., stab; puncture.

stug, v., thicken, of food: **stuggy,** adj., thick, of food.

stuil/stule, n., stool.

stummle, v., n., stumble.

stump, v., truncate: **stumpie,** n., squat person; pencil stump; adj., thickset.

sturken, v., solidify; adj., formal; stiff in manner.

sturt, v., strut; alarm; vex; n., alarm; strife; vexation.

stushie, n., squabble; tumult.

stychle, v., stifle: **stychly,** adj., stifling.

styme, n., glimpse; glimmer: **stymie,** n., short-sighted person.

styte, n., balderdash; nonsense.

subscrive, v., subscribe.

sub-tack, v., sub-lease.

sucken, adj., bound to use a certain mill to get grain milled; in debt.

suddent, adj., sudden; adv., suddenly.

Suddron/Southron, n., the English tongue; adj., English; southern.

sugaraullie, n., licorice: **sugarie willie,** n., young gull with mottled feathers.

suid/sud, v., should.

suith, n., see sooth.

summons, n., writ.

sumph, n., oafish, stupid fellow; simpleton.

sunblink/sunflaucht, n., sunbeam: **sundoun,** n., sunset: **sunkep,** n., straw hat.

Sunday braws, n., Sunday clothes; best clothes.

sune/shuin, adv., soon: **sune or late,** adv., inevitably.

sunk, n., bench; couch; turf fence; cushion filled with straw.

sunkets, n., delicacies; titbits; provisions.

supersede, v., postpone.

suppose, v., be assured that; conj., although.

surfle, v., embroider; n., embroidery.

sustain, v., confirm a call to ministry.

Suthron, n., see **Suddron.**

swabble, v., n., cane.

swack, v., brandish; wield; n., heavy blow: **swackin,** adj., hefty.

swack, adj., active; spry; supple.

swag, v., sag; walk in zigzag manner.

swage, v., assuage; relax; subside.

swaird, n., sward.

swal, v., bloat; swell; n., sea-swell: **swallin,** n., swelling.

swalla, n., swallow, the bird.

swally, v., swallow.

swank, adj., spry; supple: **swankie,** n., active lad: **swankin,** adj., hefty.

swap, v., brandish; hit smartly; n., blow; strong gust of wind.

swap, v., bear a likeness to.

swarf, v., n., swoon.

swarry, n., social gathering.

swash, v., beat; swagger; adj., showy; fuddled.

swatch, v., copy; size up; n., sample; feature; trait; kind.

swattle, v., guzzle; swill.

swats, n., ale; beer.

swaw, v., undulate; n., undulation.

swecht, n., impetus; rush.

swee/swey, v., swing; brandish; swerve;

waver; n., swing; swerve; bias; pivot used to suspend pots over fire; shoulder yoke for water pails.

sweer, v., see **sweir.**

sweesh, v., n., swish.

sweet, adj., unsalted, of butter: **sweetbreid,** n., pastries: **sweetie,** n., a sweet: **sweetie-bottle,** n., sweet-jar: **sweetie-shop,** n., confectionery shop: **sweetie wife,** n., keeper of sweetshop; purveyor of gossip.

sweevil, v., swivel; swirl.

sweil, v., rinse; swirl; swivel; n., rinse; swirl; eddy.

sweir, v., swear; n., expletive.

sweir/sweirt, adj., lazy; loath: **sweirness,** n., indolence.

sweit, v., n., sweat.

swelt, v., swelter: **sweltry,** adj., very hot and close.

swey, n., see **swee.**

swick, v., cheat; n., fraud: **swicky,** adj., deceitful.

swiff, v., whiz; sleep restlessly; n., snooze.

swinge, v., beat; whip: **swingein,** n., thrashing: **swingeour,** n., discredited person.

swingler, n., tool for scutching flax.

swipe, v., see **swype.**

swippert, adj., sudden; swift; adv., suddenly; abruptly.

swirl, v., see **swurl.**

switchpoll, n., earwig.

swith, adj., speedy; adv., speedily: **swythe,** adv., speedily.

swither, v., be very hot; swelter; n., great heat.

swither, v., doubt; hesitate; dither; n., doubt; hesitancy; quandary.

switter, v., struggle spasmodically.

swouf, v., swoop; n., swish of bird in flight.

swound, v., n., faint.

swurl/swirl, v., eddy; twist; n., eddy; swirl; vortex: **swurly,** adj., curly.

swurl, n., knot in wood.

swype, n., sweeping blow; stroke; view.

swythe, adv., see **swith.**

sybie, n., shallot.

sye, n., see **sey.**

syke, n., ditch; gutter; stream that dries up in summer.

210

syle/sile, n., soil.
syle, n., pillar.
syle, v., n., filter.
syne, adv., ago; since; thereupon.
syne, v., rinse; wash superficially; n., rinse: **syne doun**, v., wash down food with drink.
sype, v., percolate; ooze; distil; soak: **sypit**, adj., soaking wet.
sythe, n., scythe.
sythment, n., compensation.
syver/syre, n., ditch; drain; gutter; sewer; sink.

Table, n., scaffold; map: **table-clout**, n., table-cloth: **tablin**, n., coping.
tack, n., lease; tenancy: **tack-duty**, n., rent: **tacksman**, n., tenant.
tacket, n., hobnail: **tackety buits**, n., hobnailed boots.
taddy-box, n., snuff-box.
tade, n., see **taid**.
tade, n., sheep tick.
tae, n., toe; tine: **tae-girse**, n., thyme.
tae, adv., also; prep., to: **tae-faa**, n., lean-to; porch: **tae-look**, n., prospect: **tae-name**, n., sobriquet: **tae-sided**, adj., biased.
taft, n., smallholding: **taft dyke**, n., turf wall.
taid, n., cow dung.
taid, n., toad: **taid's ee**, n., jealousy.
taigle, v., delay; detain; harass; entangle: **taiglement**, n., hindrance: **taiglesome**, adj., hindering; tedious: **taigle efter**, v., hang around a girl.
taiken, n., token; badge; evidence.
tail, v., prostitute; n., rear part of skirt; train of followers; ship's stern: **tail-toddle**, n., sexual intercourse.
taings, n., tongs.
taip, v., n., tape: **taip-line**, n., tape-measure.
taird, n., sarcasm: **tairdie**, adj., sarcastic.
tairge, v., rebuke; scold; n., rebuke; virago.
tairt, n., adj., tart.
taisle, v., entangle; confuse; stir up.
tait, n., tuft: **a wee tait**, n., a small quantity.
taiver, v., rave: **taivers**, n., ravings: **taiversome**, adj., vexatious.
*tak, v., accept as fact; presume; strike

root; n., bite at bait; resource: **tak doun**, v., dilute; make infirm: **tak in**, v., take into custody; trick: **tak out**, v., enrol for a class subject: **tak up**, v., open after holidays.
talk wee, v., speak softly.
tallie, n., tallow.
Tallie, n., Italian.
tammie-noddie / norrie, n., puffin: **tammie-noddie-heid**, n., chrysalis.
tammy-book, n., credit account book.
tam-taigle, v., hobble.
tamteen, n., annuity fund.
tane, the tane . . . the tither, prons., the one . . . the other.
tangie, n., young seal.
tangs, n., tongs.
tanner-saw, n., tenon saw.
tansy, stinkin tansy, n., common tansy.
tanyaird, n., tannery.
*tap, n., top; summit: **tap-coat**, n., overcoat: **tapmaist**, adj., topmost: **tap-pickle**, n., crowning achievement; virginity: **tappit**, adj., crested: **tappit-hen**, n., decanter topped with hen's comb.
tap, n., bundle of flax on distaff: **tap o tow**, n., quick-tempered person.
tapetless, adj., heedless; dull; spiritless.
tappietourie, n., pinnacle; turret; adj., turreted.
tappiloorie, n., ornamental knob: topheavy building; adj., top-heavy.
tappin, n., tap-root.
tapsalteerie, adj., chaotic; topsyturvy; adv., upside-down.
tarbet, n., isthmus.
tare, n., frolic; spree; piece of fun.
targe, v., beat; scold; n., ill-tempered woman.
target, n., shred; strip of flesh: **targets**, n., tatters.
tarrow, v., complain.
tartle, v., scruple; shy; n., scruple.
tash, v., soil; fray; n., stain; stigma: **tashy**, adj., blustery.
tasker, n., man on piecework: **taskit**, adj., harassed.
tass, n., bunch.
tassie, n., cup; goblet.
taste, v., give relish to; n., a little, of drink.
tatterwallop, n., tatterdemalion: **tatterwallops**, n., tatters.

tattie, n., potato; **champit tatties,** n., mashed potatoes: **tattie bing,** n., potato pit: **tattie-bockie** n., potato stuck with feathers to be blown along with wind: **tattie-bogle** n., scarecrow: **tattie-howker,** n., potato digger: **tattie shaw,** n., potato haulm: **tatties an dab,** n., potatoes and salt.

tauch, n., grease; tallow: **tauchie,** adj., greasy.

taum, v., fall asleep; faint; n., fainting fit.

taur, n., tar: **taury,** adj., tarry: **taury-fingert,** adj., thievish.

taut, v., mat; tease wool for spinning: **tautit,** adj., matted.

taw, v., knead; tease out; n., fibre: **tawse,** n., fibrous roots; strap.

tawie, adj., obedient; tractable.

tawpie, n., foolish person.

tea-blade, n., tea-leaf: **tea-jenny,** n., tea-drinker: **tea skiddle,** n., tea-party.

ted, v., arrange; spread out, of hay; strew.

tedisome, adj., boring; tiresome.

tee-hee, v., giggle.

teem, v., pour heavily; n., downpour of rain.

teen, n., see **tein.**

teep, n., kind; sort: **teepical,** adj., typical.

teet, v., n., peep: **teet-about,** n., snooper.

teetle, n., title.

teil, v., till.

tein, n., grief; rage; injury: **teinfu,** adj., woeful; irate.

teind, n., levy; tax; tithe; toll.

teir, v., tear: **teirin,** adj., violent: **teir-tathers,** n., shreds.

tell, v., discern; say by heart; warn; n., account; report: **tellin-aff,** n., reprimand: **tell owre,** v., narrate; recount.

tender, v., think highly of; adj., related: **tenderness,** n., esteem; regard.

tenon, n., tendon.

tenor, v., fix tenon into mortise: **tenor/tanner-saw,** n., tenon-saw.

tent, v., listen to; notice; care for; n., attention; patience: **tentie,** adj., attentive; cautious; watchful: **tent-less,** adj., inattentive; thoughtless:

tak tent, v., take care/heed/note: **tak tent to,** v., listen to.

tent, n., adj., tenth.

terrible, adj., great; extreme; adv., extremely.

testifee, v., testify: **testification,** n., testimonial: **testment,** n., bequest.

tether, v., bind; restrain; moor a vessel; n., rope; scope.

teuch, adj., tough: **teuchle,** v., chew something tough: **teuch jean,** n., jujube.

teuchat, n., lapwing; peewit: **teuchat-storm,** n., storm in March.

Teuchter, n., Highlander, contemptuous; uncouth person.

tew, v., tire; harass; work hard; n., exhaustion.

tew, v., toughen meat: **tewed,** adj., made tough by bad cooking.

thack/theik, v., n., thatch.

thae, adj., these; those.

thaim, pron., them: **thaimsels,** pron., themselves.

thairm, n., catgut; fiddle-string: **thairm-scraper,** n., fiddler.

than, adv., then.

thane, n., pennant.

thane, adj., raw, of meat.

that, pron., who; whom; adv., so; to such an extent.

theat, v., tow; n., cord; trace: **out o theat,** adv., amiss.

thegither, adv., together.

theik, v., see **thack.**

theirsels, pron., themselves: **their lane,** adv., by themselves.

thereawa, adv., thereabouts: **therefrae,** adv., thence: **theretil,** adv., thither.

thesaurer, n., treasurer: **thesaury,** n., treasury.

thick, adj., intimate.

thieveless, adj., inactive; ineffectual; spiritless; thriftless.

thig, v., beg; borrow; plagiarise: **thigger,** n., borrower.

thing, n., kind; sort.

*****think,** v., consider; devise; n., opinion: **think on,** v., ponder; recollect.

thir, pron., adj., these.

thirdsman, n., referee; umpire.

thirl, v., bore; pierce; thrill; tingle; vibrate/cause to vibrate.

thirl, v., bind; enslave: **thirlage,** n.,

duty to have grain ground at a certain mill: **thirl-ban**, n., mortgage: **thirldom**, n., servitude: **thirlfolk**, n., servants: **thirlpin**, n., pivot.

tho, conj., though.

thocht, n., thought; very small quantity: **thochty**, adj., thoughtful.

thole, v., endure; undergo; permit: **thole wi**, v., put up with.

thon, pron., adj., that; those; yon: **thonder**, adv., yonder.

thoom, n., see **thoum**.

thorl, n., fly-wheel.

thorn, n., hawthorn.

thorough, v., see through to a conclusion: **thorough-handit**, adj., industrious.

thort, adj., transverse; adv., transversely.

thorter, v., frustrate; thwart; oppose; scotch; adj., awry.

thoum, n., thumb: **thoum-lickin**, n., the conclusion of a bargain.

thousan, n., adj., thousand: **thousantaes**, n., centipede.

thowe, v., n., thaw.

thow, n., muscle; sinew: **thowless**, adj., listless; passive; spineless; weak: **thow-pin**, n., rowlock.

thrab, v., n., throb.

thrain, n., refrain; tradition.

thrang, v., throng; n., crowd; bustle; adj., busy; crowded: **thrangerie**, n., bustle: **thrangsome**, adj., hardpressed.

thrapple, v., strangle; n., throat; windpipe: **thrapple-girth**, n., necktie.

thratch, v., get by importuning; writhe; n., death-throe.

thraw, v., n., pitch; throw; toss.

*****thraw**, v., twist; distort; screw; wring; sprain; defy; n., twist; obstinacy; setback; pique: **thrawart**, adj., adverse; stubborn: **thrawn**, adj., stubborn; surly; disobedient; adverse: **thraw-cruik**, n., tool to make straw rope.

threep, v., see **threip**.

threid, n., thread: **threid-mill**, n., flax mill.

threip, v., assert dogmatically; complain; harp; n., assertion; argument: **threipin**, adj., pertinacious: **threip at**, v., importune.

threne, n., aphorism; refrain; short story.

thresh, v., thrash.

thresh, n., rush; rush mat: **threshiewick**, n., rush wick.

thrie, n., adj., three: **thrie-plet**, adj., three-fold/ply.

thrift, n., enthusiasm at work; good luck: **thriftless**, adj., luckless.

thrissle, n., thistle: **thrissle-cock**, n., thrush.

thrist, v., n., thrust; press down; extort.

thrist, v., n., thirst.

thrive, n., prosperity.

throch/throu, v., achieve; carry through to a finish; penetrate.

throu, adj., finished; thorough; prep., through: **throu-band**, n., stone spanning thickness of wall: **throu-come**, n., ordeal: **throu-gang**, n., lobby: **throu-gate**, n., lane: **throu-gaun**, n., thorough examination: adj., thorough; spendthrift: **throuither**, adj., untidy; unruly; adv., helterskelter; confusedly: **throu-pit**, n., activity; output: **throu time**, adv., gradually.

thrum, v., n., hum; purr.

thrum, v., finger excessively; n., shred: **thrums**, n., ends of threads.

thrummle, v., grope; squeeze; foist.

thud, v., thump; blow in gusts.

thumbikins, n., thumbscrew.

thummart, n., polecat.

thummle, n., thimble.

thunner, n., thunder: **thunnert**, adj., soured, of milk: **thunner-plump**, n., sudden downpour.

tibawkie, n., tobacco.

ticht, v., tighten; secure; adj., compact; sound: **tichten**, v., tighten.

ticket, n., odd-looking person; a promissory note.

tid, v., humour; n., chance; propitious time; season; mood: **tiddy**, adj., propitious; seasonable; troublesome to work, of soil.

tide, v., befall; happen; induce.

tide, n., shore between high and low water: **tide-heid**, n., tidal current.

tiff, n., plight; state.

tift, n., mood; tedious spell: **tifty**, adj., moody.

tift/tiff, n., fit of anger; gust of wind.

tig, v., tap; touch lightly; n., tap.

tig-tag, n., suspense.

tike, n., see tyke.

til, prep., to; towards.

ti'lielick, n., sudden setback.

tillie-pan, n., scoop for baling out water; skillet.

tiltery, adj., tottery; unsteady.

timeous, adj., opportune; punctual: time about, adv., alternately.

timmer, n., timber; club; leg; adj., insensitive to music.

timorsome, adj., fearful; nervous; timid.

tin, n., receptacle made of tin: tinnie, n., small tin mug.

tin, n., prong; tine.

tinchel (guttural), v., hunt; n., trap.

tine, v., see tyne.

*tink/tinkler, n., tinker; gipsy; vagabond: tinker tongue, n., unruly tongue.

tint, adj., lost.

tip/tup, n., ram: tip-hog, n., young ram.

tip, n., best/best-dressed person: tippy, adj., stylish.

tip, n., rubbish dump.

tippence, n., twopence: tippenny, n., small beer.

tipper, v., tiptoe; totter.

tipperty, adj., flighty.

tire/tiretness, n., fatigue.

tirl, v., thrill; rattle; strip off; n., rattle: tirlin-pin, n., door knocker.

tirl, v., rotate/cause to rotate; twirl; n., rotation; twirl: tirly, adj., convoluted: tirly-wha, n., grace note: tirly-whirly, n., contrivance; flourish.

tirless, n., trellis; lattice; turnstile; wicket door.

tirr, v., pare/strip off; tear off; undress.

tirr, n., rage: tirrie, adj., querulous: tirran, n., quick-tempered person; tyrant: tirrivee, n., bustle; tantrum; rage.

tishie, n., tissue.

tit, n., teat; nipple.

tither, adj., alternative; pron., the other.

titlin, n., meadow-pipit.

titter, v., n., twitter.

tits, interj., expressing impatience.

tittie, n., sister.

tizzie, n., great effort.

toad-spue, n., frog spawn.

toby, n., valve in water or gas main.

tocher, v., give a dowry; n., purse; dowry: tocherless, adj., dowerless.

tod/tod-lowrie, n., fox.

toddle, v., waddle; saunter; glide, of stream; n., leisurely walk.

toft, n., bed of plants.

toiter, v., totter.

tolbooth, n., town jail.

toll, n., turnpike.

tollie, n., lump of excrement.

tolter, v., wobble, of building: toltery, adj., wobbly.

tongue, v., n., reprimand: tongue-deavin, adj., deafeningly loquacious: tongue-ferdy, adj., glib-tongued: tongue-tackit, adj., tongue-tied.

toog, n., tussock.

toom, adj., see tuim.

toon, n., see toun.

toorie, n., see tourie.

toosie, adj., see tousy.

toot-moot, v., whisper; n., a whispering.

torfle, v., be lost; perish.

torie, n., deceitful person; adj., noncommittal.

torie-worm, n., cranefly grub; slug.

torter, v., n., torture.

tortie-shell, n., tortoise-shell.

tosh, v., tidy up; adj., tidy; pleasant: tosht up, adj., smartly dressed.

toss, v., n., toast.

tottie, adj., tiny.

touk, v., pleat; pluck; twitch; shorten; n., pleat.

touk, n., drum-beat.

toul, n., towel.

toun, n., town; farm; hamlet: heid toun, n., county town: toun bodies, n., townspeople: toun-gate, n., main street: toun hous, n., court building; town hall: toun officer, n., officer attending town provost.

toupic, n., summit; turret; steeple.

tour, v., n., tower.

tourbillon, n., whirlwind.

tourie/tappietourie, n., tassel; tuft.

tourock, n., smoke spiral.

touse, v., handle roughly; knock about: tousy, adj., blustery; unkempt.

tousle, v., disarrange; ruffle: tousle out, v., unravel.

tove, v., converse; flatter; soar.

tow (as in "brow"), n., hemp fibre; string; rope: **tow raip**, n., hemp rope.

towdie, n., spinster.

towmond, n., year.

towt, v., tease; vex; n., short illness; tantrum: **towtie**, adj., irritable.

toy aff, v., treat summarily.

toyt, v., move feebly.

tozy, adj., drowsily warm; half drunk.

trachle, v., see **trauchle**.

track, v., break in a horse; tow with trace-horse, of a "track-boat".

track, n., period of time; spell of weather.

track, n., tract; pamphlet.

trackie, n., teapot.

traffick, v., do business; plot; n., business; intercourse.

tragullion, n., faction.

traik, v., gad; trudge; straggle; n., gadabout; long walk: **traikit**, adj., fatigued: **traik-tailed**, adj., slatternly.

*trail, v., drag water with grappling irons; n., sloven: **trailach**, n., trailing rag: **traillie-wallets**, n., slovenly person.

traisir, n., treasure.

tram, n., wooden bar; barrow shaft: **trams**, n., spectacle arms.

trammels, n., baggage.

tramp, v., tread down; n., foot tread; foot ledge on spade.

trance, n., lobby; passageway; vestibule.

transack, v., transact; n., transaction.

transcrieve, v., copy; transcribe.

transmogrify, v., transfigure; transmute.

transmue, v., convert; transfigure.

trantle, v., n., trundle.

trantles, n., miscellaneous articles; valueless odds and ends.

trap, n., hatch; pothole: **trap lether**, n., loft ladder.

traps, n., luggage.

trashery, n., rubbish: **trashlike**, adj., trashy: **trashtrie**, n., riff-raff.

trauchle, v., overburden; trudge; n., hard, heavy work; slovenly worker.

tred, v., n., trade; n., corporation of craftsmen.

tree, n., timber; beam of wood; pole; keg: **trees**, n., rafters.

treeple, adj., treble; tripple.

trekkle, n., treacle.

tress, n., frame of wood; small jetty.

trevel / traivel, v., travel; walk: **treveller**, n., gipsy; hawker.

trevis, n., partition between stable stalls; shop counter.

trewan, n., trowel.

trews, n., close-fitting tartan trousers.

trig, v., tidy up; adj., neat; smart; attractive.

trim, v., trounce.

trinch, v., n., trench.

tring, n., sequence.

trinkle, v., n., trickle.

trinkums, n., odds and ends.

trinnle, v., roll; bowl along; spin; trundle; n., cogwheel; hub.

trintle, v., n., trickle.

troch, n., platter; trencher; trough.

troddle, v., toddle; trot.

trog, v., barter: **trogger**, n., pedlar; tramp.

troke, v., exchange; deal; bargain; n., business dealings; negotiation: **troker**, n., dealer: **troke wi**, v., associate with.

trollop, v., walk in slovenly manner; n., slovenly person.

tron, n., public weighing machine; town market place.

trooan, n., see **trewan**.

trottle, v., toddle.

trottles, n., sheep dung.

trouble, n., disease; sickness.

trow (as in "brow"), n., troll: **trowie**, adj., supernatural.

trowe (as in "brow"), v., roll; spin/ cause to spin; walk with rolling gait.

trowly, n., trolley.

truan, n., see **trewan**.

truan, n., truant.

truff, n., a turf: **truff dyke**, n., turf wall.

truith, n., truth.

trummle, v., n., tremble: **trummles**, n., palsy: **trummlin tam**, n., potted meat.

trumph, n., trump card.

trumphery, trumpery.

truncher, n., trencher.

try, v., taste.

tryst, v., fix a meeting with; hire; invite; promise to marry; n.,

rendezvous; periodical fair; betrothal: **trysted**, adj., bespoken;
betrothed.
tub, n., pit hutch.
tuck, n., see touk.
tug, n., rawhide.
tuim, v., empty; unload; adj., empty:
tuim-heid, n., stupid person.
tuin, n., tune; accent; intonation.
tuith, n., tooth: **tuithfu**, n., small
amount of liquor: **tuithy**, adj., frigid;
frosty; sarcastic.
tulzie/tulyie, v., n., brawl; skirmish;
struggle.
tumfie, n., boring, insensible person.
tummle, v., n., tumble.
tummock, n., hillock; tuft.
tundle, n., tinder.
tup, n., ram: **tup-hog**, n., young ram.
turkey, n., wallet.
*****turn**, v., change, of weather; curdle,
of milk; n., bent; inclination; helping
hand; walk: **turnin-lume**, n., lathe:
turn-pike stair, n., spiral staircase.
turr, n., a turf.
turse, v., truss; bale.
tutti-tatti, n., sound of the trumpet.
*****twa/twae**, n., adj., two: **twa-faced**, adj.,
insincere: **twa-fauld**, adj., double:
twasome, n., couple: **twa-three**, adj.,
a few.
twal, n., adj., twelve: **twalt**, adj.,
twelfth: **twalmonth**, n., year: **twal-
oors**, n., noon: **twal-piece**, n., noon
snack.
tweedle, v., twiddle.
tweel, n., twill.
tweest, v., twist.
tweeze, v., nip.
twilt, n., quilt.
twin/twyne, v., divide; part; segregate.
twine, v., meander; writhe; turn; n.,
twist; turn; vicissitude.
twine, v., work hard; n., hard work.
twine, v., bind; fasten.
twirl, n., flourish: **twirliwa**, adj.,
tremolo.
tyauve, v., struggle; walk wearily; n.,
struggle: **tyauve throu**, v., survive.
tyce, v., entice.
tyde betyde, adv., alternately.
tyke, n., dog; cur; mongrel; rustic
fellow.
tyler, n., tailor.

*****tyne**, v., lose; miss a target; forfeit;
perish; n., forfeit.
type, n., symbol.
tyst, v., entice; tease.

Ug, v., abhor; disgust; n., nausea:
ugsome, adj., repulsive; macabre.
uilie, n., oil; adj., oily.
uise, v., see **yaise**.
umquhile, adj., former; late, deceased;
adv., formerly.
umrage, n., umbrage.
un-, prefix, **unable**, adj., weak: **unbekent**, adj., unbeknown; unobserved: **unbiddable**, adj., unmanageable; intractable: **unbousome**, adj., unyielding; stiff: **uncanny**, adj., careless; dangerous;
unlucky; unearthly: **unchancy**, adj.,
unlucky; threatening; ill-omened:
uncommon, adv., unusually: **uncouthy**, adj., inhospitable; strange:
undevalin, adj., unceasing: **undocht**,
n., sickly person: **unfankle**, v.,
unravel: **unfordersome**, adj., unseasonable: **unheard-tell-o**, adj., unheard-of: **unhoused**, adj., unburied: **unhanty**, adj., unwieldy:
unkennable, adj., countless; incalculable: **unkent**, adj., unfamiliar:
unkipple, v., uncouple; unleash:
unleired, adj., uneducated: **unleisome**,
adj., illegal: **unlifelike**, adj., not likely
to live: **unlikely**, adj., unacceptable:
unmarrowed, adj., unequalled: **un-
perfect**, adj., imperfect: **unsained**,
adj., unblest: **unseily**, adj., unseasonable: **unseyed**, adj., unproved:
unsiccar, adj., unsafe; undependable: **unsocht**, adj., uninvited: **unsonsie**, adj., unhealthy; unlucky:
unsteik, v., undo: **unstint**, adj.,
unrestricted: **unstowly**, adj., unsettled, of weather: **untentit**, adj.,
ignored: **untholeable**, adj., intolerable: **untimeous**, adj., premature:
unwaukit, adj., unwatched: **un-
witten**, adj., unknown: **unwittins**,
adv., inadvertently: **unwycelike**, adj.,
indiscreet: **unyirdly**, adj., unearthly;
supernatural.
unce, n., ounce.
unco, n., rarity; wonder; adj., strange;
uncouth; extraordinary; adv., ex-

ceedingly: **uncos**, n., news; tidings: **unco body**, n., stranger; foreigner.
unction, n., auction: **unctioneer**, n., auctioneer.
unnerstaun, v., understand.
up-, prefix, **upbring**, v., rear; train: **upby**, adv., up the road; up yonder: **upcast**, v., compute; n., reproach: **uphaud**, v., uphold; vouch for; n., bracket; prop: **upheize**, v., raise; elate: **upmak**, v., compensate; n., compensation; expedient: **up-pit**, v., provide with accommodation: **up-pittin**, n., lodging: **upsettin**, adj., ambitious; haughty: **upsouk**, n., sea-swell: **upsteir**, v., rouse: **uptak**, v., preoccupy; understand; n., intelligence: **upthrou**, adj., adv., inland: **upwith**, adv., upwards.
urchin, n., see **hurcheon**.
ure, n., colour; tone; ferrous oxide.
ure, n., oppressive heat.
urn, n., sepulchre.
ush, v., gush forth; issue; purify; refine.
usquebae, n., whisky.
uther, n., udder.

Vacancy, n., holiday.
vaig, v., wander about: **vaigin**, adj., vagrant: **vaigrie**, n., vagary.
vand, n., mien: **vandy**, adj., showy.
variorum, n., miscellany.
vaudie, adj., impressive; showy.
vaunty, adj., conceited; jaunty; showy; gay.
vawze, n., vase.
veem, n., spiritual uplift.
veesion, n., vision.
veesit, v., n., visit.
veeve, adj., see **vieve**.
vennel, n., lane between houses.
vent, v., vend; n., sale.
venter, v., venture.
vernish, v., n., varnish.
verra, adv., very.
vertue, n., virtue; frugality.
veshel, n., vessel: **veshel-buird**, n., dish rack.
vex, v., fret; feel grief; n., vexation: **vext**, adj., sorry.
victual, n., grain.
vieve, adj., lively; vital; vivid: **vievers**, n., provisions.

vilansie, n., violence.
virl, v., encircle; n., band.
virr, n., force; industry; vigour; impetus.
vizzy, v., inspect; pore over; survey; n., survey; view: **vizzy-hole**, n., peephole.
vocable, n., word: **vocables**, n., vocabulary.
voe, n., fiord.
vogie, adj., boastful; elated; imposing.
vou, v., n., vow.
vyce, n., voice.

Waa, n., wall.
wab, v., weave; n., web: **wabster**, n., weaver: **wab-fuitit**, adj., web-footed.
wabbit, adj., exhausted.
wabble, v., n., wobble.
wace, n., wax.
wacht, n., guard: **keep the wacht o**, v., keep guard over.
wad/wid, v., would.
wad, v., marry: **waddin**, n., wedding: **waddin-braws**, n., trousseau.
wad/wadset, v., n., bet; mortgage; wager.
wade, v., n., ford.
wadge, v., n., wedge.
wadge, v., brandish; wield.
wae, n., woe; adj., woeful: **waefu/waesome**, adj., woeful: **waelike**, adj., sad-looking: **wae's me**, interj., alas: **wae worth**, interj., woe betide.
waff, v., wave; flap; flutter; puff; n., blast of air; puff; aroma; wave of hand; adj., brief.
waff, v., wander about; n., waif; adj., feeble; forlorn; ineffectual; unprincipled: **waffie**, n., vagabond.
waffle, v., shilly-shally; adj., inert; limp.
waft, n., weft.
wag, v., shake; wield; wave; n., signal; wave: **wag-at-the-waa**, n., wall-clock with pendulum: **wag on**, v., proceed.
wa-gaun, n., departure; leave-taking.
waggle/waigle, v., n., waddle.
waik/wake, v., n., watch.
waik, adj., weak: **waikly**, adj., weakly.
wair/ware, n., spring, the season.
waird, v., guard.

wairn, v., warn: **wairnin**, n., warning.
wairsh, adj., insipid; lacking salt/zest; bitter.
waiskit, n., waistcoat.
wait on, v., await.
wal, v., well up; n., spa; water tap: **wallee**, n., spring of water.
walcome, v., n., welcome.
wald, v., wield; manage; manipulate; rule.
wald, v., weld; unite.
wale, v., select; sort out: **the wale o**, n., the pick of.
walise, n., valise.
walk, n., path; procession.
walk, v., see **wauk**.
wallie, n., porcelain dish: **wallie-dug**, n., china dog.
wallies, n., male genitals.
walloch, v., howl; wail.
wallop, v., beat; strike; n., blow.
wallop, v., n., gallop; bubble; flop; flutter; throb.
wally, v., fade; wither: **wally-draigle**, n., weakest fledgling; puny person.
wally, adj., handsome; pleasant: **wallies**, n., ornaments; wares: **bonny wally/wally-dye**, n., toy: **wally close**, n., tiled entry to block of flats.
wally-wallyin, n., wailing.
walt, n., welt; rind.
walter, v., welter; swing; wag; n., welter.
walth, n., wealth: **walthy**, adj., wealthy.
waly (wally/waily), interj., expressing sorrow.
wame, n., stomach; womb: **wamesmith**, n., obstetrician.
wammle/wamble, v., n., swing; wallow; wriggle: **wammlie**, adj., queasy.
wample, v., see **wimple**.
wan, adj., pron., one: **wance**, adv., once.
wan, n., hope: **wanless**, adj., hopeless.
wan-, prefix, **wanchance**, n., calamity: **wanchancy**, adj., ill-fated; risky: **wandocht**, n., incapable person; adj., feeble; puny: **wanearthly**, adj., unearthly: **wanease**, n., discomfort; vexation: **wangrace**, n., rascal: **wangracie**, adj., rascally: **wanhope**, n., despair: **wanluck**, n., misfortune: **wanpeace**, n., strife: **wanrest**, n., unrest: **wanricht**, n., wrong: **wanuse**,

v., misuse: **wanwordy**, adj., unworthy: **wanworth**, n., worthless thing.
wand, n., pole; rod; switch.
want, v., be deficient in; deserve; seek; n., gap; mental defect: **wantin**, prep., without: **dae wantin**, v., do without.
wap, v., fling; thrust; strike; thrash; swipe; n., blow; swipe; thrust; wrestling match: **wappin**, adj., huge; vast.
wap, v., n., strut; brawl; riot.
ward, v., n., award.
ward, n., confinement; custody; breakwater: **ward-fire**, n., beacon.
wardrop, n., wardrobe.
ware, v., spend; dissipate; waste.
wark, v., ferment; purge; control: **wark-fierdy**, adj., fit for work: **warklume**, n., tool: **wark machine**, n., mechanical contrivance.
warld, n., world: **warldlike**, adj., normal: **warld's gear**, n., worldly wealth.
warlock, n., magician; wizard: **warlockry**, n., sorcery.
warmer, n., formidable character.
warn, v., summon: **warnin**, n., augury; intimation; notice.
warp/warple, v., entangle; entwine; pleat.
warrandice, n., warranty; guarantee.
warroch, n., knot in wood; verruca.
warse, adj., worse: **warst**, adj., worst.
warsle, v., contend; wrestle; n., conflict; wrestling match: **warsle on**, v., struggle forward: **warsle throu**, v., overcome adversity.
warth, n., worth.
wash, n., stale urine for clothes bleaching: **washin-hous**, n., wash-house.
wast, n., adj., west: **wastlin/westlin**, adj., western: **wastlins**, adv., westwards.
waste, v., indulge; pamper: **wastage**, n., wilderness.
waster, n., idler; ne'er-do-well: **wastrie**, n., extravagance; waste: **wasterfu/wastrife**, adj., wasteful; profligate.
wat, v., adj., wet; n., moisture: **watshod**, adj., wetted; wet-footed.
wat, v., assure; know.
water (watter), n., lake; river; wave: **water-blackie**, n., dipper: **water-**

clearer, n., water beetle: **water-dyke**, n., embankment: **water-drucken**, adj., water-logged: **water-fuit**, n., river mouth: **water-gang**, n., millrace: **water-gate**, n., road leading to water: **watergaw**, n., incomplete rainbow, presaging bad weather: **water-hole**, n., pond: **water-shear**, n., watershed: **water-stand**, n., water barrel: **water-waggie**, n., wagtail.

wather, n., see **weather**.

wattle, v., cane; n., cane; hurdle; wand.

wauch, v., drink deeply: **waucht/guidwillie waucht**, n., hearty draught of liquor.

wauch, n., smell; adj., clammy; stale; unwell: **wauchness**, n., bad smell.

wauchle, v., shamble; stagger; tire; perplex; n., laborious effort.

wauk, v., awake/stay awake; guard: **wauken**, v., arouse; adj., awake: **wauk-rife**, adj., sleepless; vigilant.

wauk, v., full cloth; shrink: **wauker**, n., fuller: **waukit**, adj., shrunk.

waumish, adj., dizzy; faint.

waumle, v., roll; rumble; barge.

wauner, v., wander.

waur, v., defeat; worst; parry; n., defeat.

waur, adj., aware; wary.

*****waur**, adj., worse.

waur/ware, n., seaweed.

wax-cloth, n., linoleum.

waygate, n., passageway; outlet for goods; right of way; space; scope.

waygaun, n., departure.

waywart, adj., disobedient; fitful; untoward.

wean (wane), n., child; infant.

wear, v., see **weir**.

weary, v., become bored; adj., monotonous: **weary on**, v., desire; long for.

weason, n., gullet; windpipe; throat.

weather/wather, n., storm: **wathery**, adj., stormy: **saft wather**, n., wet/mild weather: **weathergaw**, n., spell of quiet weather; vain hope: **weather-gleam**, n., clear sky on horizon: **weather-set**, adj., storm-stayed.

wecht, v., weigh; n., weight; great amount: **wechts**, n., scales.

wecht, v., winnow; n., winnowing tray.

wede awa, adj., extinct.

wee, v., see **wei**.

*****wee**, adj., small; young; mean: **weecoat**, n., petticoat: **wee pickle**, n., small amount: **wee thing**, n., dear one: **wee yin**, n., child.

weedae, n., widow.

weegle, v., n., waggle; wriggle.

weel, adv., see **weill**.

weem, n., cave; tunnel.

weep, v., exude moisture, of cheese.

weer, v., see **weir**.

weerock/werrock, n., corn on foot; bunion.

weet, adj., see **weit**.

weff, adj., fusty.

wei (wee), v., weigh: **weis**, n., scales: **wei-bauks**, n., scales.

weil, n., eddy; whirlpool.

*****weill**, n., welfare; adj., adv., well: **weillness**, n., health: **weill-aff**, adj., prosperous: **weill-bred**, adj., civil: **weill-come**, adj., welcome: **weillcomed**, adj., legitimate: **weillcreished**, adj., prosperous: **weilldaein**, adj., well-behaved: **weillfaured**, adj., comely: **weill-gethert**, adj., well-off: **weill-hained**, adj., well-preserved: **weill-hertit**, adj., good-hearted; optimistic: **weill-kent**, adj., familiar: **weill/ill-willie**, adj., well/ill-disposed: **weill-wared**, adj., well-deserved; well-spent.

weir, v., wear: **weir doun**, v., wear out: **weir in**, v., pass slowly: **weir on**, v., grow late/old: **weir til**, v., approach a certain time.

weir, v., defend; shepherd: **weir aff**, v., ward off.

weir, n., war: **weiriour**, n., warrior: **weir-harness**, n., armour.

weird, v., predict; ordain by fate; invoke; n., prediction; destiny: **weird-fu**, adj., fateful: **weirdless**, adj., incompetent; thriftless; unlucky: **weirdly**, adj., eerie; sinister: **weirdit**, adj., accursed; doomed: **weirdie**, n., uncanny person: **weirdman**, n., soothsayer: **weirdrie**, n., magic.

weit, v., wet; irrigate; n., moisture; adj., wet.

weive, v., knit: **weiver**, n., knitter of stockings.

well, n., see **weil**.

welter, v., knock over; writhe.

Wensday, n., Wednesday.

werena/wurna, v., were not.

wether-hog, n., two-year-old ram: belled wether, n., flock leader.

*wey, n., way; direction; manner; mood; reason: weygate, n., exit; headway.

weys, n., see weis.

wha/whae, pron., who.

whaal/whaul, n., whale.

whack, v., n., slash; slice.

whaisk, v., wheeze: whaisky, adj., husky; wheezy.

whaizle, v., see wheezle.

whalm, v., overwhelm.

whalp, n., whelp.

wham, pron., whom.

whan, adv., conj., when.

whang, v., slice; snip; trounce; n., chunk; slice.

whang, n., band; leather bootlace; lash; thong; penis.

whase, pron., whose.

whatna, adj., what sort of.

whaup, n., curlew: whaup-nebbit, adj., sharp-nosed.

whaur, adv., where: whaurtil, adv., whither: whaurwi, adv., wherewith.

wheasel, n., weasel.

wheech, n., stink.

wheegee (whee-jee), v., shilly-shally: wheegees, n., gewgaws.

wheem, v., hum: wheemer, v., mutter.

wheen, a wheen, n., a small number of; several.

wheenge/whinge, v., n., whine.

wheep/penny wheep, n., thin beer.

wheeple, v., whistle shrilly; n., shrill whistle.

wheeram/wheeriorum, n., doll; gewgaw; trifle.

wheerie, n., female organ of generation.

*wheesh, n., whizzing sound: wheesh up, v., hush up: wheesht, v., n., hush.

wheetie-what, n., pretence; unscrupulous person.

wheezle, v., wheeze; breathe heavily; n., wheeze: wheezly, adj., asthmatic.

wheich, n., liquor.

wheich, v., dart; whiz; n., whizz: wheicher, n., large specimen.

whether-or-no, adj., indecisive.

whid, v., frisk; scamper; n., nimble spring/run.

whid, v., lie; exaggerate; n., lie; exaggeration.

whidder, v., blow in gusts.

whigmaleerie, n., bauble; contraption; gimmick; oddity; whim.

*while, conj., until.

whilk, pron., which.

whillywha, v., flatter; n., excuse; indecision; adj., undependable.

whillie-whallie, v., linger; dally.

whilom, adj., former.

whim-wham, n., trifle, the sweet.

whin, n., see whun.

whinner, v., n., crash; whizz; neigh.

whippert, adj., impatient.

whirligigums, n., ornamental appendages.

whish / whishie, n., barely audible sound: whisht, v., silence.

whisk, v., groom a horse; switch; whip.

whisky-pot, n., whisky still.

whistlin-deuk, n., widgeon.

whit, pron., what: whit for/wey, adv., conj., why: whitna, adj., what kind of.

white-airn, n., tinplate: white meat, n., poultry meat: white moss, n., sphagnum: white sark, n., surplice.

whither, conj., whether.

whitrat/whiteret/futrat, n., weasel.

whitter, n., large draught of liquor.

whitter, n., emblem; symbol.

whitter, v., n., twitter; warble.

whitter, v., whittle.

whittie-whattie, v., prevaricate; n., prevarication.

whittle, n., knife; scythe; sickle.

whittle, n., abscess near finger nail.

whuff, v., whiff; n., glimpse; instant; whiff: whuff out, v., be extinguished.

whummle, v., capsize; overthrow; overwhelm; n., tumble; upset.

whumper, v., n., whimper.

whun, n., furze; gorse: whunny, adj., whin-covered: whun-cow, n., whin tuft.

whun/whunstane, n., whinstone: whunflag, n., whinstone slab.

whup, v., n., whip: whupper-in, n., school attendance officer.

whupmadenty, n., dandy.

whuppity-scoorie, n., nimble person.

whuram, n., grace note in music.

whurl, v., whirl; n., machinery wheel: **whurly**, n., castor; chimney cowl; mechanical contrivance; pulley: **whurlie-birlie**, n., hurly-burly; toy windmill; propeller: **whurliegate**, n., turnstile.

whurr, v., whir; speak with a burr.

whusk, v., whisk: **whusker**, n., gale.

whusper, v., n., whisper.

whussle, v., whistle; n., flute; siren: **whussle-grinder**, n., organist.

whutter, n., barb.

whyles, adv., now and then; sometimes.

wi, prep., with.

wice, adj., see **wyce**.

wicht, adj., stalwart; strong; vigorous.

wicht, n., person; supernatural being; warlock.

wick, n., sea inlet.

wicker, n., hook barb.

wicker, v., n., twitch, of eye.

wicket, adj., evil: **wicketness**, n., wickedness.

wid, n., see **wuid**.

widdershins, adv., anti-clockwise; backwards.

widdie, n., cord; gallows; hangman's noose; withy: **widdiefu**, adj., rascally.

widdle, v., plod; n., strife; struggle.

wiel, n., see **weil**.

wife, n., woman: **the wife**, n., my wife.

wiggle-waggle, v., adv., zigzag.

wight, adj., see **wicht**.

wild, adj., rank in taste: **wildfire**, n., phosphorescence; lightning: **wild mustard**, n., charlock: **wildrife**, adj., violent.

will, v., bequeath; n., wish: **will-less**, adj., aimless.

willie-goo, n., lout: **williemaw**, n., guillemot.

willin-sweirt, adj., coy.

willyart, adj., bashful; reluctant; self-willed.

wilshoch, adj., unpalatable.

wimple, v., curl; meander; twine; ripple; n., curve; ripple; intricacy: **wimplin**, adj., sinuous; tortuous.

win, v., dwell; earn; gain; reach; dry hay: **winnins**, n., earnings: **win by**, v., get past: **win awa**, v., depart; die:

win forrit, v., get ahead: **win free**, v., get/set free: **win hame**, v., get home: **win in**, v., obtain entry: **win roun**, v., prevail upon: **win throu**, v., survive: **win til**, v., succeed in reaching.

*****win**, n., wind: **windgaw**, n., tumour: **windwarks**, n., lungs: **windy**, adj., flatulent; garrulous: **windy-wallets**, n., romancer.

win/wind, n., mood; prestige.

winch, v., go sweethearting; n., sweetheart; wench.

winch, v., wince; recoil.

windae, n., window: **bole windae**, n., recess window: **shot windae**, n., bay window: **storm-heid windae**, n., dormer window: **windae brod**, n., window shutter: **windae claith**, n., window curtain: **windae sole**, n., window sill.

windlestrae, n., withered grass stalk.

windrift, n., ruin.

wingle, v., hang loosely; walk in zig-zag manner.

winkie, n., flickering light: **winkle**, v., wink repeatedly.

winna/willna, v., shall not; won't.

winnister, n., winnowing fan.

winnock, n., window: **winnock-bunker**, n., window seat.

winter, n., bracket; trivet.

winterin, n., winter pasture/food for cattle.

wintle, v., stagger; upset; n., stagger; pitching of a boat.

wir/wur, pron., our.

wirly, adj., gnarled; stunted.

wirmin, n., gnawing pain.

wirmit, adj., wretched; confounded.

wirr, v., growl; fly with whizzing noise; whirr; n., growl.

wis (wiz), v., was.

wise, v., see **wyse**.

wishie-washie, n., weak tea; adj. weak and watery.

wisp, n., torch of straw: **wispin**, n., straw rope.

wiss, v., wish.

wissel, v., n., wager.

*****wit/wut**, n., good sense; reason; intelligence: **wutless**, adj., senseless.

witch-mark, n., devil's mark on witch's body: **witch-wean**, n., changeling.

wite, v., see **wyte**.

withergates / withershins, adv., contrariwise.

without/athout, conj., unless.

witter, n., waspish person.

witter, n., see **whitter**.

wittins, n., information; news.

wizzen, n., see **weason**.

wizzen, v., parch; shrink; wither: **wizzent**, adj., shrunken.

woa, interj., call to horse to stop: **woaback**, interj., call to reverse.

wolron, n., wretch.

woman body, n., adult female: **womanheid**, n., womanhood.

won, v., dwell; n., abode; home.

wonner, v., see **wunner**.

wooer-bab, n., garter worn below knee by lover: **wooster**, n., suitor; wooer.

word, n., notice; order; edict; report: **auld word**, n., proverb: **put words to**, v., express: **word anesel**, v., express oneself.

wordy, adj., worthy.

work, v., see **wark**.

worm, n., hunger; pain: **worm-etten**, adj., discontented.

worricow, n., demon.

worry, v., eat greedily; strangle; wrangle.

worset, n., see **wurset**.

wow, interj., expressing surprise/gratification.

wowff, v., bark; n., bark; booming noise.

wrack, n., couchgrass / couchgrass roots; weeds.

wrack, n., driving clouds.

wrack, v., vex; wreak.

wrack, v., wreck; demolish; n., wreck; havoc: **wrack-wuid**, n., driftwood.

wraith, v., n., wreath.

wran, n., wren.

wranch, v., wrench; n., spanner; winch; windlass.

wrang, v., injure; n., error; adj., wrong: **wrangous**, adj., wrongful.

wrapper, n., dressing-gown; smock.

wrastle/warsle, v., strive; wrestle; n., conflict; wrestling match.

wrat, n., wart.

wreath, v., pile up in snowdrifts; n., snowdrift.

wricht, n., carpenter; joiner.

wringle, v., n., wriggle.

wrist, n., instep of foot: **wristie**, n., muff for wrists.

writer, n., attorney; lawyer; notary.

wrocht bane, n., sprained joint.

wryte, v., write; n., handwriting; script: **big/smaa wryte**, n., large/small text: **haun o wryte**, n., writing style.

wrythe, v., twist; wring.

*wud, adj., crazed; raging mad: **clean wud**, adj., rabid: **wudness**, n., mania.

wuddrum, n., panic.

wuid, n., wood: **green wuid**, n., young growing trees.

wuif, n., woof.

wul/wuld, adj., wild: **wulcat**, n., wildcat: **wulfire**, n., lightning; erysipelas.

wulk, n., whelk.

wull, adj., astray; desolate: **wullgate**, n., waywardness.

wumman, n., woman.

wummle, n., auger; gimlet.

wun, v., see **win**.

wunner, v., n., wonder: **wunnerfu**, adj., wonderful.

wup, v., coil; splice.

wur, pron., see **wir**.

wur, v., were.

wurf, n., elf; puny person.

wurset, adj., worsted.

wuss, n., vegetable juice.

wut, n., see **wit**.

wutch, n., witch.

wyce, adj., shrewd; intelligent; knowing: **wycelike**, adj., sensible; comely; seemly: **wyce-spoken**, adj., sensible in speech: **wyceheid**, n., wisdom.

wyle, v., wile; lure.

wyle, n., gunwale.

wylie-coat, n., flannel shirt; vest.

wynd, n., lane between houses.

wynt, v., turn sour, of milk or butter.

wyse, v., guide; abduct; entice; obtain by guile; proceed.

wyse, v., expend: **wyse awa**, v., while away.

wyte, v., blame; n., blame; accusation: **wyteless**, adj., blameless.

Yabble, v., gabble; jabber; speak incoherently/incessantly.

yae, adj., one: **yae man**, n., a certain man.

yaird, n., yard; enclosure: **kailyaird,** n., kitchen garden.

yaise, v., use: **yaisage,** n., usage: **yaise anesel wi,** v., familiarise oneself with: **yaised tae,** adj., inured to.

yalder, v., bark loudly; make an outcry.

yammer, v., fret; complain; cry loudly; n., outcry; whine; lamentation.

yank, v., n., pluck; twitch.

yap, v., nag; whine; yelp.

yap, adj., brisk; hungry.

yare, adj., brisk; prompt.

yatter, v., n., chatter.

yauld, adj., able-bodied; hale and hearty.

ye, pron., you: **ye're/ye'se/ye've/ye'd,** v., you are/shall/have/would.

yealins, n., contemporaries; equals in age.

yearn, n., eagle.

yeddle, adj., addled.

yeld/yell, adj., barren; not yielding milk.

yella/yalla, adj., yellow: **yallochie,** adj., yellowish.

yelloch, v., n., bawl; scream; shriek.

yer, adj., your: **yersel,** pron., yourself.

yerl, n., earl.

yesk, v., hiccup; retch.

yestreen, n., yesterday evening.

yett, n., gate.

yeuk, v., n., itch: **yeuky,** adj., itchy: **yeuky-bane,** n., funny-bone.

yill, n., ale: **yill-shop,** n., alehouse.

*yin, adj., pron., one: **yince,** adv., once: **yin's lane,** adv., by oneself.

yird, v., bury: **yird/yirth,** n., earth: **yirdfast,** adj., deep-rooted.

yirk, v., n., jerk.

yirn, v., curdle: **yirnin,** n., rennet.

yiss, n., see **yuiss.**

yoke, v., fasten; n., harness: **yokin,** n., ploughman's spell of work; contest: **yoke on,** v., attack: **yoke tae,** v., begin; set to.

yoller, v., n., bawl.

yon, adj., that; those: **yondmaist,** adj., farthest.

yont, adj., distant; prep., beyond.

youth-heid, n., state of youth.

yowdendrift, n., snow driven by wind.

yowder/yowther, n., stench.

yowe, n., ewe: **yowe-hog,** n., young female sheep: **yowe-trummle,** n., spell of cold weather at sheep-shearing time.

yowl, v., n., howl; yell; yelp.

yuiss, n., use: **yuissless,** adj., useless.

Yule, n., Christmas: **Yule E'en,** n., Christmas Eve.

Aaready, adv., already.
abies, prep., besides; except.
ablach, n., dwarf.
able, adj., strong; fit.
accep, v., accept.
ace, n., best.
agent, n., solicitor.
aince-eeran, adv., for one specific errand.
aircock, n., weathercock.
aisle-tuith, n., molar tooth.
aixies, n., ague.
aizle, n., cinder.
alluterly, adv., completely.
alunt, adv., afire.
amends, tak amends o, v., take advantage of/vengeance on.
an aa, adv., as well.
anent, prep., in front of.
arena, v., are not.
arle, v., book; engage.
as, conj., than.
assle-tree, n., axle.
at, prep., "on top of," scolding.
atweesh, prep., betwixt.
auld-farrant, adj., old-fashioned.
aum, n., alum.
avizandum, n., further consideration.
awee, adv., a little.
ax, v., ask.

Backie, n., lift on someone's back.
backlins, adv., backwards.
backsey, n., sirloin.
backspang, n., mean advantage.
baikie, n., tether peg; small stool.
bairnheid, n., childhood.
bairntime, n., all the children of one mother.
baiss, v., baste; stitch loosely.
barefuit broth, n., meatless broth.
bark, v., give hard cough.
barrie, n., baby's waste band.
bassie, n., large baking bowl.
batchie, n., baker.
bate, v. beat.
bauks, n., scales.
bauldy-heidit, adj., bald-headed.
baur, n., joke.
bawtie, n., hare; dog.
beastie milk, n., first milk after calving

bedesman, n., licensed beggar; pauper.
beb/bebble, v., sip; tipple.
beddal, n., bedridden person.
beds, n., squares for "peevers."
bee-baw-babbity, n., children's party game.
beik, v., shine brightly.
belang, v., belong.
belt, v., move at speed.
Beltane, n., 1st May, a quarter day.
bensel, v., beat; thrash; n., blow; force.
beuch, n., bough; bow of ship.
beyond, adv., prep., beyond.
bicker, n., short, quick run.
biddin, n., command.
bink, n., plate-rack; peat-face.
binmaist, adj., highest.
binna, v., be not.
binner, v., n., run.
birlie-man, n., arbiter in local disputes.
birn, n., crowd.
birr, n., anger; passion.
birsie, adj., bristly.
biss, n., cow stall.
blab, n., blister; bee's honey bag.
blears, n., matter in eye.
blindrift, n., drifting snow.
blin-hooie/blin-swap, n., exchange of articles concealed, as in closed hands.
blivert, n., bilberry.
bluid-run, adj., bloodshot.
bockie, n., hobgoblin.
bogie-rowe, n., thick black tobacco.
bone, v., importune.
bouet, n., hand lantern.
brandit, adj., brindled.
branks, n., mumps.
breekums, n., small boy.
breid-and-cheese, n., inside of thistle crown.
briers/breers, n., eyelashes.
breese, v., crush stone; n., crushed stone.
bristle, v., crackle.
brizz, v., n., bruise.
brockit, adj., black-and-white-striped.
brouk, n., soot; **broukie,** adj., grimy.
breme, n., broom, the plant.
bucker, v., work fussily and to no effect.
buckie snail, n., common snail.
bude/bid, v., had to.
buffets, n., mumps.

bummle, v., hum; weep.
bung-fou, adj., quite full.
bur, n., tongue of shoe.
burble, v., n., tangle.
burdalane, adj., quite alone.
burst, n., bout of self-indulgence.
byde, v., await.
bylie, n., magistrate; farm steward.

Caip, n., coping.
cair, v., stir, broth etc.
caird, n., photograph.
candyman, n., ragman.
cannas, n., canvas sheet.
cant., n., old custom.
carron nail, n., nail holding cart to axle.
carte, n., playing card.
cassie/causey, v., pave with small stones; n. pavement.
cast, v., fade, of colour.
catch, n., acute pain; "stitch."
caup, n., wooden cup or bowl.
chances, n., tips; perks.
chapper, n., door knocker.
chat, n., small potato.
chauve/tyauve, v., n., struggle.
chawsome, adj., disappointing.
cheen/chyne, n., chain.
cheetie, n., cat.
cheiper, n., cricket.
chessart/chesset, n., cheese-press.
cheuch/teuch, adj., tough.
chirls, n., small pieces of coal.
choller, n., double chin.
chun, v., rub sprouts off potatoes.
cinner, n., cinder.
clamant, adj., urgent: clamancy, n., urgency.
clapshot, n., mashed potatoes and turnip.
clary, v., besmear; n., smear.
clatch, v., daub with mud.
claver, n., clover.
clawin-post, n., rubbing-post for cattle.
cled score, n., twenty-one, of sheep.
cleik, v., hook.
clesp, v., n., clasp.
clim, v., climb.
clink, v., strike; n., blow; fall.
clipshear, n., earwig.
clorach, v., work dirtily.
closhach, n., carcase; mess of wet stuff.

clottert, adj., clotted.
clour, v., dent.
clue, n., ball of worsted.
clyack, n., harvest supper.
clyte, play clyte, v., fall heavily.
clytrie, n., mass of wet stuff; adj., messy.
coble, n., cattle-pond.
cockie-breikie, n., boy with first pair of trousers.
cockertie-hooie, ride, v., ride on someone's shoulders.
colfin, n., wadding.
confaise, v., confuse.
consumpt, n., what is consumed.
contrair, adv., in the wrong way.
coo/cou, n., cow.
cookie shine, n., tea party.
coorgy (coorji), n., blow as challenge to fight.
caurie/corrie-haundit, adj., left-handed.
cosey, n., scarf.
courd, n., coward.
couter, n., coulter of plough.
cow, n., bush twig; a broom.
cowdle, v., rock; float.
cowld, adj., cold.
crackins, n., oatmeal fried in fat.
crampet, n., clamp; iron spike in wall.
cran, n., iron cross-piece over fire for kettle etc.
crank, adj., crooked; loose.
creenie-crannie, n., little finger.
creinge, v., cringe.
crichle, v., n., wheeze in throat.
crochle, v., limp.
cross, n., market-place.
crouse, adj., arrogant: crouseness, n., arrogance.
crowdie, n., cheese spread.
croup, v., speak hoarsely.
crub, n., manger.
cruels, n., scrofula.
cruzie, n., iron candle-holder.
cryin, n., woman's confinement.
cubbart, n., cupboard.
cuffins, n., corn chaff.
cuiter, v., pamper.
curchie, n., curtsy.
curdie, n., farthing.
curn, n., a grain.
curple, n., crupper.
currieboram, n., crowd.
cutty-cley, n., short clay pipe.

Dabbity, n., house ornament; picture transfer.
dag, n., drizzle.
daible, v., dabble.
daidle, v. fondle a child.
daily-day, adv., every day; continually.
dammish, v. stun.
deadal, adj., mortal; deadly.
deavance, n., nuisance.
debosherie, n., debauchery.
deifen, v. make sound-proof.
deister, n., agent.
dell/den, n., stopping place in "rounders."
denum, v., stupefy.
derk, adj., dark.
dert, v., n., dart.
deugs, n., shreds.
dice, v., sew wavy pattern on cloth.
dialcock, n., gnomon of sundial.
diet, n., church service.
differ, n., difference.
dim, n., dusk.
dindee, n., fuss; to-do.
dingle-douzie, n., torch waved by children.
dip, n., melted fat in which potatoes are dipped.
dippen, n., river bank steps where clothes were dipped.
ditter, v., potter about.
dixie, n., severe scolding.
dockie, adj., neat; tidy.
doctor, n., red-breasted minnow.
dodderie, adj., tottery.
doist, n., blow; bump.
donsie, adj., feeble; stupid.
dool, n., dowel; fastening pin.
doozie, n., small oil lamp.
dot, n., very small person.
dottle, n., cigarette end.
doun-throu, adv., nearer the sea.
dourles, n., sulks.
douse, v., strike; beat.
douth, adj., gloomy, of person or place.
dozie, adj., stupid.
dreip a waa, v., drop from wall with extended arms.
dribs and drabs, n., small amounts.
dumbsweir, v., cock a snook.

Easy-osy, adj., easy-going.
eeksie-peeksie, adj., much alike.
effeir, n., panoply.

emmerteen, n., ant.
etnach, n., juniper.
excamb, v., exchange.

Faiple, n., lower lip.
fairin, n., present from fair; deserts.
faut, n., lack, as in "for faut o."
fencibles, n., militia.
ferm-toun, n., farm homestead.
fillabeg, n., kilt.
fleg, v., take fright.
flet, n., plate.
flumgummery, n., ornamentation.
forritsome, adj., impudent.
fowth, n., plenty: **fowthie,** adj., plentiful.
freith, n., froth.
fulyie-man, n., refuse collector.

Gab/gob/gub, n., mouth.
gavel, n., gable.
gebbie, n., fowl's crop.
gey, adj., considerable: **geylies,** adv., very.
gibble-gabble, v., babble.
gilravage, v., over-indulge.
glabber, n., soft mud.
glim, v., shine faintly; n., gleam.
gloff, n. shock; burst of heat.
gloze v., n., blaze.
goor, n., mucus; slime.
grand-dey, n., grandfather.
grannie-mutchie, n., old woman.
grice, n., young pig.
green, n., plot of grass-covered ground.
grew, n., greyhound.
grip/greep, n., ditch; cowshed gutter.
grummly, adj., blustery; sullen.
gutterbluid, n., town native.

Haik, v. rove.
harl, v., roughcast.
hauch, v., cough to clear throat.
hauch, n., flat ground by river.
haunie, n., milk pail with longer stave for handle.
heck, n., grating across stream.
heft, v., restrain.
henner, v., challenge; disappoint.
heukbane, n., hipbone.
hey-float, n., sideless cart for bringing haystacks from field.
hilch, v., n., limp.
hind, n., farm servant.

hippen, n., baby's napkin covering hips.

hobble, v., sway.

hogger, n., footless stocking; stocking foot worn as slipper.

hogreik, n., cold mist; driving snow.

hooie, v., n., exchange; barter.

hudder, v., hang untidily; n., untidy person.

humour/eemir, n., pus; skin eruption.

humph, v., carry laboriously.

hurdy-bane, n., hipbone.

hurly, n., handcart.

hurlygush, n., diarrhoea.

hurry-burry, n., tumult.

hushle, v., fidget; work dirtily.

hush-mush, n., whisper.

ill-deedie, adj., mischievous; wicked.

ill-gabbit, adj., malicious.

ill-gien, adj., ill-disposed.

ill-hertit, adj., ill-disposed.

ill-likit, adj., disliked.

Jabble, v., splash.

jeeger, n., eccentric person.

Jenny Wullock, n., effeminate man.

jick, v., elude with jerk of body.

joco, adj., cheerful; pleased.

joogle, v., shake.

jummlie, adj., muddy.

junner, v., jolt; bump.

Kailie, n., social evening.

kenmark, n., distinguishing mark; brand.

kettle, n., large cooking-pot.

knittin, n., tape.

knock/nock, n., clock.

kyle, n., haycock.

Laldie, n., a beating; punishment.

lair/leir, v., teach; learn; n., learning; education; lore.

likely, adj., competent.

leifu lane, adj., absolutely alone.

lilly-loo, n., lullaby.

limmer, n., rogue.

lippenable, adj., dependable.

lithy, adj., thick, of porridge etc.

little, adj., low-ranking.

lorimer, n., fine-metal worker.

lot, v., allot; allocate.

loun, n., town native.

lounder, n., heavy blow.

lour, v., lower.

lowder, v., loiter.

luck-penny, n., money returned to buyer for luck.

lunkie-hole, n., sewage drain.

Maith, n., moth; maggot.

manawdge, n., people's friendly society or savings club.

man-muckle, adj., grown to manhood.

mankit, adj., faded; corrupt.

mash, n., heavy stonebreaking hammer.

mawsie, n., jersey.

megrim, n., caprice.

meh, v., n., bleat.

melt, n., spawn.

memorandum, n., memento.

mint, v., intend.

miscaa, v., slander.

mischief, n., misfortune; bodily harm.

misdout, v., disbelieve.

miss, n., loss: **miss oneself,** v., miss something good.

moggan, n., stocking foot over shoes on slippery surface.

moul/mool, n., mould.

moup, v., consort with.

mout, v., moult.

mull, n., headland.

multy, n., multi-storey building.

mump, v., grumble.

munsie, n., queer-looking person.

murnins, n., black mourning clothes.

mynd, v., remind.

Nail, v., strike; kill.

naiprie, n., household linen.

nicher/nicker, v., snigger.

nickietams, n., straps or strings tied over trouser legs below knees to keep out dust etc.

Oglet, n., theodolite.

Pandrop, n., hard smooth peppermint sweet; imperial.

pansoled, adj., in baking, hardened on under side with firing.

pant, n., caper; carry-on.

parawd, n., parade; procession.

pauchle, v., n., struggle.

paurlie, n., rectangular gingerbread biscuit.

peenge, v., complain; mope.

pellock, n., porpoise.
penny waddin, n., wedding at which guests contributed to cost.
pibroch, n., bagpipe theme and variations.
pick, v., throw.
pickfaut, n., fault-finder.
pickthank, n., flatterer; sneak.
pinchers, n., pincers.
pinglin, adj., painstaking; ineffectual.
pintle, n., penis.
pirl, v., twirl.
pizzen, v., make unpalatable.
plantry, n., ornamental garden.
pleep, n., piping cry of bird.
pluck, n., internal organs.
pock, n., smallpox.
podlie, n., tadpole.
policy, n., amenity: policies, n., estate grounds.
poshie, n., porridge.
positive, adj., adamant.
post, n., postman.
poulie, n., louse.
pout, n., young game bird.
powheid, n., tadpole.
pruch, v., scrounge; n., a perk.
pud, n., little fat child.
purls/pirls, n., sheep droppings.
pursue, v., importune; harass.
pushion, n., poison.
pyochert, adj., quite breathless.

Queer, adj., very great.
quick, adj., alive.
quickens, n., couch-grass.
quirk, n., conundrum; riddle.
quo, v., said.

Raan, n., brown-heart disease in turnips.
rack, v. stretch.
radgie, adj., lustful.
raggle, v., cut groove in stone to take slates etc.
raggyduds, n., ragamuffin.
raikin, adj., speedy.
rale, adv., extremely.
ramfoozle, v., confuse.
ramscooter, v., belabour.
rannletree/raintree, n., bar across chimney with hook for pots.
rede, n., advice.
ree, n., sieve.

reed, n., grain in wood etc.
reenge, v., swill; scour.
reif, n., robbery.
reisty, adj., stubborn.
reive, v., rend; rip.
reset, v., n., receive/reception of stolen goods for resale.
rife, adj., abundant; prodigal.
rift, v., belch.
rift, n., fissure in stone.
righteous, adj., rightful.
ripe/rype, v., search; rummage.
rit, n., groove; score.
rizzer, n., red currant.
rizzert, adj., dried in sun.
roast, n., joint of beef.
rockin, n., gathering of women to spin and gossip; merrymaking.
rokeley, n., woman's short cloak.
rook, v., rob; despoil.
rouk, n., mist; drizzle: roukie, adj., misty.
roupit, adj., hoarse.
rouse, v., become angry.
rowe-chow, v., roll down a banking.
rowst, v., roar.
royat, adj., riotous; unruly.
rudas, n., big ugly woman.
rullion, n., coarse uncouth creature.
rumgumption, n., commonsense, astuteness.
runchie, adj., stringy, of turnips etc.

Saidle, n., saddle.
Sammy dreip, n., spiritless person.
Sassenach, n., Englishman; adj., English.
saur, n., savour.
scarf, n., cormorant.
scaud, adj., shabby.
scaur, v., scare.
scran, n., refuse.
scrat, v., n., scratch.
scrauchle, v., scramble.
scree, v., n., riddle.
screenge, v., rummage.
scrimp/scrimpy, adj., scanty; mean.
scronach, v., scream.
scrunt, n., stunted person/thing.
scud, v., n., slap.
scuffed, adj., dingy; threadbare.
scug, v., trans., intrans., hide.
scunge, v., prowl; lurk.
scurryvaig, n., roaming person.

228

scutch, v., cut with knife/sickle.
seiventeen/twal hunder linen, n., very fine/fine linen.
service, n., round of drinks.
shammle, v., twist; distort.
shantrews, n., solo Highland dance.
sheil/shiel, v., shell, peas etc.
sheltie, n., Shetland pony.
shift claes/get shiftit, v., change out of working clothes.
shift, n., change of employment.
shirpit, adj., emaciated.
shivers, n., splinters.
sinnon, n., sinew.
snab, n., cobbler; shoemaker.
sneck, v., snatch; steal.
sned, n., scythe schaft.
snod adj. snug.
soo, v., ache; throb: **sooin**, n., throbbing pain.
soss, n., unpalatable mass of food.
souple, n., threshing part of flail.
sowcer, n., very large specimen.
spaik, n., spoke.
spang, n., span.
spaur, n., slat; rail.
spark, v., set alight.
spaul-bane, n., shoulder-bone.
spicketine, n., tap water used to "shed" hair.
spink, n., cowslip; primrose.
spite, n., disappointment.
spittin, n., spittle.
splatter, v., bedaub.
split new, adj., brand new.
splore, n., argument.
spree, n. disturbance.
spree adj., spry; smart.
sprig, n., tune.
sprug, n., sparrow.
spunefu, n., spoonful.
spunk-box, n., match-box.
spunkie, n., will-o-the-wisp.
squeck, v., squawk; squeak.
stack, n., weathered rock column.
stammer, v., stumble; totter.
stanes, n., testicles.
stang, v., n., ache.
stank, n., drain; drain grating.
stappit, adj., surfeited.
steg, v. stride.
stell, n., whisky still.
sterve, v., be extremely cold.
stew, v., n., stink.

stey, v., stay; support: **steys**, n., corsets.
stilt, n., plough handle.
stock, n., side of bed away from wall.
stour, adj., strong; robust.
strag, n., stray.
straik, v., stroke; smear.
strait, adj., tight, of clothes: **straiten**, v., stretch tight.
stramp, v., stamp on; trample.
strange, adj., shy towards strangers.
stunks, n., stake in marbles.
sturdies, tak the, v., take the sulks.
suddle, v., soil; n., dirty mark.
suit/sit, n., soot.
suitit, adj., pleased.
summar, n., summary.
swade, n., swedish turnip.
swarry, n., social gathering.
swatter, v., splash about.
sweel, v., wrap in clothes.
swither, v., n., swelter.

Tack, n., loose stitch.
taird, n., excrement.
taiver, v., wander: **taivert**, adj., confused.
tam-o-shanter, n., man's round flat cap with tuft.
tammie, n., tam-o-shanter-type bonnet.
tang/tangle, n., kind of seaweed.
tang, n., prong.
tarrie, n., terrier.
taste, v., tipple.
tattie grubber, n., mechanical potato digger.
taut, n., tuft: **tauty**, adj., matted.
tea dinner, n., lunch with tea, and without potatoes.
tea kitchen, n., tea urn.
teeger, n., tiger.
teeter, v., totter.
tell on, v., inform against.
thickness, n., fog.
thief, n., rascal.
thocht, n., concern.
thoumart/foumart, n., polecat.
thrave/threave, n., 24 sheaves of oats.
threeple, adj., triple: **threeplets**, n., triplets.
threshal, n., threshold.
thrissle-tap, n., thistle-down.
thriven, ill/weill-thriven, adj., under/well developed.

229

throch-stane, n., flat gravestone.
ticht, adj., mean with money.
tickler, n., difficult problem.
tiff/tift, n., quarrel.
tiller, v., send out laterals, of plant.
timmer, v., beat with stick.
timmer, adj., tone-deaf; tuneless.
tippy, adj., fashionable.
tirly-whirly, n., spinning-top.
tirr-whirr/turry-wurry, n., disturbance.
tizzie, n., troubled state of mind.
toit/toiter, v., totter.
toosht, n., heap of rags; slovenly woman.
toots/tits, interj., tut.
tot, n., total.
tot, v., toddle; totter.
totum, n., teetotum.
tour-hous, n., Border tower; "peel."
tout, v., tipple.
toy, n., kind of woman's cap.
trail, v., gad; trudge.
trait, v., n., treat.
trauchle, v. fatigue.
treesh, v., entreat.
tress, n., trestle.
trew, v., trow; believe.
troch, n., valley.
trollops n. tatters.
trummlin Tam, n., table jelly.
trump, n., Jew's harp.
tuil, n., tool.
tuim/teem, v., pour heavily, of rain.
tuin, ill/guid tuin, n., bad/good humour.
tuird/tird, n., excrement.
tulloch, n., hillock.
tumphie, n., stupid person.
tumshie, n., turnip.
twal/seiventeen hunder linen, n., fine/ very fine linen.
twasome, n., pair; couple.
tweetle, v., whistle.
twinty, adj., twenty.
tyauved, adj., fatigued.
tyle-hat, n., top-hat.
twyst/twicet, adv., twice.

U-huh, adv., yes.
unable for, adj., unfit for; having no appetite for.
unacquant wi, adj., unfamiliar with.
uncanny, adj., supernaturally malignant; treacherous.
unluesome, adj., unattractive.

unco, adj., weird; uncanny.
undeemis, adj., extraordinary; immense.
ure, n., haze; drizzle.

Vaig, n., vagrant.
vent, n., chimney flue.

Wa, adv., away.
wabble, n., insipid drink: **wabbly,** adj., insipid, of drink.
wad, n., wadding.
wae-weirdid, adj., doomed to sorrow.
waff, adj., stray.
waffle, v., flutter: **waffler,** n., indecisive person.
wage/wadge, v. pledge.
waiken, v., weaken: **waikness,** n., weakness.
wale, n., choice; the pick.
wally, adj., buxom.
wammle, v., roll; stagger.
wanrest, n., unrest: **wanrestfu,** adj., restless.
wanthriven, adj., stunted.
wanwordy, adj., unworthy.
wanner, v., wander.
wap, v., enfold; bind; tie.
wappen, n., weapon.
wappenshaw, n., review of men under arms; shooting competition.
ware-time, n., spring.
warst, adj., worst.
waucht, v., quaff; n., draught.
waygate, n., progress; "push."
weary, adj., sorrowful; dispiriting.
weave, v., knit stockings.
wedder, n., castrated ram.
wee hauf, n., a small whisky.
wee schuil, n., infant school.
wee-boukit, adj., small in size.
weill-pitten-on, adj., well-dressed.
weit, n., rain.
westlin/wastlin, adj., western.
wersh/wairsh, adj., insipid; bitter.
wham, n., blow; interj., thud!
whaup i the raip, n., snag.
wheep, v., n., whistle.
whirliwha, n., flourish in music.
whist, v., be silent.
whistle-binkie, n., non-paying guest at penny wedding not allowed to partake of entertainment.
white breid, n., loaf bread.

whupper-in, n., school attendance officer.

whurl, v., wheel.

wick, n., corner of mouth; cannon in curling.

widden, adj., wooden.

widdle, v., waddle.

windae bole, n., shuttered opening in wall for light.

winterdykes, n., clothes-horse.

witter, n., barb.

worship, n., family prayers.

wow, v., n., bark.

wrack, n., seaweed left on shore.

wrattle, n., agnail; torn shred of skin beside nail.

wrunkle, v., wrinkle.

wulsome, adj., wild; dreary.

wummle, v. upset.

wutch, n., witch.

wylie, adj., wise.

Yaff, v., chatter.

yairn, n., knitting yarn.

yaisial, adj., usual.

yaud, n., worn-out old horse.

yaupish, adj., hungry.

yawin, n., beard of barley.

yawk, v., n., ache.

yella-yite, n., yellow-hammer.

yerk, v., jerk; bind tightly; work energetically.

yetling, n., cast-iron.

yim, n., film; coating.

yirdie, adj., earthly.

yird-drift, n., snowdrift.

yirm, v., complain.

yoke, n., carriage and horses.

yokin, n., shift of work.

yokit, adj., united in marriage.

yoldrin, n., yellow-hammer.

yole, n., yawl.

younker, n., youngster.